Workplace Drug Testing

Workplace Drug Testing

Edited by
Alain Verstraete

Department of Clinical Chemistry, Microbiology and Immunology,
185 De Pintelaan, Ghent University, Ghent, Belgium
Laboratory of Clinical Biology – Toxicology, Ghent University Hospital,
185 De Pintelaan, Ghent, Belgium

London • Chicago Pharmaceutical Press

Published by Pharmaceutical Press

1 Lambeth High Street, London SE1 7JN, UK
1559 St. Paul Avenue, Gurnee, IL 60031, USA

Pharmaceutical Press is the publishing division of the Royal Pharmaceutical Society

Typeset by Thomson Digital, Noida, India
Printed in Great Britain by TJ International, Padstow, Cornwall

ISBN 978 0 85369 694 0

A catalogue record for this book is available from the British Library.

FSC
www.fsc.org
MIX
Paper from responsible sources
FSC® C013056

Contents

Preface

People who start to learn about workplace drug testing soon discover that the testing is only a small part of a drug and alcohol policy in a company. In this book, we give an overview of this complex matter, mainly from a European perspective.

The first chapter presents the epidemiology of drug use in the working population. How many workers are using drugs in different industries and in different countries? In the UK, 10–13% of the employed people reported using drugs in the last year, and 7% in the last month. The second chapter presents data on the influence of drugs on human performance. Drugs have many different effects on psychomotor function (e.g. reaction time and coordination), alertness, vision, risk-taking and aggressivity. Drugs can have influence on performance through their desired effects or side-effects. The effects of smoking cannabis can last up to 24 hours. Few people know that very heavy use of cannabis is associated with persistent decrements in neurocognitive performance even after 28 days of abstinence.

The third chapter presents the evidence base for workplace drug testing. Studies on the effects of workplace drug testing on deterring drug use, reducing the number of accidents and injuries and improving productivity or their cost-effectiveness, were mainly carried out in the late 1980s. Nearly all studies showed that workplace drug testing had a positive effect on these parameters. But many of these studies have later been criticised because of methodological flaws.

Chapter 4 describes the legal and regulatory aspects of workplace drug testing in different countries in Europe. Many European countries allow testing when there is a health, safety or security risk, or when it is deemed 'necessary' or 'proportionate', or is 'justified' or 'reasonable', or when there is a 'reasonable suspicion' that an employee is under the influence of an intoxicant (whether legal or illegal). Finland, Ireland and Norway have specific or direct legislation on drug testing in the workplace. In nearly all court cases, dismissals of employees because of a positive drug test were confirmed by the courts.

Chapter 5 discusses policies for drugs and alcohol. A workplace policy has to provide rules and solutions that address both impairment and dependency.

Testing should not be the starting point of the policy, but it has a valuable role in making people take notice of the policy.

After these chapters that set the scene for workplace drug testing, more practical aspects are considered. The key stages of workplace drug testing are specimen collection, laboratory analysis and reporting and interpreting the analytical results. The collection of donor specimens involves some of the most difficult and sensitive areas of the workplace drug testing process. Many precautions need to be taken in order to ensure that the sample is collected properly and is not tampered with. In addition to urine, other samples, such as oral fluid (saliva) and hair, are increasingly used in workplace drug testing. Oral fluid has the advantage that collection can be performed without embarrassment. Hair analysis can detect drug use over a much longer time frame (weeks to months).

Chapter 8 presents the analytical techniques that are used in workplace drug testing. When the sample is received at the laboratory, immunoassay screening tests are carried out to look for the presence of drugs. If the screening results are all negative no further analysis is necessary. In samples that test positive the presence of the drug is confirmed using a chromatographic technique, preferably in combination with mass spectrometry. All methods must be thoroughly validated as only validation can demonstrate that minimum acceptance criteria are fulfilled and that the method is suitable for a certain purpose.

Specimen adulteration is increasingly being recognised as an important issue affecting workplace drug testing programmes. When the consequences are important, people might try to dilute their urine or add some substances that will cause falsely negative results. This can occur through *in vivo* and *in vitro* methods or through specimen substitution, with a recent estimate suggesting that around 400 different products are currently available.

The effects of all these adulterants on the different tests are described, as are the ways to detect adulteration of the urine sample. After sampling and testing, the results must be interpreted. The medical review officer mainly performs this interpretation. Specialised training is needed in substance misuse and related clinical aspects including alternative medical explanations for positive drug test reports. Chapter 10 describes the interpretation of urine drug tests results, the potential causes of false positives, etc.

As the results of workplace drug testing can have important consequences, such as the loss of a job, guidelines have been produced in the last 30 years in order to ensure that the testing is performed in a reliable way and that the results are defensible in court. Chapter 11 discusses and compares the guidelines that exist in Europe, the United States and Australia. Chapter 12 presents examples of three companies in the UK, Germany and Sweden that use workplace drug testing.

The last three chapters describe the experience in Australia, Canada and New Zealand. In Australia (Chapter 13), workplace drug testing is well established in heavy industries and its main aim is to manage risk of accident or injury in the workplace. However, there is continuing controversy from union groups as how to best measure impairment.

In Canada (Chapter 14), employee testing can only be initiated if it is part of a comprehensive alcohol and drug policy tailored to meet the specific needs of each workplace. In addition, the programme should be seen as a reasonable and responsible response to those stated needs, presenting an appropriate balance between health and safety (due diligence) and respect for individual rights and privacy.

In New Zealand (Chapter 15), most 'safety-critical' industry sectors are embracing drug and alcohol testing as part of comprehensive programmes which also have a strong focus on education and rehabilitation.

Alain Verstraete
January 2011

About the editor

Alain Verstraete studied medicine at Ghent University, and specialised in clinical biology. Since 1987 he has been responsible for the Toxicology Laboratory of Ghent University Hospital. Since 2002, he has been a part-time professor at the Faculty of Medicine and Health Sciences of Ghent University.

His main research interests are in analytical toxicology and driving under the influence. He was the coordinator for the laboratories in the Belgian Toxicology and Trauma Study (BTTS) and the coordinator of the EU-funded Rosita (1999–2000) and Rosita-2 (2003–2005) studies on roadside drug testing and plays an important role in the EU-funded DRUID project (2006–2011). He is author of more than 80 peer-reviewed papers.

He was a founding member of the European Workplace Drug Testing Society (EWDTS) and was board member until 2009.

He is vice-president of the Toxicological Society of Belgium and Luxembourg and president-elect of the International Association of Forensic Toxicologists (TIAFT).

Contributors

Ronald Agius Department of Forensic and Clinical Toxicology, Labor Krone, Bad Salzuflen, Germany.

Per Björklöv CEO, Drugtest Scandinavia AB, Bromma, Sweden.

Daniëlle Borrey Department of Laboratory Medicine, AZ Sint-Jan Brugge-Oostende AV, Brugge, Belgium.

Barb Butler President, Barbara Butler & Associates Inc., Toronto, Ontario, Canada.

Claire George Concateno, Abingdon, Oxfordshire, UK.

Lindsay Hadfield Policy and Education Services, Concateno, London, UK.

Pascal Kintz X-Pertise Consulting, Oberhausbergen, France.

John H Lewis Visiting Fellow, National Drug and Alcohol Research Centre, UNSW, Sydney and Honorary Associate, University of Technology, Sydney, Australia.

Leendert J Mostert Van Weel-Bethesda Hospital, Department of Clinical Chemistry and Hematology, Dirksland, The Netherlands.

Susan Nolan DrugFree Sites, Susan Nolan and Associates Ltd, Auckland, New Zealand.

John O'Sullivan Managing Director, Claymon Biomnis Laboratories, Sandyford Business Estate, Dublin, Ireland.

Elke Raes Department of Clinical Chemistry, Microbiology and Immunology, Ghent University, Ghent, Belgium.

Helen Vangikar Independent Toxicology Consultant, London, UK, www.helenvangikar.com.

Alain Verstraete Department of Clinical Chemistry, Microbiology and Immunology, Ghent University and Laboratory of Clinical Biology – Toxicology, Ghent University Hospital, Ghent, Belgium.

Abbreviations

1-TPC	*N*-trifluoroacety-1-prolylchloride
11-OH-THC	11-hydroxy-tetrahydrocannabinol
6-AM	6-acetylmorphine
AADAC	Alberta Alcohol and Drug Abuse Commission (Canada)
ACLU	American Civil Liberties Union
ADA	Americans With Disabilities Act of 1990
AEME	androhydroecgonine methylester
AIRC	Australian Industrial Relations Commission
AMIA	Ascend Multiimmunoassay
ARIMA	Autoregressive, integrated moving-average
AS/NZS 4308	Standards Australia and Standards New Zealand, Procedures for specimen collection and the detection and quantitation of drugs of abuse in urine
ATS	amphetamine type substances
bfor	bona fide occupational requirement
BSTFA	*N*-*O*,-bis-(trimethylsilyl) trifluoroacetamide
BVG	Betriebsverfassungsgesetz, Works Constitution Act (Germany)
BZE	benzoylecgonine, metabolite of cocaine
BZP	benzylpiperazine
CAD	collision-activated dissociation
CBI	Confederation of British Industry
CCF	custody and control form
CDSA	Controlled Drugs and Substances Act
CDUW	Committee on Drug Use in the Workplace
CEDIA	cloned enzyme donor immunoassay
CID	collision-induced dissociation
CPRG	chlorophenol red-β-D-galactopyranoside
CRI	Crown Research Institute (New Zealand)
DAD	diode-array detector
DAFWP	drug and alcohol-free workplace programme

DAP	drug abuse policy
DCSSA	Direction Centrale du Service de Santé des Armées, Central direction of the health service of the army (France)
DEA	Drug Enforcement Administration
DFSA	drug facilitated sexual assault
DHHS	US Department of Health and Human Services
DMAA	1,3-dimethylamylamine
DOT	US Department of Transportation
EAP	Employee Assistance Programme
ECHR	European Convention on Human Rights
EDDP	2-ethylidene-3,3-diphenylpyrrolidine, metabolite of methadone
EEA	European Economic Area
ELDD	European Legal Database on Drugs
ELISA	enzyme-linked immunosorbent assay
EMCDDA	European Monitoring Centre for Drugs and Drug Addiction
EMDP	2-ethyl-5-methyl-3,3-diphenyl-1-pyrrolidine, metabolite of methadone
EMIT	enzyme multiplied immunoassay technique
EQAS	external quality assessment schemes
ESPAD	European School Survey Project on Alcohol and Drugs
ESR	Environmental Science and Research Limited (New Zealand)
EWDTS	European Workplace Drug Testing Society
FAA	Federal Aviation Administration (USA)
FAEE	fatty acid ethyl esters
FDA	Food and Drug Administration (USA)
FHWA	Federal Highway Administration (USA)
FPIA	fluorescence polarisation immunoassay
FRA	Federal Railway Administration (USA)
G6P-DH	glucose-6-phosphate dehydrogenase
GC	gas chromatography
GC-MS	gas chromatography-mass spectrometry
GHB	gamma-hydroxybutyrate
GMC	General Medical Council
HFBA	heptafluorobutyric anhydride
HPLC	high-performance liquid chromatography
HR	human resource
HSA	Health and Safety Authority
IA	immunoassay
IANZ	International Accreditation New Zealand
IDRS	illicit drug reporting system

IFDAT	International Forum for Drug and Alcohol Testing
IOC	International Olympic Committee
ISO	International Organisation for Standardisation
ITS	interrupted time series
IUPAC	International Union of Pure and Applied Chemistry
KIMS	kinetic interaction of microparticles in solution
LC-MS	liquid chromatography-mass spectrometry
LC-MS/MS	liquid chromatography-tandem mass spectrometry
LOD	limit of detection
LOQ	(lower) limit of quantification
LPME	liquid-phase microextraction
LSD	lysergic acid diethylamide
MA	methamphetamine
MBDB	1-(1,3-benzodioxol-5-yl)-*N*-methylbutan-2-amine
MDMA	methylenedioxymethylamphetamine, ecstasy, XTC
MDPPP	3′,4′-methylenedioxy-α-pyrrolidinopropiophenone
MPHP	4′-methyl-α-pyrrolidinohexanophenone
MPPP	4′-methyl-α-pyrrolidinopropiophenone
MRM	multiple reaction monitoring
MRO	medical review officer
MUNZ	Maritime Union (New Zealand)
NAD	nicotinamide adenine dinucleotide
NATA	National Association of Testing Authorities (Australia)
NHSDA	National Household Survey on Drug Abuse
NIDA	National Institute on Drug Abuse
NSDUH	National Surveys on Drug Use and Health
NTSB	National Transportation Safety Board
NZQA	New Zealand Qualification Authority
OH	occupational health
OHA	occupational health advisers
ONPG	*o*-nitrophenyl-β-D-galactopyranoside
OR	odds ratio
OTC	over the counter
PAR	population attributable risk
PCP	phencyclidine
PFP	pentafluoropropionic acid
PHPD	post-hallucinogen perceptual disorder
POCAT	point-of-care or point-of-collection adulterant test strips
POCT	point-of collection drug testing
PRHO	pre-registration house officers
PST	poppy seed tea
PTP	proficiency testing programmes
PVP	α-pyrrolidinovalerophenone

QA	quality assurance
RCT	randomised controlled trial
RIA	radioimmunoassay
ROSITA	roadside testing assessment, EU-funded project that evaluated roadside drug tests
RSAP	rapid site access programme
RSD	relative standard deviation
SAMHSA	Substance Abuse and Mental Health Services Administration
SAP	substance abuse professionals
SDLP	standard deviation of the lateral position
SNCF	Société nationale des chemins de fer français, French National Railway Corporation
SPME	solid-phase microextraction
SRM	single reaction monitoring
SVT	specimen validity tests
TEEU	Technical Engineering and Electrical Union
TFAA	trifluoroacetic anhydride
TFMPP	trifluoromethylphenylpiperazine
THC	Δ9-tetrahydrocannabinol
THC-COOH	11-nor-Δ-9-tetrahydrocannabinol-9-carboxylic acid, metabolite of THC
THCV	Δ9-tetrahydrocannabivarin
TLNZ	Toll Owens Limited (New Zealand)
TMCS	trimethylchlorosilane
TRO	toxicology review officer
TUC	Trade Unions Congress
UKWDTF	United Kingdom Workplace Drug Testing Forum
UNODC	United Nations Office on Drugs and Crime
USPS	US Postal Service
UV	ultraviolet
WAIRC	Western Australian Industrial Relations Commission
WDT	workplace drug testing
XTC	ecstasy, MDMA, methylenedioxymethylamphetamine

1

Epidemiology of drug use in the working population

Alain Verstraete

Key points

- In Europe, 22.5 million people (6.8% of all adults) have used cannabis in the last year, 4 million have used cocaine, 2.5 million people have used ecstasy and 1–2 million people have used heroin.
- In the UK, 10–13% of the employed people reported using drugs in the last year, and 7% in the last month. Fifty-four per cent of the regular cannabis users in the 15–24 age group are students, 30% are employed and 12% are unemployed.
- In Europe, 41% of people who go into rehabilitation are employed and 7.5% are students.
- In a series of samples obtained during workplace drug testing, the percentage of positives varies from less than 1% to 20%. Pre-employment testing in different industries shows around 5% of positives.
- Very high percentages (25%) of current drug users were seen in some surveys of junior medical doctors and dentists in the UK.
- In university students, the prevalence of regular weekly cannabis use varied between 9% and 28%.
- In European prisons, 1–50% of inmates report having used drugs while incarcerated, and up to 27% report regular use inside prison.
- In the United States, 8.2% of the full-time workers aged 18–64 years reported past-month illicit drug use. The highest prevalence of past-month illicit drug use was observed in food service workers (17.4%) and in construction workers (15.1%).

Introduction

This chapter will focus on the question of how many working people in Europe use drugs. Some data on alcohol use will also be given. Detailed data are available for the United States, but for Europe fewer data are available on the number of drug users who are employed.

In order to estimate the number of employed people who use drugs, two approaches are possible: surveys based on self-report and results of workplace drug testing. In surveys on drug use in different populations or age groups a question about employment status is asked. Unfortunately there are very few surveys in Europe where the employment status of the respondents was reported. The available data from the younger age group (15- to 34-year-olds) will also be given. The data on past-month and past-year use will be discussed, because they are more relevant for the working population than the data on the people who have ever used drugs. Estimates of past-month prevalence include those using the drug more regularly, though not necessarily in an intensive way. Some data will also be given about the employment status of people who go into rehabilitation.

Another approach is to use the results of workplace testing in different industries, and results of the available studies will be given. In these types of studies one should be aware of potential biases. If a drug policy that includes testing is in place in a company, the prevalence of drug users is likely to be lower than in companies that do not have such policies (see the results of the US survey later in this chapter).

Drug use on a global scale

Drug use has increased very significantly in the world in recent decades, but it seems to have stabilised or somewhat decreased in Europe in the last few years. The 2009 World Drug Report[1] estimates that between 172 and 250 million persons used illicit drugs at least once in 2007. The total number of people aged 15–64 years in 2007 was 4343 million. Eighteen to 38 million people (15–64 years old) were 'problem drug users' and 11–21 million people aged 15–64 years injected drugs. The number of people who used opiates at least once in 2007 is estimated at between 15 and 21 million people at the global level. The total number of people who used cocaine at least once in 2007 is estimated to range between 16 and 21 million. The global number of people who used cannabis at least once in 2007 is estimated to be between 143 and 190 million.

The highest levels of use remain in the established markets of North America and Western Europe, although there are signs from recent studies that the levels of use are declining in developed countries, particularly among young people. Between 16 and 51 million people aged 15–64 used amphetamine-group substances at least once in 2007; the number who used ecstasy-group drugs at least once is estimated at between 12 and 24 million worldwide. The width of these ranges is far greater than those for cocaine and heroin, given the high level of uncertainty in relation to this drug group in terms of both use and production.

Drug use in Europe

Tables 1.1 and 1.2 show the past-month prevalence (percentage) of drug use among all adults (15–64 years old) and among young people (15–34 years old) in nationwide surveys among the general population based on the last survey available for each member state of the European Union. These results will be discussed for each drug class in the next paragraphs.

Use of amphetamine-type substances (ATS) in Europe

Significant ecstasy consumption was first reported in Europe in the 1990s and use has now grown to equal or surpass that of amphetamine in most countries. The European Monitoring Centre for Drugs and Drug Addiction (EMCDDA) estimates that around 2 million adults have used amphetamines (0.5% of all adults) in the past year. National surveys show that between 0.1% and 15.3% of young adults report having tried amphetamines and 0.2–7.7% report having used it in the last year. The highest rates of past-year amphetamines use among young adults are reported in the Czech Republic (7.7%), Estonia (3.7%) and the UK (3.1%).

It is estimated that about 2.5 million adults in Europe (0.8% of all adults) have used ecstasy in the last year. Considerable variation exists between countries, with recent surveys suggesting that past-year use ecstasy varies across Europe from 0.1% to 3.5%. On all measures, and as with most other illicit drugs, reported use is far higher among males than among females.

After general increases in the 1990s, population surveys now point to an overall stabilisation, or even moderate decrease, in the popularity of both drugs, although this pattern is not seen in all countries.[3]

Use of cannabis in Europe

The use of cannabis in Europe has evolved considerably over the last decade, as has the debate on how to respond appropriately to the widespread use of this drug. In the early and mid 1990s, a few countries stood out as having a high prevalence, whereas the European norm was levels of use that, by today's standards, were low. In most countries, cannabis use increased during the 1990s and early 2000s, and this has resulted today in a less varied European picture, even if important differences between countries still exist. Moreover, the last few years have seen a growing understanding of the public health implications of the long-term and widespread use of this drug, and rising

Table 1.1 Past-month percentage prevalence of drug use among all adults (aged 15–64 years) in nationwide surveys among the general population: last survey available for each member state (from 2000 onwards)[2]

Country	Geographical area	Year	Age range all adults	Sample size all adults	Cannabis (%)	Cocaine (%)[a]	Amphetamines (%)[b]	Ecstasy (%)[c]	LSD (%)
Austria	National	2004	15–64	3980	3.8	0.4	0.4	0.4	0.1
Belgium	National	2004	15–64	NA	3.0	NA	NA	NA	NA
Bulgaria	National	2007	15–64	6027	1.2	0.3	0.2	0.2	0.0
Cyprus	National	2006	15–64	3504	1.4	0.4	0.3	0.6	0.3
Czech Republic	National	2004	18–64	3526	4.8	0.0	0.2	1.1	0.1
Denmark	National	2008	16–64	3408	2.2	0.2	0.3	0.1	0.0
Estonia	National	2003	15–64	NA	1.4	0.0	0.3	0.4	0.0
Finland	National	2006	15–64	2802	1.6	0.1	0.2	0.1	0.0
France	National	2005	15–64	25879	4.8	0.2	0.1	0.1	0.0
Germany	National	2006	18–64	7912	2.2	0.2	0.3	0.2	0.0
Greece	National (except Aegean and Ionian Islands)	2004	15–64	4351	0.9	0.0	0.0	0.0	0.0
Hungary	National	2007	18–64	2710	1.2	0.2	0.3	0.2	0.1
Ireland	National	2006–07	15–64	4967	2.6	0.5	0.1	0.3	0.0
Italy	National	2007	15–64	7289	7.2	0.8	0.1	0.2	NA
Latvia	National	2007	15–64	4500	1.8	0.2	0.2	0.4	0.0

Lithuania	National	2004	15–64	4207	0.7	0.1	0.1	0.2	0.0
Luxembourg	NA	NA	NA	NA	NA	NA	NA	NA	NA
Malta	National	2001	18–64	1755	0.5	0.1	0.0	0.2	0.0
Netherlands	National	2005	15–64	4516	3.3	0.3	0.2	0.4	0.0
Norway	National	2004	15–64	2669	2.2	0.3	0.2	0.1	0.0
Poland	National	2006	15–64	2859	0.9	0.1	0.2	0.1	0.0
Portugal	National	2007	15–64	12202	2.4	0.3	0.1	0.2	0.1
Romania	National	2007	15–64	6797	0.1	0.0	0.0	0.0	0.0
Slovakia	National	2006	15–64	1305	2.0	0.2	0.2	0.5	NA
Slovenia	NA	NA	NA	NA	NA	NA	NA	NA	NA
Spain	National	2007–08	15–64	23715	7.1	1.1	0.3	0.4	NA
Sweden	National	2007	16–64	4401	0.6	NA	NA	NA	NA
United Kingdom	England and Wales	2007–08	16–59	28688	4.2	1.0	0.4	0.5	0.1
United Kingdom	Northern Ireland	2006–07	16–64	2439	3.0	0.5	0.3	0.4	0.1
United Kingdom	Scotland	2006	16–59	3157	6.8	1.8	0.9	1.6	0.2
United Kingdom	United Kingdom	2006	16–59	NA	4.9	1.3	0.5	0.9	0.1

NA, data not available.

[a] Cocaine, any form.

[b] For Belgium National 2001 and for Metropolitan France 1995: amphetamine and ecstasy.

[c] For Spain: ecstasy and other synthetic drugs.

Table 1.2 Past-month prevalence of drug use among young adults (aged 15–34 years) in nationwide surveys among the general population: last survey available for each member state (from 2000 onwards)[2]

Country	Geographical area	Year	Age range young adults	Sample size young adults	Cannabis (%)	Cocaine (%)[a]	Amphetamines (%)[b]	Ecstasy (%)[c]	LSD (%)
Austria	National	2004	15–34	1754	6.4	0.5	0.6	0.8	0.2
Belgium	National	2004	15–34	NA	7.6	NA	NA	NA	NA
Bulgaria	National	2007	15–34	2591	2.7	0.5	0.5	0.6	0.1
Cyprus	National	2006	15–34	1753	2.1	0.4	0.3	0.8	0.3
Czech Republic	National	2004	18–34	1414	9.8	0.1	0.5	2.3	0.2
Denmark	National	2008	16–34	1744	4.8	0.5	0.8	0.3	0.1
Estonia	National	2003	15–34	646	3.3	0.0	0.8	0.9	0.0
Finland	National	2006	15–34	1387	3.5	0.3	0.6	0.2	0.1
France	National	2005	15–34	10855	9.8	0.5	0.1	0.3	0.1
Germany	National	2006	18–34	3306	5.5	0.4	1.0	0.5	0.1
Greece	National (except Aegean and Ionian Islands)	2004	15–34	2620	1.5	0.1	0.1	0.0	0.0
Hungary	National	2007	18–34	1111	2.7	0.2	0.5	0.3	0.0
Ireland	National	2006-07	15–34	1989	4.2	1.0	0.2	0.6	0.1
Italy	National	2007	15–34	4243	10.4	1.2	0.2	0.3	NA
Latvia	National	2007	15–34	2497	3.6	0.3	0.3	0.8	0.1

Lithuania	National	2004	15–34	1814	1.5	0.2	0.2	0.4	0.1
Luxembourg	NA	NA	NA	NA	NA	NA	NA	NA	NA
Malta	National	2001	18–34	640	NA	NA	NA	NA	NA
Netherlands	National	2005	15–34	NA	5.6	0.4	0.4	0.8	0.0
Norway	National	2004	15–34	1238	4.5	0.7	0.3	0.1	0.0
Poland	National	2006	15–34	2031	1.9	0.1	0.3	0.3	0.0
Portugal	National	2007	15–34	4765	4.5	0.6	0.2	0.4	0.1
Romania	National	2007	15–34	2262	0.3	0.0	0.0	0.1	0.0
Slovakia	National	2006	15–34	556	4.2	0.4	0.4	0.1	NA
Slovenia	NA	NA	NA	NA	NA	NA	NA	NA	NA
Spain	National	2007-08	15–34	9843	13.4	1.9	0.6	0.8	NA
Sweden	National	2007	16–34	1432	1.3	NA	NA	NA	NA
United Kingdom	England and Wales	2007-08	16–34	10 021	7.8	2.1	0.6	1.1	0.2
United Kingdom	Northern Ireland	2006-07	16–34	920	5.9	1.2	0.7	0.7	0.2
United Kingdom	Scotland	2006	16–34	1115	12.6	4.1	1.5	3.3	0.4
United Kingdom	United Kingdom	2006	16–34	NA	9.3	2.7	1.0	1.9	0.2

NA, data not available.

[a] Cocaine, any form.

[b] For Belgium National 2001 and for Metropolitan France 1995: amphetamine and ecstasy.

[c] For Spain: ecstasy and other synthetic drugs.

reported levels of treatment demand for cannabis-related problems. Europe may now be moving into a new phase, as data from general population and school surveys point to a stabilising or even decreasing situation. Levels of use remain high by historical standards.

It is conservatively estimated that cannabis has been used at least once (lifetime prevalence) by around 74 million Europeans, over one in five of all 15- to 64-year-olds. Considerable differences exist between countries, with national prevalence figures varying from 1.5% to 38.6%. For most of the countries, the prevalence estimates are in the range 10–30%.

Many countries report comparatively high prevalence levels of past-year and past-month use of cannabis. The highest percentages of past-month use are observed in Italy (7.2%), Spain (7.1%) and Scotland (6.8%). It is estimated that around 22.5 million Europeans have used cannabis in the last year, or on average 6.8% of all 15- to 64-year-olds. It is estimated that about 12 million Europeans used the drug in the last month, on average about 3.6% of all 15- to 64-year-olds. It is estimated that over 1% of all European adults, about 4 million, are using cannabis daily or almost daily. Most of these cannabis users, about 3 million, are aged between 15 and 34 years, representing approximately 2–2.5% of all Europeans in this age group.

Use of cannabis in Europe is lower, however, than on other continents. In the United States, the lifetime prevalence of cannabis use is 49% among young adults and the past-year prevalence of 21%. For the same age group, lifetime prevalence of cannabis use was 58% and past-year prevalence 28% in Canada in 2004, while in Australia (2007) the figures were 47% and 16%. All these figures are above the corresponding European averages, which are respectively 31.1% and 12.5%. Among school students, only Spain and the Czech Republic report levels of lifetime prevalence of cannabis use that are comparable to those reported in the United States and Australia.[3]

Use of cocaine in Europe

An overall increase in cocaine use and cocaine seizures has been observed in the European Union during the last decade, although this has been largely confined to western member states, and major differences exist between countries. The data available also indicate considerable diversity among cocaine users, both in terms of patterns of use and in terms of socio-demographics. Those who only experiment with the substance on one or a few occasions make up the largest group. Another group includes socially integrated regular users who, in some countries, account for a relatively large number of young people. Some of them will intensify their use of cocaine, or use it over a long period, which may lead to chronic health and social problems and to the need for treatment. A third set of users includes members of socially excluded groups, including current and former opioid users. Most of them have intensive patterns of cocaine use, possibly using crack or injecting the drug, which may perpetuate or exacerbate existing health and social problems, and may complicate their treatment for opioid use. Because of the diversity of profiles among cocaine users, assessing the prevalence of the drug's use, its health and social consequences and the necessary responses presents a unique set of challenges.

Overall, cocaine remains the second most used illicit drug in Europe, after cannabis, though levels of use vary greatly between countries. It is estimated that around 13 million Europeans have used it at least once in their lifetime, on average 3.9% of adults aged 15–64 years. National figures vary from 0.1% to 8.3%, with 12 out of 23 countries, including most central and eastern European countries, reporting low levels of lifetime prevalence among all adults (0.5–2%).

Around 4 million Europeans have used cocaine in the last year (1.2% on average), although again with variation between countries. Recent national surveys report past-year prevalence estimates of between 0 and 3.1%, although in 18 out of 24 countries levels of use do not exceed 1%. The prevalence estimate for past-month cocaine use in Europe represents about 0.4% of the adult population or around 1.5 million individuals. The highest percentages are observed in Scotland (1.8%), Spain (1.1%) and Italy (0.8%). These estimates are likely to be conservative.

Overall, cocaine use appears to be concentrated in a few countries, notably Denmark, Spain, Italy, Ireland and the UK, while use of the drug remains relatively low elsewhere in Europe. In countries where amphetamines dominate the market in illicit stimulant drugs, estimates of cocaine use are low in nearly all cases. Conversely, in most countries where cocaine is the main illicit stimulant, low levels of amphetamine use are reported.

The past-year prevalence of cocaine use is lower among young adults in the European Union than among their counterparts in Australia and the United States. However, two countries, Spain and the UK (England and Wales), report higher figures than Australia, and only Spain reports a higher estimate than that of the United States.[3]

Box 1.1 *Cocaine use in the German and European Parliaments*

In June 2000 a journalist filmed himself with a small digital camera while carrying out a 'wipe-test' in toilets used by members of the German Parliament. The reporter wiped the toilets using a Sagrotan cloth. The laboratory tests of these cloths revealed traces (around 1–3 micrograms) of cocaine in 22 out of 28 cubicles tested, but in extremely minute quantities. The investigation of other public buildings, such as the Berlin Stock Exchange, had found cocaine traces at far higher levels – one of Berlin's leading hotels found over 30 times as much.

(continued overleaf)

In 2005, the German Sat-1 channel sent reporters to take 46 swabs from toilets and other public areas of the Brussels buildings of the European parliament. They polished toilet roll dispensers, door handles and other areas in the Brussels building. Nearly all (41 out of 46) tested positive for cocaine. The concentrations found were higher than in the Bundestag. Ten of the swabs were smeared with between 20 and 30 micrograms. Professor Sorgel, who analysed the swabs, stated that the amount was too high and found in too many spots. It showed that cocaine was brought in deliberately. As the buildings are cleaned regularly, it appeared that cocaine had been used recently in the places where the traces were found. As the toilets are freely accessible, it was not possible to say who brought in the cocaine. With journalists, invited guests and cleaners all having access to the area, it was hardly conclusive evidence for use by the members of parliament.

Professor Sorgel tested for traces of cocaine at five German secondary schools and insignificant amounts of the drug were found at only two of the sites, which illustrates that contamination with cocaine is not a general phenomenon.

Use of opiates in Europe

Heroin use, particularly injecting the drug, has been closely associated with problem drug use in Europe since the 1970s. Today, this drug still accounts for the greatest share of morbidity and mortality related to drug use in the European Union. A decline in heroin use and associated problems has been observed in the last ten years, although more recent data suggest that, in some countries, the trend may have changed direction. In addition, reports of the use of synthetic opioids, such as fentanyl, and the injection of stimulant drugs, such as cocaine or amphetamines, reflect the increasingly multi-faceted nature of problem drug use in Europe.

Estimates of the prevalence of problem opioid use in European countries during the period 2002–2007 range roughly between one and six cases per 1000 population aged 15–64. Overall prevalence of problem drug use is estimated to range from under three cases to ten cases per 1000. The countries reporting the lowest well-documented estimates of problem opioid use are the Czech Republic, Latvia, Poland and Finland (though both the Czech Republic and Finland have large numbers of problem users of amphetamines), while the highest estimates are reported by Malta, Italy, Austria and Spain. The available data suggest that the downward trend in opioid use observed prior to 2003 has levelled off. This is perhaps most clearly visible since 2003 among seizures and drug-induced deaths, and after 2004 in new treatment demands related to heroin use. These changes have occurred alongside increased opium production in Afghanistan, raising concerns that these events might be linked through increased availability of heroin on the European market.[3]

Use of LSD and hallucinogenic mushrooms in Europe

Lifetime prevalence of lysergic acid diethylamide (LSD) use among the adult population (15–64 years) ranges from almost 0 to 5.2%. Among young adults (15–34 years), lifetime prevalence estimates are a little higher (0–6.6%), although much lower prevalence ranges are reported for past-year use. In contrast, in the few countries providing comparable data, the use of LSD is often exceeded by that of hallucinogenic mushrooms, where lifetime prevalence estimates for young adults range from 0.3% to 8.3%, and past-year prevalence estimates between 0.2% and 2.8%.

Employment status of respondents in drug use surveys

The only large study that provides some data on drug use according to employment status is the Eurobarometer survey,[4] which was conducted in 2004 among 7859 young people aged 15–24 in the 15 countries of the European Union. The data are given in Table 1.3.

Past-month cannabis use was reported by 20% of the unemployed, 12% of the manual workers, 11% of 'other white collar' workers, 10% of self-employed and 5% of the managers. Fifty-four per cent of the regular cannabis users aged 15–24 years were students, 30% were employed and 12% were unemployed.

Table 1.3 Results of the Eurobarometer study. Percentage of young people (aged 15–24) who have tried or used drugs according to their employment status[4]

	n	Have tried cannabis	Last month cannabis use	Have tried other drugs	Past month other drug use	Regular alcohol consumption
Houseperson	144	37	16	20	5	34
Students	4580	29	10	7	2	22
Unemployed	533	44	20	23	6	32
Self-employed	108	36	10	5	2	30
Manager	139	33	5	2	0	28
Other white collar	568	30	11	10	3	34
Manual worker	1460	40	12	14	4	33
Never worked	72	27	9	18	5	23

Past-month other drug use was 6%, 4%, 3%, 2% and 0% in the different age groups respectively. Forty-three per cent of the other drug users aged 15–24 years were students, 36% were employed and 15% were unemployed.

Other studies describe the situation in the UK. An analysis of the British Crime Survey data of 2008/09[5] showed that among people aged 16–59 and 16–24, those who were unemployed had significantly higher reported levels of past-year usage of any drug, any Class A drug or any stimulant drug compared with those in employment or economically inactive. The percentages of people reporting any drug use in the past year were 10.1% in the study populations, 7.7% in managerial and professional occupations, 7.6% in intermediate occupations, 10.4% in routine and manual occupations, 12.9% in long-term unemployed or people who have never worked and 21.6% in full-time students[5] (Figure 1.1).

In a large survey in the UK[6] of 7979 people (aged 18 years or more, selected at random from the electoral registers for Cardiff and Merthyr Tydfil), 4620 (58%) of whom were employed, it was shown that 38% of the employed people reported ever having used drugs, 13% reported using drugs in the last year and 7% in the last month. Cannabis was the most commonly reported drug used (11% in the last year), followed by ecstasy, amphetamines and cocaine (2.5%, 2.3% and 2.2% respectively). In that population, 35% drank more than the recommended limits of alcohol. The prevalence of drug use decreased with age: past-year use was 28% in workers younger than 30 years, 15% in 30- to 40-year-olds, 5% in 40- to 50-year-olds and 3% in people older

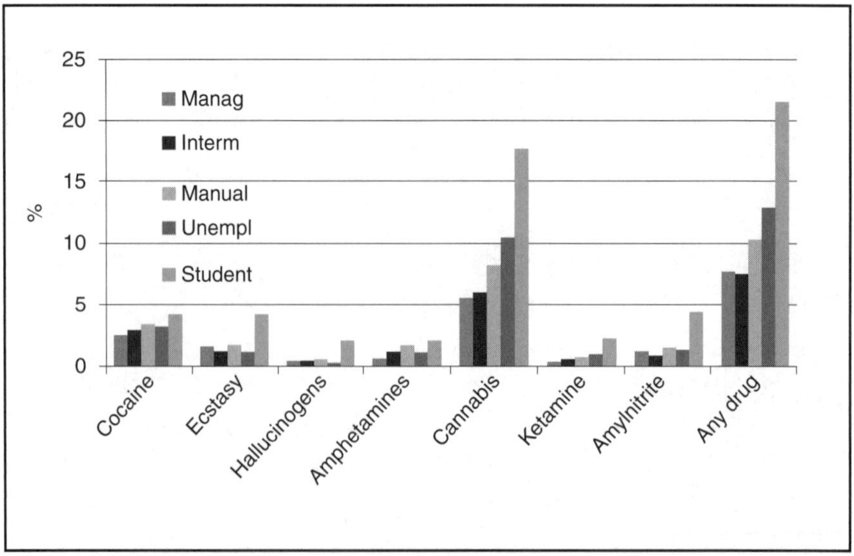

Figure 1.1 Past-year prevalence of the use (%) of different drug (classes) in different occupations in the UK in 2008/2009. Manag: managerial & professional occupations; Interm: intermediate occupations; Manual: routine and manual occupations; Unempl: never worked and long-term unemployed; Student: full-time students.[5]

than 50 years. Using multivariable logistic regression modelling the authors showed that, among workers, drug use was independently associated with being male, younger (i.e. under 25), unmarried, having a higher education qualification, living in Cardiff, having a higher neuroticism score, drinking more than the recommended weekly limits (14 units for women and 21 for men) and smoking. The strongest associations were with heavy drinking and, in particular, smoking.

In a survey in 1996 in the UK Hadfield found that 52% of males and 42% of females aged 11–35 had ever used drugs. Between 40 and 50% of the employed people in this age group had ever used drugs: 43% in the professional/managerial category, 49% clerical/administrative, 47% skilled manual, 46% unskilled manual and 51% in people on state benefits.[7]

Studies in workplace fatalities

Szwarc *et al.*[8] measured the prevalence of psychoactive drugs (alcohol excepted) among victims of occupational fatalities (including workplace accidents plus traffic accidents on the way to and from work) that occurred in the Alsace region over the period 2000–2005. Data were collected by compiling files on occupational accidents from two different public agencies together with those from the Medico-Legal Institute of Strasbourg over the period tested. Toxicological analyses were requested by the authorities in 41% of traffic victims and only 15% of workplace victims. Data analysis showed that 3% of the victims of workplace fatalities and 5% of the victims of occupational traffic accidents were under the influence of drugs (alcohol excluded) at the time of the accident.

Studies of people who start rehabilitation

A survey between 1998 and 2002 of 12 000 patients under substitution treatment in the Reggio-Emilia region of Italy showed that 32% were permanently employed, 32% were occasionally employed and 35% were unemployed. According to a survey carried out in 2000 on a sample of 158 patients in a treatment centre in Venice and Mestre (Italy), 62% of the subjects who were employed were working as generic manual workers, 21% as specialised workers, 9% as traders and 1.8% were employees.[9]

Table 1.4 presents the data on the employment status of people who go into rehabilitation based on EMCDDA data.[10] Overall, out of the nearly 200 000 people who entered outpatient treatment in 2007 40.8% were regularly employed and 7.5% were pupils or students.

Studies in prisoners

Compared with the general community, drug use is much more widespread in European prison populations. Data available from several studies carried out

Table 1.4 Labour status of clients entering outpatient treatment, 2007 or most recent year available[10]

Country	Regular employment	Pupil/student	Economically inactive	Unemployed	Other
Austria	38.5	5.2	5.2	46.8	4.3
Belgium	39.2	11.1	21.9	26.0	1.8
Bulgaria	37.4	9.8	16.7	34.8	1.2
Croatia	33.6	12.8	3.4	49.8	0.5
Cyprus	35.2	6.7	2.2	46.1	9.7
Czech Republic	29.2	22.2	6.3	34.6	7.7
Denmark	18.7	3.2	20.8	50.1	7.2
Finland	15.5	10.5	4.8	62.9	6.3
France	26.5	14.2	20.1	22.9	16.3
Germany	27.5	6.1	18.5	47.3	0.6
Greece	30.5	8.4	1.0	48.1	12.0
Hungary	43.6	23.0	2.7	20.4	10.3
Ireland	18.7	6.7	8.9	61.3	4.4
Italy	58.9	5.8	4.1	29.8	1.3
Lithuania	NA	NA	NA	NA	NA
Luxembourg	44.9	18.9	7.1	18.9	10.2
Malta	38.7	5.7	1.3	54.3	0.0
Netherlands	38.6	2.9	0.4	36.6	21.4
Poland	NA	NA	NA	NA	NA
Portugal	NA	NA	NA	NA	NA
Romania	14.3	12.4	0.2	46.3	26.8
Slovakia	24.3	19.9	1.6	52.9	1.4
Slovenia	25.2	9.5	0.4	58.2	6.7
Spain	45.0	4.4	9.9	34.6	6.1
Sweden	22.1	7.0	19.3	36.9	14.7
UK	NA	NA	NA	NA	NA
Total	40.8	7.5	10.3	35.3	6.0

NA, not available.

from 2002 onwards, mostly in Western European countries, show that between a third and half of those surveyed reported regular drug use of any illicit drug prior to imprisonment. Studies carried out between 2000 and 2007 in Europe show that 1–50% of inmates report having used drugs while incarcerated (Table 1.5), and that up to 27% report regular use inside prison. Those injecting within prison represent 1–31% of inmates.[10]

A study in Belgium in 2003 showed that 29% of prisoners took cannabis, 13% used heroin, 11% used amphetamine, 11% used cocaine and 10% used ecstasy.[11]

Workplace drug testing in different countries, regions or industries

These studies give information about the percentage of active workers who test positive on workplace drug tests. One should be aware that there is evidence that once a workplace drug testing programme is in place, the number of positives decreases, probably because of the deterrent effect (see, for example, the results for the Spanish railways below). The percentages shown probably underestimate the number of drug users in the industry sector because one can expect a higher percentage of positives in companies where no tests are performed.

Reports from unspecified industries

George published the results of the analysis of 1617 specimens from 82 workplace drug testing sources in the UK in 2002.[12] The samples originated from male subjects in 89.9% of the cases. The most commonly detected drugs were cannabis (11.6%), opiates (3.0%), benzodiazepines (1.5%), methadone (1.4%), cocaine (1.1%) and amphetamines (0.4%). There were no significant differences between the age ranges. Of the 308 (19%) positive samples, only 9 could be explained by declared prescription. Globally, 19% of the samples were positive for illicit drug use. Unfortunately, no data were available on the indication for workplace drug testing (pre-employment, for cause, etc.). Some bias is also possible because some industries may test with on-site devices and only send the positive samples to the lab for confirmation, which could increase the percentage of positives.

Clarke[13] presented the results of 4780 oral fluid specimens collected for workplace drug testing: 3.5% were positive (1.25% for cannabinoids, 1.21% for opiates (0.3% for 6-acetylmorphine), 0.6% for cocaine and metabolites, 0.2% for benzodiazepines, 0.1% for amphetamines and 0.1% for methamphetamines).

Drug use in the chemical and petrochemical industries

In 1999, one German company in the chemical industry tested 4900 employees, including all job applicants, all trainees after completion of their job

Table 1.5 Prevalence of lifetime drug use among prisoners[10]

Country	Year	Size of the sample	Any illicit drug (%)	Cannabis (%)	Cocaine (%)	Heroin (%)	Amphetamines (%)	Ecstasy (%)	Crack (%)
Belgium	2006	902	60	52	39	27	27	28	
Bulgaria	2007	7780	10						
Spain	2006	4934		65	53	39	25	24	39
Latvia	2003	2867	53	51	15	21	22	17	
Lithuania	2003	1304	49						
(a) Hungary	2004	609	32	26	11	7	16	16	
(b) Hungary	2004	609	34	27	11	8	16	17	
(b) Netherlands	2002–03	205		78	11	4	8	18	2
(a) Netherlands	2003	355	79						
Poland	2007	1240	49	43	21	8	39	29	
(a) Portugal	2007	1986	55	48	35	30	15	18	
(b) Portugal	2007	1986	59	55	40	34	16	20	
Romania	2006	3218	16	15	6	8	1	4	
United Kingdom	2004–05	1457	79	70	43	37	37		41
Norway	2002	1074	70	65	51	37	59	45	

Data for Bulgaria, Spain, Latvia, (a) Hungary, the Netherlands, Poland, (a) Portugal and Romania refer to prevalence lifetime drug use prior to imprisonment. Data for (b) Hungary and (b) Portugal refer to prevalence lifetime drug use prior/inside prison.

training programmes, all workers who were moving to jobs with new occupational hazards and all workers whose behaviour led to suspicion of drug abuse. In job applicants, positive test results were found in 2–3% of the cases. In the other tested groups, 4–9% were positive. Cannabis was most frequently found.[14]

In another German chemical company, 906 samples from job applicants (who were warned beforehand that they would be tested) were tested, and 4.1% were positive. Two-thirds of the positives were positive for cannabis, 13.5% for amphetamines, 13.5% for opiates and 4.5% for cocaine. In another sample, where no advance warning was given, 17% of pre-employment tests were positive.[15]

A survey of 8364 tests among 2091 workers in a chemical company in Germany showed that 3.1% of the pre-employment tests and 8.5% of the tests performed in other circumstances were positive. In the great majority of the cases (91% of pre-employment positives and 83% of other positives), cannabis was found.[16]

In 2000, a survey of tests found that the number of pre-employment positives in two large chemical companies in Germany was between 6 and 8% (Gerold Kauert, Institute of Forensic Toxicology, Frankfurt, Germany, personal communication).

In a large petrochemical company in 1998, the results of 16 265 alcohol and drug tests on employees, conducted inside and outside the United States showed that 28 employees (0.18%) were positive. This percentage was the lowest reported since worldwide testing was implemented. Marijuana was detected in 47% of the 28 positive tests in 1998. In the United States, marijuana (38%) was the substance most frequently detected, followed by cocaine (23%). Outside the United States, marijuana (57%) was followed by alcohol (36%) and cocaine (7%).[14]

Drug use in the metallurgy and automobile industries

In 2000 in two major car manufacturers in Germany, the number of positive pre-employment tests was 1 and 2%, while at a large metallurgy company it was 17% (Gerold Kauert, Institute of Forensic Toxicology, Frankfurt, Germany, personal communication).

Drug use in the transport sector

Airlines

Pre-employment and for cause workplace drug testing in a French airline found cannabis was positive in 4–5% of the cases (no systematic confirmation was performed).[17]

Railways

Over an eight-year period (1990–1997), 477 workers consuming alcohol and drugs were detected in the Spanish National Railway Company, which corresponds to 1.1% of workers.[18] In the south-eastern region of Spain, 3.6% of the railway workers tested positive in 1998–1992, 1.4% in 1993–1995, 1.1% in 1996–1997 and 0% in 1999.[14]

In unannounced tests performed on British Railways workers between 1994 and 1997, the positive rate varied between 0.18 and 0.36%. Cannabis was the number one drug detected (68% of the positives), followed by alcohol (14%) and opiates (10%).[19]

In 2000 in the German railways, 5.8% of the pre-employment tests were positive (Gerold Kauert, Institute of Forensic Toxicology, Frankfurt, Germany, personal communication).

In 2001 in the Belgian Railways Company, out of 2953 tests, 280 were confirmed positive (9.5%). In decreasing order of frequency, the positives were: cannabis 6.3%, opiates 1.8%, benzodiazepines 0.6%, cocaine 0.4% and methadone 0.14%.

Public transport

The percentages of positive random tests (10% were randomly tested at the time of the survey) among employees of public transport in Stockholm, where pre-employment, post-accident and return to duty testing is performed, were 0.8% in 1998, 0.2% in 1999 and 0.3% in 2000.[19] Pre-employment testing gave positive results in about 0.5% through the years.[20]

In a study of 262 bus drivers (99.2% males) in Hungary, Varga *et al.*[21] reported that 50% drank alcohol on a daily basis, but the breath alcohol was negative at the time of the test in 100%. Very few positives were found: 0.8% for opiates and 1.5% for benzodiazepines. In addition, one driver was prescribed benzodiazepines, one was prescribed opiates and one was positive for opiates because of poppy seed consumption.

Trucking and road transport

Labat *et al.*[22] published the results of workplace drug testing in 1000 truck drivers in 2003–2004 in the north of France. The tests were performed on a voluntary basis as part of the annual medical visit (75%), pre-employment (20%) and return to duty (5%). The population was 99.2% male and the mean age was 36.7 ± 9.8 years. Cannabis was detected in 8.5% of the cases, ethanol in 5.0%, opiates in 4.1%, amphetamines in 0.3% and cocaine in 0.1%. Buprenorphine was detected in 1.8%. Among the drivers aged 18–25, 22.6% were positive for cannabis. In pre-employment testing of the 18- to 25-year-olds, 14.7% were positive. In one centre 30% of urine samples were positive during the annual visit. Overall, 2.2% of the drivers were in substitution treatment, which is 8 times higher than the national average, but concomitant use of other drugs was lower in the employed than in pre-employment testing.

Drug use in the medical sector

A survey of 90 junior house officers in 18 National Health Service (NHS) hospitals in the north-east of England showed that 35% of males and 19% of females were currently using cannabis, with 11% taking it weekly or monthly and 15.6% very occasionally. Use of other drugs (hallucinogenic mushrooms, LSD, ecstasy, amyl nitrite, cocaine and amphetamines) was also reported: 13% in males and 10% in females. In addition to that, among the 93% who drank alcohol, 60% (of both sexes) exceeded recommended safe limits.[23]

In 1997 in Belarus, of 2032 officially registered drug abusers, 28 were physicians (mainly surgeons and anaesthesiologists) and 6 were nurses.[17]

A study in Newcastle, UK showed that 41% of recently qualified dentists and 54% of pre-registration house officers (PRHOs) used higher than recommended doses of alcohol.[24] Fifty-one per cent of the dentists and 66% of the PRHOs reported having experimented with cannabis. Current use of cannabis was reported by 16% of dentists and 24% of PRHOs. Other illicit drugs currently used by dentists were amphetamines (4%), ecstasy (13%), cocaine/crack (13%), amyl/butyl nitrite (4%) and magic mushrooms (4%). Illicit drug use by PRHOs included amphetamines (1%), ecstasy (4%), cocaine/crack (3%), amyl/butyl nitrite (1%), LSD (1%) and temazepam/diazepam (3%).

A study among 3476 French anaesthetists[25] showed that 6.5% were dependent on or abusing alcohol and 4.3% were dependent on or abusing tranquillisers or hypnotics. For cannabis, 2.6% had used it in the last 12 months, and 0.7% were dependent or abusing. For opiates, the percentages were 0.9 and 0.6%, respectively, and 0.2% were abusing amphetamines or cocaine.

Among 144 doctors who had received treatment for drug and alcohol dependency in the UK,[26] alcohol was the major substance abuse problem for 42%, drugs for 26% and alcohol and drugs for 31%. Twenty-five per cent had misused injectable drugs. After alcohol, the most frequent agents misused were opiates (26%), barbiturates (24%), benzodiazepines (21%) and amphetamines (15%). Drugs were mainly obtained by self-prescription (66%); only 5% were obtained from the black market.

Drug use in the military

A study performed by the General Directorate of Health Services of the French army (Direction Centrale du Service de Santé des Armées, DCSSA) in 1996 showed that 12% of 1972 urine tests were positive for cannabis and 0.1% for ecstasy. Cocaine was never detected. Out of the 2031 subjects who were questioned about their current drug use, 17% declared that they used cannabis and 0.5% used ecstasy. Use of cocaine and heroin was very infrequent (0.05%).[27]

A French study in 17- to 18-year-olds who underwent tests in order to determine whether they were fit for military service showed that, regarding recent use, after alcohol (80.2% had used it in the last 30 days) and smoking (48%), cannabis use was most frequent (32.3%), followed by psychoactive substances (11.8%). Only 1.6% used ecstasy and 0.3% had used crack recently. Experimentation with other drugs was infrequent: 4.4% had experimented with inhalants, 0.3% with ketamine and γ-hydroxybutyric acid (GHB). Between 2000 and 2002, regular use of cannabis (at least 10 times in the last 30 days) increased, but it decreased in 2003, mainly in boys (14.6% in 2000, 17.7% in 2002 and 14.6% in 2003). The decrease was less pronounced in girls where regular cannabis use was as frequent as regular alcohol use.[28]

Use of drugs to increase performance or cope with work stress

There are occasional reports that some people use drugs to improve their performance at work. Lapeyre-Mestre *et al.* analysed 2106 questionnaires from workers taken during their annual compulsory occupational medical examination in the Toulouse (France) metropolitan area. One third of the workers used licit psychoactive substances (alcohol, coffee, drugs) in the context of work: 20% used drugs in order to be in good condition for work, 12% used drugs at the workplace for an awkward symptom and 18% used drugs to relax after a difficult day at work. They mainly used psycholeptic drugs. The highest percentages were seen in employees and manual workers.[29]

Drug use in schools

The 2007 European School Survey Project on Alcohol and Drugs (ESPAD) project provided data on drug use among European schoolchildren (15–16 years). ESPAD data for 2007 reveal that on average, 23% of the boys and 17% of the girls have tried illicit drugs (cannabis, amphetamines, cocaine, crack, ecstasy, LSD and heroin) at least once during their lifetime. Reported use of illicit drugs varies considerably across the countries. In the Czech Republic, almost half (46%) of the students report such use and many students (roughly a third) did so also in France, the Isle of Man, the Slovak Republic and Switzerland. Only around 6% reported illicit drug use in Cyprus, the Faroe Islands, Norway and Romania. Lower prevalence rates are often found among the Nordic countries and in Eastern Europe.

The vast majority of the students who have tried illicit drugs have used cannabis. Lifetime cannabis use was reported by 19% of the students while 7% had tried one or more of the other drugs included in the index. Ecstasy, cocaine and amphetamines followed in joint second place (3% each) and less commonly reported were LSD, crack and heroin (1–2%). Bulgaria, Estonia, the Isle of Man, Latvia and the Slovak Republic are the top five countries regarding lifetime ecstasy use in 2007 (prevalence rates around 6–7%). Lifetime use of magic mushrooms was reported by 3%, while GHB and steroids were mentioned by 1%, which is of the same magnitude as the reported experience of intravenous drug use.

Use of cannabis in the past 12 months was reported by 14% of all students while use in the past 30 days was stated by 9% of the boys and 6% of the girls (7% mean). In the two top-prevalence countries (the Czech Republic and the Isle of Man) one in six students reported cannabis use in the past 30 days, indicating more regular cannabis consumption in those countries. Only 1–2% in Armenia, the Faroe Islands, Finland, Norway, Romania and Sweden reported such recent use. High-prevalence countries are most often found in Western Europe.

Overall, one out of seven past-year cannabis users (14%) was classified as having a high risk of developing cannabis-related problems, and the average prevalence of high-risk users across countries was 2%.

In those ESPAD countries with comparable data for all four waves, 12% of the students reported lifetime prevalence of illicit drugs in 1995 and this figure rose to 21% in 2003. However, the 2007 results indicate that the upward trend in illicit drug use has come to a halt since only 18% of the students reported such experiences this year. This development is practically the same for both genders, and the girls are consistently about five percentage points below the boys.[30]

Drug use in university students

Webb *et al.* conducted a survey of alcohol and drug use in the faculties of several UK universities in 1997.[31] The results are shown in Table 1.6. Alcohol consumption was greatest in biological science students: 23% of those who drank exceeded 'hazardous' levels compared with 10–16% in all other faculties. Prevalence of cannabis use was highest in arts and social science students, of whom 28% reported regular weekly use compared with 9–22% in other faculties. Experience with other illicit drugs was greatest among arts, social science and physical science students, of whom 64–71% reported experience at least once or twice, and least among veterinary students (42%).

A questionnaire survey in 136 second-year medical students at the University of Leeds (UK)[32] showed that 86% drank alcohol, with a high proportion exceeding the weekly limit of alcohol consumption (53% of

Table 1.6 Prevalence of drug use in different faculties in UK universities[31]

Faculty	Alcohol (mean weekly consumption (units)	Cannabis regular use	Amphetamines[a]	Ecstasy[a]	Cocaine[a]	LSD[a]	Mushrooms[a]	Heroin[a]	Nitrites[a]
Arts	28	28	27	19	9	30	22	5	18
Biological science	38	22	21	14	6	38	17	5	16
Engineering	27	16	13	9	9	52	14	2	11
Law/accountancy/ economics	24	15	13	12	3	51	10	1	12
Mathematics/statistics	31	12	11	6	4	53	11	3	10
Medicine/dentistry/ allied disciplines	27	11	10	7	2	53	7	1	11
Physical science	33	21	20	13	4	40	16	3	18
Social sciences	34	26	26	17	9	34	19	4	20
Veterinary science	25	9	13	8	1	58	10	5	0

[a] Experience with.

men and 51% of women). Illicit drug use was reported by 33% of the students, with cannabis being the most commonly used drug.

A study in 1998 among dental school students[33] showed that 82% of male and 90% of female undergraduates reported drinking alcohol. Of those drinking, 63% of males and 42% of females drank in excess of sensible weekly limits (14 units for females, 21 units for males), with 56% of males and 58.5% of females 'binge drinking'. Fifty-five per cent of undergraduates reported cannabis use at least once or twice since starting dental school, with 8% of males and 6% of females reporting current regular use at least once a week. After cannabis the next most commonly used drugs by dental undergraduates were amphetamines (16%), amyl nitrite (13%), ecstasy and magic mushrooms (8%), LSD (5.5%), cocaine (4.5%) and inhalants (2.5%).

Current regular drug use other than cannabis was rarely reported, with 2.9% of fourth- and fifth-year males using amphetamines and 1.4% of first- to third-year females using ecstasy at least once a month.

Another study in a dental school in Newcastle, UK[24] in 1995 and 1998 showed that 47% of second-year students and 25% of the final-year students drank alcohol above the recommended level. In medical students the respective percentages were 33% and 43%. Experimentation with illicit drugs ranged from 47% as second-year students to 54% as final-year students. Current use of cannabis in the final year of their degree was reported by 8% of the dental student group and 22% of the medical student group. Other illicit drugs currently used by the dental student group included amphetamines (4%), ecstasy (6%) and cocaine/crack (6%). Illicit drug use by medical students included amphetamines (1%), ecstasy (3%) and cocaine/crack (1%).

Data from the United States

The report on 'Worker Substance Use and Workplace Policies and Programs'[34] presents findings on substance use among workers and on workplace drug policy and programmes from the 2002, 2003 and 2004 National Surveys on Drug Use and Health (NSDUH). The NSDUH are annual surveys of the civilian, non-institutionalised population of the United States aged 12 years or older. They analyse the worker information in conjunction with the substance use data collected in the survey to investigate substance use among full-time employed US workers aged 18–64 during the period 2002–2004.

The prevalence of substance use behaviours and substance use disorders was higher among unemployed persons than among full-time workers, part-time workers and those with other employment status. However, because full-time workers constitute about two-thirds of the population aged 18–64 (or 114.7 million persons), most substance users and most of those with substance use disorders were employed full time.

The prevalence of past-month illicit drug use among full-time workers aged 18–64 was estimated to be 8.2% in 2002, 2003 and 2004. Nineteen per cent of workers aged 18–25 used illicit drugs during the past month. This was a higher percentage than among the 26–34 (10.3%), 35–49 (7.0%) and 50–64 (2.6%) age groups.

Males were more likely than females to report past-month illicit drug use (9.7 vs. 6.2%). Males accounted for about two-thirds (6.4 million) of the workers who reported past-month illicit drug use.

Workers with a college education had a lower prevalence of past-month illicit drug use compared with those without a college education. The prevalence of past-month use of illicit drugs was lower among college graduates (5.7%) than those with less than high school education (11.2%).

The prevalence of past-month illicit drug use was lower among workers with higher family incomes than among workers with lower family incomes. An estimated 13.2% of workers who reported family income that was less than $20 000 had used illicit drugs during the past month. In contrast, 6.0% of workers who reported income in the highest category – US$75 000 or more – had used illicit drugs during the past month.

An estimated 8.8% of full-time workers (10.1 million) reported past-month heavy alcohol use. Among younger workers (18- to 25-year-olds), 16.3% reported past-month heavy alcohol use compared with 10.4% of 26- to 34-year-olds, 8.1% of 35- to 49-year-olds and 4.7% of 50- to 64-year-olds.

Of the major occupational groups (Table 1.7, Figure 1.2), food service workers (17.4%) and construction workers (15.1%) exhibited a higher prevalence of past-month illicit drug use than other occupational groups. Those working in education, training and library occupations (4.1%), community and social services occupations (4.0%), and protective service occupations (3.4%) had the lowest prevalence of past-month illicit drug use among the major occupational groups.

The major occupational groups with the highest prevalence of past-month heavy alcohol use were construction and extraction occupations (17.8%) and installation, maintenance and repair occupations (14.7%). Community and social services occupations (2.8%) had the lowest prevalence of past-month heavy alcohol use of the major occupations.

The major industry groups with the highest prevalence of past-month illicit drug use were accommodations and food services (16.9%) and construction (13.7%) (Figure 1.3). Public administration (4.1%), educational services (4.0%) and utilities (3.8%) had the lowest prevalence.

The industry groups with the highest prevalence of past-month heavy alcohol use were construction (15.9%); arts, entertainment and recreation (13.6%); and mining (13.3%) industries. Healthcare and social assistance (4.3%) and educational services (4.0%) had the lowest prevalence of past-month heavy alcohol use compared with the other major industries.

Table 1.7 Illicit drug, marijuana and heavy alcohol use in the past month among full-time workers aged 18–64, by occupational categories: percentages and numbers in thousands, annual averages based on 2002–2004[34]

Occupational category	Past month illicit drug use[a]		Past month marijuana use		Past month heavy alcohol use[b]	
	Percentage	Number (thousands)	Percentage	Number (thousands)	Percentage	Number (thousands)
Total[c]	8.2	9413	6.4	7293	8.8	10 113
Management occupations	6.1	876	4.5	641	7.9	1121
Chief executives	3.6	35	3.1	30	5.5	53
Advertising, marketing, promotions, public relations, and sales managers	6.2	50	3.5	28	10.5	84
Financial occupations	4.9	133	3.3	91	6.2	170
Mathematical and computer scientists	6.9	222	5.5	178	5.9	191
Engineering, architecture, and surveyors	6.9	199	6.0	172	8.3	238
Drafters and engineering technicians	12.7	76	10.2	61	13.2	79
Life, physical, and social science occupations	7.0	95	5.0	68	5.3	73
Physical scientists	7.2	50	4.6	32	4.7	32
Social scientists and related workers	7.4	24	6.7	22	6.3	21

(continued overleaf)

Table 1.7 *(continued)*

Occupational category	Past month illicit drug use[a]		Past month marijuana use		Past month heavy alcohol use[b]	
	Percentage	Number (thousands)	Percentage	Number (thousands)	Percentage	Number (thousands)
Community and social services occupations	4.0	80	2.4	49	2.8	56
Legal occupations	4.8	68	3.9	55	5.9	82
Lawyers	4.3	33	3.0	23	6.5	49
Education, training, and library occupations	4.1	254	3.2	198	3.7	231
Elementary and middle school teachers	3.1	76	2.3	57	3.3	82
Secondary school teachers	4.4	44	3.3	33	4.7	48
Special education teachers	5.3	19	2.9	10	6.4	22
Other teachers and instructors	5.1	82	4.4	70	3.4	54
Arts, design, entertainment, sports, and media occupations	12.4	267	10.1	218	7.5	161
Healthcare practitioners and technical occupations	6.1	463	3.9	293	3.9	294
Health diagnosing and treatment practitioners	4.4	159	2.6	95	2.5	92
Registered nurses	4.6	95	3.3	68	2.2	46
Health care technical and support occupations	7.6	303	4.9	198	5.1	202

Nursing, psychiatric, and home health aides	7.5	117	5.7	89	4.6	71
Protective service occupations	3.4	89	2.4	63	8.7	227
Protective service managers and supervisors, firefighter and prevention workers, law enforcement workers	1.5	25	1.1	19	9.1	158
Other protective service workers	7.4	63	5.2	44	8.0	69
Food preparation and serving related occupations	17.4	809	14.2	661	12.1	564
Food preparation supervisors and managers	12.6	75	10.1	60	8.6	51
Cooks	16.8	294	14.2	248	11.9	208
Food preparation workers	9.2	53	7.4	42	6.9	39
Food and beverage serving and other food preparation serving related occupations	22.2	388	17.7	310	15.2	265
Building and grounds cleaning and maintenance occupations	8.2	284	6.6	225	9.5	328
Personal care and service occupations	7.7	181	5.7	135	5.4	127
Personal appearance workers	8.2	51	7.0	44	6.6	41

(continued overleaf)

Table 1.7 *(continued)*

Occupational category	Past month illicit drug use[a]		Past month marijuana use		Past month heavy alcohol use[b]	
	Percentage	Number (thousands)	Percentage	Number (thousands)	Percentage	Number (thousands)
Child care workers	6.9	64	4.6	43	3.3	31
Personal and homecare aides	6.6	30	5.2	23	4.4	20
Sales and related occupations	9.6	1,114	7.4	857	10.2	1,183
Retail sales	11.7	229	9.1	179	12.4	242
Sales representatives, services	9.8	46	7.3	34	14.7	69
Sales representatives, wholesale and manufacturing	9.8	137	7.0	98	14.6	204
Office and administrative support occupations	7.5	1,172	5.7	892	6.9	1,071
Farming, fishing, and forestry occupations	8.7	89	3.3	34	9.5	97
Construction and extraction occupations	15.1	1,247	12.9	1,063	17.8	1,467
Carpenters	20.0	378	16.5	312	17.9	338
Carpet, floor, tile installers, and finishers	18.7	45	17.4	42	17.6	42
Construction laborer	14.8	137	11.6	107	17.6	164
Construction equipment operator	8.6	35	6.1	25	12.8	53

Electricians	13.0	106	12.7	104	19.0	155
Roofers	16.9	37	14.1	31	25.7	56
Other construction related workers	15.1	359	13.0	310	17.4	415
Extraction workers	9.9	12	5.9	7	[d]	[d]
Installation, maintenance, and repair occupations	9.5	468	8.1	401	14.7	724
Production occupations	7.4	663	5.7	510	9.7	865
Transportation and material-moving occupations	8.4	569	6.3	427	11.2	760
Motor vehicle operators	7.2	17	5.4	13	8.6	20
Bus drivers	1.5	6	*	*	2.7	11
Truck drivers, heavy and tractor-trailer	7.4	249	5.2	176	11.2	380
Material-moving workers	12.7	255	10.1	204	14.1	284

[a] Illicit drugs include marijuana/hashish, cocaine (including crack), heroin, hallucinogens, inhalants, or prescription-type psychotherapeutics used nonmedically.

[b] Heavy alcohol use is defined as drinking five or more drinks on the same occasion (i.e. at the same time or within a couple of hours of each other) on each of 5 or more days in the past 30 days.

[c] Estimates in the total row include respondents with unknown or other occupational information.

[d] Low precision; no estimate reported.

Data from SAMHSA, Office of Applied Studies, National Survey on Drug Use and Health, 2002, 2003 and 2004.

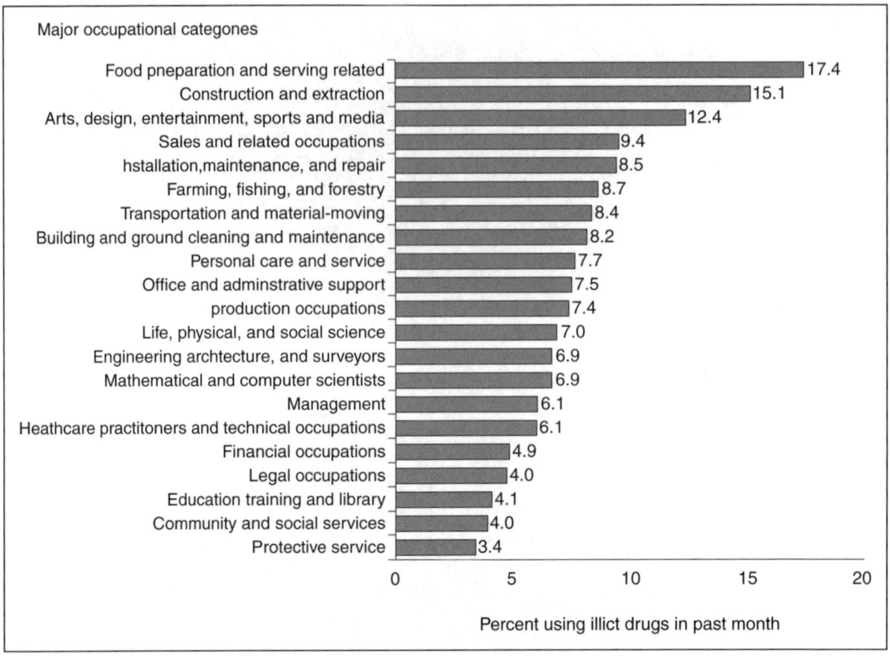

Figure 1.2 Past-month illicit drug use among full-time workers aged 18–64 by major occupational categories: 2002–2004 combined.[34]

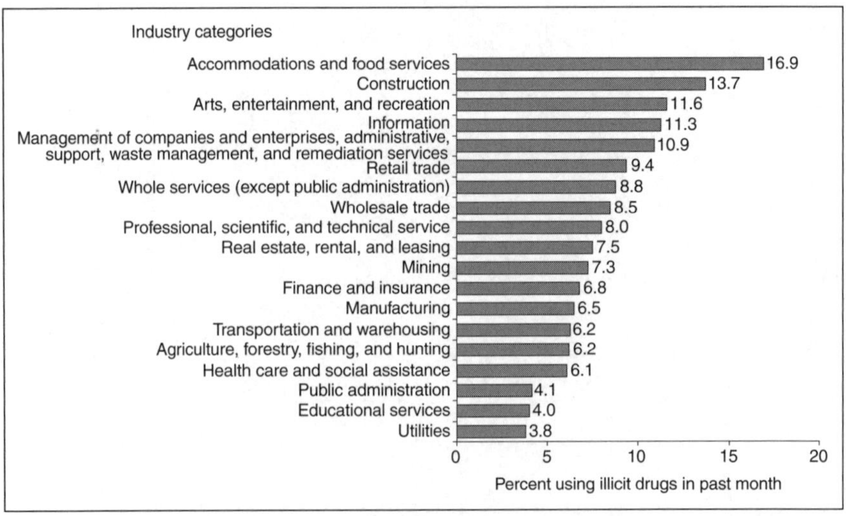

Figure 1.3 Past-month illicit drug use among full-time workers aged 18–64, by industry categories: 2002–2004 combined.[34]

Prevalence of past-month illicit drug use was lower as establishment size increased. The prevalence among workers in establishments with 25–99 employees was 8.2%, compared with 6.7% among workers in establishments with 100–499 employees and 5.7% among workers in establishments with 500 or more employees. A similar pattern was found for past-month heavy alcohol use.

Nearly 3 million (32.1%) full-time workers between the ages of 18 and 64 who had used an illicit drug in the past month reported that they worked for an employer who offered educational information about alcohol and drug use. An Employee Assistance Programme (EAP) was reported to be available to 3.9 million (45.4%) workers who were past-month users of an illicit drug, while 6.5 million (71.0%) reported working for employers who had a written policy about drug and alcohol use.

In general, past-month illicit drug users were less likely to report working for employers who offered workplace drug or alcohol programmes or policies compared with those who did not use an illicit drug in the past month. An estimated 45.4% of past-month illicit drug users reported that there was an EAP at their place of employment compared with 59.6% of workers who had not used an illicit drug in the past month.

Among the US full-time workers, 42.9% reported that tests for illicit drug or alcohol use occurred at their place of employment during the hiring process, or 'prehire' testing. This equates to more than 47 million adults who worked in settings where testing for illicit drug or alcohol use occurred during the hiring process.

A total of 29.6%, or 32 million, of full-time workers in the United States reported random drug testing in their current employment setting during the study period.

Hersch *et al.*[35] found that nearly 17% of construction workers (60% of whom were apprentices) reported current drug use.

Conclusion

Drug use remains an important problem in Europe, even if the number of people who use drugs has stabilised or decreased a little recently. Ten to 13% of the employed people in the UK reported using drugs in the last years. Forty-one per cent of people who go into rehabilitation are employed. If the situation in the United States is similar to that in Europe, the industry groups with the highest prevalence of past-month illicit drug use were accommodations and food services (16.9%) and construction (13.7%). Public administration (4.1%), educational services (4.0%) and utilities (3.8%) had the lowest prevalence of past-month illicit drug use.

References

1. United Nations Office on Drugs and Crime (UNODC) (2009) *World Drug Report 2009*. New York: United Nations. www.unodc.org/documents/wdr/WDR_2009/WDR2009_eng_web.pdf (accessed November 2010).
2. European Monitoring Centre for Drugs and Drug Addiction (EMCDDA) (2010) *General Population Surveys (GPS)*. www.emcdda.europa.eu/stats09/gps (accessed 5 April 2010).
3. European Monitoring Centre for Drugs and Drug Addiction (EMCDDA) (2010) *Analysis of the Drug Situation in Europe*. www.emcdda.europa.eu/situation/analysis (accessed 5 April 2010).
4. Eurobarometer (2004) *Young People and Drugs*. Flash Eurobarometer no. 158. Wavre, Belgium: European Commission. http://ec.europa.eu/public_opinion/flash/fl158_en.pdf (accessed November 2010).
5. Hoare J. Drug misuse declared: results from the 2008/09 British Crime Survey. England and Wales. *Home Office Statistical Bulletin*, 2009. http://rds.homeoffice.gov.uk/rds/pdfs09/hosb1209.pdf (accessed November 2010).
6. Smith A, Wadsworth E, Moss S, Simpson S. *The Scale and Impact of Illegal Drug Use By Workers*. Cardiff: HSE Books, 2004.
7. Hadfield L. Drugs, alcohol and the workplace in the year 2000. *Syva Drug Monitor* 2000; 3 (7): 49–51.
8. Szwarc E, Tracqui A. Ludes BAC. Occupational workplace and traffic fatalities in Alsace, France (2000–2005): results of toxicological investigations. *Forensic Sci Int Suppl* 2009; 1: 15–16.
9. Mariotti O. Drug addiction and working. *G Ital Med Lav Ergon* 2004; 26(3): 247–250.
10. European Monitoring Centre for Drugs and Drug Addiction (EMCDDA) (2010) *Statistical Bulletin 2009*. www.emcdda.europa.eu/stats09 (accessed 5 April 2010).
11. Sleiman S. *Belgian National Report on Drugs 2004*. Report No.: 2004–022. Brussels: Scientific Institute on Public Health, 2005.
12. George S. A snapshot of workplace drug testing in the UK. *Occup Med Oxford* 2005; 55(1): 69–71.
13. Clarke JB. Workplace drug testing using oral fluid – the UK experience. Poster presented at the Fourth European Workplace Drug Testing Society Symposium in Dublin, 2005.
14. Verstraete AG, Pierce A. Workplace drug testing in Europe. *Forensic Sci Int* 2001; 121(12): 2–6.
15. Kauert G, Breitstadt R, Falke B, Filippi G. Drugtesting in applicants for a job – prevalence and strategies. Presentation at the First European Symposium on Drugtesting at Workplace, Huddinge, Stockholm, Sweden, 30 March–1 April 1998.
16. Kauert G. Quantitative aspects in workplace drug testing. Paper presented at the European Workplace Drug Testing Society meeting in Rimini, 2000.
17. Dalen P, Beck O, Bergman U, Bjorklov P, Finer D, Garle M *et al.* Workplace drug testing (WDT) likely to increase in Europe. Report from the First European Symposium on WDT including selected abstracts. *Eur J Clin Pharmacol* 2000; 56(1): 103–120.
18. Cabrero E, Gomez-Acebo A, Garcia-Alcazar I, Luna JD, Luna A. Detection methods of the drug-addiction and alcoholism treatment programme of the Spanish National Railway Company (RENFE). *Med Lav* 2003; 94(4): 364–373.
19. Anon. Drug use by European and US rail and transit workers. *ICADTS Reporter* 2000; 11 (4): 2–3.
20. Norbeck H-E. Experience of three years of drug testing at Stockholm Transport. Paper presented at the second European Workplace Drug Testing Society meeting in Rimini, 2000.
21. Varga T, Mágori K, Tárkáni I, eds. Workplace testing of the drivers of a public transport company in Hungary. Paper presented at the ICADTS Conference, 2004, Glasgow, 2004.
22. Labat L, Fontaine B, Delzenne C, Doublet A, Marek MC, Tellier D *et al.* Prevalence of psychoactive substances in truck drivers in the Nord-Pas-de-Calais region (France). *Forensic Sci Int* 2008; 174(2–3): 90–94.

23. Birch D, Ashton H, Kamali F. Alcohol, drinking, illicit drug use, and stress in junior house officers in north-east England. *Lancet* 1998; 352(9130): 785–786.
24. Newbury-Birch D, Lowry RJ, Kamali F. The changing patterns of drinking, illicit drug use, stress, anxiety and depression in dental students in a UK dental school: a longitudinal study. *Br Dental J* 2002; 192(11): 646–649.
25. Beaujouan L, Czernichow S, Pourriat JL, Bonnet F. Prevalence and risk factors for substance abuse and dependence among anaesthetists: a national survey. *Ann Fr Anesth Reanim* 2005; 24(5): 471–479.
26. Brooke D, Edwards G, Taylor C. Addiction as an occupational hazard: 144 doctors with drug and alcohol problems. *Br J Addict* 1991; 86(8): 1011–1016.
27. Observatoire français des drogues et des toxicomanies (OFDT) (2006) Suivi epidémiologique des conduites toxicophiles dans les armées: Enquàte auprès des appelés (fin 1996). www.ofdt.fr/BDD_len/Bd_stats/7_Doc.xhtml (accessed 10 April 2010).
28. Beck F, Legleye S, Spilka D. Drogues à l'adolescence. Niveaux et contextes d'usage de cannabis, alcool, tabac et autres drogues à 17–18 ans en France. ESCAPAD. Saint-Denis (France): Observatoire français des drogues et des toxicomanies (OFDT), 2004.
29. Lapeyre-Mestre M, Sulem P, Niezborala M, Ngoundo-Mbongue TB, Briand-Vincens D, Jansou P *et al.* Taking drugs in the working environment: A study in a sample of 2106 workers in the Toulouse metropolitan area. *Therapie* 2004; 59(6): 615–623.
30. Hibell B, Guttormsson U, Ahlström S, Balakireva O, Bjarnason T, Kokkevi A *et al.* *The 2007 ESPAD Report – Substance Use Among Students in 35 European Countries.* Stockholm: The Swedish Council for Information on Alcohol and Other Drugs (CAN), 2009.
31. Webb E, Ashton H, Kelly P, Kamali F. Patterns of alcohol consumption, smoking and illicit drug use in British university students: interfaculty comparisons. *Drug Alcohol Depend* 1997; 47(2): 145–153.
32. Pickard M, Bates L, Dorian M, Greig H, Saint D. Alcohol and drug use in second-year medical students at the University of Leeds. *Med Educ* 2000; 34(2): 148–150.
33. Underwood B, Fox K. A survey of alcohol and drug use among UK based dental undergraduates. *Br Dental J* 2000; 189(6): 314–317.
34. Larson SL, Eyerman J, Foster MS, Gfroerer JC. *Worker Substance Use and Workplace Policies and Programs.* DHHS Publication No. SMA 07–4273. Rockville, MD: Substance Abuse and Mental Health Services Administration, Office of Applied Studies, 2007.
35. Hersch RK, McPherson TL, Cook RF. Substance use in the construction industry: a comparison of assessment methods. *Subst Use Misuse* 2002; 37(11): 1331–1358.

2

Effects of drugs on human performance

Elke Raes and Alain Verstraete

Key points

- Controlled experimental studies of the effect of illicit drugs on human performance give a clear picture of the effects that can be expected. Drugs can have an influence on performance through their desired effects (e.g. hallucination in LSD and cannabis users or sedation in heroin users) or their side-effects (e.g. miosis in heroin users or tremor in amphetamine users). Drugs have many different effects on psychomotor function (e.g. reaction time and coordination), alertness, vision, risk taking and aggressivity.
- Low doses of (meth)amphetamine can improve mental and motor performance in fatigued persons. Tests in driving simulators revealed that the intake of amphetamine causes a decrease in overall simulated performance by inducing problems such as incorrect signalling, failing to stop at a red traffic light and slow reaction times. The chronic use of amphetamines causes depression and has obvious negative effects on cognitive and psychomotor skills, which last longer than the period of intoxication and are often correlated to the severity of use. It is also linked to psychiatric problems, such as depression, hallucinations, schizophrenia and paranoia.
- The use of MDMA (ecstasy) can cause a decrease in attention, short-term and long-term memory, verbal memory, visuospatial skills, executive functioning and prediction of object movement under divided attention. Chronic ecstasy use can lead to higher impulsivity.

- Cannabis affects working performance, as it impairs several cognitive and psychomotor functions in a dose-dependent way. A user is aware of the impairment, but can only partially compensate for the decrements. The effects of cannabis can last up to 24 hours, indicating that a person using cannabis in the evening can still experience residual impairment the following day at work. Chronic use of cannabis also affects work performance, even when intoxication is no longer present, particularly among individuals in occupations requiring high levels of cognitive capacity. The work performance of a chronic cannabis user can be impaired, even during a period of abstinence. Very heavy use of marijuana is associated with persistent decrements in neurocognitive performance even after 28 days of abstinence.
- The use of cocaine can partially reverse performance decrements in sleep-deprived persons. In rested persons, some studies found no effect of the use of cocaine on psychomotor or cognitive skills, while other studies observed an improvement in psychomotor performance (decreased reaction time), attention and learning. Negative consequences for work performance are mostly expected with chronic use of cocaine, as this can lead to cognitive defects, impaired psychomotor performance, impulsive behaviour and even psychosis.
- LSD users are unable to perform at work during intoxication, as they experience perceptual distortions and an increase in reaction time. LSD users can suffer from post-hallucinogen perceptual disorder (PHPD), spontaneous recurrences of LSD-like states in subjects following cessation of drug use. It can occur up to five years after last ingestion, even after a single LSD ingestion.

Introduction

It is estimated that some 172–250 million people (in the 15–64 age group), have used drugs at least once in the last 12 months. About half of these (2.7%) use drugs at least once per month. Between 18 and 38 million persons worldwide, or 0.6% of world's population, are considered to be drug addicts or problem drug users.[1]

The effects of drugs on performance can be the consequence of the acute effect of the drug (including the 'crash' phase after drug use), but also of the impairment caused by withdrawal or by chronic use.

How can one assess these effects? In this chapter, we will briefly explain the methods to detect performance impairment, and describe the impairment caused by the major classes of illicit drugs. An important aspect that should be taken into consideration is the duration of these effects, as most people will not use drugs at work but more likely when going out or at home.

Methods for measuring the effect of drugs on performance

The effect of drugs on performance is mainly studied in experimental studies. However, in some cases epidemiological surveys can also give information. Many studies have looked at the effects of drugs on driving behaviour, and can also provide information on performance at the workplace.

Experimental studies

In experimental studies, the drug is administered in different doses to volunteers and the effects on performance are measured and compared to placebo or a positive control (for example alcohol). The tests evaluate the different psychomotor and cognitive functions of the volunteers. Several publications have reviewed the available tests.[2–4] The tests that are most often used are as follows.

Attention tests

These can be subdivided into simple and divided attention tasks. In a simple attention task, the subject is asked to monitor one process and to respond appropriately to specific stimuli. In a divided attention task a subject is asked to monitor two or more simultaneous processes and to respond appropriately to specific stimuli. For instance, the test may involve a tracking task and a visual search for a target. The subject is graded on his or her tracking error, the number of targets correctly detected and response time for detection.

Vigilance tests

This task is generally performed by means of an electronic device that presents a visual stimulus, moving in a rather monotonous pattern on a screen. The subject must observe and report deviations in this pattern over a prolonged period of time without feedback from the apparatus. An auditory pattern of signals may be used instead of the visual stimulus.

Auditory and visual tests

An example of an auditory test is a test concerning auditory discrimination. A series of pairs of auditory tones is presented to the subject, who must indicate whether the second tone is higher or lower than the first. An example of a visual test is the assessment of visual acuity. The subject is shown a series of test patterns of increasing complexity or decreasing size and is asked to identify or discriminate between the patterns. The distance, lighting conditions or degree of contrast may be varied (Figure 2.1).

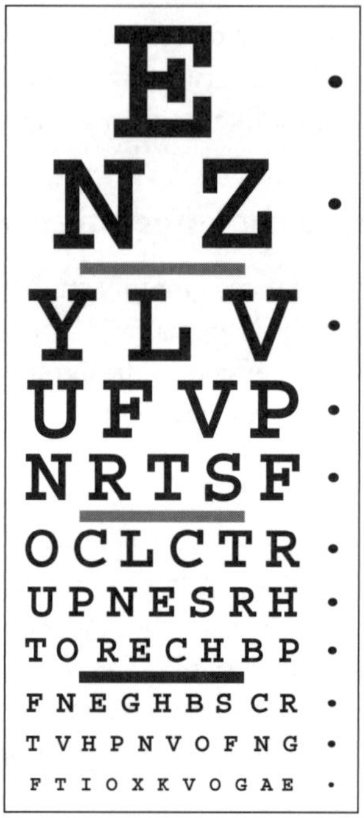

Figure 2.1 A visual acuity test.

Reaction time

There are simple, go/no go and choice reaction time tasks. The simple reaction time is the interval elapsing between the mental receiving of a sensory impression (such as visual, auditory and somatosensory) and the execution of a movement in response to that impression. In a go/no go reaction time task the participants respond to one particular event (e.g. a red colour or a horn sound) but ignore other events (e.g. a blue colour or a rooster sound). In a choice reaction time task, a series of stimuli, which may be auditory and/or visual, are presented to the subject using an electronic apparatus or a computer screen. The subject is instructed to respond appropriately and rapidly through hand or foot movements to pre-selected signals. The test may include disturbance signals to distract the subject, and it may involve two or more simultaneous tasks. The subject is graded on the speed and accuracy of his or her performance.

Cognitive tests

There is a large variety in cognitive tests. For example the Tower of London task is a task to measure the planning function (Figure 2.2). Another is the digit symbol substitution task, during which the subject is shown a code sheet

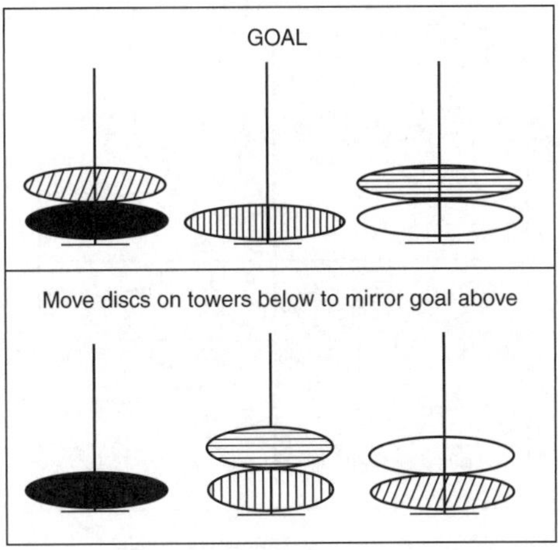

Figure 2.2 A Tower of London test.

containing a series of numbers assigned to a series of symbols. Afterwards the subject is shown those symbols in random order and is asked to assign the corresponding number. During repetitions of the task, the pattern of the digit–symbol pairings is usually scrambled. In the Stroop word/colour test the subject is asked to depress one of four keys labelled with a different colour in response to a stimulus. The stimulus is the name of one of the four colours or of a non-represented colour or does not represent a colour at all. During the letter cancellation test the subject is given a page filled with random letters and is asked to strike through one or more specific target letters whenever they appear (Figure 2.3). In logical reasoning tests a series of simple sentences, such as 'Birds grow on trees', is presented and the subject must indicate whether each statement is true or false.

Critical flicker fusion

The subject is asked to view one or more lights on a computer screen or electronic apparatus and to indicate whether the light appears to be flickering or continuous. The rate of flicker is increased or decreased, and the frequency of the subject's discriminative threshold is recorded.

Visual-motor coordination tests

The circular lights task typically employs an electronic device with a series of 10–20 lights arranged in a circular pattern. As each light is illuminated in random order, the subject must trigger a switch corresponding to that light. During the simplest form of a tracking task the subject is asked to control the position of a light bar on a screen using a hand-operated device. More sophisticated versions involve variable speed control of the visual stimulus and/or a computerised representation of a vehicle moving along a road. The parameter

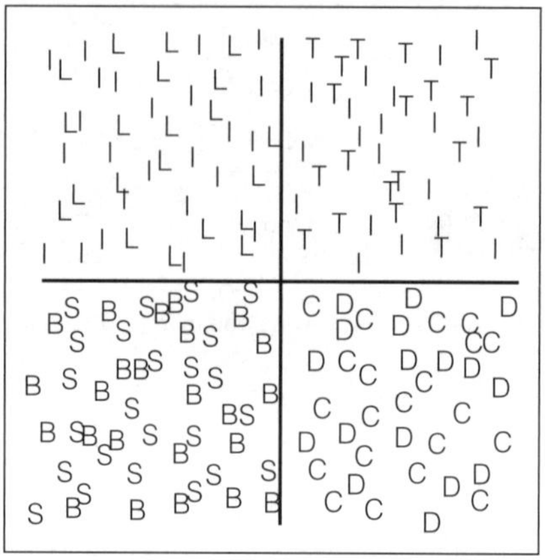

Figure 2.3 Four examples of forms of a letter cancellation task.

that can be used to express performance is the standard deviation of the lateral position (SDLP).

Body sway

The measurements of body movement of the subject with or without eyes closed are usually taken in both the lateral and sagittal directions over a specified period of time using some type of metering device such as an electronic platform.

Physiological measurements

The parameters that can be assessed are electroencephalogram, eye movements, pupillary response, pulse and blood pressure.

Self-assessment of some functions

The subject themselves report their observations on visual analogue scales. These scales are a measurement instrument that tries to measure a characteristic or attitude that is believed to range across a continuum of values (Figure 2.4).

While laboratory studies give invaluable information, one should be aware of their limitations:

- Often the doses administered are low compared with the doses used in the street. For example, performance studies for cannabis have traditionally been using low-potency marijuana (maximum 4%).[5–24] Recently, Ramaekers *et al.*[25] discovered in their study that, when using high-potency marijuana (13% THC (tetrahydrocannabinol)) additional cognitive functions were diminished, and that the influence on performance was more distinct when compared to the traditional studies using low-potency marijuana. The concentration of THC in cannabis is nowadays much

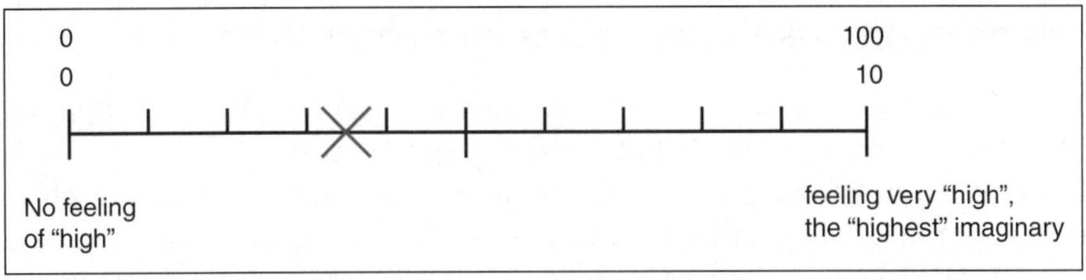

Figure 2.4 A visual analogue scale for the subjective feeling of 'high'.

higher than it was 20 or 30 years ago because of the new cultivation techniques. The effects of cannabis are thus no longer comparable with those that were described in the 1970s. This emphasises the importance of using realistic doses to estimate the effects of drugs in real life.

- Experimental studies measure only a part of the performance needed to complete a task, and the selection of specific tests can influence the results of the study. For example when the effect of the combination of cannabis and alcohol was studied, sometimes an additive or even synergistic effect was found, while other studies found the contrary. Liguori *et al.*[17] found no significant additive effects of alcohol and marijuana on brake latency. The authors mentioned that this may be due to the selection of reaction time as the key dependent variable, as several other studies found additive or multiplicative marijuana and alcohol effects on other aspects of performance, such as visual search and road tracking.[23,26,27]

Epidemiological studies

Epidemiological studies can complement the findings from experimental studies concerning the effects associated with the use of drugs by examining the incidence of drugs in various populations. Some studies have investigated the prevalence of drugs in the general population, while others have focused on certain subpopulations, such as persons admitted to an emergency department because of a car crash. By comparing the prevalence of a certain drug in the general population with the prevalence in persons admitted to an emergency department, some studies have even made estimations of the risk of being admitted while under the influence of a certain drug. These figures can indicate whether or not a person under the influence of a certain drug has a higher risk than a 'sober' person of being involved in a work or traffic accident. The prevalence of drugs in the various populations can be assessed by analysing biological samples of the involved subjects, but also by means of questionnaires. The problem in the last method can be an underestimation of the prevalence, while using the first method there may be a higher percentage of drop-outs.

Effects of different drug classes on performance

Illicit drugs are often taken to feel a 'high' or a rush. This is hardly a situation of optimal control of one's fine psychomotor functions. Thus drugs will decrease psychomotor performance because of their desired effects, such as euphoria, relaxation, apathy, hallucinations, but they can also impair because of their 'side-effects', such as shaking, trembling (decreased coordination), dizziness, anxiety and effects on vision (e.g. blinding due to mydriasis with amphetamines, cannabis or cocaine).

For each drug class, the duration of the effects will be described, but the reader should bear in mind that the duration depends on many factors such as the dose, the route of administration and the individual characteristics and susceptibility of the users. Moreover, co-ingestion of different drugs makes predictions even more difficult (e.g. cocaine users often use alcohol concomitantly to increase the duration of the effects (explained by the formation of the longer acting metabolite cocaethylene)).

Amphetamine and MDMA (ecstasy) (Tables 2.1 and 2.2)

Amphetamines are mostly used orally, but they can also be administered intranasally, intravenously or by smoking.[28] They are often taken as a pill or capsule at mega-discotheques or rave parties. Some people will spend the whole weekend dancing, moving from discotheques to after-clubs, using amphetamine or ecstasy to increase their energy for dancing and cannabis or

Table 2.1 Characteristics of amphetamine

Administration		Intranasally (intravenously, orally, smoking)
Typical use	Occasional user	±60 mg/dose
	Heavy user	250 → 5000 mg/day
Desired effects		Rush: intense euphoria, high energy, sexual stimulation Duration: <24 hours
Side-effects	Acute	Mydriasis, irritability, insomnia, tremors, anxiety, paranoia, aggression, lack of coordination, poor impulse control, fatigue, positive and negative effects on cognition and psychomotor performance Duration: several days
	Chronic	Cognitive defects, depression, hallucinations, schizophrenia, paranoia Duration: some effects minimum 2 years since last use
Combination with fatigue		Positive effect on psychomotor performance, effects on cognition unclear

Table 2.2 Characteristics of ecstasy (XTC, MDMA, methylenedioxymethylamphetamine)

Administration		Orally (intranasally, intravenously, smoking)
Typical use	Occasional user	10–150 mg/dose
	Heavy user	?
Desired effects		Rush: intense euphoria, high energy, empathy Duration: <24 hours
Side-effects	Acute	Mydriasis, sensory disturbances, nausea, restlessness, tremors, fatigue Positive and negative effects on cognition and psychomotor performance Duration: several days
	Chronic	Defects in cognitive functions, increased impulsivity and depression Duration: some effects minimum 2 years since last use
Combination with alcohol		Alcohol: reinforces negative effects of ecstasy + causes some additional defects. Ecstasy can diminish some but not all negative effects of alcohol

benzodiazepines to calm down. It is not surprising that after such a weekend they will be exhausted at work or at school on Monday morning. The drug is also sometimes used by professional drivers and students to stay awake.[29–31]

Acute effects

Amphetamine causes a strong central stimulation. Two phases can be observed in a person who has consumed this drug[28] – the rush phase and the crash phase.

- During the rush phase the user will experience some psychological effects, such as overestimation of one's abilities, more risk taking, loss of the sense of reality, euphoria, insomnia, reduced fatigue or drowsiness and poor impulse control. The physiological effects that characterise this phase are mydriasis (dilated pupils), increased heart rate and blood pressure, increased respiration rate and a suppression of thirst and appetite.
- During the crash phase psychological effects are dysphoria, residual stimulation, restlessness, paranoia, aggression, lack of coordination, psychosis and drug craving. Physiological effects are fatigue, exhaustion, falling asleep and itching.

Ecstasy (methylenedioxymethylamphetamine, MDMA, XTC) is a 'designer' amphetamine, indicating that it is synthesised to resemble the effects of amphetamine. It has been suggested that MDMA belongs to the 'entactogens', which produce feelings of empathy, love and emotional closeness.[32] MDMA causes a weaker stimulation of the central nervous system than amphetamine, but beside the stimulating effect, it can also cause sensory disturbances, nausea, dizziness, ataxia, muscular rigidity, sweating, restlessness and tremor.[28]

Amphetamine

The effects of (dextro)amphetamine have been less investigated in experimental studies. The use of amphetamine can improve some cognitive functions such as divided attention performance and verbal interaction.[33,34] One study found that administration of amphetamine produces little effect on performance on a psychomotor test battery.[20] Tests in driving simulators, however, revealed that the intake of dexamphetamine causes a decrease in overall simulated driving by inducing problems such as incorrect signalling, failing to stop at a red traffic light and slow reaction times. The decrease in simulated driving ability was only observed during the day-time, however, which is consistent with the tunnel vision that is associated with amphetamine consumption.[33,35] The doses of amphetamine administered in these experimental studies were very low (10–30 mg) and thus not representative for realistic 'street' situations (100–1000 mg/day).[28] A series of studies showed low-level amphetamine-related enhancement of function but also less conservative movement estimation that might contribute to amphetamine-related road fatalities.[36]

Studies investigating the effect of dextroamphetamine in sleep-deprived persons revealed a positive effect on psychomotor functions.[37–39] Dextroamphetamine also appears to be effective for sustaining helicopter pilot performance during short periods of sleep loss without producing adverse side-effects.[38,39] The effects of dextroamphetamine on cognitive functions in sleep-deprived persons are less obvious. Both positive, negative as well as no effects have been observed.[33,37]

Ecstasy

Most experimental studies concerning the effects of amphetamines on performance administered ecstasy to the volunteers. The results indicated that the use of ecstasy can have an acute effect on some cognitive functions. Studies mention a decrease in attention, short-term and long-term memory, verbal memory, visuospatial skills, executive functioning and prediction of object movement under divided attention.[40–44] One study, however, found no effect of ecstasy on visual search, planning or retrieval from semantic memory.[42] Ecstasy leads to improved psychomotor performance on a battery of tests, such as movement speed and tracking performance in a single, as well as in a divided attention task.[42] Tests in driving simulators, however, revealed that the intake of ecstasy can decrease performance by increasing speed and speed variation, and inducing problems in car following, while some tasks are not influenced (reaction time, lateral control), or even better performed (lateral control).[43,45] Nocturnal doses of MDMA may produce impairment of tracking performance and divided attention throughout the night that are additive to performance impairment produced by sleep loss.[46]

Other psychoactive substances such as alcohol can reinforce the deleterious effects of ecstasy, and even cause some additional negative effects.[47] On the other hand, the use of ecstasy can diminish some, but not all deleterious effects of alcohol, while other negative effects of alcohol can be reinforced.[43] Co-administration of MDMA and ethanol did not show greater impairment of performance compared with the single-drug conditions. Impaired memory function was consistently observed after all drug conditions. Co-administration of MDMA and ethanol did not exacerbate the effects of either drug alone. Although the impairment of performance was relatively moderate, all induced significant impairment of cognitive function.[48]

Duration of the effects

The duration of the subjective 'positive' effects is less than 24 hours,[49] but thereafter the crash phase starts, with the subject feeling very tired, unable to combat sleep and even depressed which can last for several days.[40,41,49] The effects on psychomotor performance can last for more than 5 hours,[42] and studies in flight simulators revealed positive effects in sleep-deprived pilots for up to 9 hours after last intake.[38,39] The duration of the cognitive effects is unclear. Some studies show that the negative effects on cognitive performance, especially verbal memory, can last for several days,[40,41,44] while other studies could no longer find impairment about 24 hours after last use.[43]

Chronic effects

Ecstasy users are aware of the consequences of their chronic use. They report the development of tolerance, impaired ability to concentrate and depression.[49] Experimental studies revealed that the consequences of chronic amphetamine or ecstasy use for the cognitive functions are a decrease in executive functioning, attention, memory (spatial, semantic, long-term and short-term) and verbal intelligence. Some of these defects become more prominent with increasing severity of use, and could be assessed up to two years since last use.[50–56] Stimulant-dependent individuals exhibit altered time processing in several domains, one of which can be explained by increased impulsivity.[57]

The chronic use of ecstasy can also lead to higher levels of impulsivity.[58] The chronic use of (meth)amphetamine (not ecstasy) is aetiologically linked to psychiatric problems, such as depression, hallucinations, schizophrenia and paranoia.[59,60] In a large study from a psychiatric hospital and a detention centre in Taiwan, researchers found that 40% of the methamphetamine users met the criteria for amphetamine-induced psychosis. The risks for the development of psychosis were younger age at onset, larger dosage and premorbid schizoid/schizotypal traits.[61]

Workplace context

Some individuals who work irregular or rotating shifts use stimulants (before going to work) and sedatives (before going to sleep) to offset mood and performance decrements related to shift changes. During a simulated shift work study, Hart *et al.*[62] assessed the acute effects of the stimulant methamphetamine (10 mg) and the effects of the hypnotic zolpidem (10 mg), and the combination of both during the shift after drug administration. The results indicated that shift changes produce performance impairments and mood alterations that are improved by a single low to moderate dose of methamphetamine. Zolpidem, given alone or in combination with methamphetamine, did not alleviate most mood and performance effects related to shift changes. Nevertheless, shift workers may use the combination of stimulants and sedatives on consecutive days, thus the authors recommend that future studies should assess the effects of (a combination of) these substances administered over consecutive days.[62]

Conclusion

The use of amphetamines reduces sleepiness and causes a stimulating effect. Both positive and negative effects are observed on the cognitive and psychomotor skills. The negative effects are reinforced after additional intake of other psychoactive substances such as alcohol. The positive effects are mostly observed in fatigued or sleep-deprived persons. The chronic use of amphetamines causes depression and has obvious negative effects on cognitive and psychomotor skills, which last longer than the period of intoxication and are often correlated to the severity of use.

One single dose of amphetamines can thus have partially positive and partially negative effects on working performance. Amphetamine use during the weekend can, however, lead to performance deficits during the working week and chronic use can even lead to psychiatric problems that are obviously not reconcilable with an appropriate work performance.

Cannabinoids (Table 2.3)

Cannabis is usually smoked as a cigarette ('joint') or in a pipe or bong. Hollowed out cigars packed with cannabis are called 'blunts'. To a lesser degree cannabis is ingested orally, for example by eating 'space-cake'.[28]

Table 2.3 Characteristics of cannabis

Administration		Smoking (joint, pipe or bong) (orally)
Typical use		Highly variable and depending on potency (marijuana: 2–25%, hashish: 5–15%, hashish oil: ≥20%)
Desired effects		Euphoria, relaxation, increased social interaction with frequent laughing and changes in perception Duration: 2 hours
Side-effects	Acute	Mydriasis, dry mouth, anxiety, decrements in cognitive and psychomotor functions Duration: up to 24 hours
	Chronic	Defects in cognitive functions and psychomotor functions, amotivational behaviour and schizophrenia Duration: some effects minimum 1 month since last use
Combination	Alcohol	Some negative effects of cannabis: additive or even synergistic relation with negative effects of alcohol
	Cocaine	The combination of cannabis and cocaine causes additional impairment compared to the use of cannabis or cocaine alone

Acute effects

The effects of marijuana vary with dose, route of administration, experience of the user, vulnerability to psychoactive effects and setting of use. A user will feel euphoria, relaxation, increased social interaction with frequent laughing and changes in perception (visual, auditive, sensory or time perception). Occasionally, the use of cannabis can cause anxiety that may escalate to panic attacks and paranoia. A sense of enhanced well-being may alternate with depressive phases.[63] The users are aware of the effects of the drug, and this awareness increases with higher doses.[14,17,18,22,64]

The physiological effects of cannabis use are increased heart rate and arterial pressure, red eyes, mydriasis, dry mouth and throat, increased appetite, vasodilatation and decreased respiratory rate. Cannabis also affects the immune and endocrine systems, produces lung damage and EEG alterations, and influences neonatal and child development.[63]

Cannabis reduces some cognitive and psychomotor skills such as learning, equilibrium, coordination, tracking ability, memory, perception, motor impulsivity and vigilance, and these effects are mostly dose-dependent.[6,8–10,13,17,18,20–22,25,64] The impairment depends on the experience of the user (with more impairment in inexperienced users).[5,65] Hunault *et al.* studied acute cognitive and psychomotor effects of THC among recreational users after smoking cannabis cigarettes containing up to 69 mg of THC. The THC dose in smoked cannabis was linearly associated with a slower response time in simple reaction time, visuospatial selective attention, sustained attention, divided attention and short-term memory tasks and motor control impairment in the motor control task and the number of errors increased significantly with increasing doses in the short-term memory and the sustained attention tasks. However, some participants showed no impairment in motor control even at THC serum concentrations higher than 40 ng/mL. High feeling and drowsiness differed significantly between treatments. Response time slowed down and motor control worsened, both linearly, with increasing THC doses.[66]

Studies with pilots in flight simulators found clear impairing effects of cannabis on performance, with significant impairment in number and size of aileron changes, size of elevator changes, distance off centre on landing, vertical and lateral deviation on approach to landing and radio navigation errors.[12,15,16,24] However, the pilots were not aware of their impaired performance (Figure 2.5).[24]

Cannabis can also have an effect on behaviour. The influence of cannabis on human risk taking is unclear. The results of experiments in a laboratory setting are contradictory.[14,19,25] However, in some driving studies (with rather low doses) it has been observed that the user is aware of the impairment and compensates his or her driving style by driving more slowly, overtaking less or keeping longer distances. Nevertheless the driver is still unable to compensate for the loss of capability in some psychomotor skills.[5,22,23] The use of cannabis can influence social behaviour, for example acute marijuana use can decrease the amount of time subjects engage in verbal exchanges.[11,67]

In a study[68] of neurocognitive performance during acute THC intoxication in heavy and occasional cannabis users, THC significantly impaired performance of occasional cannabis users on critical tracking, divided attention and the stop signal task. THC did not affect the performance of heavy

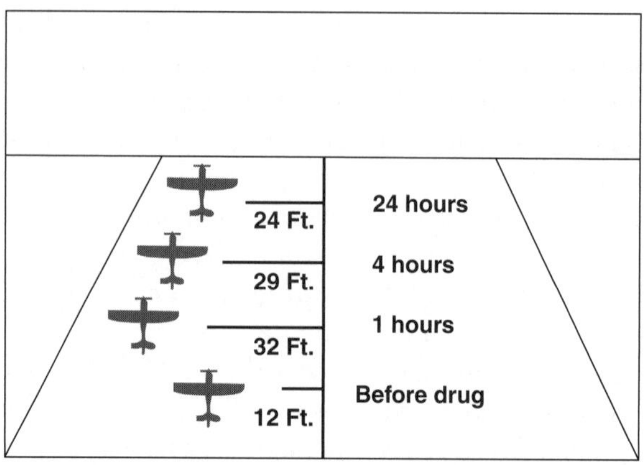

Figure 2.5 Average distance from the centre of the runway before, 1, 4 and 24 hours after smoking one marihuana cigarette of 2% THC.[24]

cannabis users except in the stop signal task (i.e. stop reaction time increased), particularly at high THC concentrations. Group comparisons of overall performance in occasional and heavy users did not reveal any persistent performance differences due to residual THC in heavy users. The authors concluded that cannabis use history strongly determines the behavioural response to single doses of THC. However, another study that used a virtual reality maze task found that in regular marijuana users, the immediate effects of marijuana may have an impact on cognitive-motor skills and brain mechanisms that modulate coordinated movement and driving.[69]

Some deleterious effects of cannabis appear to be additive or even synergistic with those of alcohol, and the combination of both agents results in a prolongation as well as enhancement of their effect.[2] For example, stronger subjective effects are generated after the use of a combination of alcohol and cannabis than after the use of alcohol or cannabis alone.[23,70] Driving studies revealed that drivers under the influence of both alcohol and cannabis were less attentive for traffic approaching from side streets, while the use of either cannabis or alcohol had no effect[26] and that the combination of cannabis and alcohol generates an additional decrement in lateral control on top of the decrement caused by either cannabis or alcohol.[23,27] Nevertheless, Liguori *et al.*[17] found no additive effects of alcohol and cannabis on brake latency or body sway.

The combined use of cocaine and marijuana can cause performance decrements in a repeated acquisition task while the use of cocaine or marijuana alone caused no effect on this task.[71]

Duration of effects

Effects from smoking cannabis products are felt within minutes and reach their peak in 10–30 minutes. Typical cannabis smokers experience a high that lasts approximately 2 hours.[28] Most studies assessed significant negative effects of cannabis maximum 7 hours after use.[6,8,9,13,14,18–22,25,64] However, some studies found impairing effects caused by cannabis use 10 (tracking ability), 12 (time estimation, verbal working memory or divided attention) or 24 hours (arithmetic and recall tasks, flight simulator landing task) after last use.[10,16,24,64,72] This may be due to the use of more sensitive and complex measurements, as two studies that assessed performance decrements up to 24 hours after use were performed in a flight simulator. Yesavage *et al.*[24] conducted a study with ten volunteer pilots who practised on a flight simulator landing an airplane on the centre of the runway. The study showed that the average distance from the centre of the runway before smoking marijuana was 12 feet (3.6 m). The pilots averaged 32, 29 and 24 feet (9.8, 8.8 and 7.3 m) from the centre of the runway respectively 1, 4 and 24 hours after smoking one marijuana cigarette of 2% THC (Figure 2.5). It is important to note that the pilots were judged normal by physicians and psychologists conducting that survey and also reported that they felt 'fine' the second day.

Very heavy use of marijuana is associated with persistent decrements in neurocognitive performance even after 28 days of abstinence.

Neuropsychological decrements may persist in chronic cannabis users during multiple days of abstinence.[73–78] Significantly larger deficits were observed in 77 chronic cannabis users on abstinence days 0, 1 and 7 but not 28 as compared to former cannabis users.[73,79] In contrast, others reported decreases in cortical motor activity[80] and neurocognitive impairment[76] after 28 days or more of documented abstinence in chronic, heavy cannabis users. In addition, duration rather than frequency of cannabis use has been suggested as the key factor in performance impairment.[75] Karschner *et al.* have suggested that the THC presence in plasma in chronic cannabis users (they measured THC concentrations 2 ng/mL after seven days of abstinence) may be the mechanism for residual neurocognitive impairment observed in chronic cannabis smokers after multiple days of abstinence.[81]

Chronic effects

The chronic use of cannabis can lead to deficiencies in memory, attention, information processing, visual perception and construction, manual dexterity, executive functioning, verbal expression and psychomotor speed.[75–77,82–87] These effects last longer than the period of intoxication and worsen with either increasing number of years or frequency of cannabis use. These defects are partially reversible with prolonged abstinence, but some impairment may be permanent. However, persons with a high IQ could somewhat compensate for the impairing effects, so there are individual differences in vulnerability.[83,85]

Long-term cannabis users tend to become withdrawn and indifferent and develop an amotivational syndrome. Lane *et al.*,[88] for example, examined motivation in a sample of regular cannabis users and a sample of controls. Both groups of participants were compared on a two-option experimental task designed to measure motivation. One option (work), which required systematically increasing response output, initially produced greater rates of monetary reinforcement than an alternative option (non-work) that required no response output to earn money. Switching to the non-work option was interpreted as a measure of reduced motivation. The cannabis-smoking participants switched earlier to the non-work option, and derived a greater percentage of their earnings from the non-work option. These differences persisted when controlling for differences in cognitive aptitude, gender, and the presence of conduct disorder.

The use of cannabis is even associated with an increased risk of developing schizophrenia.[89–92] Two meta-analyses and systematic reviews[93,94] found a consistent, twofold greater risk for psychosis among cannabis users. Persons with a higher vulnerability to develop psychosis have a greater likelihood to develop psychosis after cannabis use.[95]

A study by Kanayama *et al.*[96] revealed that the observed effects of long-term cannabis use on spatial working memory may be underestimated by studies using conventional neuropsychological tests. Their study suggested that long-term, heavy cannabis users display increased cortical brain activity and even recruit additional brain regions when performing a working memory task, and thus may superficially perform as well as control subjects but only at the cost of 'working harder'.

Workplace context

The acute and chronic effects of cannabis that were assessed by experimental studies with volunteers were confirmed within the context of work and everyday life by Wadsworth *et al.*[97] The study involved drug users and controls completing a battery of laboratory-based computer tasks during pre- and post-work sessions at the start and end of a working week. The results revealed that cannabis use was associated with impairment in both cognitive function and mood, though cannabis users reported no more workplace errors than controls. Cannabis use was associated with lower alertness and slower response organisation. In addition, users experienced working memory problems at the start, and psychomotor slowing and poorer episodic recall at the end of the working week. The authors suggest two possible effects, namely first a 'hangover'-type effect, which may increase with frequency of use, and second a subtle effect on cognitive function, perhaps more apparent under cognitive load and/or fatigue, which may increase with more prolonged use.

In another study, the same research group conducted a postal questionnaire among people selected at random from the electoral registers. Cannabis use was associated with both minor injuries and accidents, particularly among those with high levels of other associated risk factors. There was, however, no association between cannabis use and cognitive failure.[98] These studies suggest measurable cognitive performance deficits among cannabis users but relatively little awareness by users of any detrimental performance effects at work.

Breitstadt and Kauert[99] concluded that cannabis use at work can lead to misbehaviour by indecisiveness or by misinterpretation of colour or acoustic signals. The authors also point out the danger of inadequate psychomotor capacities caused by cannabis use in the operation of certain machines.

A study by Blows *et al.*,[100] for example, revealed that there is a strongly significant association between habitual use of cannabis and car crash injury, even after adjustment for the influence of possible confounders (acute use prior to driving, age, gender, ethnicity, education level, passenger carriage, driving exposure, time of day and other risky driving at the time of the crash such as blood alcohol concentration, seat-belt use, travelling speed and sleepiness score). The results showed that habitual cannabis use is associated with a tenfold increase in car crash injury.

Conclusion

Cannabis can clearly affect working performance, as it impairs several cognitive and psychomotor functions in a dose-dependent way. A user is aware of the impairment, but can only partially compensate for the decrements. The effects of cannabis can last up to 24 hours, indicating that a person using cannabis in the evening can still experience residual impairment the following morning at work. The combined use with alcohol causes some additional decrements and also a prolongation of these effects. Chronic use of cannabis can affect work performance, even when intoxication is no longer present, particularly among individuals in occupations requiring high levels of cognitive capacity. The work performance of a chronic cannabis user can be impaired, even during a period of abstinence.

Cocaine (Table 2.4)

Cocaine is usually administered by nasal insufflation. It is rarely injected subcutaneously (skinpopping). In some areas, crack, the free base of cocaine,

Table 2.4 Characteristics of cocaine

Administration		Intranasally (skinpopping, crack smoking)
Typical use	Occasional user	10–120 mg/dose
	Heavy user	≥5000 mg/day
Desired effects		Euphoria, excitation, increased alertness, sexual stimulation Duration: maximum 30 min
Side effects	Acute	Mydriasis, dizziness, motor restlessness, aggressiveness Duration: up to 4 hours (binge use: several days)
	Chronic	Defects in cognitive and psychomotor functions, increased impulsive behaviour, paranoia, hallucinations Duration: some effects: minimum 1 year since last use
Combination	Alcohol	Cocaine partially diminishes decrements caused by alcohol, chronic combined use doesn't cause additional decrements
	Cannabis	The combination of cannabis and cocaine causes additional impairment compared to the use of cannabis or cocaine alone

is smoked in a glass pipe. Cocaine can also be used topically for use as a local anaesthetic.[28]

Acute effects

The desired effects of cocaine are similar to those of amphetamine, but the onset is slower and the duration is longer. One can also observe two phases in a person that has consumed this drug:[28]

- A rush phase: during this phase the user experiences some psychological effects such as euphoria, excitation, feelings of well-being, general arousal, increased sexual excitement, dizziness, increased focus and alertness, mental clarity, increased talkativeness and motor restlessness, but also some physiological effects such as reduced appetite and fatigue, increased heart rate, blood pressure and body temperature, mydriasis and increased light sensitivity. Higher doses may, however, produce a pattern of psychosis with confused and disoriented behaviour, delusions, hallucinations, irritability, fear, paranoia, antisocial behaviour and aggressiveness.
- A depressive phase: the psychological effects intrinsic to this phase are dysphoria, agitation, nervousness, drug craving, general CNS depression, fatigue and insomnia. The physiological parameters intrinsic to this phase experienced are itching/picking/scratching, normal heart rate and normal pupils.

The use of cocaine can partially reverse performance decrements in sleep-deprived persons.[101] In rested persons, some studies found no effect of the use of cocaine on psychomotor or cognitive skills,[101–106] while other studies assessed an improvement in psychomotor performance (decreased reaction time), attention and learning.[104,107–110] A study by Hopper *et al.*,[102] however, found no effect of a low dose of cocaine (0.2 mg/kg) on attention, recall and recognition task performance, while cortisol induced marginal dose–response effects on these functions. The effects of cocaine may thus be influenced by the induction of hypercortisolaemia. Cocaine-dependent subjects displayed significantly poorer ability to copy three-dimensional objects (e.g. Necker cube, a smoking pipe, a hidden line elimination cube, a pyramid and a dissected pyramid). Decreased three-dimensional copying ability has been found to be associated with fatal injuries.[111]

Cocaine can partially diminish performance decrements caused by alcohol consumption. The use of a combination of alcohol and cocaine decreases psychomotor impairment and improves performance on cognitive tests when compared to the use of alcohol alone.[71,108] Cocaine also decreases the subjective feeling of drunkenness caused by alcohol,[71,108] and a combination of alcohol and cocaine causes a higher increase in heart rate and blood pressure than is observed following the use of alcohol or cocaine alone.[105,108] The combined use of cocaine and marijuana can cause performance decrements in a repeated acquisition task, while the use of cocaine or marijuana alone caused no effect on this task.[71]

Duration of effects

The faster the absorption of cocaine, the more intense and rapid the feeling of 'high' appears, but the shorter the duration of the desired effects. Injecting cocaine produces an effect within 15–30 seconds. A hit of smoked crack produces an almost immediate intense experience and will typically produce effects lasting 5–15 minutes. Similarly, snorting cocaine produces effects almost immediately and the resulting high may last 15–30 minutes.[28] Experimental studies assessed the effects on cognitive or psychomotor performance for a maximum of 4 hours after use.[104,108–110]

The late-phase effects following binge use may, however, last for several days,[28] with the subject feeling very tired and unable to combat sleep.

Chronic effects

Chronic use of cocaine can affect performance in abstinent users. Cocaine-dependent subjects have lower grey matter volumes in cerebellar hemispheres as well as in frontal, temporal cortex and thalamus.[112] Chronic users can experience difficulties in processing cognitive tasks concerning cognitive flexibility, memory (long-term, short-term and visual), problem solving and abstraction, calculating and learning. The results concerning the effects on attention, executive functioning, verbal and spatial memory are contradictory, with some studies finding negative effects, none or even positive effects.[113–122] The chronic use of cocaine can also result in detrimental effects on psychomotor performance, such as a decrease in psychomotor speed and perception.[113,115–120] Cocaine addiction is associated with reduced error processing and impaired behavioural correction of errors after an error is made.[123] However, one study found that abstinent cocaine-dependent males performed better than controls on a task assessing simple visual-motor speed.[119]

Chronic cocaine use is also associated with an effect on behaviour, namely an increase in impulsive behaviour.[124]

Chronic use of alcohol and cocaine each selectively affect performance on different neurobehavioural tests in a dose-dependent way.[125] However, the combined use of alcohol and cocaine does not cause additional negative effects on the brain, as singly addicted cocaine abusers demonstrate similar or greater neurocognitive impairment than individuals who abuse both alcohol and cocaine.[115,116,118,126]

Studies on cocaine abusers in clinical settings report that more than half of such individuals experience paranoia and hallucinations. Those who develop psychosis with cocaine use are likely to be men, have a greater duration and amount of use, have greater proneness to psychosis and have a lower body mass index. Cocaine-induced psychosis shows sensitisation, with psychosis becoming more severe and occurring more rapidly with continued cocaine use.[59]

Conclusion

The use of cocaine can improve performance in fatigued or sleep-deprived persons, but the drug does not necessarily enhance performance in rested persons. Cocaine can partially reverse some negative effects of alcohol, while detrimental effects of other drugs such as marijuana can be reinforced. Negative consequences for work performance are mostly expected with chronic use of cocaine, as this can lead to cognitive defects, impaired psychomotor performance, impulsive behaviour and even psychosis.

LSD (Table 2.5)

Lysergic acid diethylamide (LSD) is a hallucinogenic drug. The drug is primarily used orally, but it can be inhaled, injected and applied transdermally.

Acute effects

The effects are unpredictable and depend on the dose ingested, the user's personality and mood, expectations and the surroundings. The psychological effects include hallucinations, increased colour perception, altered mental

Table 2.5 Characteristics of LSD

Administration		Orally (inhalation, intravenously, transdermally)
Typical use		25–200 micrograms/dose
Desired effects		Hallucinations, impaired depth, time and space perceptions, increased colour perception Duration: 2–4 hours (peak), diminishes over 6–8 hours
Side-effects	Acute	Anxiety, terrifying thoughts (bad trip), sweating, tachycardia, mydriasis, sleeplessness, cognitive and psychomotor impairment Duration: up to 5 hours
	Chronic	Impairment of visual functions (colour discrimination, palinopsia), psychosis (paranoia, hallucinations, depression), post-hallucinogen perceptual disorder Duration: some effects: minimum 5 years since last use
Combination with alcohol		LSD causes a partial to complete blockade of subjective alcohol effects

state, thought disorders, temporary psychosis, delusions, body image changes, and impaired depth, time and space perceptions. Users may feel several emotions at once or swing rapidly from one emotion to another. 'Bad trips' may consist of severe, terrifying thoughts and feeling, fear of losing control and despair. The drug also causes some physiological effects, such as tachycardia, hypertension, mydriasis, sweating, loss of appetite, sleeplessness, dry mouth, tremors, speech difficulties and piloerection.[28]

Experimental studies have shown that the use of LSD can cause several cognitive effects. Users can experience visual effects such as prolonged after-images during LSD intoxication (palinopsia),[127] increased elicitation of subjective colours and patterns by flickers and pure tones,[128] enhancement of illusions[129] and distortions.[130] LSD users also have decreased critical flicker frequencies, meaning that the frequency at which a flickering light is indistinguishable from a steady light is lower than in control subjects.[131]

LSD can also negatively affect psychomotor performance by increasing reaction time.[129,132] This effect is even dose-related.[132] A study by Key[133] illustrated that the effect of LSD on the response time for a simple conditioned avoidance response depends upon the presence or absence of stimuli other than these used in the conditioning procedure. When the conditioning stimulus was presented alone, administration of LSD even caused a decrease in response time. However, in the additional presence of tonal pips at three different levels of intensity, the administration of LSD potentiated the lengthening of reaction time and increase in the number of incorrect responses.

Other impairments in reaction in LSD users are impairment in skin sensitivity[129] and a decrease in kneejerk threshold.[134]

Experimental studies in animals showed that LSD can have a negative influence on time estimation and on motivation, and only in high doses (0.03 mg/kg) on short-term memory.[135]

Concerning the combination of LSD with other psychoactive substances, LSD users themselves report a partial to complete blockade of subjective alcohol effects when using both substances at the same time.[136]

Duration of effects

The onset of the desired effects of LSD is rapid following intravenous administration (10 minutes). Following oral ingestion, onset of the first effects is experienced in 20–30 minutes, peaking at 2–4 hours and gradually diminishing over 6–8 hours.[28] Effects on reaction time and skin sensitivity have been assessed up to 5 hours after use.[129,132]

Chronic effects

The use of LSD can cause some long-term visual effects. Abraham[137] found that an average of two years after their last exposure to the drug, LSD users performed worse than controls on a test of colour discrimination, and that

LSD users without flashbacks performed better than users with flashbacks. Kawasaki and Purvin[127] found that three individuals experiencing palinopsia during LSD intoxication continued to be symptomatic three years after they ceased to ingest the drug. Depressed critical flicker frequencies can be found in past LSD users at least 2.3 years since their last use.[138]

The use of LSD can lead to prolonged psychosis. Abraham and Aldridge[139] found in their review that the incidence of prolonged psychosis following LSD in clinical settings falls in a range of 0.08–4.6%, with a median of 2.7%. Some individuals can even become psychotic after a single dose of LSD, suggesting a peculiar vulnerability to the drug in certain individuals. Possible psychotic reactions include labile moods, paranoid delusions, hallucinations, fear, depression with suicidal ideas and schizophrenia, and these can last for more than a year. Many individuals developing prolonged psychosis after LSD use had prior histories of psychosis, indicating that LSD use may precipitate the onset of psychotic illness.[139]

Another long-term effect that has been observed in LSD users is the occurrence of post-hallucinogen perceptual disorder (PHPD), namely spontaneous recurrences of LSD-like states in subjects following cessation of drug use. PHPD is predominantly visual and can occur up to five years after last ingestion, even after a single LSD ingestion.[139] Batzer *et al.*[140] concluded that findings indicate a statistically significant relation between the number of doses taken and the incidence of flashbacks.

Conclusion

It is clear that LSD users are unable to perform at work during intoxication, as they will experience perceptual distortions and an increase in reaction time. More important is that the use of LSD can have long-lasting effects on perception, and even can lead to prolonged psychosis. These effects can last several years even after a single ingestion of LSD, meaning that (a single) use of LSD by an individual during his or her free time may have long-lasting detrimental effects on work performance.

Heroin (Table 2.6)

Heroin is an opiate that can be smoked, snorted, injected and administered subcutaneously.[28]

Acute effects

Following intravenous administration, the user generally feels intense euphoria ('rush') accompanied by a warm flushing of the skin, dry mouth and heavy extremities. The user then alternates between a wakeful and drowsy state. The

Table 2.6 Characteristics of heroin

Administration		Smoking, snorting, injecting and subcutaneous administering
Typical use	Occasional user	10–15 mg/dose
	Heavy user	Up to 400 mg/day
Desired effects		Euphoria, relaxation, drowsiness, delirium, mental clouding Duration: several minutes
Side-effects	Acute	Miosis, analgesia, nausea, cold turkey, psychomotor and cognitive decrements Duration: up to 6 hours
	Chronic	Cognitive and psychomotor decrements, depression, anxiety Duration: some effects minimum 1 year since last use
Combination with methadone		Methadone maintenance can cause impairment over and above that associated to the long-term use of heroin

psychological effects are euphoria, feeling of well-being, relaxation, drowsiness, sedation, lethargy, disconnectedness, self-absorption, mental clouding and delirium. Heroin users also experience some physiological effects, such as analgesia, depression of heart rate, depressed respiration and central nervous system, nausea and vomiting, fixed and constricted pupils (miosis), sweating and cramping. Six to twelve hours later, an unpleasant feeling of abstinence ('cold turkey') appears which may last for several days. Early symptoms include watery eyes, runny nose, yawning and sweating. Forty-eight to 72 hours after the last dose the major withdrawal symptoms peak, including drug craving, restlessness, dysphoria, loss of appetite, tremors, diarrhoea, nausea and vomiting, elevated heart rate and blood pressure, chills alternating with flushing and excessive sweating, muscle and bone pain, muscle spasms and insomnia.[141]

Few experimental studies have investigated the acute effects of heroin in humans. Several studies confirmed the acute effect of heroin on subjective sedation and of miosis.[142–145] One study found a trend towards a decreased performance on the circular lights task, which is an indicator for psychomotor performance.[145] In another study the administration of heroin impaired performance on a reaction time task.[142] However, the doses used in these experimental studies ranged from 2 to 20 mg, while average daily doses range from 300 to 500 mg of heroin.[28]

Duration of effects

The desired effects of heroin, namely the intense euphoria, last from 45 seconds to several minutes.[28] The effects on performance can last up to

6 hours.[142–145] The duration of the effects is dependent on the dose and the route of administration. For example Jenkins *et al.*[142] assessed subjective effects of sedation, miosis and increased reaction time that lasted during 2 hours after smoking, and 4 hours after intravenous administration.

Chronic effects

Chronic heroin use can have long-lasting effects in humans. Studies have found an impairment of the planning function,[146] reaction time,[147] time perception,[148] spatial working memory,[54] pattern recognition memory,[54] executive functioning[54,55,149] and right–left discrimination.[150] Chronic heroin users also tend to be reckless and ignore the rules and regulations of tasks.[151] For some of these defects there is a significant relationship between the severity of heroin dependence or duration of use and the impairment.[55,146,149] For example, male addicts with duration of use longer than 1.5 years perform worse on a Tower of London task than addicts with a shorter duration of use.[146] The performance deficits caused by chronic heroin use are gender-related. For example heroin-dependent females demonstrate greater impairment of right–left discrimination than males.[150] The effects of heroin abuse on the simple reaction time are also gender-related, as the effects remitted after three months of abstinence in males, while females still had slower reaction times after six months of withdrawal.[147]

Some chronic effects can persist more than a year since last use,[151] while for example the effect on time perception had disappeared after 15 days of abstinence.[148]

The chronic use of heroin is also associated with depression, as studies of heroin users on treatment have documented elevated rates of comorbid depression that far exceed general population estimates. The reported prevalence of lifetime major depression among treated opiate users ranged from 38% to 56%, and the reported prevalence of current major depression from 16% to 30%.[152–160] A handful studies have indicated that individuals who regularly use heroin are at risk for elevated levels of anxiety and its disorders.[155,161–163]

Studies have also shown that methadone maintenance, used in substitution therapy, may be associated with additional impairment over and above that associated with long-term abuse of heroin.[164,165] Nevertheless, one must not forget that employment is associated with improved treatment outcome for opioid-dependent outpatients receiving methadone maintenance treatment.[166]

Conclusion

Heroin users are obviously not able to perform at work during intoxication, considering the many psychological and physiological defects. And during the

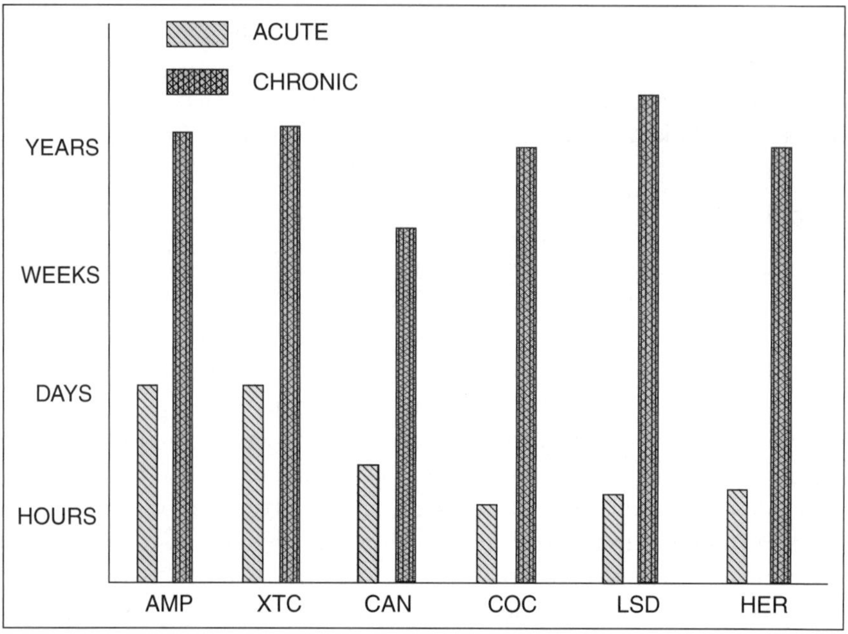

Figure 2.6 The duration of the acute and chronic effects of amphetamine (AMP), XTC, cannabis (CAN), cocaine (COC), LSD and heroin (HER).

withdrawal phase, performance remains impaired through restlessness, tremors and nausea, meaning that a person using heroin in the weekend can be unable to work during the week because of the withdrawal symptoms. Chronic effects, including cognitive and psychomotor defects, can persist for more than a year, indicating that an abstinent heroin user may perform worse than a non-user for a very long time.

The durations of the acute and chronic effects of the different kinds of drugs are presented in Figure 2.6.

Conclusion

There is a lot of evidence from experimental studies that drugs impair performance by decreasing psychomotor and cognitive functions and by causing some physiological effects. Only some drugs (cocaine or methamphetamine) are able to improve performance, and these positive effects have mostly been found in sleep-deprived persons. It can thus be concluded that a person under the influence of drugs is unable to perform well at work. Drug use, however, mostly takes place during leisure, for example at a party or at home. One could think that this drug use during leisure does not affect working performance. The above-mentioned data, however, show that, even if a person is no longer intoxicated, their performance can still be impaired when they go to work one or a few days later. This can be caused by residual effects, or by decrements caused by chronic drug use. An extreme example of long-lasting effects is the withdrawal phase that follows heroin use, causing restlessness, tremor and nausea. For cannabis, impaired performance on a flight simulator task was assessed in pilots up to 24 hours after use. The crash phase following amphetamine use makes the subject feel very tired, unable to combat sleep and even depressed, which can last for several days.

An example of decrements caused by chronic use is the possibility of the development of PHPD in LSD users. This disorder can develop even after a single use of LSD, and cause long-term spontaneous occurrences of LSD-like states after cessation of use. The chronic use of amphetamines, cannabis, cocaine, LSD or heroin can cause detrimental effects on cognitive and/or psychomotor functions, and for some drugs these defects lasted up to several years after last use. The performance deficits become more apparent as the complexity of the required task increases, indicating that deleterious effects of drug use will be more obvious in persons performing a complex and demanding job. The chronic use of these drugs is also associated with an increased risk for developing psychosis. These examples show that the use of drugs during leisure can negatively influence working performance during the week.

References

1. United Nations Office on Drugs and Crime (UNODC). *World Drug Report 2009*. New York: United Nations, 2009.
2. Baselt RC. *Drug Effects on Psychomotor Performance*. Foster City, CA: Biomedical Publications, 2001.
3. Irving A, Jones W. Methods for testing impairment of driving due to drugs. *Eur J Clin Pharmacol* 1992; 43(1): 61–66.
4. Ferrara SD, Giorgetti R, Zancaner S. Psychoactive substances and driving: state of the art and methodology. *Alcohol Drugs Driving* 1994; 10(1): 1–55.
5. Robbe HWJ, O'Hanlon JF. Marijuana and actual driving performance: US Department of Transportation 1993. National Highway Traffic Safety Administration Final Report no. DOT-HS-808078.
6. Fant RV, Heishman SJ, Bunker EB, Pickworth WB. Acute and residual effects of marijuana in humans. *Pharmacol Biochem Behav* 1998; 60(4): 777–784.
7. Foltin RW, McEntee MA, Capriotti RM, Pedroso JJ, Fischman MW. Effects of cocaine, alone and in combination with task performance, on heart rate and blood pressure. *Pharmacol Biochem Behav* 1988; 31(2): 387–391.
8. Hart CL, van Gorp W, Haney M, Foltin RW, Fischman MW. Effects of acute smoked marijuana on complex cognitive performance. *Neuropsychopharmacology* 2001; 25(5): 757–765.
9. Heishman SJ, Arasteh K, Stitzer ML. Comparative effects of alcohol and marijuana on mood, memory, and performance. *Pharmacol Biochem Behav* 1997; 58(1): 93–101.
10. Heishman SJ, Huestis MA, Henningfield JE, Cone EJ. Acute and residual effects of marihuana: profiles of plasma THC levels, physiological, subjective and performance measures. *Pharmacol Biochem Behav* 1990; 37(3): 561–565.
11. Higgins ST, Stitzer ML. Acute marijuana effects on social conversation. *Psychopharmacology (Berl)* 1986; 89(2): 234–238.

12. Janowsky DS, Meacham MP, Blaine JD, Schoor M, Bozzetti LP. Simulated flying performance after marihuana intoxication. *Aviat Space Environ Med* 1976; 47(2): 124–128.
13. Kurzthaler I, Hummer M, Miller C, Sperner-Unterweger B, Gunther V, Wechdorn H *et al.* Effect of cannabis use on cognitive functions and driving ability. *J Clin Psychiatry* 1999; 60(6): 395–399.
14. Lane SD, Cherek DR, Tcheremissine OV, Lieving LM, Pietras CJ. Acute marijuana effects on human risk taking. *Neuropsychopharmacology* 2005; 30(4): 800–809.
15. Leirer O, Yesavage JA, Morrow DG. Marijuana, aging, and task-difficulty effects on pilot performance. *Aviat Space Environ Med* 1989; 60(12): 1145–1152.
16. Leirer VO, Yesavage JA, Morrow DG. Marijuana carry-over effects on aircraft pilot performance. *Aviat Space Environ Med* 1991; 62(3): 221–227.
17. Liguori A, Gatto CP, Jarrett DB. Separate and combined effects of marijuana and alcohol on mood, equilibrium and simulated driving. *Psychopharmacology* 2002; 163 (34): 399–405.
18. Liguori A, Gatto CP, Robinson JH. Effects of marijuana on equilibrium, psychomotor performance, and simulated driving. *Behav Pharmacol* 1998; 9(7): 599–609.
19. McDonald J, Schleifer L, Richards JB. de Wit H. Effects of THC on behavioral measures of impulsivity in humans. *Neuropsychopharmacology* 2003; 28(7): 1356–1365.
20. Pickworth WB, Rohrer MS, Fant RV. Effects of abused drugs on psychomotor performance. *Exp Clin Psychopharmacol* 1997; 5(3): 235–241.
21. Robbe HWJ, ed. Marijuana's effects on actual driving performance. *Proceedings of the 13th International Conference on Alcohol, Drugs and Traffic Safety*, 1995. http://casr.adelaide.edu.au/T95/paper/s1p2.html (accessed 8 December 2010).
22. Sexton BF, Tunbridge R, Brook-Carter N, Jackson PG, Wright K. The influence of cannabis on driving. TRL report no. 477. Crowthorne: TRL Ltd, 2000.
23. Sexton BF, Tunbridge RJ, Board A, Jackson PG, Wright K, Stark MM *et al.* The influence of cannabis and alcohol on driving. TRL report no. 543. Road Safety Division, Department of the Environment, Transport and the Regions, 2002.
24. Yesavage JA, Leirer VO, Denari M, Hollister LE. Carry-over effects of marijuana intoxication on aircraft pilot performance: a preliminary report. *Am J Psychiatry* 1985; 142(11): 1325–1329.
25. Ramaekers JG, Kauert G, van Ruitenbeek P, Theunissen EL, Schneider E, Moeller MR. High-potency marijuana impairs executive function and inhibitory motor control. *Neuropsychopharmacology* 2006; 31(10): 2296–2303.
26. Lamers CT, Ramaekers JG. Visual search and urban driving under the influence of marijuana and alcohol. *Hum Psychopharmacol* 2001; 16(5): 393–401.
27. Robbe H. Marijuana's impairing effects on driving are moderate when taken alone but severe when combined with alcohol. *Hum Psychopharmacol Clin Exp* 1998; 13: S70–S8.
28. Couper FJ, Logan BK. Drugs and human performance fact sheets. Report no. DOT HS 809 725. National Highway Traffic Safety Administration (NHTSA), 2004.
29. Boys A, Marsden J, Strang J. Understanding reasons for drug use amongst young people: a functional perspective. *Health Educ Res* 2001; 16(4): 457–469.
30. Gerstner-Stevens JF, Davies C, eds. The prevalence of drugs in surviving truck drivers involved in fatal accidents. Poster presented at the 41st International Meeting of the International Association of Forensic Toxicologists, Melbourne, Australia, 2003.
31. Golob TF, Hensher DA. Driver behaviour of long distance truck drivers: the effects of schedule compliance on drug use and speeding citations. Institute of Transport Studies, Graduate School of Business, the University of Sydney, Australia, 1994.
32. Nichols DE. Differences between the mechanism of action of MDMA, MBDB, and the classic hallucinogens. Identification of a new therapeutic class: entactogens. *J Psychoactive Drugs* 1986; 18(4): 305–313.
33. Mills KC, Spruill SE, Kanne RW, Parkman KM, Zhang Y. The influence of stimulants, sedatives, and fatigue on tunnel vision: Risk factors for driving and piloting. *Human Factors* 2001; 43(2): 310–327.

34. Ward AS, Kelly TH, Foltin RW, Fischman MW. Effects of d-amphetamine on task performance and social behavior of humans in a residential laboratory. *Exp Clin Psychopharmacol* 1997; 5(2): 130–136.
35. Silber BY, Papafotiou K, Croft RJ, Ogden E, Swann P, Stough C. The effects of dexamphetamine on simulated driving performance. *Psychopharmacology* 2005; 179(3): 536–543.
36. Silber BY, Croft RJ, Papafotiou K, Stough C. The acute effects of d-amphetamine and methamphetamine on attention and psychomotor performance. *Psychopharmacology (Berl)* 2006; 187(2): 154–169.
37. Wesensten NJ, Killgore WDS, Balkin TJ. Performance and alertness effects of caffeine, dextro amphetamine, and modafinil during sleep deprivation. *J Sleep Res* 2005; 14(3): 255–266.
38. Caldwell JA, Caldwell JL, Crowley JS, Jones HD. Sustaining helicopter pilot performance with Dexedrine(R) during periods of sleep-deprivation. *Aviat Space Environ Med* 1995; 66(10): 930–937.
39. Caldwell JA, Caldwell JL. An in-flight investigation of the efficacy of dextroamphetamine for sustaining helicopter pilot performance. *Aviat Space Environ Med* 1997; 68 (12): 1073–1080.
40. Curran HV, Travill RA. Mood and cognitive effects of ±3,4-methylenedioxymethamphetamine (MDMA, 'ecstasy'). Week-end 'high' followed by mid-week low. *Addiction* 1997; 92(7): 821–831.
41. Parrott AC, Lasky J. Ecstasy (MDMA) effects upon mood and cognition: Before, during and after a Saturday night dance. *Psychopharmacology* 1998; 139(3): 261–268.
42. Lamers CTJ, Ramaekers JG, Muntjewerff ND, Sikkema KL, Samyn N, Read NL *et al.* Dissociable effects of a single dose of ecstasy (MDMA) on psychomotor skills and attentional performance. *J Psychopharmacol* 2003; 17(4): 379–387.
43. Ramaekers JG, Kuypers KPC, Wood CM, Hockey GRJ, Jamson S, Jamson H, *et al.* Experimental studies on the effects of licit and illicit drugs on driving performance, psychomotor skills and cognitive function. Deliverable D-R4.4. Impaired Motorists, Methods of Roadside Testing and Assessment for Licensing (IMMORTAL), 2004.
44. Smith RM, Tivarus M, Campbell HL, Hillier A, Beversdorf DQ. Apparent transient effects of recent 'ecstasy' use on cognitive performance and extrapyramidal signs in human subjects. *Cogn Behav Neurol* 2006; 19(3): 157–164.
45. de Waard D, Brookhuis KA, Pernot LMC, eds. A driving simulator study on the effects of MDMA (Ecstasy) on driving performance and traffic safety. International Council on Alcohol Drugs and Traffic Safety (ICADTS), Stockholm, Sweden, 2000.
46. Kuypers KP, Wingen M, Samyn N, Limbert N, Ramaekers JG. Acute effects of nocturnal doses of MDMA on measures of impulsivity and psychomotor performance throughout the night. *Psychopharmacology (Berl)* 2007; 192(1): 111–119.
47. Brookhuis KA, de Waard D, Samyn N. Effects of MDMA (ecstasy), and multiple drugs use on (simulated) driving performance and traffic safety. *Psychopharmacology* 2004; 173(3–4): 440–445.
48. Dumont GJ, Wezenberg E, Valkenberg MM, de Jong CA, Buitelaar JK, van Gerven JM *et al.* Acute neuropsychological effects of MDMA and ethanol (co-)administration in healthy volunteers. *Psychopharmacology (Berl)* 2008; 197(3): 465–474.
49. Verheyden SL, Henry JA, Curran HV. Acute, sub-acute and long-term subjective consequences of 'ecstasy' (MDMA) consumption in 430 regular users. *Hum Psychopharmacol Clin Exp* 2003; 18: 507–517.
50. Rizzo M, Lamers CTJ, Sauer CG, Ramaekers JG, Bechara A, Andersen GJ. Impaired perception of self-motion (heading) in abstinent ecstasy and marijuana users. *Psychopharmacology* 2005; 179(3): 559–566.
51. Bolla KI, McCann UD, Ricaurte GA. Memory impairment in abstinent MDMA ('Ecstasy') users. *Neurology* 1998; 51(6): 1532–1537.
52. McCann UD, Mertl M, Eligulashvili V, Ricaurte GA. Cognitive performance in (±) 3,4-methylenedioxymethamphetamine (MDMA, 'ecstasy') users: a controlled study. *Psychopharmacology* 1999; 143(4): 417–25.

53. Wareing M, Murphy PN, Fisk JE. Visuospatial memory impairments in users of MDMA ('ecstasy'). *Psychopharmacology* 2004; 173(34): 391–397.
54. Ornstein TJ, Iddon JL, Baldacchino AM, Sahakian BJ, London M, Everitt BJ *et al.* Profiles of cognitive dysfunction in chronic amphetamine and heroin abusers. *Neuropsychopharmacology* 2000; 23(2): 113–126.
55. Verdejo A, Orozco-Gimenez C, Sanchez-Jofre MM, de Arcos FA, Perez-Garcia M. The impact exerted by the severity of recreational drug abuse on the different components of the executive function. *Rev Neurol* 2004; 38(12): 1109–1116.
56. de Sola S, Tarancon T, Pena-Casanova J, Espadaler JM, Langohr K, Poudevida S *et al.* Auditory event-related potentials (P3) and cognitive performance in recreational ecstasy polydrug users: evidence from a 12-month longitudinal study. *Psychopharmacology (Berl)* 2008; 200(3): 425–437.
57. Wittmann M, Leland DS, Churan J, Paulus MP. Impaired time perception and motor timing in stimulant-dependent subjects. *Drug Alcohol Depend* 2007; 90(2–3): 183–192.
58. Morgan MJ. Recreational use of 'Ecstasy' (MDMA) is associated with elevated impulsivity. *Neuropsychopharmacology* 1998; 19(4): 252–264.
59. Thirthalli J, Benegal V. Psychosis among substance users. *Curr Opin Psychiatry* 2006; 19(3): 239–245.
60. Sommers I, Baskin D, Baskin-Sommers A. Methamphetamine use among young adults: health and social consequences. *Addict Behav* 2006; 31(8): 1469–1476.
61. Chen CK, Lin SK, Sham PC, Ball D, Loh EW, Hsiao CC *et al.* Pre-morbid characteristics and co-morbidity of methamphetamine users with and without psychosis. *Psychol Med* 2003; 33(8): 1407–1414.
62. Hart CL, Haney M, Nasser J, Foltin RW. Combined effects of methamphetamine and zolpidem on performance and mood during simulated night shift work. *Pharmacol Biochem Behav* 2005; 81(3): 559–568.
63. Huestis MA. Cannabis (Marijuana) – effects on human performance and behavior. *Forensic Sci Rev* 2002; 14(12): 15–60.
64. Menetrey A, Augsburger M, Favrat B, Pin MA, Rothuizen LE, Appenzeller M *et al.* Assessment of driving capability through the use of clinical and psychomotor tests in relation to blood cannabinoids levels following oral administration of 20 mg dronabinol or of a cannabis decoction made with 20 or 60 mg Delta9-THC. *J Anal Toxicol* 2005; 29 (5): 327–338.
65. Berghaus G, Scheer N, Schmidt P, eds. Effects of cannabis on psychomotor skills and driving performance – a metaanalysis of experimental studies. In: Kloeden CN, McLean AJ, eds. *Proceedings of the 13th International Conference on Alcohol, Drugs and Traffic Safety*, Vol. 1. Adelaide: NHMRC Road Accident Research Unit, 1995: 403–409.
66. Hunault CC, Mensinga TT, Bocker KB, Schipper CM, Kruidenier M, Leenders ME *et al.* Cognitive and psychomotor effects in males after smoking a combination of tobacco and cannabis containing up to 69 mg delta-9-tetrahydrocannabinol (THC). *Psychopharmacology (Berl)* 2009; 204(1): 85–94.
67. Foltin RW, Fischman MW. Effects of smoked marijuana on human social behavior in small groups. *Pharmacol Biochem Behav* 1988; 30(2): 539–541.
68. Ramaekers JG, Kauert G, Theunissen EL, Toennes SW, Moeller MR. Neurocognitive performance during acute THC intoxication in heavy and occasional cannabis users. *J Psychopharmacol* 2009; 23(3): 266–277.
69. Weinstein A, Brickner O, Lerman H, Greemland M, Bloch M, Lester H *et al.* Brain imaging study of the acute effects of Delta9-tetrahydrocannabinol (THC) on attention and motor coordination in regular users of marijuana. *Psychopharmacology (Berl)* 2008; 196(1): 119–131.
70. Chait LD, Perry JL. Acute and residual effects of alcohol and marijuana, alone and in combination, on mood and performance. *Psychopharmacology* 1994; 115(3): 340–349.
71. Foltin RW, Fischman MW, Pippen PA, Kelly TH. Behavioral-effects of cocaine alone and in combination with ethanol or marijuana in humans. *Drug Alcohol Depend* 1993; 32(2): 93–106.

72. Chait LD. Subjective and behavioral effects of marijuana the morning after smoking. *Psychopharmacology (Berl)* 1990; 100(3): 328–333.
73. Pope HG, Gruber AJ, Hudson JI, Huestis MA, Yurgelun-Todd D. Neuropsychological performance in long-term cannabis users. *Arch Gen Psychiatry* 2001; 58(10): 909–915.
74. Pope HG, Gruber AJ, Yurgeluntodd D. The residual neuropsychological effects of cannabis – the current status of research. *Drug Alcohol Depend* 1995; 38(1): 25–34.
75. Solowij N, Stephens RS, Roffman RA, Babor T, Kadden R, Miller M *et al.* Cognitive functioning of long-term heavy cannabis users seeking treatment. *JAMA* 2002; 287(9): 1123–1131.
76. Bolla KI, Brown K, Eldreth D, Tate K, Cadet JL. Dose-related neurocognitive effects of marijuana use. *Neurology* 2002; 59(9): 1337–1343.
77. Block RI, Ghoneim MM. Effects of chronic marijuana use on human cognition. *Psychopharmacology* 1993; 110(1–2): 219–228.
78. Fletcher JM, Page JB, Francis DJ, Copeland K, Naus MJ, Davis CM *et al.* Cognitive correlates of long-term cannabis use in Costa Rican men. *Arch Gen Psychiatry* 1996; 53 (11): 1051–1057.
79. Pope HG, Gruber AJ, Hudson JI, Huestis MA, Yurgelun-Todd D. Cognitive measures in long-term cannabis users. *J Clin Pharmacol* 2002; 42(11): 41S–47S.
80. Pillay SS, Rogowska J, Kanayama G, Gruber S, Simpson N, Pope HG *et al.* Cannabis and motor function: fMRI changes following 28 days of discontinuation. *Exp Clin Psychopharmacol* 2008; 16(1): 22–32.
81. Karschner EL, Schwilke EW, Lowe RH, Darwin WD, Herning RI, Cadet JL *et al.* Implications of plasma delta(9)-tetrahydrocannabinol, 11-hydroxy-THC, and 11-nor-9-carboxy-THC concentrations in chronic cannabis smokers. *J Anal Toxicol* 2009; 33 (8): 469–477.
82. Pope HG, Jr Yurgelun-Todd D. The residual cognitive effects of heavy marijuana use in college students. *JAMA* 1996; 275(7): 521–527.
83. Solowij N. Do cognitive impairments recover following cessation of cannabis use? *Life Sci* 1995; 56(23–24): 2119–2126.
84. Solowij N, Michie PT, Fox AM. Differential impairments of selective attention due to frequency and duration of cannabis use. *Biol Psychiatry* 1995; 37(10): 731–739.
85. Pope HG Jr, Gruber AJ, Hudson JI, Huestis MA, Yurgelun-Todd D. Neuropsychological performance in long-term cannabis users. *Arch Gen Psychiatry* 2001; 58(10): 909–915.
86. Mendhiratta SS, Varma VK, Dang R, Malhotra AK, Das K, Nehra R. Cannabis and cognitive functions a re-evaluation study. *Br J Addict* 1988; 83(7): 749–753.
87. Fisk JE, Montgomery C. Real-world memory and executive processes in cannabis users and non-users. *J Psychopharmacol* 2008; 22(7): 727–736.
88. Lane SD, Cherek DR, Pietras CJ, Steinberg JL. Performance of heavy marijuana-smoking adolescents on a laboratory measure of motivation. *Addict Behav* 2005; 30(4): 815–828.
89. Andreasson S, Allebeck P, Engstrom A, Rydberg U. Cannabis and schizophrenia. A longitudinal study of Swedish conscripts. *Lancet* 1987; 2(8574): 1483–1486.
90. Zammit S, Allebeck P, Andreasson S, Lundberg I, Lewis G. Self reported cannabis use as a risk factor for schizophrenia in Swedish conscripts of 1969: historical cohort study. *BMJ* 2002; 325(7374): 1199.
91. Weiser M, Knobler HY, Noy S, Kaplan Z. Clinical characteristics of adolescents later hospitalized for schizophrenia. *Am J Med Genet* 2002; 114(8): 949–955.
92. Arseneault L, Cannon M, Poulton R, Murray R, Caspi A, Moffitt TE. Cannabis use in adolescence and risk for adult psychosis longitudinal prospective study. *BMJ* 2002; 325 (7374): 1212–1213.
93. Semple DM, McIntosh AM, Lawrie SM. Cannabis as a risk factor for psychosis: systematic review. *J Psychopharmacol* 2005; 19(2): 187–194.
94. Arseneault L, Cannon M, Witton J, Murray RM. Causal association between cannabis and psychosis: examination of the evidence. *Br J Psychiatry* 2004; 184: 110–117.

95. Verdoux H, Gindre C, Sorbara F, Tournier M, Swendsen JD. Effects of cannabis and psychosis vulnerability in daily life: an experience sampling test study. *Psychol Med* 2003; 33(1): 23–32.
96. Kanayama G, Rogowska J, Pope HG, Gruber SA, Yurgelun-Todd DA. Spatial working memory in heavy cannabis users: a functional magnetic resonance imaging study. *Psychopharmacology* 2004; 176(3–4): 239–247.
97. Wadsworth EJK, Moss SC, Simpson SA, Smith AP. Cannabis use, cognitive performance and mood in a sample of workers. *J Psychopharmacol* 2006; 20(1): 14–23.
98. Wadsworth EJK, Moss SC, Simpson SA, Smith AP. A community based investigation of the association between cannabis use, injuries and accidents. *J Psychopharmacol* 2006; 20(1): 5–13.
99. Breitstadt R, Kauert G. *Der mensch als risiko und sicherheitsreserve*. Aachen, Germany: Shaker Verlag GmbH, 2004.
100. Blows S, Ivers RQ, Connor J, Ameratunga S, Woodward M, Norton R. Marijuana use and car crash injury. *Addiction* 2005; 100(5): 605–611.
101. Fischman MW, Schuster CR. Cocaine effects in sleep-deprived humans. *Psychopharmacology (Berl)* 1980; 72(1): 1–8.
102. Hopper JW, Karlsgodt KH, Adler CM, Macklin EA, Lukas SE, Elman I. Effects of acute cortisol and cocaine administration on attention, recall and recognition task performance in individuals with cocaine dependence. *Hum Psychopharmacol Clin Exp* 2004; 19(7): 511–516.
103. Rush CR, Baker RW, Wright K. Acute physiological and behavioral effects of oral cocaine in humans: a dose-response analysis. *Drug Alcohol Depend* 1999; 55(1–2): 1–12.
104. Higgins ST, Bickel WK, Hughes JR, Lynn M, Capeless MA, Fenwick JW. Effects of intranasal cocaine on human learning, performance and physiology. *Psychopharmacology (Berl)* 1990; 102(4): 451–458.
105. Foltin RW, Fischman MW. Ethanol and cocaine interactions in humans: cardiovascular consequences. *Pharmacol Biochem Behav* 1988; 31(4): 877–883.
106. Herning RI, Hooker WD, Jones RT. Cocaine effects on electroencephalographic cognitive event-related potentials and performance. *Electroencephalogr Clin Neurophysiol* 1987; 66(1): 34–42.
107. Johnson B, Overton D, Wells L, Kenny P, Abramson D, Dhother S *et al.* Effects of acute intravenous cocaine on cardiovascular function, human learning, and performance in cocaine addicts. *Psychiatry Res* 1998; 77(1): 35–42.
108. Farre M, Delatorre R, Llorente M, Lamas X, Ugena B, Segura J *et al.* Alcohol and cocaine interactions in humans. *J Pharmacol Exp Ther* 1993; 266(3): 1364–1373.
109. Stillman R, Jones RT, Moore D, Walker J, Welm S. Improved performance 4 hours after cocaine. *Psychopharmacology* 1993; 110(4): 415–420.
110. Burns M. Cocaine effects on performance. In: *Proceedings of the 12th International Conference on Alcohol, Drugs and Traffic Safety*. Cologne, Germany: Verlage TUV Rheinland, 1992: 612–619.
111. Elman I, Chi WH, Gurvits TV, Ryan ET, Lasko NB, Lukas SE *et al.* Impaired reproduction of three-dimensional objects by cocaine-dependent subjects. *J Neuropsychiatry Clin Neurosci* 2008; 20(4): 478–484.
112. Sim ME, Lyoo IK, Streeter CC, Covell J, Sarid-Segal O, Ciraulo DA *et al.* Cerebellar gray matter volume correlates with duration of cocaine use in cocaine-dependent subjects. *Neuropsychopharmacology* 2007; 32(10): 2229–2237.
113. Toomey R, Lyons MJ, Eisen SA, Xian H, Chantarujikapong S, Seidman LJ *et al.* A twin study of the neuropsychological consequences of stimulant abuse. *Arch Gen Psychiatry* 2003; 60(3): 303–310.
114. Goldstein RZ, Leskovjan AC, Hoff AL, Hitzemann R, Bashan F, Khalsa SS *et al.* Severity of neuropsychological impairment in cocaine and alcohol addiction: association with metabolism in the prefrontal cortex. *Neuropsychologia* 2004; 42(11): 1447–1458.
115. Lawton-Craddock A, Nixon SJ, Tivis R. Cognitive efficiency in stimulant abusers with and without alcohol dependence. *Alcohol Clin Exp Res* 2003; 27(3): 457–464.

116. Di Sclafani V, Tolou-Shams M, Price LJ, Fein G. Neuropsychological performance of individuals dependent on crack-cocaine, or crack-cocaine and alcohol, at 6 weeks and 6 months of abstinence. *Drug Alcohol Depend* 2002; 66(2): 161–171.
117. Smelson DA, Roy A, Santana S, Engelhart C. Neuropsychological deficits in withdrawn cocaine-dependent males. *Am J Drug Alcohol Abuse* 1999; 25(2): 377–381.
118. Di Sclafani V, Truran DL, Bloomer C, Tolou-Shams M, Clark HW, Norman D *et al.* Abstinent chronic crack-cocaine and crack-cocaine/alcohol abusers evidence normal hippocampal volumes on MRI despite persistent cognitive impairments. *Addict Biol* 1998; 3(3): 261–270.
119. Gillen RW, Kranzler HR, Bauer LO, Burleson JA, Samarel D, Morrison DJ. Neuropsychologic findings in cocaine-dependent outpatients. *Progr Neuro-Psychopharmacol Biol Psychiatry* 1998; 22(7): 1061–1076.
120. Hoff AL, Riordan H, Morris L, Cestaro V, Wieneke M, Alpert R *et al.* Effects of crack cocaine on neurocognitive function. *Psychiatry Res* 1996; 60(2–3): 167–176.
121. Kelley BJ, Yeager KR, Pepper TH, Beversdorf DQ. Cognitive impairment in acute cocaine withdrawal. *Cogn Behav Neurol* 2005; 18(2): 108–112.
122. Rahman Q, Clarke CD. Sex differences in neurocognitive functioning among abstinent recreational cocaine users. *Psychopharmacology* 2005; 181(2): 374–380.
123. Franken IHA, van Strien JW, Franzek EJ, de Wetering BJV. Error-processing deficits in patients with cocaine dependence. *Biol Psychol* 2007; 75(1): 45–51.
124. Moeller FG, Barratt ES, Fischer CJ, Dougherty DM, Reilly EL, Mathias CW *et al.* P300 event-related potential amplitude and impulsivity in cocaine-dependent subjects. *Neuropsychobiology* 2004; 50(2): 167–173.
125. Bolla KI, Funderburk FR, Cadet JL. Differential effects of cocaine and cocaine plus alcohol on neurocognitive performance. *Neurology* 2000; 54(12): 2285–2292.
126. Robinson JE, Heaton RK, O'Malley SS. Neuropsychological functioning in cocaine abusers with and without alcohol dependence. *J Int Neuropsychol Soc* 1999; 5(1): 10–19.
127. Kawasaki A, Purvin V. Persistent palinopsia following ingestion of lysergic acid diethylamide (LSD). *Arch Ophthalmol* 1996; 114(1): 47–50.
128. Hartman AM, Hollister LE. Effect of mescaline, lysergic acid diethylamide and psilocybin on color perception. *Psychopharmacologia* 1963; 65: 441–451.
129. Edwards AE, Cohen S. Visual illusion, tactile sensibility and reaction time under LSD-25. *Psychopharmacologia* 1961; 2: 297–303.
130. Kohn B, Bryden MP. The effect of lysergic acid diethylamide (LSD-25) on perception with stabilized images. *Psychopharmacologia* 1965; 7(5): 311–320.
131. Holliday AR, Hall GM, Sharpley RP. The effects of lysergic acid diethylamide I: critical flicker frequency. *Proc West Pharmacol Soc* 1965; 8: 48–50.
132. Wikler A, Haertzen CA, Chessick RD, Hill HE, Pescor FT. Reaction time ('mental set') in control and chronic schizophrenic subjects and in postaddicts under placebo, LSD-25, morphine, pentobarbital and amphetamine. *Psychopharmacologia* 1965; 7(6): 423–443.
133. Key BJ. The effect of LSD-25 on the interaction between conditioned and non-conditioned stimuli in a simple avoidance situation. *Psychopharmacologia* 1964; 6(5): 319–326.
134. Wikler A, Rosenberg DE, Hawthorne JD, Cassidy TM. Age and effect of LSD-25 on pupil size and kneejerk threshold: Studies in chronic schizophrenic and nonpsychotic subjects. *Psychopharmacologia* 1965; 7(1): 44–56.
135. Frederick DL, Gillam MP, Lensing S, Paule MG. Acute effects of LSD on rhesus monkey operant test battery performance. *Pharmacol Biochem Behav* 1997; 57(4): 633–641.
136. Barrett SP, Archambault J, Engelberg MJ, Pihl RO. Hallucinogenic drugs attenuate the subjective response to alcohol in humans. *Hum Psychopharmacol Clin Exp* 2000; 15(7): 559–565.
137. Abraham HD. A chronic impairment of color-vision in users of LSD. *Br J Psychiatry* 1982; 140: 518–520.

138. Abraham HD, Wolf E. Visual function in past users of LSD: psychophysical findings. *J Abnorm Psychol* 1988; 97(4): 443–447.
139. Abraham HD, Aldridge AM. Adverse consequences of lysergic-acid diethylamide. *Addiction* 1993; 88(10): 1327–1334.
140. Batzer W, Ditzler T, Brown C. LSD use and flashbacks in alcoholic patients. *J Addict Dis* 1999; 18(2): 57–63.
141. Drummer OH, Bentliff G, Elliot Z, McAllister L. *The Forensic Pharmacology of Drugs of Abuse*. London: Arnold, 2001.
142. Jenkins AJ, Keenan RM, Henningfield JE, Cone EJ. Pharmacokinetics and pharmacodynamics of smoked heroin. *J Anal Toxicol* 1994; 18(6): 317–330.
143. Jasinski DR, Preston KL. Comparison of intravenously administered methadone, morphine and heroin. *Drug Alcohol Depend* 1986; 17(4): 301–310.
144. Martin WR, Fraser HF. A comparative study of physiological and subjective effects of heroin and morphine administered intravenously in postaddicts. *J Pharmacol Exp Ther* 1961; 133: 388–399.
145. Cone EJ, Holicky BA, Grant TM, Darwin WD, Goldberger BA. Pharmacokinetics and pharmacodynamics of intranasal 'snorted' heroin. *J Anal Toxicol* 1993; 17(6): 327–337.
146. Bryun EA, Gekht AB, Polunina AG, Davydov DM, Gusev EI. Neuropsychologic deficit in chronic heroin abusers. *Zh Nevropatol Psikhiatr Im S S Korsakova* 2001; 101(3): 10–19.
147. Liu N, Zhou DM, Li B, Ma YY, Hu XT. Gender related effects of heroin abuse on the simple reaction time task. *Addict Behav* 2006; 31(1): 187–190.
148. Alexandrov SG. Dynamics of time intervals evaluation in heroin addicts. *Zh Nevropatol Psikhiatr Im S S Korsakova* 2004; 104(3): 21–24.
149. Lyvers M, Yakimoff M. Neuropsychological correlates of opioid dependence and withdrawal. *Addict Behav* 2003; 28(3): 605–611.
150. Ning L, Bo L, Fraser FAW, Ma YY, Hu XT. Gender effect on the right-left discrimination task in a sample of heroin-dependent patients. *Psychopharmacology* 2005; 181(4): 735–740.
151. Pau CWH, Lee TMC, Chan SFF. The impact of heroin on frontal executive functions. *Arch Clin Neuropsychol* 2002; 17(7): 663–670.
152. Brienza RS, Stein MD, Chen MH, Gogineni A, Sobota M, Maksad J *et al.* Depression among needle exchange program and methadone maintenance clients. *J Subst Abuse Treat* 2000; 18(4): 331–337.
153. Brooner RK, King VL, Kidorf M, Schmidt CW, Bigelow GE. Psychiatric and substance use comorbidity among treatment-seeking opioid abusers. *Arch Gen Psychiatry* 1997; 54 (1): 71–80.
154. Croughan JL, Miller JP, Wagelin D, Whitman BY. Psychiatric-illness in male and female narcotic addicts. *J Clin Psychiatry* 1982; 43(6): 225–228.
155. Darke S, Ross J. Polydrug dependence and psychiatric comorbidity among heroin injectors. *Drug Alcohol Depend* 1997; 48(2): 135–141.
156. Havard A, Teesson M, Darke S, Ross J. Depression among heroin users: 12-Month outcomes from the Australian Treatment Outcome Study (ATOS). *J Subst Abuse Treat* 2006; 30(4): 355–362.
157. Khantzian EJ, Treece C. DSM-III Psychiatric-diagnosis of narcotic addicts – recent findings. *Arch Gen Psychiatry* 1985; 42(11): 1067–1071.
158. Rounsaville BJ, Weissman MM, Critschristoph K, Wilber C, Kleber H. Diagnosis and symptoms of depression in opiate addicts – course and relationship to treatment outcome. *Arch Gen Psychiatry* 1982; 39(2): 151–156.
159. Teesson M, Havard A, Fairbairn S, Ross J, Lynskey M, Darke S. Depression among entrants to treatment for heroin dependence in the Australian Treatment Outcome Study (ATOS): prevalence, correlates and treatment seeking. *Drug Alcohol Depend* 2005; 78 (3): 309–315.

160. Weissman MM, Slobetz F, Prusoff B, Mezritz M, Howard P. Clinical depression among narcotic addicts maintained on methadone in community. *Am J Psychiatry* 1976; 133 (12): 1434–1438.
161. Grenyer BFS, Williams G, Swift W, Neill O. The prevalence of social-evaluative anxiety in opioid users seeking treatment. *Int J Addict* 1992; 27(6): 665–673.
162. Darke S, Swift W, Hall W, Ross M. Drug-use HIV risk-taking and psychosocial correlates of benzodiazepine use among methadone-maintenance clients. *Drug Alcohol Depend* 1993; 34(1): 67–70.
163. Lejuez CW, Paulson A, Daughters SB, Bornovalova MA, Zvolensky MJ. The association between heroin use and anxiety sensitivity among inner-city individuals in residential drug use treatment. *Behav Res Ther* 2006; 44(5): 667–677.
164. Mintzer MZ, Copersino ML, Stitzer ML. Opioid abuse and cognitive performance. *Drug Alcohol Depend* 2005; 78(2): 225–230.
165. Verdejo A, Toribio I, Orozco C, Puente KL, Perez-Garcifa M. Neuropsychological functioning in methadone maintenance patients versus abstinent heroin abusers. *Drug Alcohol Depend* 2005; 78(3): 283–288.
166. Platt JJ. Vocational rehabilitation of drug abusers. *Psychol Bull* 1995; 117(3): 416–433.

3

The evidence base for workplace drug testing

Alain Verstraete

Key points

- The effects of workplace drug testing on deterring drug use, reducing the number of accidents and injuries and improving productivity or being cost-effective were mainly studied in the late 1980s. Nearly all studies showed that workplace drug testing had a positive effect on these parameters. But many of these studies have later been criticised for their methodological flaws.
- Analysis of the data from various years of the National Surveys on Drug Use and Health (NSDUH) shows that workplace testing deters worker drugs use. A 24% lower rate of drug use was measured among employees at work sites with a drug testing programme relative to work sites without a drug testing programme. Employees at work sites with a drug testing programme were 38.5% less likely to be chronic drug users.
- Workplace urine surveillance is successful in detecting employees with significant substance abuse-related problems, and referral to standard treatment is associated with substantial improvements in those problems.
- A Cochrane review about injury prevention in the construction industry found evidence for the effectiveness of a multifaceted safety campaign and a multifaceted drug testing programme.
- A Cochrane review on alcohol and drug screening of occupational drivers for preventing injury or work-related effects such as sickness absence related to injury showed that mandatory random drug testing was significantly associated with an immediate change in injury level following the intervention in one of the two included studies. In the long term, random drug testing was

associated with a significant increase in the downward trend and with a significant improvement in the long-term downward trend.
- However, time-series studies of higher quality and of long duration are needed to increase the level of evidence.

Introduction

One of the important questions about workplace drug testing is whether it makes a difference, whether it reaches its objective of reducing the number of work-related accidents and whether it is cost-effective.

Alcohol and drug testing may prevent workplace-related injuries by deterring the misuse of illicit substances among employees, thereby reducing risks to health and safety in the work environment. Other purported benefits of testing include: improved employee welfare, reduced risks to the production process, enhanced public confidence in the organisation and improved medical fitness, thereby reducing healthcare costs.[1]

The costs of substance abuse programmes can be divided into direct and variable costs. Direct costs are related to the cost of collection, laboratory testing and the medical review officer report. The variable costs include those associated with the Employee Assistance Programme (EAP), time lost due to drug abuse as well as to the collection of specimens, training of supervisors and overheads involved in administering the programme. However, these costs are offset by increased productivity, decreased absenteeism, decreased turnover, decreased costs for healthcare benefits, decreased disciplinarian action, and improvements in safety and employee morale.[2]

Several authors have studied the question, and many pros and cons have been given.

In this chapter, we will review the studies that have evaluated the effectiveness of workplace drug testing and summarise the results.

We will look for an answer to three questions:

- Does drug testing deter drug use in employees?
- Does drug testing reduce the number of accidents and injuries?
- Does drug testing improve productivity?

To answer these questions, we searched the peer-reviewed literature and we will end with meta-analyses and Cochrane reviews.

In 1994, a report of the National Academy of Sciences stated that: 'The preventive effects of drug testing have never been adequately demonstrated. There is as yet no conclusive scientific evidence from properly controlled studies that employment drug testing programs widely discourage drug use or encourage rehabilitation.' And 'Despite beliefs to the contrary, the preventive effects of drug testing programs have never been adequately demonstrated.'[3] Since that time, studies using the National Survey on Drug Use and Health (NSDUH) have indicated a consistent and inverse relationship between employee reports of workplace drug testing and self-reported drug use. More studies have been performed and they will be reviewed in this chapter.

Does drug testing deter drug use in employees?

The Quest Diagnostics Drug Testing Index[4] gives data on the number of positive samples in the United States for workplace drug testing. It examines positivity rates to provide a comprehensive analysis of workplace drug-use trends among three major testing populations: (1) federally mandated, safety-sensitive workers, (2) the general workforce and (3) a combined US workforce. These statistics show a nearly continuous decrease in the number of positives and suggest that drug testing does have a deterrent effect, because the percentage of positives decreases over time (Figure 3.1).

Mehay and Pacula[5] (also cited in [6]) performed a study that rigorously analysed the effects of workplace drug testing on drug use. They looked at the deterrence effect of an aggressive random drug testing policy implemented by the military in 1981 and concluded that after the introduction of the programme, military personnel were about 20% less likely to report past-year

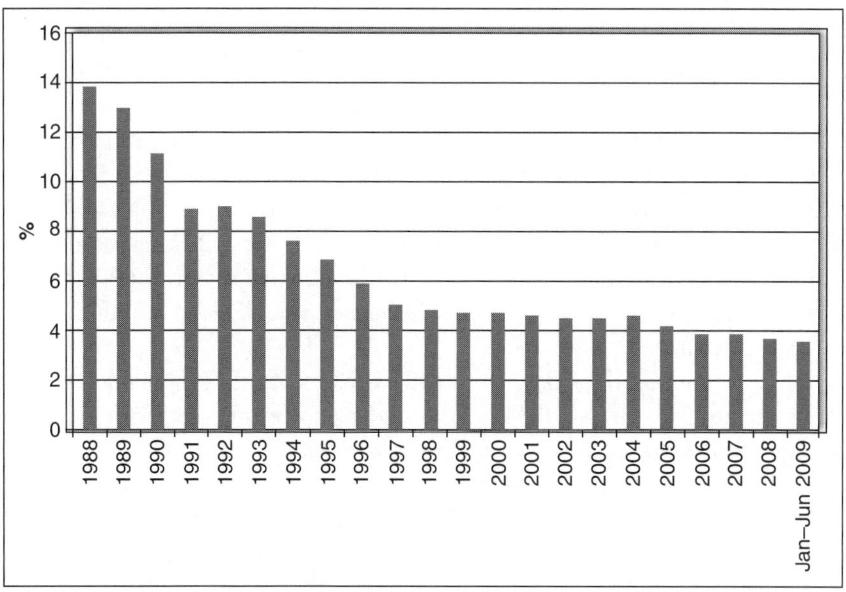

Figure 3.1 Quest Drug Testing Index. Annual positivity rate of urine drug tests for the combined US workforce.[4]

drug use then civilians, with other factors held constant at their means. Moreover, they attributed about 30% of this difference to the deterrent effect of the testing programme itself.

Using the US military's policy of random drug testing and zero tolerance, they found that a strict employer anti-drug programme was a highly effective means of deterring illicit drug use both among current users as well as potential users. However, the size of the deterrence effect varied considerably depending on the age group, drug use measure and data set. Based on these considerations, the deterrence effect for the military programme would range between 4% and 16%. They noted that even the strictest workplace anti-drug programme cannot eliminate illicit drug use among employees. Although drug participation rates in the military are low, they are not zero. This raises the question as to whether or not such strict anti-drug programmes are worth their cost.

The primary cost of zero tolerance is the cost of replacing terminated workers. The programme the military used in 1984 involved a 'two strikes' policy, and in the case of the Army, lower random testing rates, yet still produced a sizeable deterrence effect. These results suggest that policies that would be feasible today in the private sector can be expected to reduce drug use in a cost-effective manner.

In the US military, use of any illicit drugs in the past 30 days was reduced from about 29% in 1980 to less than 3% in 1995 (cited in [7]).

A case study in the southern Pacific transportation company showed that in the first year of testing (1984) in the Transportation department, 22.9% of the tests were positive for drugs and alcohol.[25] In 1985 and 1986, 11.6% and 5.8% were positive. Between 1983 (the year before initiation of testing) and 1988, personal injuries per 200 000 man-hours worked dropped from 15.5 to 5.8. Personal injuries were dramatically reduced after the initiation of drug testing – from 2234 in 1983 to 322 for the first six months of 1988. Similarly, train accidents attributable to human failure dropped from 911 in 1983 to 54 for the first seven months of 1988. In 1983, there were 22.2 human factor train accidents per 1 million train miles. During the first seven months of 1988 there were 2.2. The cost of the damage decreased from US$6.4 million in 1983 to US$600 000 in 1988.

Three studies used the data from various years of the National Surveys on Drug Use and Health (NSDUH), and found a significant association between testing and drug use. These studies are described in Chapter 1.

Past-month illicit drug users were less likely to report working for employers who offered workplace drug or alcohol programmes or policies, compared with those who did not use an illicit drug in the past month. An estimated 45.4% of past-month illicit drug users reported that there was an EAP at their place of employment, compared with 59.6% of workers who had not used an illicit drug in the past month.

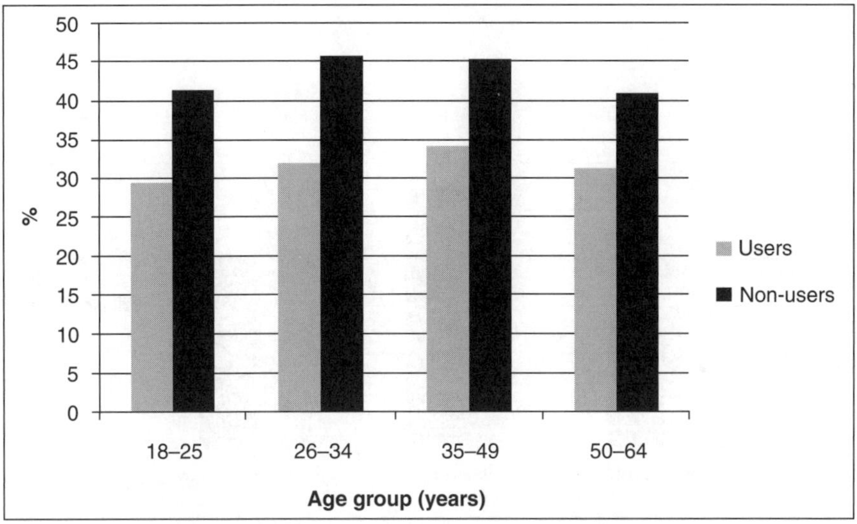

Figure 3.2 Percentage of illicit drug users and non-users reporting working for employers who conducted pre-employment testing.[8]

In the United States, among full-time workers 42.9% reported that tests for illicit drug or alcohol use occurred at their place of employment during the hiring process or 'prehire' testing.

For each age group, past-month illicit drug users were less likely than non-users to report working for employers who conducted prehire drug or alcohol tests (Figure 3.2). Past-month illicit drug users were less likely to report working for employers who conducted random drug or alcohol tests than were non-drug users (Figure 3.3). Among full-time workers who

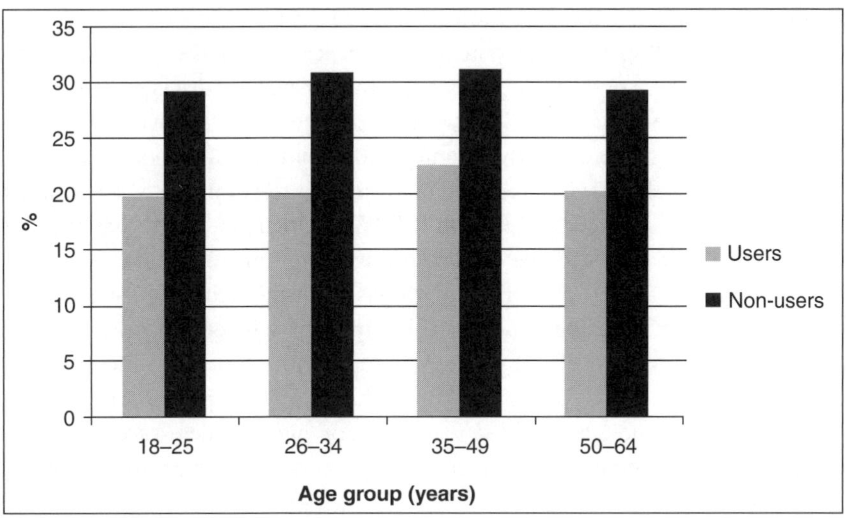

Figure 3.3 Percentage of illicit drug users and non-users reporting working in a random testing environment.[8]

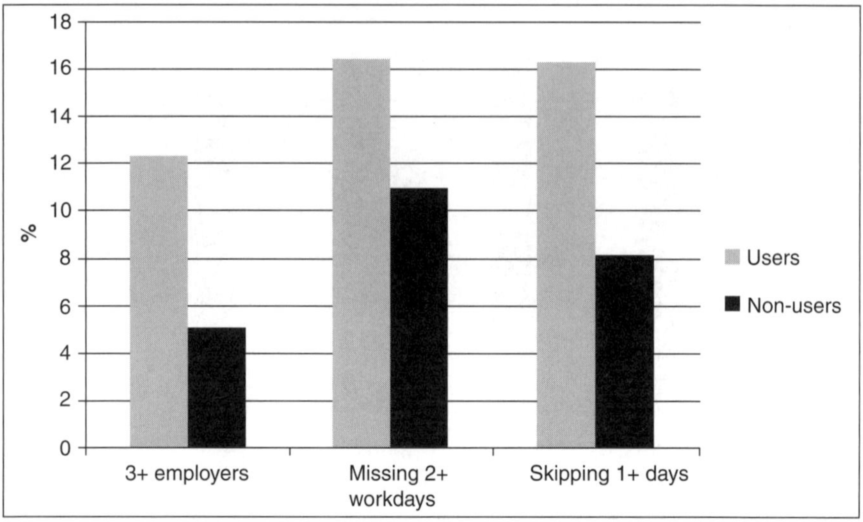

Figure 3.4 Percentage of illicit drug users and non-users reporting working for three or more employers in the past year, missing 2 or more workdays in the past month due to illness or injury and skipping 1 or more days of work in the past month.[8]

reported past-month illicit drug use, 12.3% reported working for three or more employers in the past year, compared with 5.1% of workers without past-month drug use. They also were more likely to report missing two or more workdays in the past month due to illness or injury when compared with workers without past-month use (16.4 vs. 11.0%). Finally, 16.3% of workers who used illicit drugs in the past month reported skipping one or more days of work in the past month (vs. 8.2% of workers who did not use an illicit drug during the past month) (Figure 3.4).

More than half of US workers reported that it would make no difference to them if an employer tests employees randomly after hire for drug or alcohol use. An estimated 45.5 million (39.8%) workers reported that they would be more likely to work for such an employer, while 10.0 million (8.7%) reported that they would be less likely to work for an employer who tests randomly for drug or alcohol use. An estimated 58.8 million (51.4%) workers indicated that random testing would not influence their decision to work for an employer.

An estimated 29.1% of workers with past-month illicit drug use reported that they would be less likely to work for employers who conduct drug testing randomly, while only 6.9% of workers who did not report past-month illicit drug use selected this response category. This relationship was consistent in the multivariate models while controlling for age, gender, race/ethnicity, educational attainment, family income, region and county type (metropolitan statistical area).[8]

Carpenter[9] performed a multivariate logistic regression of the likelihood of marijuana use estimated as a function of several different workplace drug policies, including drug testing. Individuals whose employers perform drug tests were significantly less likely (adjusted odds ratio 0.634, $P = 0.01$) to report past-month marijuana use, even after controlling for a wide array of worker and job characteristics. However, large negative associations were also found for variables indicating whether a firm had drug education, an Employee Assistance Programme, or a simple written policy about substance use. Accounting for these other workplace characteristics reduced but did not eliminate the testing differential. Frequent testing and severe penalties reduce the likelihood that workers use marijuana. He concluded that while previous studies have interpreted the large negative correlation between workplace drug testing and employee substance use as representing a causal deterrent effect of drug testing, his results, using more comprehensive data, suggest that these estimates have been slightly overstated due to omitted variables bias. The overall pattern of results remains largely consistent with the hypothesis that workplace testing deters worker drugs use.

Lange *et al.*[10] compared pre-employment drug screening results in all applicants for employment at a major teaching hospital during identical two-month periods in 1989 and 1991. In 1989, of 593 applicants screened, 64 (10.8%) were confirmed positive for one or more drugs. Marijuana metabolites were detected with the greatest frequency (35 samples, 55% of positive screens), followed by cocaine (36%), then opiates (28%). In 1991, after a formal pre-employment testing programme was in place, 365 applicants were screened, and 21 (5.8%) were confirmed positive. Opiates were most often detected (48% of positive screens), followed by cocaine (38%), then marijuana metabolites (28%). During both periods, positive urine screens were associated with ethnicity (non-White) and occupational category (blue-collar). Whereas in 1989 positive screens were associated with male gender, in 1991 females were more likely to test positive. The authors concluded that the decline in prevalence following implementation of a screening programme supports the notion that pre-employment testing can serve as a deterrent for drug-using persons in applying for employment.

French *et al.*[11] analysed nationally representative data on over 15 000 US households to determine whether various types of workplace drug testing programmes influenced the probability of drug use by workers. The study estimated several empirical specifications using both univariate and bivariate probit techniques. Estimated marginal effects of drug testing on any drug use were negative, significant and relatively large, indicating that drug testing programmes are achieving one of the desired effects. The results suggested a 24% lower rate of drug use among employees at work sites with a drug testing programme relative to work sites without a drug testing programme. Employees at work sites with a drug testing programme were 38.5% less likely to be chronic drug users.

A European study also showed a reduction in the number of positives after the start of a workplace drug testing programme. In 2004, the French national railway company SNCF started a long-term action of drug information and detection. It has been well-understood by the workers and all the firm's operators achieved appropriate conditions, with a strict respect of medical confidentiality. In four years, the number of detected drug users decreased by half.[12]

What is the follow-up of employees who participate in treatment programmes after a positive workplace drug test?

With the advent of on-site urine testing and other initiatives designed to reduce substance abuse at the workplace, employees who are found to have used alcohol and/or drugs have been coerced into substance abuse treatments under threat of job loss. This widespread practice has produced three questions relative to these practices:

1. Do these employees have significant substance abuse problems or are they merely 'recreational users' who have been caught?
2. Will these employees participate in standard treatments or will they resist them?
3. Will standard substance abuse treatments provide any benefits to these coerced patients relative to other self-referred patients in treatment?

Lawental *et al.*[13] compared the pre-treatment problems, during treatment performance and post-treatment outcomes of 96 employed, insured participants who were coerced into treatment at four private treatment programmes due to detection of drug use on the job, to the same measures collected on a comparison group of 161 patients from the same job sites who were self-referred admissions to the same four treatment programmes. Results showed that the coerced group had significant substance abuse and other life problems at the start of treatment, but that these problems were generally less severe or chronic than those of the self-referred group. Coerced participants were significantly more likely to remain in treatment (either inpatient or outpatient) than the self-referred participants. Post-treatment follow-up of coerced patients indicated marked improvements in alcohol and drug use, employment, medical, family and psychiatric problems. These levels of improvement were comparable to those shown by the self-referred patients.

This study suggests that workplace urine surveillance was successful in detecting employees with significant substance abuse related problems, and that referral to standard treatment was associated with substantial improvements in those problems.

Weisner *et al.*[14] examined the role of workplace mandates to chemical dependency treatment in treatment adherence, alcohol and drug abstinence, severity of employment problems, and severity of psychiatric problems. The study population included 448 employed members of a private, non-profit US managed care health plan who entered chemical dependency treatment with a workplace mandate ($n = 75$) or without one ($n = 373$); 405 of these individuals were followed up at one year ($n = 70$ and $n = 335$, respectively), and 362 participated in a five-year follow up ($n = 60$ and $n = 302$, respectively). Participants with a workplace mandate had 1- and 5-year outcomes similar to those without such a mandate. Having a workplace mandate also predicted longer treatment stays and improvement in employment problems. When other factors related to outcomes were controlled for, having a workplace mandate predicted abstinence at one year, with length of stay as a mediating variable. They concluded that workplace mandates can be an effective mechanism for improving work performance and other outcomes. Study participants who had a workplace mandate were more likely than those who did not have a workplace mandate to be abstinent at follow-up, and they did as well in treatment, both short and long term. Pressure from the workplace likely gets people to treatment earlier and provides incentives for treatment adherence.

Lindseth *et al.*[15] performed a descriptive–correlational study of civilian student pilots' attitudes toward urinalysis drug testing over a ten-year period and the pilots' opinions regarding effectiveness, adequacy and fairness of the testing as a deterrent for substance abuse among pilots. The pilots continue to believe that alcohol use by pilots within the civilian piloting training programme has decreased since testing was mandated and that drug use also showed a significant decrease ($P = 0.01$), although not as significant ($P = 0.0001$) as the decrease in alcohol use. A previous study[16] by the same group had also shown that the mandatory urine drug testing appeared to decrease substance abuse among pilots on the flight schedule.

Does workplace drug testing reduce the number of accidents and injuries?

Crouch and co-authors[17] described a model of a cost–benefit analysis of the Utah Power and Light Co. (UP&L) drug programme which provides additional data on the relationship between drug use and job performance. There were 28 positive drug screens, 25 of which only contained marijuana. Drug-using employees were found to be absent more often than controls (Table 3.1), with drug-positive employees taking sick leave at a rate 35% greater than control employees and unexcused absences at a rate 240% greater than control employees. While medical cost data analysis was inconclusive (employees who tested positive subsequently cost the company slightly less in medical claims, but the reverse was true for those who had volunteered for the EAP), drug-positive employees were 5 times more likely to have a reportable vehicle accident than controls.

Table 3.1 Comparison of different parameters between drug-positive employees at Utah Power and Light Co. and their matched controls[17]

	Drug positive ($n = 12$)	Matched controls ($n = 47$)	Employees who volunteered for the EAP ($n = 27$)	Matched controls ($n = 108$)
Sick (hours/employee)	75.3[a]	55.7	81.7[a]	56.3
Unexcused (hours/employee)	63.8[a]	18.7	32.2[a]	10.1
Medical expenses (employee/year)	US$677	US$823	US$1267	US$568
Accidents (*n*)	5	4	3	11
Accidents (employee)	0.42	0.08	0.11	0.10
Damages due to accidents	US$49 800	US$200	US$700	US$6000

[a] Significantly different from controls.

The authors provide a detailed cost–benefit analysis in which the programme was found to provide a potential yearly cost savings to the company of US$660 000 if the differences in these measures between drug users and non-users could be eliminated. In addition this paper provides an analysis of the potential costs of a comprehensive drug programme. The authors enumerate contributing factors such as planning meetings, legal fees, analytical testing, quality assurance expenses, implementation of EAPs and grievance procedures. For the UP&L Co. these expenses were reported to total US$482 327.

At a state mass transit agency, drug testing effectively reduced workplace injuries. When the programme was instituted in 1985, 20.5% of post-incident drug and alcohol tests were positive. By 1989, the percentage of positives had dropped to 2–3%.[18]

An overview[19] of the relationship between drug testing and accident rates over five years in 48 Wisconsin business facilities found that post-accident drug testing was significantly related to a decrease in accident rates compared to the pre-testing period and to facilities using only pre-employment testing, while 'reasonable cause' testing was not. However, ordinary least squares regression results indicated that the 12 locations that installed a drug testing programme during this period did not experience a significant reduction in accident and illness rates compared to the 36 non-testing facilities.

Wickizer *et al.*[20] performed a controlled interrupted time series study (ITS) that evaluated a drug-free workplace programme targeted at workers, work teams and organisations, on the risk of non-fatal injuries in construction workers. The intervention consisted of the following components: a formal written substance abuse policy, payment for drug testing, a worker assistance programme for referral to treatment, no termination of worker employment when they agreed to receive treatment, an annual educational programme on substance abuse and a minimum of 2 hours of training for supervisors and managers. The programme used informational, educational, facilitative (for example, financial incentive) and compulsory (drug testing) implementation strategies. Outcome data were obtained from state administrative databases. They showed a significant initial intervention effect of a drug-free workplace programme with non-fatal injury rate difference of –7.59 per 100 person-years between the intervention and control group; the study had a downward trend of injuries over time. A sustained effect of the intervention was observed with an injury rate difference of –1.97 per 100 person-years per year between the intervention and control group. This yielded effect sizes of –6.78 (95% confidence interval (CI) –10.02 to –3.54) and –1.76 (95% CI –3.11 to –0.41) for initial effect and sustained effect respectively.

A study among contractors (cited in [21]) showed that the average decline in rate of occupational injury and illnesses from 1985 to 1988 was 2.14 per 200 000 hours, or a prevented fraction of 19.1%. The rate difference was not statistically significant. Twenty-one companies experienced declines in rates, one company had no change, and nine companies experienced increases in incidence rates from the pre-test to the post-test periods. Those companies that had initially had incident rates much higher than the US national average for all construction companies (15 per 200 000 work-hours) showed a significant decline, from 25.1 to 14.2 per 200 000 work-hours.

In his doctoral thesis, Messer (cited in [21]) reported on a comparison of random with non-random drug testing programmes. The study population consisted of about 16 000 employees, and results were evaluated for the 1987–1989 (the non-random) and 1992–1993 (random) periods. Results were also presented for drug users versus employees not identified as users. The accident rate per 1 million transport miles decreased from 1.9% to 1.5% and the passenger injury rate per day per 100 000 miles decreased from 5.2% to 3.9%. Differences in testing period data were not statistically significant overall or for vehicular accident rates. The difference in rates for passenger injuries was marginally significant ($P = 0.045$). They also reported an increase in prevalence from 2.1% in all employees in the non-random period to 5.2% in the random test period. For vehicle operators, the prevalence rate of positive drug tests increased from 7.4% to 9.7%. For the intervention group alone, an initial effect of a drug-free workplace programme was found with a reduction in non-fatal injuries of –4.62 per 100 person-years; no sustained intervention effect was found.

Miller *et al.*[22] estimated the effectiveness and cost–benefit ratio of a peer-based substance abuse prevention programme at a US transportation company (employing 26 000 people), implemented between 1988 and 1990. The programme focused on changing workplace attitudes toward on-the-job substance use in addition to training workers to recognise and intervene with co-workers who have a problem. It was a union–management partnership and was strengthened by federally mandated random drug and alcohol testing (implemented, respectively, in 1990 and 1994). With time-series analysis, the study analysed the association between monthly injury rates and costs with phased programme implementation, controlling for industry injury trends. The combination of the peer-based programme and testing was associated with an approximate one-third reduction in injury rate, avoiding an estimated US$48 million in employer costs in 1999. The results suggested that the peer-based substance abuse prevention programme and random drug testing were complementary and interdependent. That year, the peer-based programme cost the company US$35 and testing cost another US$35 per employee. The programme avoided an estimated US$1850 in employer injury costs per employee in 1999, corresponding to a benefit–cost ratio of 26 : 1. These findings suggest that peer-based programmes buttressed by random testing can be cost-effective in the workplace.

Construction companies with drug testing programmes experienced a 51% reduction in incident rates within two years of implementation.[23]

Implementation of a drug-screening programme at General Motors led to a 50% decline in workplace injuries.

Kesselring and Pittman[24] performed a state-by-state analysis of statutory law applicable to drug testing, combined with state and industry data to isolate how drug testing laws affect workplace injury rates. Their evidence strongly suggests that the most overwhelming determinant of an occupational injury is the industry of employment. In this model neither the legal environment of the state nor any of its demographic characteristics had any significant statistical effect on injuries. This does not necessarily mean that drug testing has no effect on workplace injuries. It means that within the confines of their model no statistical evidence was produced that could verify such an effect.

Taggart[25] reviewed the implementation of a drug testing policy for Southern Pacific Railroad. He found that overall, 8.4% of all workers hired had a positive drug test; 13.3% of workers who had positive drug tests were fired within six months compared with 9.5% of workers with negative drug tests. There was a decline in personal injury rates (from 2234 to 322) and the number of train accidents attributed to human failure decreased (from 911 to 54) in the five-year period following the introduction of random workforce drug testing policies. There has been some criticism of these data, pointing out that the study did not take account of other non-programme workplace developments like massive engineering improvements in the tracking system, the implementation of crew risk reduction programmes, the expansion of training programmes and other safety improvements, which occurred simultaneously with the use of the drug-screening programme. Other criticisms of the study include an absence of rigorous controls and absence of data regarding on-the-job use.

Spicer *et al.*[26] found a weak relationship between problem substance use and occupational injury when problem behaviours were controlled for. This suggests that this relationship, observed in previous studies, may be explained by a worker's tendency towards problem behaviours. They performed a nested case–control study in which cases (3994) were workers suffering an occupational injury. Five controls per case were selected from the cohort of workers active on the day of the injury and matched on the job title. Conditional logistic regression modelled the association of problem substance use with occupational injury, controlling for problem behaviours and worker characteristics. Problem substance use was indicated if EAP visit, excused absence or disciplinary action were alcohol- or drug-involved. The odds of injury among workers with an indicator of problem substance use were 1.55 ($P = 0.015$) times greater than the odds among workers without an indicator. This ratio declined to 1.21 ($P = 0.138$) when problem behaviours were also controlled for. Minor and serious problem behaviours were significantly associated with occupational injury (odds ratio (OR) = 1.73, $P < 0.001$, OR 2.19, $P < 0.001$, respectively) after controlling for demographics and substance use.

Cunradi *et al.*[27] estimated the impact of employee alcohol and drug use on crashes in the transit industry from 1995 to 2000. They performed a secondary analysis of federally mandated post-crash and random alcohol and drug testing results in the US transit industry. For drugs, the estimated population attributable risk (PAR%) ranged from 0.38% (1998) to 0.67% (1997). Based on these calculations, the estimated number of crashes per 1000 crashes attributable to drugs was about 4–6 during 1995–2000. The number of crashes attributable to either alcohol or drugs did not vary greatly from 1995 to 2000. They concluded that approaches to transit safety based on reducing employee use of alcohol and other drugs have modest potential for reducing number of fatalities, injuries and crashes.

Ozminkowski *et al.*[7] performed an empirical investigation of the consequences of drug testing by estimating its impact on medical care expenditures and injury rates at a large manufacturing firm in 1996–1999. Multiple regression analyses of a pooled cross-sectional time-series data set were used to separate the impact of drug testing from other factors and to help find the optimal level of testing that was associated with minimum medical expenditures. They found a marginally significant ($P = 0.0532$) relationship between drug testing and injury rates. Results indicated that medical expenditures would be minimised when 42% of the employees in a calendar quarter were drug tested. This implies that, on average, employees should be tested 1.68 times a year. The results also indicated that doubling the testing rate would reduce the odds of incurring any injuries on the job by over half, but the injury rate was already so low that this impact was very small.

Jacobson[6] used a set of 'natural experiments' created by the passage of the US Department of Transportation drug testing mandate and 13 State testing laws between 1987 and 1989, to examine the effects of testing truckers for illicit substances on highway safety. She found that testing led to a 9–10% reduction in truck accident fatalities. This responds to 527 lives saved per year. The total cost of the programme was estimated to be US$257 million while the benefits of mandated testing for the country were estimated to be between US$527 million and US$2.6 billion per year. The benefits of mandated testing appeared to outweigh the costs of the programme. However, the similarity between the effect of mandating testing and simply clarifying state laws suggests that extending the right to perform drug tests may have been as effective at lower cost.

Swena[28] performed an evaluation of federally mandated random drug testing on fatal truck accidents in an interrupted time-series design from 1983 to 1997. The data were obtained from the Fatality Analysis Reporting System database that is maintained by the National Highway Traffic Safety Administration. The number of active truck drivers (i.e. number of participants exposed to the intervention) was not actually known with a sufficient degree of accuracy. The study duration was 14 years, from 1984 to 1997. The primary outcome measure was the rate of large truck fatal accidents per 100 million vehicle miles travelled. A large truck was defined as weighing over 10 000 pounds gross vehicle weight, including single unit trucks and truck tractors. There was no immediate statistically significant effect for mandatory random drug testing (–1.36/injuries/100 person-years, 95% CI –1.69 to 0.41), but the intervention was associated with a significant further improvement of the downward trend (–0.83 fatal accidents/100 million vehicle miles/year, 95% CI –1.08 to –0.58).

Wickizer *et al.*[20] evaluated the effect of a publicly sponsored drug-free workplace programme in Washington State on reducing the risk of occupational injuries. The workers' compensation programme offered a 5% discount in workers' compensation premiums for up to three years for private employers who enrolled in the programme. They used workers' compensation claims data from the Washington State Department of Labor and Industries covering the period 1994 through 2000. Work-hours data reported by employers served as the data sources for the analysis. A pre–post design with a non-equivalent comparison group was used to assess the impact of the intervention on injury risk, measured in terms of differences in injury incidence rates. Two hundred and sixty-one companies that enrolled in the drug-free workplace programme during the latter half of 1996 were compared with approximately 20 500 non-intervention companies. Autoregressive, integrated moving-average (ARIMA) models were tested to assess the robustness of the findings.

The drug-free workplace intervention was associated ($P < 0.05$) with a statistically significant decrease in injury rates for three industry groups: construction, manufacturing and services. It was associated ($P < 0.05$) with a reduction in the incidence rate of more serious injuries involving four or more days of lost work time for two industry groups: construction and services. The ARIMA analysis supported these findings. For a company with 50 employees the injury risk reduction associated with the drug-free workplace programme would generate estimated annual savings of approximately US$11 600 for construction companies, US$3800 for manufacturing companies and US$11 450 for service companies. Depending upon the frequency of testing and the cost of EAP services, these gross cost savings figures could be reduced by US$1500–2000.

They concluded that the drug-free workplace programme was associated with a selective, industry-specific preventive effect. The strongest evidence of an intervention effect was for the construction industry. Estimated net cost savings for this industry were positive, though small in magnitude.

One possible explanation for the differences between the studies is that certain occupations and industries carry a higher risk of injury than others. Certain jobs may be riskier for persons whose cognitive or cycle motor skills may be impaired by substance use. The transportation industry may see a higher relation between alcohol and substance use and accidents due to the nature of the work, schedules that limit employee use of sick days when high or drunk, and schedules conducive to good use of stimulants to stay awake on the job.

Does drug testing improve productivity?

The third and last question raises more ethical questions. Where most people would agree to use drug testing in order to reduce injuries and fatalities, using it for cost savings and improving productivity is more controversial.

There are reasonable arguments that can be constructed suggesting either positive or negative effects on productivity from drug testing. The arguments suggesting a positive effect are: drug testing reduces illicit drug use (by weeding out users or providing them with a strong incentive to stop), which, in turn, enhances productivity. Potentially positive effects could also result if highly productive workers or managers prefer to work at companies that conduct drug tests, believing it provides a safer, drug-free work environment, with lower risk of accident, injury or interaction with other employees who use drugs. These companies may attract better workers, and the workers there may exhibit greater loyalty towards the company.

It is also possible that drug testing lowers productivity. There are several reasons why this could be the case. The first reason is that drug tests can be expensive and take time to administer. It is important to consider all of the economic costs associated with drug tests. The second possible reason for a negative effect is that drug testing could undermine worker morale, motivation, loyalty or effort towards the company. A third reason is if workers who use illicit drugs are either more productive than workers who do not use illicit drugs, or more productive than they would be if they didn't use drugs. A fourth reason why drug tests may result in lower productivity is if workers (rather than give up drug use altogether because of the drug tests) substitute other drugs that are more harmful to performance in the workplace.[29]

Commonwealth Edison, a Chicago-based electric utility, started an anti-drug education and rehabilitation programme in 1982, offering treatment to users who came forward and threatening to fire those caught with drugs at work. The company also gives urine tests to job applicants. Since the programme started absenteeism dropped by 25% and medical claims, which had been rising steadily at an average rate of 23% annually, rose only 6% in 1988. Moreover, the company had fewer on-the-job accidents in 1985 than in any previous year.[30]

General Motors has claimed a greater than 40% reduction in absenteeism, 50% fewer disciplinary actions and 50% fewer accident claims by employees after implementation of a drug testing programme.[31]

A comprehensive review of scientific studies on drug testing and productivity was conducted by a committee of the National Research Council and Institute of Medicine under the sponsorship of the National Institute of Drug Abuse (NIDA). The Committee on Drug Use in the Workplace (CDUW) was assembled in 1991 with a broad mandate to analyse existing scientific knowledge about drug consumption in the workforce and the effectiveness of work-site prevention and treatment programmes. The CDUW consisted of experts from several disciplines and evaluated hundreds of studies in a multiyear effort, which culminated in the report *Under the Influence? Drugs and the American Work Force*.[3]

Overall, the findings of the CDUW do not provide strong support for drug testing. The CDUW evaluated studies related to drug testing and productivity and found 'few systematic studies relating drug testing programs to workers' productivity, and those that had been done were often flawed in significant ways.' There was some evidence from prior studies of pre-employment testing that employees testing positive for illicit drugs had higher rates of absenteeism, turnover and disciplinary actions. However, several important problems with the methods applied in prior research were identified:

- The magnitude of the relationships between drug use and negative outcomes was generally small and the evidence was mixed.

- The research designs and methods were not amenable to establishing causality, and variables left out of the models may explain the observed correlations.
- Results obtained from evaluation of drug testing at specific job sites (e.g. post offices, the military) may not be representative of the population as a whole (i.e. work sites nationwide).
- Even with a positive association with some outcomes (e.g. lower absenteeism or turnover), effects on overall productivity are uncertain.

Thus, until more empirical studies are conducted, it is unknown to what extent these results can be generalised to other organisations. Furthermore, given the costs of drug testing and low incidence of test-positive results, the CDUW argued that pre-employment drug testing might not be cost-effective. The committee also expressed concern that many companies use drug testing procedures that are not approved by NIDA, increasing the chances of incorrect test results.

The committee also reviewed prior studies on 'for cause' drug testing programmes and found that they 'suffer from serious methodological problems that preclude any scientific assessment of the impact . . . on work force productivity.' Thus they concluded that 'there are few empirically based conclusions that may be reached concerning the effectiveness of drug testing programs in improving workplace productivity' and that companies 'should be cautious in making decisions on the basis of the evidence currently available.'

Blank and Fenton[32] compared 500 US Navy recruits who had tested positive for marijuana at the time of induction yet were allowed to continue in service and to be treated equally, with a matched group who tested negative. If the accession urinalysis test was positive for THC, recruits were warned, counselled and perhaps put on a surveillance programme of regular urinalysis. The sailors who tested positive for marijuana upon entry into the Navy recruit training centre were 2.5 times as likely to attrite from Naval service before the end of their enlistment. After two and a half years, only 57% of those who tested positive for marijuana were still in the Navy, compared to 81% for those who showed no sign of illicit drug use at the time of induction. Results also showed that 14% of those who tested positive for marijuana had left the Navy for drug and alcohol-related problems, and an additional 21% were discharged early for other behavioural or performance problems (Figure 3.5). In comparison, only 1% of the group that tested negative for marijuana were removed for alcohol or drug-related difficulties, and only an additional 8% were discharged for behavioural or performance problems. The researchers projected that only about 38% of the marijuana-positive group would complete their full four years enlistment. No significant differences in retention patterns for three groups (based on the concentration of cannabis

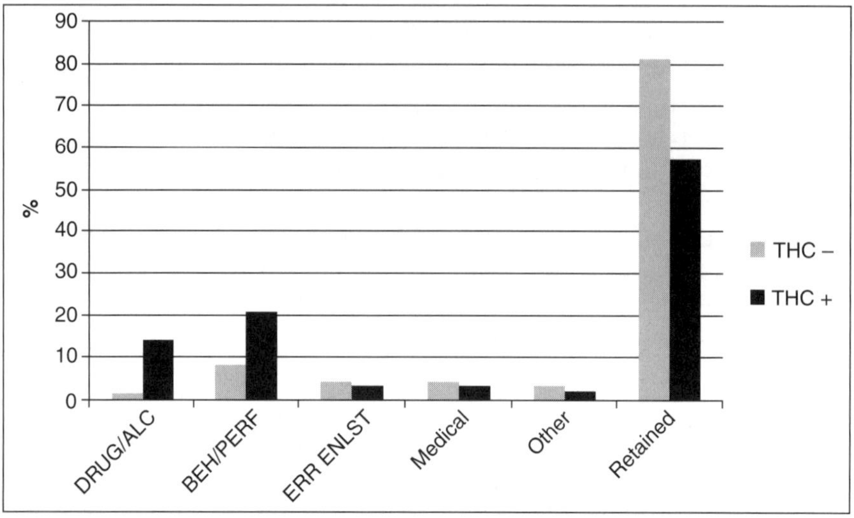

Figure 3.5 Attrition and retention of THC positive vs. THC negative Navy recruits.[32] DRUG/ALC: discharge for drug or alcohol abuse, distribution, manufacturing, etc. BEH/PERF: discharge for behavioural or performance reasons (misconduct, commission of a serious crime, security breech, discreditable incidents, fraudulent entry, trainee discharge due to entry-level performance, and discharge for the good of the service). ERR ENLST: discharge for erroneous enlistment.

metabolites in urine: between 100 and 200, >200 and >>200 ng/mL by radio-immunoassay) were observed.

Sheridan and Winkler[33] studied the previous performance of 198 employees of the Georgia Power Company. They found similar rates of absenteeism amongst those testing positive and negative, although they found variations within some occupational categories. They found that employees who had tested positive had averaged 165 hours of absenteeism, compared with 47 hours for the control group and 41 for the workforce as a whole, a ratio of 4 to 1. The company estimated that it saved as much as US$1.7 million by discharging and replacing the employees who had failed drug tests between 1983 and 1987. This figure represents a saving in medical claims, absenteeism and workers' compensation payments.

Elmuti[34] performed a longitudinal field study that compared changes in perceptions of productivity and attendance behaviours for participants in a drug testing programme in a manufacturing plant in the mid-western United States. Employee efficiency, productivity and absenteeism changes related to the implementation of the drug testing programme were measured by collecting and analysing actual organisational data. Data for each of the measures were collected for a 42-month period, ranging from 18 months prior to the implementation of the programme to 24 months after the programme began. The attitudinal results provide, at best, circumspect support for the claims of drug testing proponents that the programme reduces drug abuse in the workplace and improves overall productivity. A majority of the employees perceived the following as positive benefits that resulted from their firm's drug testing programmes: increased awareness of problems resulting from drug abuse (68%), reduced drug abuse in the workplace (59%), lowered medical costs in the long run (45%), reduced property damages resulting from accidents due to drug abuse (53%), reduced tardiness and absenteeism (48%), reduced drug-related injury (43%) and improved performance and overall productivity (56%). Thirty-two per cent of respondents felt that the drug testing lowered employees' morale and had disruptive effects on employees in their organisations. More than half of the respondents were not sure of the costs and the reliability of drug testing programmes in their organisations. A majority of the respondents either agreed or strongly agreed with the statement 'both employers and employees benefit from drug testing programmes.' Over 69%, however, thought that employers benefit more than employees from drug testing.

The performance results, however, document a positive and substantial impact of drug testing initiative on employee productivity and absenteeism rates. *T*-tests were computed in order to see how significant the changes were across time periods for each measure between the 12 months preceding the drug testing programme and the 24 months after the programme was introduced. The results indicate there were significant differences ($P < 0.01$) between the two periods in percentage of hours spent on production, absenteeism and drug-related injuries (Figure 3.6).

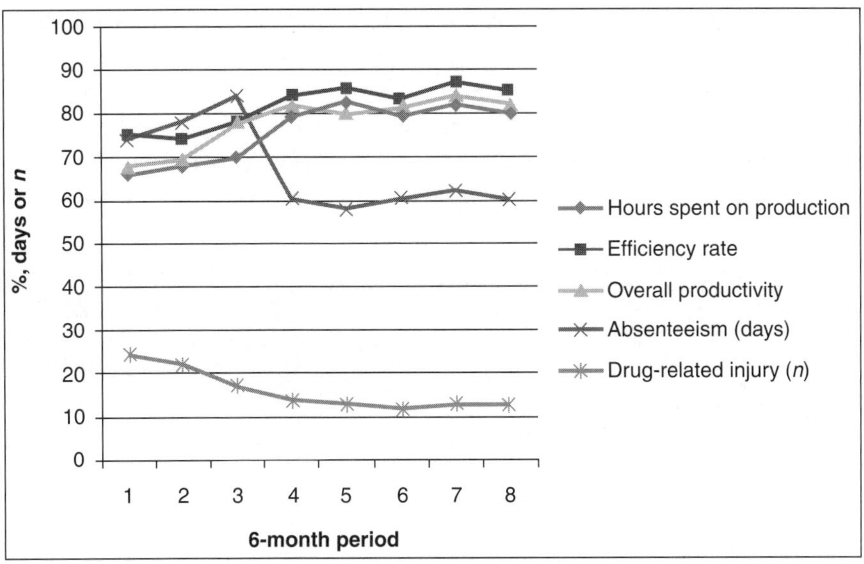

Figure 3.6 Data from organisational records before (period 1–3) and after (period 4–8) introduction of a workplace drug testing programme at a manufacturing plant.[34] Periods 1–3 were before the introduction of workplace drug testing, periods 4–6 after workplace drug testing was introduced. *Y*-axis: %, except for absenteeism (days) and drug-related injury (number).

It was estimated that the total cost of the drug testing programme 24 months after it began was about US$250 000 in fees for urinalysis tests and other additional tests, US$28 000 for treatment and counselling for persons tested positive on drug tests. The plant was realising approximately US$250 000–300 000 per year in continued cost savings from reduction in waste, sick-leave, drug-related injury and worker compensation payments. Other advantages as a result of the implementation of the drug testing programme were 12% lower medical costs, 20% reduction in accidents related to drug abuse during a one-year period, reduced property damage resulting from accidents due to drug abuse and 18% improved sales and labour productivity 12 months after the drug testing programme began.

Zwerling *et al.*[35] reported on a prospective, controlled study of the association between pre-employment drug screening results and employment outcomes in 2537 postal employees. The results are given in Table 3.2.

The mean absence rate of marijuana users was 7.1%, it was 9.8% for cocaine users, compared with 4.0% for non-users.

This study showed that a pre-employment drug screen positive for marijuana or cocaine is associated with adverse employment outcomes. The level of risk, however, was much less than previously estimated.

Peat[2] reported on the results of another study performed by the US Postal Service (USPS). More than 5000 applicants were drug tested between September 1987 and May 1988. A total of 4396 of these applicants were eventually hired. Over the next three years, absenteeism, turnover, referrals to the EAP, medical claims and disciplinary actions were monitored. After three years, the mean absenteeism was 11.4% for the employees who had tested positive versus 6.85% for the drug-negative group. Over the first year, employees who tested positive for marijuana were 1.5 times more likely to be heavy leave-of-absence users (219 hours) than those who tested negative (132 hours). Those who tested

Table 3.2 Comparison of the relative risk for turnover, accidents, injuries and being disciplined in workers that tested positive for marijuana and cocaine compared to those that tested negative (95% confidence interval between parentheses)[35]

	Marijuana users	Cocaine users
Turnover	1.56 (1.17 to 2.08)	1.15 (0.65 to 2.05)
Accidents	1.55 (1.16 to 2.08)	1.59 (0.95 to 2.67)
Injuries	1.85 (1.30 to 2.64)	1.85 (1.01 to 3.39)
Discipline	1.55 (1.03 to 2.32)	1.40 (0.62 to 3.17)

positive for cocaine were more than four times as likely to be heavy users of leave-of-absence. After three years, the drug-positive group had 77% higher rates of involuntary turnover compared with the drug-negative group. After three years, 14.4% of the positives were referred to the EAP for assistance versus 2.7% for the negatives. Marijuana positives were twice as likely, and cocaine positives 6.3 times as likely as a drug-free group to be referred to EAP. The mean number of medical claims filed by the positives was 51% higher than the negatives. The median dollar amount of these claims was 83% higher for the positives (US$487) then the negatives (US$265). The odds of being disciplined were 2.4 times higher for those testing positive than for those testing negative. Cocaine positives were 5.5 times more likely to be disciplined then their drug-negative peers. The authors estimated that the savings from a drug testing programme over a 10-year period would be US$105 000 000 or a saving of about US$19 000 for every positive applicant who was not hired.

Zwerling *et al.*[36] pointed out that a cost–benefit analysis is sensitive to changes in its underlying assumptions. In one study, drug screening would have saved the US Postal Service US$162 per applicant hired, but the results were sensitive to the assumptions in the model. If the prevalence of drug use in the population screened were 1% rather than 12%, the programme would lose money. Similarly, if the cost per urine sample screened were US$95 rather than the US$49 assumed, then the programme would lose money, even if the prevalence of drug positives was as high as 9%. Any company considering pre-employment drug screening should carefully weigh the costs and benefits in its own industry.

A 1989 study by Parish[37] looked for a correlation between urine toxicology examination results and job performance in newly hired hospital employees at a large teaching hospital in a moderate sized urban area in Georgia. Prospective employees were notified during the interview process that drug screening would be part of their physical examination and that the results would not have any bearing on their job, and would be used as part of a study of the usefulness of urinary drug testing. One year later information was extracted from personnel folders regarding disciplinary actions, promotions, commendations, absenteeism, job retention, supervisor evaluations, and reasons for termination. Of the 195 employees screened, 12% (22) tested positive for drugs, the majority (14), for THC. None were positive for cocaine or heroin. This study could not show a relation between positive pre-employment drug screens and substandard job performance; however, the size of the drug-positive group was not large enough to allow valid comparisons. Furthermore, there was no medical review of positive tests to determine which ones could have had medical explanations, so a significant number of the positives may have been users of prescription medications, not illicit substances, but were nevertheless included in the drug user cohort. Parish concluded that hospital money could be better spent on programmes other than drug testing if larger studies that include more variables to detect subtler differences in job performance could reproduce his findings.

Shepard and Clifton[29] studied the economic effects of drug testing programmes by applying a production function model to a test sample of 63 firms within the computer and communications equipment industries in the US economy. Data on drug testing used for this study was collected at an Internet site where employees reported their employer's drug policy. The accuracy of the data was checked. They used the Cobb–Douglas (CD) production function (the most common form used in applied studies because it is simple to estimate and is consistent with the economic theory of production) to estimate the effects. It is commonly used in empirical studies to analyse effects of varying workplace characteristics on productivity. The dependent variable used the log of net sales divided by number of employees, as a proxy for productivity. Two types of drug testing variables were used, the first was coded for drug testing, and the second categorised them into two groups: (1) pre-employment screening testing and (2) random testing of current employees and pre-employment screening.

Surprisingly, companies adopting drug testing programmes were found to exhibit lower levels of productivity than their counterparts that did not. The regression coefficients representing potential effects of drug testing programmes on productivity were both negative and significant. Both pre-employment and random testing of workers were found to be associated with lower levels of productivity. A change from not drug testing to using drug testing would reduce productivity by 19% (confidence interval –4 to –33%). Similarly, the regression estimates also suggested a large and significant decline in productivity with pre-testing use associated with 16% drop and random testing with 29%.

The authors discuss possible causes of bias and explanations, such as non-representativeness of the sample and rather imprecise estimate of the mean effect given the relatively small sample size. A third possible reason is that there are omitted variables that are correlated with drug testing associated with companies of lower productivity. One possibility is that companies with low levels of productivity are more likely to adopt productivity-enhancing programmes, such as drug testing, in the hopes of improving performance. Another is that companies with inferior management are more likely to adopt drug testing.

Their results showed that drug testing programmes did not succeed in improving productivity. One should point out that this study was performed in the computer and communications equipment industries, where the risk of accidents that cause considerable damage is probably much lower than in the construction or transportation industries.

Meta-analyses and Cochrane reviews

In 2001, Kraus[21] evaluated published evidence relevant to the effect of introducing a workplace drug testing programme (other than for pre-employment purposes) on injury or accident outcomes. Articles from peer-reviewed journals, technical and government reports, and unpublished documents were systematically retrieved. Papers with data allowing comparison of non-testing versus testing or a change in testing method were evaluated for independent measures of effect of the programme. From the 740 abstracts reviewed, 101 papers were selected and read. Six of them addressed the objective to greater or lesser degrees; five provided data on the impact of a new drug testing programme on injuries or accidents and one addressed the effect of random versus non-random testing. He did not include studies limited to the effects of pre-employment drug screening only, but four studies included pre-employment testing as well. No report of a randomised controlled trial was identified among the reviewed articles. All used ecologic databases that did not allow independent analyses for aggregate measure of effect. Thus, it was not possible to separate the effects of one type of testing (random and for cause) from the effects of pre-employment testing. Four reports indicated that the total drug testing programmes (which included several types of testing protocols) were effective in reducing injuries or injury rates. The only report that addressed whether random or 'for cause' drug testing programmes resulted in lower injuries suggested that accident rates declined following the change from a non-random to a random drug testing protocol. Shortcomings in study designs and limitations of the data included and/or tests of significance preclude conclusions regarding the effect of drug testing programmes on injury reduction.

All the reports were based on group exposures, not on individual exposures. All study designs were of the pre-test/post-test variety, which is subject to numerous potential sources of bias, most notably the mixed effects from factors other than the introduction (or change) in testing programme per se. He concluded that: 'Despite the extensive use of and management support for worksite-based drug testing, the published evidence for effects such as reduced injury or accident rates lacks scientific detail. Better studies and careful reassessment of this issue appear warranted.'

A Cochrane systematic review about injury prevention in a different occupational setting, the construction industry,[38,39] performed a systematic review of the effectiveness of interventions for preventing occupational injuries among construction workers. They searched seven databases, from the earliest available dates through June 2006, for published findings of injury prevention in construction studies. Acceptable study designs included randomised controlled trials, controlled before–after studies, and interrupted time series. Effect sizes of similar interventions were pooled into a meta-analysis in January 2007.

Of 7522 titles found, four interrupted time series studies and one controlled interrupted time series study met the inclusion criteria. Three studies evaluated the effect of regulations, one evaluated a safety campaign, and one a drug-free workplace programme on fatal or non-fatal injuries compared to no drug-free workplace programme. The overall methodological quality was low. No indications of publication bias were found. The studies that evaluated legislation did not show either an initial or sustained effect on fatal or non-fatal injuries, with effect sizes of 0.69 (95% CI –1.70 to 3.09) and 0.28 (95% CI 0.05 to 0.51).

Findings from a safety campaign study and a drug-free workplace study indicated that both interventions significantly reduced the level and the trend of injuries. The safety campaign did have an initial and sustained effect, reducing non-fatal injuries with effect sizes of –1.82 (95% CI –2.90 to –0.75) and –1.30 (95% CI –1.79 to –0.80), respectively. The drug-free workplace programme[20] did have an initial and sustained effect, reducing non-fatal injuries compared to no intervention, with effect sizes of –6.78 (95% CI –10.02 to –3.54) and –1.76 (95% CI –3.11 to –0.41), respectively.

A Cochrane review[1] on alcohol and drug screening of occupational drivers for preventing injury or work-related effects such as sickness absence related to injury searched the literature up to June 2007 for randomised controlled trials (RCTs), cluster-randomised trials, controlled clinical trials, controlled before and after studies (more than three time points to be measured before and after the study) and interrupted time series studies that evaluated alcohol or drug-screening interventions for occupational drivers (compared to another intervention or no intervention) with an outcome measured as a reduction in injury or a proxy measure thereof. Two review authors independently extracted data and assessed study quality.

They included two interrupted time series studies conducted in the United States.[22,40,41] One study was conducted in five large US transportation companies ($n = 115\,019$) that carried passengers and/or cargo. Monthly injury rates were available from 1983 to 1999. In the study company, two interventions of interest were evaluated: mandatory random drug testing and mandatory random and for cause alcohol testing programmes. The third study focused only on mandatory random drug testing and was conducted on Federal injury data that covered all truck drivers of interstate carriers. They recalculated the results from raw data provided by the study authors. Following reanalysis, they found that in one study mandatory random and for cause alcohol testing was associated with a significant decrease in the level of injuries immediately following the intervention (–1.25 injuries/100 person-years, 95% CI –2.29 to –0.21) but did not significantly affect the existing long-term downward trend (–0.28 injuries/100 person-years per year, 95% CI –0.78 to 0.21).

Mandatory random drug testing was significantly associated with an immediate change in injury level following the intervention (1.26 injuries/100 person-years, 95% CI 0.36 to 2.16) in one study, and in the second study there was no significant effect (–1.36/injuries/100 person-years, 95% CI –1.69 to 0.41). In the long term, random drug testing was associated with a significant increase in the downward trend (–0.19 injuries/100 person years/year, 95% CI –0.30 to –0.07) in one study; the other study was also associated with a significant improvement in the long-term downward trend (–0.83 fatal accidents/100 million vehicle miles/year, 95% CI –1.08 to –0.58).

The authors concluded that there is insufficient evidence to advise for or against the use of drug and alcohol testing of occupational drivers for preventing injuries as a sole, effective, long-term solution in the context of workplace culture, peer interaction and other local factors. Cluster-randomised trials are needed to better address the effects of interventions for injury prevention in this occupational setting. The Cochrane review concluded that there is limited evidence that in the long term mandatory drug testing interventions can be more effective than no intervention in reducing injuries in occupational drivers. For mandatory alcohol testing there was evidence of an immediate effect only.

Given the widespread practice of alcohol and drug testing and the paucity of evaluation studies found, more evaluation studies are needed. Interrupted time series is a feasible study design for evaluating interventions that aim at preventing alcohol and drug-related injuries. However, time series studies of higher quality and of long duration are needed to increase the level of evidence. A cluster-randomised trial would be the ideal study design to evaluate the effects of interventions for injury prevention in this occupational setting.

Conclusion

The effects of workplace drug testing on deterring drug use, reducing the number of accidents and injuries and improving productivity or being cost-effective, have mainly been studied in the late 1980s. Nearly all studies showed that workplace drug testing had a positive effect on these parameters. But many of these studies were later criticised because of methodological flaws. Recently, two Cochrane reviews have examined this question. Very few studies met the methodological criteria, but there were some indications that workplace drug testing had some positive effects. Future studies based on sound methods should be able to answer this question definitively.

References

1. Cashman CM, Ruotsalainen JH, Greiner BA, Beirne PV, Verbeek JH. Alcohol and drug screening of occupational drivers for preventing injury. *Cochrane Database Syst Rev*, CD006566.

2. Peat MA. Financial viability of screening for drugs of abuse. *Clin Chem* 1995; 41(5): 805–808.
3. Normand J. *Under the Influence? Drugs and the American Work Force*. Washington, DC: National Academy Press, 1994.
4. Quest Diagnostics (2009) *Drug Testing Index*. www.questdiagnostics.com/employersolutions/dti/2009_11/dti_index.html (accessed 4 March 2010).
5. Mehay S, Pacula RL. The effectiveness of workplace drug prevention policies: does 'zero tolerance' work? Report no.: W7383 Contract no.: W7383. National Bureau of Economic Research, Cambridge, MA, 1999.
6. Jacobson M. Drug testing in the trucking industry: the effect on highway safety. *J Law Econ* 2003; 46(1): 131–156.
7. Ozminkowski RJ, Mark TL, Goetzel RZ, Blank D, Walsh JM, Cangianelli L. Relationships between urinalysis testing for substance use, medical expenditures, and the occurrence of injuries at a large manufacturing firm. *Am J Drug Alcohol Abuse* 2003; 29(1): 151–167.
8. Larson SL, Eyerman J, Foster MS, Gfroerer JC. Worker substance use and workplace policies and programs. DHHS Publication no. SMA 07-4273. Substance Abuse and Mental Health Services Administration, Office of Applied Studies, Rockville, MD, 2007.
9. Carpenter CS. Workplace drug testing and worker drug use. *Health Serv Res* 2007; 42(2): 795–810.
10. Lange WR, Cabanilla BR, Moler G, Bernacki EJ, Frankenfield DL, Fudala PJ. Preemployment drug screening at the Johns-Hopkins Hospital 1989 and 1991. *Am J Drug Alcohol Abuse* 1994; 20(1): 35–46.
11. French MT, Roebuck MC, Kebreau Alexandre P. To test or not to test: do workplace drug testing programs discourage employee drug use? *Soc Sci Res* 2004; 33(1): 45–63.
12. Ricordel I, Wenzek M. [Cannabis and safety of work: Evolution of its detection within the controls of narcotics since 2004 to the SNCF]. *Ann Pharm Fr* 2008; 66(4): 255–260.
13. Lawental E, McLellan AT, Grissom GR, Brill P, O'Brien C. Coerced treatment for substance abuse problems detected through workplace urine surveillance: is it effective? *J Subst Abuse* 1996; 8(1): 115–128.
14. Weisner C, Lu Y, Hinman A, Monahan J, Bonnie RJ, Moore CD *et al.* Substance use, symptom, and employment outcomes of persons with a workplace mandate for chemical dependency treatment. *Psychiatr Serv* 2009; 60(5): 646–654.
15. Lindseth PD, Vacek JJ, Lindseth GN. Urinalysis drug testing within a civilian pilot training program: did attitudes change during the 1990s? *Aviat Space Environ Med* 2001; 72(7): 647–651.
16. Lindseth PD, Lindseth G. Attitudes toward urinalysis drug testing within a civilian pilot training program. *Aviat Space Environ Med* 1995; 66(9): 837–840.
17. Crouch DJ, Webb DO, Peterson LV, Buller PF, Rollins DE. A critical-evaluation of the Utah Power and Light company substance-abuse management program – absenteeism, accidents and costs. In: Gust S, Walsh JM, eds. *Drugs in the Workplace: Research and Evaluation Data*. NIDA Research monograph 91. Rockville, MD: National Institute on Drug Abuse, 1989: 169–193.
18. Kertesz L. Two firms curb losses from drug abuse. *Business Insurance* 1990; 24(24): 16–18.
19. Feinauer DM, Havlovic SJ. Drug-testing as a strategy to reduce occupational accidents – a longitudinal analysis. *J Safety Res* 1993; 24(1): 1–7.
20. Wickizer TM, Kopjar B, Franklin G, Joesch J. Do drug-free workplace programs prevent occupational injuries? Evidence from Washington State. *Health Serv Res* 2004; 39(1): 91–110.
21. Kraus JF. The effects of certain drug-testing programs on injury reduction in the workplace: an evidence-based review. *Int J Occup Environ Health* 2001; 7(2): 103–108.
22. Miller TR, Zaloshnja E, Spicer RS. Effectiveness and benefit-cost of peer-based workplace substance abuse prevention coupled with random testing. *Accid Anal Prev* 2007; 39(3): 565–573.
23. Gerber JK, Yacoubian GS Jr. An assessment of drug testing within the construction industry. *J Drug Educ* 2002; 32(1): 53–68.

24. Kesselring RG, Pittman JR. Drug testing laws and employment injuries. *J Labor Res* 2002; 23(2): 293–301.
25. Taggart RW. Results of the drug testing program at Southern Pacific Railroad. In: Gust S, Walsh JM, eds. *Drugs in the Workplace: Research and Evaluation Data.* NIDA Research monograph 91. Rockville, MD: National Institute on Drug Abuse, 1989: 97–108.
26. Spicer RS, Miller TR, Smith GS. Worker substance use, workplace problems and the risk of occupational injury: a matched case-control study. *J Stud Alcohol* 2003; 64(4): 570–578.
27. Cunradi CB, Ragland DR, Greiner B, Klein M, Fisher JM. Attributable risk of alcohol and other drugs for crashes in the transit industry. *Inj Prev* 2005; 11(6): 378–382.
28. Swena D. Effect of random drug screening on fatal commercial truck accident rates. *Int J Drug Testing* 1999; 2(1): 1–13.
29. Shepard E, Clifton T. Drug testing and labor productivity: estimates applying a production function model. Research paper number 18. Le Moyne College Institute of Industrial Relations, 1998: 1–30.
30. Castro J, Beaty J, Dolan B. Battling the enemy within. *Time* 1986: 52–61.
31. Osterloh J. Drug testing in the workplace. *Occup Med* 1990; 5(3): 617–632.
32. Blank DL, Fenton JW. Early employment testing for marijuana – demographic and employee retention patterns. In: Gust S, Walsh JM, eds. *Drugs in the Workplace: Research and Evaluation Data.* NIDA Research monograph 91. Rockville, MD: National Institute on Drug Abuse, 1989: 139–150.
33. Sheridan J, Winkler H. An evaluation of drug-testing in the workplace. In: Gust S, Walsh JM, eds. *Drugs in the Workplace: Research and Evaluation Data.* NIDA Research monograph 91. Rockville, MD: National Institute on Drug Abuse, 1989: 195–216.
34. Elmuti D. Effects of a drug testing programme on employee attitudes, productivity and attendance behaviours. *Employee Couns Today* 1994; 6(5): 24–32.
35. Zwerling C, Ryan J, Orav EJ. The efficacy of preemployment drug screening for marijuana and cocaine in predicting employment outcome. *JAMA* 1990; 264(20): 2639–2643.
36. Zwerling C, Ryan J, Orav EJ. Costs and benefits of preemployment drug screening. *JAMA* 1992; 267(1): 91–93.
37. Parish DC. Relation of the pre-employment drug-testing result to employment status – a one-year follow-up. *J Gen Intern Med* 1989; 4(1): 44–47.
38. van der Molen HF, Lehtola MM, Lappalainen J, Hoonakker PL, Hsiao H, Haslam R *et al.* Interventions for preventing injuries in the construction industry. *Cochrane Database Syst Rev* 2007; 4: CD006251.
39. Lehtola MM, van der Molen HF, Lappalainen J, Hoonakker PL, Hsiao H, Haslam RA *et al.* The effectiveness of interventions for preventing injuries in the construction industry: a systematic review. *Am J Prev Med* 2008; 35(1): 77–85.
40. Spicer RS, Miller TR. Impact of a workplace peer-focused substance abuse prevention and early intervention program. *Alcohol Clin Exp Res* 2005; 29(4): 609–611.
41. Swena D. Effect of random drug screening on fatal commercial truck accident rates. *Int J Drug Testing* 1999; 2: 1–13.

4

Legal and regulatory aspects of workplace drug testing

John O'Sullivan

Key points

- Many European countries allow testing when there is a health, safety or security risk, or when it is deemed 'necessary' or 'proportionate,' or is 'justified' or 'reasonable', or when there is a 'reasonable suspicion' that an employee is under the influence of an intoxicant (whether legal or illegal).
- In many European countries the occupational health physician can only inform the employer whether an employee is 'fit for work' or 'unfit for work' rather than revealing the full results of a particular test.
- There are wide differences in practice between countries on the issue of pre-employment testing in comparison with the testing of existing members of the workforce.
- In common law jurisdictions in Europe, such as Ireland and the UK, employers have had a common law duty of care to employees to provide a safe place of work and not expose them to reasonably foreseeable harm arising out of the work duties they undertake.
- Three countries have specific or direct legislation on drug testing in the workplace: Finland, Ireland and Norway. In Italy, the main drug law contains an article addressing specifically drug testing in the workplace. In all other countries, there is indirect legislation in the areas of privacy and data protection that regulate to some extent the type of testing that can take place.
- Several court cases have examined different aspects of workplace drug testing in Europe and in general the outcome was favourable to the practice of workplace drug testing. In nearly all cases, dismissals of employees because of a positive drug test were confirmed by the courts.

Introduction

The issue of whether a company should introduce a workplace drug testing programme is one that involves commercial, moral, ethical, social and legal considerations. This chapter will be solely concerned with the legal and regulatory context surrounding drug (and alcohol) testing policies in a workplace setting. Note that for the purposes of clarity in this chapter, where the term 'drug' is used, alcohol is included unless specifically stated. Similarly, the term 'intoxicant' when used will include alcohol and drugs whether legal (e.g. over-the-counter medications) or illicit drugs.

An examination of the legal issues is particularly important in the context of corporations and other commercial entities operating within and across many European Union (EU) countries and thus in differing legal codes (e.g. common law jurisdictions, such as in UK and Ireland, versus civil law jurisdictions, such as Spain and France) and subject to a variety of national laws dealing either directly or indirectly with workplace drug testing through legislation. International legal differences aside, membership of the EU has ensured that there are common legal threads relating to workplace drug testing in member states in the areas of employment, health and safety, data protection and disability discrimination.

The main focus here will be to look at some of the legal tensions with regard to the issue of drug testing in a workplace or corporate setting under the headings of:

- Health and safety legislation
- Labour/employment legislation
- Occupational health law, practice and guidelines
- Workplace privacy
- EU data protection directives
- Discrimination/disability legislation.

We will see that superimposed on these categories are legal authorities, both national and supra-national that impose imperatives and constraints with respect to the how, who, why, where and when of drug testing and will obviously influence the decision-making process whether at occupational health (OH) or human resource (HR) level in deciding to introduce a workplace drug testing programme in a particular country, and if so, how to ensure legal compliance. Thus the European Convention on Human Rights and Fundamental Freedoms has been given affect in most European nations through various 'Human Rights' Acts and in the context of testing for intoxicants in the workplace, Article 8 and the right to privacy will be seen to be a focal point for challenges.

It goes without saying that, notwithstanding international norms and comparisons, the best advice is still to retain an eminent local employment lawyer to review the draft form of any substance abuse or drug abuse policy, especially if it contains provisions for the testing of intoxicants. How positive drug tests are or may be treated in courts of law or industrial/employment tribunals will also be looked at by way of reference to some established international case law. An overview of the legal situation in a number of countries will also be undertaken with a review of some of the European Legal Database on Drugs (ELDD) categorisations.

It is recognised that workplace drug testing can be a potentially divisive issue, and this is reflected in much of the commentary about it; it is, of course, considered differently depending on the standpoint of the commentator. Shehandeh and Caborn[1] analysed arguments for and against workplace drug testing under the following headings:

- Safety
- Morals
- Deterrence
- Privacy
- Data protection
- Discrimination.

The morals and deterrent arguments will not be dealt with here and for the purposes of clarity, the phrase 'workplace drug testing' will be taken to include alcohol, although it may be the case that some companies in different countries across Europe who introduce testing as part of an overall substance abuse policy, treat alcohol in a different manner to the taking of drugs at work, in as much as alcohol is a legal 'drug', whereas the majority of drugs tested for are illegal in most jurisdictions. As for the other headings, there is no doubt that testing for intoxicants in the workplace can raise issues regarding privacy, data protection and discrimination (particularly in the area of disability).

Many of the ethical concerns around intoxicant testing relate to a cohort of recurring issues across all jurisdictions:

- Testing is invasive (physical invasion, invasion of privacy).
- Testing may amount to discrimination in some circumstances.
- Testing may reveal more than workplace behaviour in that intoxicants may never be consumed during work, but traces of consumption outside of work can still be detected (especially in case of cannabis consumption using urine as a test matrix).
- Testing (particularly using urine as a matrix) is not a measurement of impairment.
- Testing may be abused in certain circumstances, whereby other information relating to the employee is revealed (e.g. use of prescription medication).

The challenge for transnational companies

One of the challenges facing a company seeking to introduce testing for intoxicants in the workplace in different locations throughout Europe is that there are many different national legal systems, and although more countries have recently transposed common EU Directives in the fields of data protection, equality and, importantly, the European Convention on Human Rights and Fundamental Freedoms, there are still many arrangements at the level of national labour law and industrial relations that, while allowing drug testing in one jurisdiction, preclude its introduction in another.

In effect, the European Union can be considered to be a 'mixed jurisdiction' where 'there is a growing convergence within the Union between Europe's two major legal traditions, the civil law of the continental countries and the common law of England, Wales, Northern Ireland and The Republic of Ireland'.[2] This can be very problematic when 'The Very Big Global Corporation (VBGC)' wants to implement a single strategy with respect to, for example, pre-employment recruitment worldwide. In common law countries, the individual contract of employment is at the core of the employment relationship, whereas in the rest of Europe it varies from countries such as France or Belgium which have labour codes over-pinning collective agreements, internal regulations and practices, to countries such as Denmark, where labour courts rule in disputes according to custom and practice in a particular industry.[3]

Overall though, at EU level, it can be said that there is a high degree of harmonisation across differing legal codes with respect to the legal principles that will effect the introduction of workplace drug testing, especially in the areas of health and safety, data protection and discrimination legislation, and terms such as 'necessity', 'proportionality' and 'reasonableness' when applied to intoxicant testing will be familiar to all.

As we shall see, the testing regimes that a company may want to introduce can be subject to more stringent requirements in different countries, depending on the particular requirements. For example, should testing be performed only on employees working in 'safety-critical' or 'safety-sensitive' roles within a company, or is the testing to be conducted on a random (perhaps 5–10%) selection of the workforce? A company with a workforce in London and Amsterdam will be able to conduct pre-employment medicals (including intoxicant testing) on applicants in London, but will be precluded from doing so in Amsterdam, as under Dutch law, such testing is deemed unconstitutional. This obviously poses the question of how to uniformly implement a common and coherent policy across the workforce and is no small challenge in this age of the migratory worker.

Furthermore, in an era of global mergers and acquisitions, it is important that common policies arising from corporate headquarters do not fall foul of local employment law and practice (remedies for unfair dismissals arising out of positive drug or alcohol tests is a case in point).

Workplace testing modalities

The modalities of workplace testing have been dealt with in detail elsewhere. For the purposes of examining the potential legal ramifications of introducing intoxicant testing as part of a corporate substance abuse policy, it is vitally important to distinguish the types of testing that are to be undertaken as there may be a hierarchy of legal rights attached, depending on whom and how the testing is conducted.

On one level, there are two main categories of testing: pre-employment or during employment. During employment, testing can take the form of:

- with cause/for cause/reasonable suspicion
- random (announced and unannounced)
- post-accident
- return to duty.

If one is to assign a hypothetical scale of justification or legal onus to be overcome in introducing the various types of testing into a company, intuitively one can see that pre-employment testing (generally under the rubric of the pre-employment medical), because of the lack of an employment contract is the easiest to introduce and justify. Note that one must take care in the common scenario that the testing procedure as part of the pre-employment medical assessment takes place after a firm job offer, in which case the requirement for a fully informed consent.

From a health and safety perspective, with cause and post-accident testing can be objectively justified in certain industries and it is the case across many jurisdictions in the EU that there has been agreement between unions and employers as to the scope of this type of testing in particular sectors. Random testing of a fixed cohort of employees (conventionally 5–10% per annum) is common across a number of industry sectors (e.g. military, transportation (air, road and rail), mining, nuclear, among others). But there is a difference between randomly testing 5–10% of a safety-critical cohort of workers and testing 5–10% of a total workforce. It may be easier to objectively justify the former on health and safety grounds, but in some unionised workforces, the implementation of workplace drug testing as part of a corporate substance abuse policy may necessitate all tiers of the company hierarchy being amenable to testing (including managers) in order to make its introduction more acceptable. It is axiomatic that random testing must mean exactly that – random. The selection procedure must be statistically robust in order to counter potential accusations of bias and unfair procedures, which could lead to legal challenge.

Craig[4] has classified the drug testing policy options of a company without the distinction (based on privacy alone) of candidate versus employee, and looks at:

- Who is tested – all employees or a subcategory
- Reason for testing – e.g. post-accident, with or without cause
- Method of testing – random v. universal
- When testing is carried out – scheduled (announced) or surprise (unannounced) testing.

To the above categories I would add a further more technical category: whether testing is carried out 'on site' or is primarily laboratory-based. The distinction is important from a recognised international accreditation standard (e.g. ISO 17025, ISO 15189) standpoint and therefore may be an important consideration with respect to defending potential litigation into the future.

Ferguson[5] has looked at the 'competing interests' between employers and employees on the issue of testing in the workplace and suggests that national and international legal systems can act as balances to these interests directly or indirectly in either encouraging or restricting the ability to test. Examples of 'direct legal authorisation' can be via health and safety legislation (e.g. Safety, Health and Welfare at Work Act, 2005 – Ireland), while 'indirect' encouragement may also be construed via the 'duty of care' in common law countries to provide a safe place of work for employees (e.g. Health and Safety at Work Act 1974 – UK). Acting as a counterbalance to express and indirect legislative provisions are internationally agreed conventions, national constitutional rights and directives transposed into national pertaining to data protection, privacy and discrimination due to disability.

In broad terms, the globalisation of commercial transactions has meant that there are now more and more companies operating in a multinational milieu. This has prompted the European Monitoring Centre for Drugs and Drug Addiction (EMCDDA) to categorise and stratify the possible legal heads under which workplace drug and alcohol testing may be classified in countries throughout Europe, looking at the International, European and, where applicable, local national legislation in its web publication.[6] It says that, in its broadest terms, 'On an international level, the matter might be covered by Universal Declaration of Human Rights, art 12 – No one shall be subjected to arbitrary interference with his privacy.'

The European Convention on Human Rights and the EU Directives on data protection and health and safety at work have been transposed into national law in most of the EU. This is in keeping with one of the EU aims of harmonisation of laws. National data protection authorities have made clear statements on workplace drug testing in some of the countries. The ELDD[6] has categorised testing under the following headings:

Health and safety

Many countries allow testing when there is a health, safety or security risk, or when it is deemed 'necessary' or 'proportionate', or is 'justified' or 'reasonable', or when there is a 'reasonable suspicion' that an employee is under the influence of an intoxicant (whether legal or illegal). Regulations arising from EU legislation put an onus on employers to carry out health and safety risk assessments in the workplace. Ferguson suggests that drug and alcohol testing programmes in the workplace may be 'an effective form of risk assessment'.[5]

Focus on occupational health

In many countries the occupational doctor (occupational health physician) can only inform the employer whether an employee is 'fit for work' or 'unfit for work' rather than revealing the full results of a particular test. Also, in some countries, consent must be obtained from the employee to allow the results of a particular health screen or intoxicant screen to be given to the employer (via the human resource department).[7]

Employment aspects

There are wide differences in practice between countries on the issue of pre-employment testing in comparison with the testing of existing members of the workforce. Pre-employment testing is allowed for job applicants in some countries. In general the testing is considered a part of the 'pre-employment medical', in which case, the practice in a number of countries is that if a candidate tests positive at pre-employment stage, they will be deemed to have 'failed' the medical and would no longer be considered for the position. (Note: Notwithstanding this, the issues of whether the consent given to testing was informed may be a factor in whether a pre-employment medical intoxicant test is procedurally sound.) With regard to existing employees, an existing term in the employment contract or the insertion of a new term to change a contract, agreeing to testing is in general only allowable after consultation with worker representatives or collective bargaining with unions.

The employment contract

In the 'very big corporation of America' scenario, in which the multinational company with headquarters in the United States and facilities and offices across the EU wishes to implement a global policy for substance abuse prevention, there are very large differences between the EU and United States regarding the contract of employment which may be pertinent when considering the implementation of a testing regime across all regions. In the United States there is no requirement for a contract, whether written or verbal, and employment is in general treated as being 'at will'. In the EU, the employment relationship can be viewed from the perspective of the Anglo-Saxon common law, or the civil law of mainland EU countries. In common law countries, a number of fundamental principles are apparent, arrived at either by court judgments in contract law developed over the years or protective statutory employment enactments, whether domestic or transposed into national legislation through EU Directives. Examples of the former are a number of 'implied terms', such as duty of employer to give reasonable notice of termination of employment, duty of mutual trust and confidence between employer and employee, and duties of fidelity and good faith. The latter includes legislation giving protection against unfair dismissal, discrimination (e.g. on grounds of sex, race, religion, sexual orientation, and disability among others), health and safety legislation and statute pertaining to data protection.

These legal protections, deriving as they do from EU Directives, are also common to civil law jurisdictions, but in general, the employment relationship tends to be guided by labour codes (e.g. code du travail in France), collective agreements and local custom and practice. So, for example, there is no specific legislation in Denmark, and disputes are resolved in the courts in accordance with the industry-specific custom and practice.

Despite the convergence between common law and civil law jurisdictions in the areas of protective employment law legislation via EU Directives, there still remains the fundamental difference in that in the UK and Ireland there is an individual contract of employment, while in most of mainland, EU members have adopted a collective approach. Thus, there will be a different emphasis required when it comes to the introduction of an intoxicant testing regime in companies. As we shall see later in some common law cases, the fact that testing provisions are included in individual employment contracts is enough to give it efficacy.[8]

From first principles, one of the best protections for a company wishing to introduce testing is to insert a relevant clause in the contract of employment from the outset, referring to the company drug and alcohol policy, and where appropriate, to the particular provisions for the testing of employees. This clause should expressly state the nature of intoxicant testing required in the particular workplace, and an explanation of the testing methodology, including the full list of intoxicants that will be tested.

It is much more difficult to introduce testing for all of a designated workforce (e.g. safety-critical identified after a risk assessment) retrospectively, requiring as it would, insertion of new terms into existing contracts of employment. Companies would need to take cognisance of local industrial relations requirements, and/or the requirements for collective bargaining in the case of unionised workforces.

It must be recognised that in some countries in Europe, the employment contract is considered to be imbalanced per se, in that the balance of power lies with the employer (see Switzerland and Germany trade unions approach) and as such, the worker or employee may not be in a strong bargaining position to reject the implementation of testing or indeed to refuse to undergo a test following the introduction of a testing regime. But in a large number of EU countries, the tradition of collective bargaining regarding national agreements at a sectoral level and local workplace agreements based on industry custom and practice is a safeguard to employee rights.

Employer's duty of care

In common law jurisdictions in Europe, such as Ireland and the UK, employers have had a common law duty of care to employees to provide a safe place of work and not expose them to reasonably foreseen harm arising out of the work duties they undertake. This duty of care has in general been subsumed into various health and safety legislative initiatives, and can be seen in similar guises across Europe. For example, in Slovenia, under the Law on Safety and Health at the Workplace (1999), the employer is obliged to provide a safe place of work.

Does workplace drug testing infringe the privacy of workers?

Craig[4] states that 'employment drug testing is perhaps the most controversial of today's workplace privacy issues' and in his review on privacy and employment law in the United States, UK, Canada and France, he notes the widely varied treatment by the courts and tribunals in the area of drug and alcohol testing in the workplace.

Privacy is a constitutional right in a number of jurisdictions (in Ireland for example, it is described as unenumerated – i.e. it is not explicitly referred to in the Constitution but it has been accepted that article 40.3 of the Constitution implicitly guarantees a right to privacy). Article 8 of the European Convention on Human Rights explicitly states that a person has a right to respect for private and family life.

European Convention on Human Rights and Fundamental Freedoms

The European Convention on Human Rights has been given effect in a number of EU countries via legislation such as the Human Rights Act (UK), whereby one can complain of a breach of the Convention to the European Court of Human Rights in Strasbourg, but only after having first exhausted all available domestic remedies. The Convention has been ratified by all the EU member states. Its provisions can be relied on by a worker directly as against public bodies or public authorities. Thus the provisions of Article 8, as enacted via national legislation (various 'Human Rights Acts') may be relied upon by an individual directly against public bodies, or such entities the functions of which are public in nature.

Article 8 of the European Convention on Human Rights is acknowledged by experts as being of most relevance to the issue of drug and alcohol testing:

1 Everyone has the right to respect for his private and family life, his home and his correspondence.
2 There shall be no interference by a public authority with the exercise of this right except as in accordance with the law and is necessary in a democratic society in the interests of national security, public safety or the economic well-being of the country, for the prevention of disorder or crime, for the protection of health or morals, or for the protection of the rights and freedoms of others.

Article 8 gives the right to privacy, but is a qualified right and gives way to the prevention of crime, the protection of health or morals, and the protection of the rights and interests of others.

The first thing to note in Article 8.2 is the reference to a 'public authority' and thus from a labour law perspective is on its face limited to the public sector.[9] It is also directly enforceable against bodies which, although not public authorities per se, carry out functions of a public nature (e.g. privatised rail undertakings, ferry companies, etc.). However, it is submitted that courts and industrial tribunals will in all likelihood interpret legislative provisions dealing with, for example, unfair dismissals in the spirit of Article 8, even in actions against private undertakings.

While Article 8 does not provide an absolute guarantee of privacy it does mean that any invasion of an individual's privacy should be necessary and proportional. Article 8.1 can also be said to protect 'bodily integrity', therefore for testing not to fall foul of the European Convention on Human Rights it must satisfy Article 8.2.

The European Convention of Human Rights is now part of national law across the EU (e.g. Human Rights Act in UK). Thus in the context of a company drug testing policy, one can apply the derogations in Article 8.2 to measure if it is able to overcome the privacy issues, thus:

- Is it 'in accordance with law'?
- Is it 'necessary in a democratic society' in the 'interests of . . . public safety'?
- Is it 'necessary in a democratic society'. . . for the 'protection of Health'?
- Does it comply with the principle of proportionality?

However, if drug use did come to be seen as an essentially private matter, the right to private life could still be overridden under Article 8.2. This can be seen below in the *Wretlund* v. *Sweden* decision by the European Court of Human Rights.[10] There is also justification for interference in the private life of a worker if a third party is likely to be harmed as a result of intoxication. Intuitively, air passengers would like to feel sure that an airline pilot is not under the influence of drugs on any given day and may feel that he or she being subjected to testing certainly comes under the rubric of 'public safety' and very safely clears the proportionality hurdle; similarly rail and ferry passengers (cf. Zeebrugge disaster of 6 March 1987, where the *Herald of Free Enterprise* ferry capsized with the deaths of 193 passengers and crew, because the bow doors were left open after departure). Thus, in many cases there is often a tension between the public policy defending every citizen's right to privacy, and the public policy supporting health and safety in the workplace.[4]

The principle of proportionality also underpins the intoxicant testing provision of the Irish Safety, Health and Welfare at Work Act, 2005 (Section 13(1)c). It thus will determine such issues as who can be tested, when tests should be conducted and what action should be taken based on positive results.

Right to privacy

Is the behaviour of an employee outside the workplace a proper concern for the employer? It could be argued that it is only to the extent that it affects the employee's work. In *Walton* v. *TAC Construction Materials*[11] it was held that it was fair to dismiss a registered heroin addict employed in construction because he constituted a health and safety risk. This author has, however, noted some examples of companies hiring former heroin addicts who have successfully transitioned to methadone as part of a state programme and who submit themselves to testing on a once weekly basis with the knowledge of their employer.

What of the situation with respect to use of drugs outside of work time or used for recreational purposes with little evidence of them affecting the employee's work? Should that be a concern of an employer? In the UK Employment Appeals Tribunal case of *Mathewson* v. *Wilson Dental Laboratory*[12] an employee was dismissed for being convicted for buying cannabis in his lunch break: the dismissal was deemed to be fair.

Consent[13] to being tested for intoxicants

Before any prospective or current employee can be asked to undergo a drug or alcohol (or both) test, it is vitally important that informed consent is obtained, 'informed' meaning that the individual concerned will be told, at a minimum, the nature of the testing, what tests are to be carried out and what will be done with the test results. Further, the consent should be expressly given, in writing and should be full and free. (Note: We have seen elsewhere argument that consent in the context of employer/employee can never be totally free.[14])

Consent to testing is required whether or not there is an express contractual term in existence. Thus, an employer may obtain consent from a safety-critical employee to test for alcohol and a listed number of other intoxicants, pursuant to an agreed policy. Any deviation from the list of drugs (e.g. by mistakenly or otherwise testing for other biological parameters) could result in an offence. In common law jurisdictions, these can range from trespass to the person, to assault and battery or an action for negligence, for which the employer may be sued in a court of law.

In order for a medical review officer to make an informed decision on all aspects of a positive drug test on an employee or a prospective candidate, consent forms or chain-of-custody forms invariably enquire as to a donor's current medication if any, taken in the previous 3–4 weeks, with a view to ascertaining if this medication may have cross-reacted to give a presumptive positive screen (onsite or laboratory immunoassay) or confirmation by gas chromatography-mass spectrometry (GC-MS) or liquid chromatography-mass spectrometry (LC-MS), both of which are considered legal 'gold standards' for evidential purposes in courts, industrial tribunals or courts of arbitration. Thus, information potentially relating to an ongoing medical condition may be furnished that may have no relevance to the drug testing procedure. This may give rise to data protection and confidentiality issues depending on who receives the information and may also have implications with regard to disability legislation.

Privacy and bodily integrity

One of the criticisms levelled by opponents of workplace drug testing is that it is 'invasive'. One must draw a distinction between the requirement of a candidate/worker to provide a biological sample as a result of a drug and alcohol policy (in which case consent is fundamental) and the physical invasiveness or otherwise of the sampling procedures for the various biological matrices that can be tested (e.g. urine, saliva/oral fluid, hair, sweat). Thus, it is argued that within the employment setting the mere imbalance between employer and employee is enough to imply a coercive element to a drug and alcohol policy and therefore makes it invasive. The recent European workplace experience, however, with an emphasis on collective bargaining in the case of unionised workforces, has been to introduce drug and alcohol policies (with and without testing elements) on an agreed basis.[15]

From a purely technical standpoint, it is often argued that a saliva swab of the oral cavity is less invasive than providing a urine sample, although in the former, a device actually enters the body, whereas in the latter situation this is not the case. In any case, there is an element of subjectivity on the matter.

The European Convention on Human Rights also protects bodily integrity and requires free and informed consent to drug testing. Bodily integrity would also be violated if a blood or other sample was taken under another pretext and subsequently used for drug testing purposes without the consent of the individual.[16] Private information which was irrelevant to the workplace could be disclosed, and there is a risk of mistakes if the test was not conducted properly or if the information was misused.

In France, the decision of the Conseil d'Etat in *Ministre du Travail* v. *Société Peintures Corona*[17] looked at rights of bodily integrity and dignity in the context of alcohol blood tests. In that case, a work rule was instigated by the employer whereby employees would be subjected to blood alcohol testing if suspected of being intoxicated at work, and where refusal to submit to a test was in itself treated as a positive result resulting in disciplinary procedure. The Conseil d'Etat said that obliging a worker to submit to blood alcohol testing was a violation of bodily integrity, and testing should only be carried out on employees who performed certain tasks with health and safety implications or who are considered to perform safety-critical tasks, and not, as in this case, across the whole workforce. This decision in effect would seem to rule out random testing of all staff in a company per se, but in reality, random testing of safety-critical cohorts of workers is performed across many industrial, manufacturing and transportation industries.

In the UK Employment Appeals Tribunal case of *Whitefield* v. *General Medical Council*[18] certain conditions regarding a GP's continuing ability to practice were imposed by the General Medical Council as a result of his ongoing alcoholism and depressive illness. These included abstaining from alcohol and undergoing a testing regime. The Privy Council said that his right to respect for private life under Article 8(1) was not infringed by these conditions. They said 'His "right" to an unrestricted social life must give way to the wider public interest in ensuring that he does not present a risk to his patients.'

Some commentators such as Craig[4] have expressed concern that samples obtained for the purpose of testing for a panel of drugs could reveal, for example, that a candidate for a job or a current employee is on specific medication or is pregnant or is infected with HIV or another sexually transmitted disease. It is convention that in most cases the procedure of obtaining consent for drug testing an individual through a specific consent form will have provisions for outlining current medication not from the point of view of eliciting further information which may be used against an employee or candidate, but as a safeguard in the situation that one of the constituents of the medication may cause a cross-reaction with one of the drugs on the screening panel. For example, it is widely known that over-the-counter or prescription medications that contain codeine will invariably yield a positive screen test for opiate class compounds, and thus prior knowledge of the use of such medications is essential for a medical review officer to decide if a case such as this should be designated as negative in all the circumstances.

Also on consent form, the panel of tests to be performed should be clearly set out. Testers employed or trained by companies should not be allowed to deviate from this agreed panel, which it can be argued is implied into the employment contract. A further safeguard for a candidate who, on undergoing a drug screen as part of pre-employment medical (which is usually the case) having to reveal current medication, is that it is possible that failure to successfully get an employment contract having passed a drugs test but because of an underlying medical condition revealed through medical history, may leave the company open to challenge based on disability legislation. As we shall discover later, while most countries look on pre-employment medicals (with or without a drug testing element) relatively benignly from a legal standpoint, the Netherlands does not allow pre-employment testing of applicants under any circumstances.

In practical terms also, the majority of workplace drug tests are performed in the first instance as screens using specific drug testing lateral flow devices that cannot test for any other substances. Further, even in the event of positive screen, the sample (usually urine) is sent, under conditions to maintain a chain of evidence, to specific drug testing laboratories with competencies to test generally only for drugs of abuse. It is highly implausible that a company that has invested time and money in developing a corporate 'no drugs' policy that is legally defensible, in some cases in a unionised environment through collective bargaining, would jeopardise industrial relations by surreptitiously testing for various other medical conditions/disease states.

The International Labour Organization has issued guidelines on alcohol and drug testing in the workplace, dealing the requirements of a testing policy.[13]

EU data protection legislation

Information obtained by drug testing is considered sensitive personal data according to many of the EU states data protection legislation. EU Directive 95/46/EC on data protection, Article 8.1 states the processing of personal data related to health is banned, though it gives a number of exceptions to this. The Working Party of Article 29 has issued an opinion on the processing of personal data in the employment context which addresses the processing of health data in a employment relationship. Workplace drug testing shall be carried out in compliance with data protection principles as laid down in Directive 95/46/EC. A consultation in November 2002 by DG Employment identified workplace drug testing as one of the upcoming areas in the field of protection of workers' personal data. In light of this, the Commission indicated in its European Social Agenda adopted in February 2005 that it will launch an initiative concerning the protection of the personal data of workers.

In the UK, the Information Commissioner issued the Employment Practices Data Protection Code Part IV.[19] One of its provisions says that testing for drugs and/or alcohol must be proportionate to the aim to be achieved and should only be carried out on workers whose drug or alcohol consumption would put at risk the safety of others. The UK Data Protection code of practice stipulates that:

- the only justification for testing is a health and safety risk
- drug tests must be of the highest technical quality and subject to rigorous quality control
- the testing must be conducted and interpreted under the direction of a competent doctor, the medical review officer
- there should be two samples, one given to the worker, and there should be a right of appeal.

Directive 2002/58/EC Privacy and Electronic Communications has been transposed into national law in the respective EU Member States. The European Data Protection Rules can be examined under the following headings:

- Fair obtaining and processing consent
- Specified purpose
- No disclosure unless 'compatible'
- Safe and secure
- Accurate, up-to-date
- Relevant, not excessive
- Retention period
- Right of access
- Independent supervisory authority.

Thus, data pertaining to a drug or alcohol test that is recorded and processed by an employer or prospective employer will be subject to data protection legislation and must comply with the appropriate principles laid out in the Directive, via the national legislation. Thus, the data must be processed fairly and lawfully, must be obtained for a specified purpose which must be legal, and must be adequate, relevant and not excessive. Further, the data must only be obtained and processed with consent (defined in Article 2(h) as 'freely given specific and informed indication of his/her wishes by which the data subject signifies his agreement to personal data relating to him/her being processed') or as a result of a legal obligation.

The concept of proportionality is important in relation to the data protection legislation. In Ireland the Office of the Data Protection Commissioner has said that testing should be proportionate to the risks identified. Data protection may be defined as the safeguarding of the privacy rights of individuals in relation to the processing of personal data.

What effect does equality legislation have on workplace drug testing?

Employers should also exercise caution in their handling of employees with alcohol or drug dependence because in cases taken under different equality legislation, tribunals such as the Irish Equality Tribunal have categorised alcoholism as a disability.[20] Section 6(2)(g) of the Employment Equality Act, 1998 defines disability as:

> (a) The total or partial absence of a person's bodily or mental functions, including the absence of a part of a person's body . . .
>
> (b) a condition, illness or disease which affects a person's thought processes, perception of reality, emotions or judgement or which results in disturbed behaviour, and shall be taken to include a disability which exists at present, or which previously existed but no longer exists, or which may exist in the future or which is imputed to a person;

EU equality legislation requires the employer to take appropriate measures to assist an employee with a disability in being accommodated into the workplace. Thus the concept of reasonable accommodation is recognised in numerous jurisdictions both in Europe and globally.[21]

Health and safety

EU membership has led to a constant flow of directives that have to be implemented at national level with a view to setting common standards across member states. The European Directive 89/391/EEC on the introduction of measures to encourage improvements in the safety and health of workers at work, applies to all sectors of activity, both public and private (Article 2). Artical 6 states that the employer shall have a duty to ensure the safety and health of workers in every aspect related to the work, with Article 6(5) exonerating the workers from liability for financial cost. Article 11 states that 'Employers shall consult workers and/or their representatives and allow them to take part in discussions on all questions relating to safety and health at work.' Article 13(2)(d) states that employees must immediately inform the employer and/or the workers with specific responsibility for the safety and health of workers of any work situation they have reasonable grounds for considering represents a serious and immediate danger to safety and health.[22]

In Ireland the Safety, Health and Welfare at Work Act, 2005 represents a major step in legislating directly for workplace intoxicant testing. Although the testing provisions have not yet been enabled by ministerial order, thc relevant section (Section 13(1)) allows for 'reasonable suspicion' testing of employees in the workplace.

Occupational health and workplace drug testing

The occupational health department, certainly in the larger, multinational corporations, has been at the fulcrum of workplace drug and alcohol testing in recent years from the point of view of its execution within the workplace and so it is important to look at the dynamic between the occupational health professional, whether physician/doctor or nurse, and their employer on the one hand and the issue of doctor/patient confidentiality on the other, because in practical terms, this is a contentious area whenever positive tests arise if the drug and alcohol policy is not clear and precise as to the flow of information pertaining to results.

In most European countries, pre-employment medicals are a fact of life for prospective job candidates (the main exception being the Netherlands, where pre-employment medical assessments and testing of any kind are deemed unconstitutional) and more and more, drug testing may be an integral part of the pre-employment process. So can a job applicant refuse to undergo pre-employment tests?

In the landmark case of *X* v. *The European Commission*,[23] in an appeal to the Court of Appeal from a decision of the Court of First Instance it was held that prospective job applicants have a right to know what tests are to be carried out as part of pre-employment medical assessment, and have the right to refuse to participate in the process thereafter. In this case, the candidate, a male, refused to undergo HIV testing as part of a medical assessment for work as a temporary typist with the European Commission. Having provided blood samples as part of the medical, the doctor ordered blood tests for HIV (T4 and T8 lymphocyte counts) having reviewed X's medical records. The subsequent results were consistent with an immune deficiency and the candidacy was rejected on the grounds of the applicant having 'full-blown' AIDS. The European Court of Justice held that:

> The Court of First Instance had incorrectly held that, in view of the abnormalities found in the medical examination of the appellant... the Commission's medical officer was entitled to request that a T4/T8 lymphocyte count be carried out, notwithstanding that the appellant had expressly refused to undergo an HIV test. The manner in which the appellant had been medically examined and declared physically unfit constituted an infringement of his right to respect for his private life as guaranteed by Article of the European Convention on Human Rights.

The Court went on to say that the right to respect for private life is a fundamental right and includes the right of a person to maintain secrecy in respect of the state of his or her health. It importantly continued that

> although the pre-employment medical examination serves a legitimate interest of the Community Institutions and if the person concerned, after being properly informed, withholds his consent to a test which the medical officer considers necessary in order to evaluate his suitability for the post for which he has applied, the institutions cannot be obliged to take the risk of recruiting him, nevertheless that interest does not justify the carrying out of a test against the will of the person concerned.

Full-time occupational physicians owe a duty to the employee as patient but also to their employers. A problem can arise when the interests of the employer and employee are not the same; this can be as true for a potential medical condition that the employee may not want to reveal (whereas the company may feel it is in the interests of other employees' health and safety to have knowledge of this), as it is for the results of a drug test result. In the UK case of *Kapfunde* v. *Abbey National*[24] it was held that an occupational health physician, in carrying out pre-employment medicals, only has a duty of care to her or his employer and not to prospective employees.[25]

It is important to note also, that at pre-employment level, failure to award a prospective employee a job based on their medical assessment (whether including a drug screen or not) may constitute discrimination on the grounds of a disability (EU Equal Treatment Directive 76/207/EEC). Recent case law in some jurisdictions has ruled alcoholism a disability under employment equality legislation giving effect to EU Directives[26] and it is not too fanciful to suggest that local industrial tribunals will treat substance abuse in general in a like manner.

In general terms, occupational health professionals have a duty of confidentiality to employees, breach of which is both a legal and an ethical wrong. But if an employee constitutes a risk to others, the doctor or nurse may breach confidence by reporting this to the employer. The International Code of Ethics for Occupational Health Professionals[27] enumerates some duties and responsibilities of occupational health professionals. Thus no. 8 on health surveillance (under which if in a particular jurisdiction, drug test results go through the occupational health department and are resulted as a worker being declared 'fit' or 'unfit' for work, and therefore come under the rubric of health surveillance) states that 'surveillance must be carried out with the informed consent of the workers. The potentially positive and negative consequences of participation in screening and health surveillance programmes should be discussed as part of the consent process.' Basic principle (no. 9) says that 'The results of examinations, carried out within the framework of health surveillance must be explained to the worker concerned.' It goes on to say that a worker has a right to challenge conclusions relating to their fitness to work and says that an appeals procedure 'must be established'. It is fair to say that both of these are carved from fairly universal labour or employment law principles, at least at EU level.

In Finland, France, Germany, Belgium and Austria, the results of an intoxicant test are communicated to the occupational health physician and not the employer. It is interesting to also note the situation in France, whereby the occupational health physicians ('médecins du travail') are the arbiters with respect to whether a company introduces a drug testing policy. Thus in France, one finds the anomalous situation whereby in two similar companies with the same processes, worker profiles, risks and health and safety issues, one company has a comprehensive testing regime as part of drug and alcohol policy whereas the other has none, because the occupational health physician deems it so. This is in stark contrast to the French nuclear industry, in which testing, on health and safety grounds, can be as high as 80% of workforce per year (JM O'Sullivan, personal communication, market research in French occupational health market, 2006).

In many jurisdictions the outcome of a drug test result is couched in terms of whether the worker is 'fit' or 'unfit' for work and the drug test results are not directly given to the 'human resource' department for processing via company disciplinary procedure (e.g. Finland, Act on the Privacy of Working Life 2001). It is also important to point out that the various data protection legislative provisions across the EU ensure that workers will have access to any report on file about them that is in the hands of the company.[28]

Global background

It is readily acknowledged that the United States has led the way both legally and commercially in the whole area of workplace drug testing in the so-called 'war on drugs'. This had its genesis in the Drug Free Workplace Act, 1988 (became law on 18 March 1989), whereby it became a statutory requirement for companies or organisations with federal contracts of US$100 000 or more to introduce drug-free workplace programmes. Drug testing is not required under this law, but other provisions of a drug-free workplace are. It must be acknowledged that workplace drug testing in the United States, although widespread, is not as homogeneous as imagined by European standards, and is regulated to some extent by legislation such as Title VII of the Civil Rights Act of 1964, individual State drug testing laws,[29] the Americans With Disabilities Act of 1990 (ADA) and State Workers' Compensation laws. The ADA prohibits discrimination against an employee on the grounds of a disability: it is important to note that a 'qualified person' with a disability for the purposes of the Act does not include an applicant or employee currently abusing drugs or alcohol but may include those who are deemed in recovery.

Notwithstanding the above legal constraints, workplace drug testing soon became a major factor for the private sector bidding for lucrative government contracts. The Omnibus Transportation Employee Testing Act of 1991 allowed for enabling regulations by the Secretary of Transportation that required employers in the transportation industry with safely-sensitive workforces to set up testing programmes for drugs and alcohol. Thus, pre-employment, random, post-accident and reasonable suspicion testing of safety-sensitive employees for drugs and alcohol was mandated for transportation sector employees.

The US Department of Transportation has issued rules and regulations that require the implementation of drug- and alcohol-free workplaces, including drug and alcohol testing, by employers in the transportation industry.[29] The rules and regulations are applicable to employers regulated by one or more of the following transportation regulators:

- Federal Aviation Administration (FAA)
- Federal Highway Administration (FHWA)
- Federal Railway Administration (FRA)
- United States Coast Guard
- Urban Mass Transportation Administration
- Research and Special Programs Administration (pipelines).

Thus it is the case in the United States that there is a considerable remit for workplace drug testing across a number of work sectors encompassing public and private (sector) employees but, as can be seen below, workplace drug testing is procedurally regulated from the centre and thus, unlike in the EU at the moment, employers and employees alike are under no misapprehension as to the application and effect of workplace drug testing in the workplace.

The Department of Transportation has established strict testing procedures that must be followed. All drug testing must be conducted in laboratories certified by the US Department of Health and Human Services. Specific requirements vary from administration to administration, but basic guidelines under the Department of Transportation regulations include:

1 Circumstances under which testing is required:
   - pre-employment
   - reasonable suspicion
   - random
   - post accident
   - return-to-duty and follow-up.

2 Five classes of drugs (the so-called 'NIDA 5') must be tested for: marijuana, cocaine, amphetamines, opiates and phencyclidine (PCP).
3 Cut-off levels established by Department of Transportation must be used in drug testing.
4 Alcohol testing of employees must be conducted using only devices and equipment approved by the Department of Transportation and in accordance with procedures established by the Department. Alcohol testing of applicants is not required.
5 Depending on the agency, employees must receive drug awareness training, including information about the company's drug- and alcohol-free workplace programme. Employees must also be provided awareness information about alcohol misuse.
6 Employees determined to have drug and/or alcohol abuse problems must be referred by the employer to a substance abuse professional for evaluation. Before the abusing employee can be returned to duty, a recommendation of 'return to duty' must be made by the substance abuse professional.

Specific workplace drug testing legislation in Europe

The following is a synopsis and comparative look at some of the recent legislative developments and 'highlights' affecting workplace drug testing in a selection of European countries and is not intended to be an exhaustive review of the legal situation pertaining to workplace drug testing across the EU and EEA. For a complete country by country guide, the European Legal Database on Drugs (ELDD) compiled by the European Monitoring Centre for Drugs and Drug Addiction database (EMCDDA) is a very useful compendium of legal information.[22]

There has been a relatively recent flurry of activity with three countries adopting specific or direct legislation on drug testing in the workplace: Finland, Ireland and Norway. In Italy, the main drug law contains an article addressing specifically drug testing in the workplace. In all other countries, we can see indirect legislation in the areas of privacy and data protection that regulate to some extent the type of testing that can take place. Importantly also, a number of countries with written constitutions have enshrined provisions for privacy, in similar terms to Article 8 of the European Convention on Human Rights. Again, in some jurisdictions, the concept of 'bodily integrity' also has constitutional protection.

To summarise, the following countries have no 'direct' or specific workplace drug testing legislation (although they may have industry-specific legislation, as in the UK Railway Transport Act 1992): Germany, France, Belgium, Denmark, Greece, Sweden, UK, Slovenia, Portugal, Austria, The Netherlands (pre-employment drug testing of all applicants is prohibited by law; testing of the successful applicant is permitted in certain circumstances), Hungary, Luxembourg, Spain and the Czech Republic.

Finland

A recent article has outlined the Finnish guidelines for workplace drug testing.[30] The guidelines are based on the Act on the Protection of Privacy in Working Life (759/2004), the Occupational Health Care Act (1383/2001) and the Decree on Workplace Drug Testing (218/2005). They define when workplace testing is allowed and deal with the issuing of drug test certificates to employers. The role of the occupational healthcare system is crucial in the procedure. The guidelines include the best practice procedures to be followed by laboratories providing workplace drug testing services which are based on international best practice. The guidelines make laboratory accreditation a necessity for any workplace drug testing laboratory. This covers specimen collection, laboratory organisation, analysis procedure, quality assurance and quality control measures. These largely conform to the European laboratory guidelines for legally defensible workplace drug testing published by the European Workplace Drug Testing Society (EWDTS), but there are differences. In addition to urine, blood is also included in the Finnish guidelines.

It must be stressed that participation of employees is voluntary, but an obligation to undergo a test may arise if there is a justified suspicion of an employee being impaired at work on health and safety grounds. Looking in more detail at the Act, Sections 7 and 8 deal with the issue of who can be tested, and permit workplace drug testing for successful job applicant or employees.

During recruitment the employer may request a certificate of drug test from the applicant, but the job applicant is not obliged to submit a certificate. The employer may also request a certificate if the job applicant will be working in a safety-sensitive role, where intoxication or addiction may endanger life, health, national or traffic safety, security of information in the public interest, or business or professional confidentiality.

During the employment relationship the employee is obliged to produce proof of undergoing a drug test when the employer has a justified suspicion that the employee is addicted to drugs or when the employee's work consists of tasks which require special accuracy, independent judgement and where intoxication may endanger. The employer may also set a moderate time limit to submit the certificate. It is important to note that the test is assessed by a healthcare professional (Section 6) and is paid for by the employer. Furthermore, the employer is obliged to prepare a written comprehensive prevention programme on alcohol and drugs policy in the company in consultation with the employees.

Norway

Under the Working Environment Act of 17th June 2005 (Act No. 62), relating to the working environment, working hours and employment protection, an employee or job applicant may be tested for intoxicants:

a when provided by statutes and regulations
b for positions associated with risks
c when employers find it necessary to protect the life or health of employees or a third party.

The 'control measures' must be objectively justified and not a disproportionate burden on the employee and must have been discussed with the elected representatives of the employees as early as possible and to provide information to the employees themselves.

It is important to note that in Norway, the consent of the employee is not a sufficient basis for drug testing.

Ireland

Recent Irish legislative initiatives

In the 2005 Safety, Health and Welfare at Work Act, Section 13, the Act contains duties of employees in relation to appropriate behaviour in the workplace: employees should not be under the influence of an intoxicant defined as drugs or alcohol and any combination of drugs and alcohol.

> General Duties of Employee and Persons in Control of Places of Work
>
> 13. (1) An employee shall, while at work:
>
> (a) comply with the relevant statutory provisions, as appropriate, and take reasonable care to protect his or her safety, health and welfare and the safety, health and welfare of any other person who may be affected by the employee's acts or omissions at work,
>
> (b) ensure that he or she is not under the influence of an intoxicant to the extent that he or she is in such a state as to endanger his or her own safety, health or welfare at work or that of any other person,
>
> (c) if reasonably required by his or her employer, submit to any appropriate, reasonable and proportionate tests for intoxicants by, or under the supervision of, a registered medical practitioner who is a competent person, as may be prescribed.

Thus, Section 13 of the 2005 Act deals with the duties of employees. Thus, Section 13(1)(b) says that an employee shall, while at work 'ensure that he or she is not under the influence of an intoxicant to the extent that he or she is in such a state as to endanger his or her own safety, health or welfare at work or that of any other person.' Section 13(1)(c) further says that employee shall 'if reasonably required by his or her employer, submit to any appropriate, reasonable and proportionate tests for intoxicants by, or under the supervision of, a registered medical practitioner who is a competent person,' as may be prescribed. Of major importance here are the pre-conditions of testing being appropriate, reasonable and proportionate (all concepts that are familiar to the legal systems of most EU member states).

A number of questions have arisen subsequent to the enactment. Who does the policy apply to? Is it reasonable to test all staff or just a selection of occupations in a workforce? Does the situation require testing to ensure the safety of employee or co-workers? What sanction applies to workers who are in violation of the company policy? Is it instant dismissal on grounds of misconduct, or will the company take a more rehabilitative approach?

The meaning of 'under the supervision of' in the Act has caused confusion, but it has been interpreted as meaning that occupational health staff and people trained in the procedures can perform the requirements of testing under the supervision of what will probably be prescribed as a medical doctor with an occupational health background ('competent person'). Furthermore, the Health and Safety Authority (HSA) will issue a Guidance Code of Practice for practitioners in the area. It is likely that there will be a requirement for medical review officers – qualified occupational health physicians with specific training in workplace drug and alcohol toxicology, whose function it will be to review toxicology reports on employees and give a professional opinion, for instance, if a positive drug screen result should in fact be reported as negative due to interferences (e.g. from over-the-counter preparations which may contain codeine, ingestion of poppy seeds or so-called 'false positives').

In the context of employee assistance programmes, Section 8(2)f of the Act obliges employers to ensure that the workplace has 'facilities and arrangements for the welfare of his or her employees at work'. Furthermore, Section 22(1) of the 2005 Act provides that 'every employer shall ensure that health surveillance appropriate to the risks to safety, health and welfare that may be incurred at the place of work identified by the risk assessment . . . is made available to his or her employees.' Some legal commentators say that this may mean a requirement for an employer to make available an employee assistance programme or a counselling service.[31] Importantly, the Irish High Court, in *Maher* v. *Jabil Global Services Ltd.*,[32] has followed the position as enunciated by the UK Court of Appeal in *Hatton* v. *Sutherland* that an employer who provided confidential services with referral to counselling or treatment services, would in all probability not be found to be in breach of duty to employees.[33]

Although enacted, the regulations pursuant to ministerial order were never introduced. It has been argued by some commentators that no testing pursuant to the Act can be carried out unless relevant secondary legislation is enacted, but it is most likely that, once the testing provisions are part of the employment contract, any such testing will be upheld if it is appropriate, reasonable and proportionate. Questions arising from the intoxicant testing provisions of the Act are what will be the outcome vis-à-vis the description of 'safety-critical' occupations. Will it be defined broadly or narrowly? In practical terms, will it apply to miners, construction workers, firemen, ambulance crew, construction workers, oil-rig workers? Will it apply to some or all of these occupations? Is a hospital doctor not working in a safety-critical capacity? Should junior doctors working 80–100 hour weeks be subjected to testing?

Railway Safety Act 2005 (Ireland)

By way of comparison to the 2005 Safety, Health and Welfare at Work Act, the Railway Safety Act 2005, treats comprehensively all aspects of intoxicant testing and defines the scope of a safety-critical task and what category of worker falls under the definition of a 'safety critical worker' (driving a train, maintenance of a train, control/management of passenger movement in transit or on/off trains). Section 37(2) states that there is a general duty on rail workers not to be 'under the influence of an intoxicant to such an extent as to expose a person (including himself or herself) to danger or risk of danger as a consequence of being under such influence.' Section 84 sets out, among others, definitions of 'analysis' and what specified level is allowable in relation to blood, urine or breath alcohol. Section 87 makes a code of conduct in relation to intoxicants and establishment of procedures in relation to the provision of samples, mandatory. Section 89 prescribes how, when, where and by whom sampling can be undertaken, while Section 90 deals with disciplinary measures arising from testing, including non-compliance and failure to provide a sample. Section 91 importantly deals with proof of certificate of analysis, which document would be used in evidence in any disciplinary hearing arising from Section 90. Thus, for the safety-critical rail undertakings sector, Part 9 of the Railway Safety Act 2005 deals comprehensively and in some detail with the legislative requirements for dealing with the issue of intoxicant testing in the workplace.

It is worth noting that the Irish Health and Safety Authority (HAS) will be publishing a guidance document on workplace intoxicant testing in lieu of governmental regulations, after consultation with the social partners (employer and employee representative bodies and unions), and with professional stakeholders. The HSA have stated that they will look at developments in other EU countries and also will have regard to the EWDTS Guidelines for Legally Defensible Drug Testing.[34]

In a separate development, the Technical Engineering and Electrical Union (TEEU), at a recent conference, discussed a motion calling for any drug testing in Ireland to be based on the EWDTS Guidelines. The motion said this was to 'ensure that specimen collection, laboratory organisation, laboratory analysis procedures, quality assurance/quality control and interpretation of results was robust and uniform.' It went on the say that this would 'ensure that the "zero tolerance policy" adopted by many companies operating in Ireland does not conflict with the proposed national policy.'[34]

Slovakia

The issue of workplace drug testing is regulated by the law on safety and health protection at work. In the Safety and Health Protection at Work Act (No. 330/1996 Coll) an employer has a legal duty to test if the employee is under the influence of drugs at work. Section 14 states that the employee has a duty to be subject to examination by the competent state authority or employer to establish if he or she is under the influence of intoxicants. Procedural aspects of testing methodology should be set out in internal work practices or standards issued by each employer as long as they meet with the approval of relevant trade union. Thus, the importance of collective bargaining and implementation by agreement can be seen once more.

Italy

According to Article 125 of Law No. 162 (26 June 1990) workers holding positions that involve a threat to security, and the physical safety and health of third parties may be tested for intoxicants in public undertakings. In such cases, the testing is paid for by the employer, and if a test is positive the worker will be suspended. An employer may be fined up to 25 000 euros if found liable. A new Italian legislation for workplace drug testing has been introduced (Unified Conference no. 99/2007, Legislative decree n. 81/2008 on health and safety in workplaces, Agreement Stato-Regioni of 18 September 2008). These laws establish mandatory procedures for screening tests (performed by occupational health specialists), and for confirmatory tests (performed by laboratories identified by regional Directives), for at-risk workers (public/private transportation, oil/gas companies, and explosives/fireworks industry).

Germany

There is no single legislation on drug testing in the workplace, although various laws refer to it, and there is some case law from the Federal Labour Court. The Federal Labour Court (Bundesarbeitsgericht) developed the 'right to ask questions'. During the pre-employment medical exam, the employer can ask about drug consumption and conduct tests to discover information about drug addiction. The doctor is only allowed to inform the employer whether or not the person is fit for work.

Drug testing is much more common in the pre-employment setting. The German Labour Protection Law (Arbeitsschutzgesetz) and related regulations do, however, give guidance to the workplace setting. Section 38(2) of the

Arbeitsschutzgesetz prohibits employment of persons who are under the influence of intoxicants such that they are a danger to themselves or others. Breitstadt and Kauert[35] review some of the legal problems associated with workplace intoxicant testing in Germany at both pre-employment and employment level. A number of important points can be summarised:

- Pre-employment testing: There is a balance between the constitutional right to privacy and the right to bodily integrity versus the health and safety requirements of the employer. As there is no existing contract of employment, the employer may perform such testing with the full, free and informed consent of the candidate. Consent here also gives the right of the occupational physician to view the results and declare if a candidate is medically 'fit' for the work.
- Drug screening on an employee can only be performed in narrow circumstances and given the constitutional right to bodily integrity, a urine sample for a drug test cannot be requested against a worker's will.
- Thus a worker may refuse to participate in a drug screening test. However they may still be subject to disciplinary action by the company, subject to the disciplinary action for refusal being stipulated in the contract of employment or through a labour agreement.
- An employee who tests positive for intoxicants can be removed from workplace, but as part of employers duty to workers welfare, the employee must be accommodated with regard to treatment.
- If a supervisor is aware that a worker is under the influence of intoxicants and takes no action, he or she may be liable under criminal or civil law if intoxicated employee causes damage or an accident in workplace.
- Random testing is prohibited.

The provisions of the Occupational Safety and Health Act oblige the employer to ban drugs at work if there is a considerable danger. The Accident Prevention Regulations by the Occupational Accident Insurance Funds oblige the employee not to be in a state that endangers him- or herself or others, and the Works Constitution Act (BVG) Section 87 permits a ban and testing for the influence of drugs during working hours. The Federal Labour Court accepts an obligation to test due to the employee's 'general duty of loyalty', provided the employer has a legitimate reason to test (e.g. suspicion). Routine testing is not allowed except in dangerous or security-sensitive workplaces.

France

Workplace drug testing in France is in the main carried out under the direction of the company occupational physician, and is focused primarily on 'safety-critical' occupations. Notwithstanding this, there are anomalies in some sectors whereby in one company there may be no testing, and another company in the same sector may test 10% of the workforce on a yearly basis, solely on the direction of the company occupational health physician.

The right to privacy, incorporated into the French Civil Code in 1970 (Article 9), as well as in domestic legislation through Article 8 of the European Convention on Human Rights, is the main legal counterbalance to workplace drug testing. Furthermore, Article L120-2 of the Labour Code states: 'no one may limit the rights of the individual, or individual and collective freedoms, unless the limitations are justified by the task to be performed and are in proportion to the goal towards which they are aimed.' Thus an employer seeking to introduce a testing regime needs to ensure it is relevant to the work or occupation and that testing is proportionate to the aim of the policy.[17] A Ministry of Labour circular in 1990 (no. 90/13 of 9 July) effectively considered that workplace drug testing would only be allowable for safety-sensitive jobs, both at the recruitment and regular health check stage.

Interestingly, the Ministry of Transport Arrêté of 30 July 2003 provided for a testing under the supervision of an occupational doctor to detect psychoactive substances for safety-sensitive employees in the national rail system (SNCF employees). At the Fourth Symposium on Workplace Drug Testing in Dublin in 2005, the statistics for SNCF employees since the introduction of testing is such that of approximately 165 000 employees, as many as 92 000 considered safety-sensitive, had undergone workplace drug testing.

Belgium

The national collective agreement no. 100 (April 1, 2009) obliges each company to have a policy on alcohol and drugs. The focus is on prevention. Alcohol and drug tests are permitted under some conditions defined in the agreement. But with drug tests, psychomotor tests (skills tests and simple reaction tests) are meant, not drug screening. There is also some 'indirect' legislation, which can affect the implementation of workplace drug testing by a company. The National Collective Agreement No. 38 on recruitment (1983) provides that interference in the private life of applicants can be justified only when relevant to employment relationship. Articles 3, 79 and 91(3) of the Royal Decree of 28 May 2003 on health surveillance on workers state that the results of a test (whether drug or medical) must be given to the occupational doctor and not to the employer. In common with a great many European countries, the occupational health doctor can only inform the employer whether or not the person is 'fit' or 'unfit' for work, and not give the actual result of the drug test. Under Article 14 of the same law, pre-employment drug testing can be performed where workers are considered to carry out 'safety-sensitive' or 'safety-critical' roles.

Denmark

The Danish industrial relations system (also known as the 'Danish Model') is such that the relations between employers and employees is basically governed by collective agreements, individual agreements, and principles of labour law, as well as statute. The September Agreement of 1899 between the Danish Federation of Trade Unions and the Danish Employers Federation laid down five main principles governing employer/employee interactions.

There is no 'direct' legislation for workplace drug testing, but under employment law the employer's right to manage and control work does give the employer the right to carry out control measures and regulatory provisions. The measures have to be necessary and proportionate, otherwise they will be deemed unlawful.[36]

The Act on the Use of Health Data (no. 286 of 24 April 1996, Lov om brug af helbredsoplyninger påarbejdsmarkedet) defines when an employer can request health data from an employee. In explanatory notes to the Bill (Paragraph 3, Section C) it is stated 'This Bill does not affect the employers right to institute general control measures affecting employees, e.g. in the form of tests to detect the abuse of alcohol or drugs, provided that such tests are not intended as health examinations.'

The Work Environment Law of 11 October 1999 (LBK 784/99), Chapter 11, allows the Minister of Labour to pass regulations regarding medical examinations of employees in specific sectors whose work is associated with health risks which may include testing for drug and alcohol testing.

Greece

While no 'direct' workplace drug testing legislation exists in Greece, as in other countries, the Data Protection Authority's 'Code of Conduct' does make reference to it.

Article 7 of law 2683/1999 (Code for Civil Servants) regarding health permits testing individuals at the pre-employment stage, while a law of 1997 permits testing of private individuals at the pre-employment stage for security services.

Sweden

There is no 'direct' workplace drug testing legislation in Sweden, but there is some labour court case law on the subject.[10] Employers and employees may stipulate conditions, such as security reasons, that could justify an employer to oblige an employee to undergo a drug test.

Section 30 of the 1994 Public Employment Act allows an employer to conduct regular health tests, following a special request if health problems of an employee at work poses a risk to human life, personal security or health, or of substantial damage to the environment or property.

United Kingdom[37]

There is no specific workplace drug testing legislation in the UK, apart from the provisions of the Transport and Works Act 1992 dealing with railway undertakings. Under this, it is an offence for defined workers (e.g. train drivers or conductors) to work while unfit to do so because of drink or drugs (Section 27(1)), or when their breath, blood or urine alcohol levels exceed a certain amount (Section 27(2)).

The Human Rights Act 1998 and the Data Protection Act 1998 do, however, give effect to the relevant EU Directives, which can indirectly affect workplace drug testing. Similarly, since drug testing can reveal the taking of prescription medication (or the information may be given to employers in the process of giving consent to testing), provisions of the Disability Discrimination Act 1995 may come into play, whereby a failed drug test, with consequent disciplinary sanction up to and including dismissal, may be considered to be discriminatory on the ground of a disability. (Note that under the Disability Discrimination (Meaning of Disability) Regulations 1996, current alcohol and drug dependency is excluded.) Compensation may then be awarded to a complainant.

Pre-employment testing of applicants, whereby there is no contract of employment in existence at the time of the test (albeit the offer of employment has been made subject to 'passing' the company medical examination), will in general not give rise to legal challenges unless the procedure fails with respect to the issue of consent or falls foul of disability legislation. So for example, an unsuccessful job applicant, who revealed, as part of the testing process (e.g. through a pre-test questionnaire) medication being taken that indicates a pre-existing condition or disease state, may subsequently claim that they have been discriminated on the grounds of disability.

A positive result following an intoxicant test that results in dismissal of an employee may give rise to a claim for unfair dismissal under existing legislation (Employment Rights Act 1996). Most cases tend to focus on potential weaknesses in the procedural aspects of the testing policy than on the technical efficacy of the tests themselves. It is fair to say that dismissals following evidence of intoxication of an employee resulting in deterioration in performance or giving rise to health and safety issues will, in the absence of procedural irregularities in the process, be considered fair and will be upheld by employment tribunals, especially in safety-critical industries or pertaining to workers undertaking safety-critical work.[38]

Data protection legislation does have a bearing on workplace drug testing with regard to the results of the tests themselves, how they are obtained, how they are stored (e.g. in 'hardcopy' or computerised), what purpose they are used for and who has access to the information.

For employers and employees in the UK, a Draft Code of Practice on the Use of Personal Data in Employer/Employee Relationships was published in 2000.[39] It deals with, among other things, issues such as justification for testing, impairment and the requirement for evidence, and technical requirements for testing. Subsequently, guidelines on drug testing in the workplace were published by the Information Commissioner.[40]

Review of selected international case law

It is now apparent that there is a very strong momentum for the introduction of workplace drug testing on health and safety grounds in certain industries across Europe. The problem that arises will be the prescription of what exactly is a 'safety-sensitive' occupation.

Some international case law in recent years gives us some indication of what can be expected. There has been over the last 5–10 years an increase in cases relating to workplace drug testing in courts and employment tribunals or industrial relations type commissions, particularly in countries with the common law legal system (e.g. United States, Canada, UK and Australia). These cases are useful in that, although not authoritative, it may well be looked at persuasively, particularly in common law jurisdictions when a similar type cases arise.

In *EEOC* v. *Exxon*,[41] an appeal under the Americans with Disabilities Act (ADA), one of the legal sequelae to the 1989 Exxon Valdez oil disaster in Alaska, after which Exxon faced numerous lawsuits (one of which, *Alaska* v. *Exxon* resulted in the company being fined US$125 million in 1994), the Equal Employment Opportunities Commission alleged on behalf of certain Exxon employees that the company substance abuse policy violated the ADA in that it removed from safety-sensitive positions employees who had undergone treatment for substance abuse. Exxon successfully argued that the policy was justified by business necessity and would be liable if it placed recovering drug and alcohol addicts in safety-sensitive positions and another accident was to occur. The Court held that in *Alaska* v. *Exxon*, the company was found liable because it knew that the ship's captain was in treatment for alcohol abuse and depression, but had relapsed before the disaster. The jury concluded that Exxon did not act although aware of the relapse. Exxon subsequently amended their drug and alcohol policy to ensure that employees in treatment cannot resume employment in safety-sensitive areas with limited supervision.

In *Harrison* v. *Tucker Wool Processors*, a New Zealand case from 1998, the Employment Court found clauses in a collective agreement providing for inter alia, 'compulsory unrestricted drug testing' to be 'harsh and oppressive'. This decision was subsequently overturned by the Court of Appeal in 1999.

In *Entrop* v. *Imperial Oil Co.*,[42] the plaintiff, a former alcoholic, upon informing his employers of his history, was reassigned from a safety-sensitive position. (Imperial Oil had implemented a comprehensive drug and alcohol policy post the Exxon Valdez oil disaster, at its Canadian Refineries.) In a series of cases stemming from a complaint by the plaintiff that his human rights had been violated, with counter-appeal by Imperial Oil, the Appeal Court of Ontario looked at and compared the company's alcohol testing policy with its drug testing policy in reviewing whether the alcohol and drug testing provisions were reasonably necessary. It held that the employee had been discriminated against on the grounds of a handicap (alcoholism). Furthermore, in looking at the reasonableness of the drug testing and alcohol testing regimes for employees in safety-sensitive positions, the court distinguished the random drug testing (did not measure present impairment – only recent past use) with the breath alcohol test, which did measure impairment. It held that random drug testing for employees in safety-sensitive positions cannot be justified with respect to the companies goal of a 'safe workplace free of impairment'. In contrast, random alcohol tests could show present impairment and thus were allowable. This illustrates the importance of clarity in the drug and alcohol policy with respect to testing provisions (with cause and post-accident testing was looked at separately).

In *PF Worden* v. *Diamond Offshore Mining Co.*,[43] an unfair dismissal case arising out of a termination of employment due to a positive drug test, the Australian Industrial Relations Commission (AIRC) held inter alia that the dismissal was unfair despite testing positive, because the company had a history of 'condonation' in that employees who had tested positive even at pre-employment level had previously been hired. It was found that the drug and alcohol policy was hardly ever enforced. The plaintiff in this case admitted to being a chronic cannabis user, but denied ever being in breach of the company policy by using drugs on-board the oil rig and/or being impaired from the use of drugs while at work. The Commission, on hearing expert evidence went on to hold that there was no evidence of impairment such as to breach the policy, but that if the policy had stated that an indication of the presence of cannabis in the system was a breach of the policy, then dismissal may have been allowed.

This can be contrasted with a 1998 decision of the AIRC in *BHP Iron Ore*,[44] where it looked at trade union objections to the random drugs testing component of the drug and alcohol policy on the grounds that it constituted an unreasonable intrusion into the privacy of employees. The company here acknowledged that the tests did not measure impairment, but that a positive test was an indicator of a risk of impairment which it had a duty to eliminate in the interests of safety. On the evidence before it, the Commission concluded that the company programme was fair and reasonable. It added the caveat that this decision was in the context of the mining industry.

The importance of testing procedures being followed properly by service providers such as laboratories cannot be overstated. In the *Bosela* case, an airline captain's licence was revoked following an allegation that he tampered with his urine specimen, submitted under a US Department of Transportation mandated random drug test. In essence the charge was one of adding a substance (nitrite) in order to invalidate the testing methods. The case centred on the collection and testing of the specimen by the designated laboratory. The National Transportation Safety Board (NTSB) reinstated Bosela after it was held that the laboratory had not appropriately validated the dipstick adulteration test as per the guidelines then in force (see also *Ishikawa* v. *Delta Air Lines, and LabOne Inc.*[45]).

A debate very current in the drug testing industry is whether urine should be replaced by saliva, which is being marketed as 'less intrusive'. In the Australian case *Pioneer Construction*[46] where one of the unions wanted saliva testing instead of urine testing in the proposed testing policy, the Western Australian Industrial Relations Commission (WAIRC), held that saliva testing was not accurate enough and there was no standard for the detection of drugs in saliva, unlike for urine, and thus declared that the proposal 'to conduct urine testing as part of the fitness for duty policy is reasonable'.

Recently, the Federal Aviation Authority of the United States proposed to impose an $100 000 fine on Delta Airlines when on inspection the airline was found to have failed to provide all records to an employee relating to his drug tests over a period of five years.

In a landmark Canadian case,[47] where in general the attitude to corporate drug testing is in marked contrast to that prevailing in the United States, a three-member bench of the Canadian Human Rights Tribunal unanimously declared that random and pre-employment drug testing conforms with Canadian human rights legislation as a legitimate aim to promote workplace safety, but only in the context of accommodating existing or prospective employees who suffer from substance-related disabilities and who test positive in drug tests. Milazzo, a bus driver who failed a drugs test, appealed his dismissal on the grounds of a disability (i.e. drug dependence). He failed to invoke the Canadian Human Rights Act, because he did not show that he had a disability. The tribunal found that Autocars' drug testing policy was 'reasonably necessary to accomplish the companies work-related goal of promoting road safety' and in order to comply with the requirements of coach companies travelling into the United States to comply with American drug testing legislation. The issue of urine drug testing and its inability to directly correlate with impairment was raised. The tribunal stated that 'although a positive drug test does not indicate that a bus driver was actually impaired on the job . . . we are satisfied that a positive test result is a "red flag"' and went on to say that 'the presence of cannabis metabolite in an employee's urine does assist in identifying drivers who are at an elevated risk of an accident.'

This is an important concession in the whole 'just because you find some drug doesn't mean I can't do my job argument'. Drug testing technology (especially for urine as a sample) is acknowledged as being limited to what conclusions can be drawn from screen and confirmed positive results; this does not mean that it has no utility, especially in the context of a corporate risk assessment strategy as part of corporate health and safety. It is finally important to note that the tribunal found that in the context of 'automatically withdrawing an offer of employment or terminating the employment of drivers suffering from substance-related disabilities who test positive', the practice was discriminatory in not accommodating these drivers.

In *Eastern Associated Coal Corp.*[48] the US Supreme Court upheld a Court of Appeal's decision to affirm an arbitrators award to reinstate a coal miner each time, after two occasions in which he tested positive for marijuana. They said that 'public policy considerations do not require courts to refuse' such actions by an arbitrator. This demonstrates that even with very stringent regulations, summary dismissal of employees who fail drugs tests is not always an option.

The Alaskan Supreme Court decision in *Luedtke* v. *Nabors Alaska Drilling Inc.*[49] concerned two oil-rig workers who refused to undertake 'without cause' drug testing, and were subsequently dismissed. They claimed the dismissals were wrongful and in contravention of public policy with respect to the constitutional right to privacy. The Court held a balance is required between public policy for employee privacy and public policy supporting health and safety in the workplace, finding that public policy was in favour of drug testing with the caveats that:

- testing must be conducted with regard to on-duty behaviour
- there must be reasonable notice to employees.

The US Supreme Court looked at privacy in the context of workplace drug testing in the case of *National Treasury Employees Union* v. *Von Raab*[50] concerning the constitutionality of a US Customs Service drug testing programme whereby all employees who applied for transfer or promotion to positions involving use of firearms or work involving illegal drugs would be tested. Positive drug tests would act as a bar to transfer or promotion and could lead to dismissal. The net question before the Court was: is chemical drug testing of US Customs Service employees (considered a 'search') constitutionally intrusive and irregular under the provisions of the Fourth Amendment? In a 5–4 verdict, the Court held that the Fourth Amendment rights of US Customs Service employees were not violated by drug screening for employees serving in or applicants applying for positions in which they might perform 'sensitive tasks' or for employees applying for promotion to sensitive positions. The Supreme Court found the requirement to submit a urine sample as a condition to performing Customs

Service duties appropriate, and that Governmental interest superseded the 'sanctity of privacy'.

Neither of these Supreme Court cases involved random drug testing. In other cases from lower courts, however, random drug testing of public employees in 'safety-sensitive' positions has been frequently upheld.[51] Public sector random drug testing has withstood challenge for certain employees involved in sensitive transportation positions (flight crews, maintenance workers, air traffic controllers), medical personnel, employees with secret security clearances, employees involved in drug interdiction, correctional employees who have contact with prisoners, those who handle hazardous materials, firefighters and fire-protection inspectors.[51] On the other hand, it has been held that a governmental employer has

> no legitimate interest in the random drug testing of prosecutors or other federal court employees who have access to grand jury or court records, certain motor vehicle operators, a transportation system's maintenance custodian, the Army's civilian drug-testing laboratory personnel, or the air-conditioning and elevator mechanics at the Veteran's Administration.[51]

European case law

In the last few years across Europe, a number of legal developments have taken place pertaining directly or indirectly to workplace drug testing. In the UK the Railway and Transport Safety Act has been enacted, covering air, road, rail and sea transport, allowing for drug and alcohol testing. Also in the UK earlier this year the Information Commissioners 'Employment Practices Data Protection Code Part IV' was published.[19] One of its provisions says that testing for drugs and/or alcohol must be proportionate to the aim to be achieved and should only be carried out on workers whose drug or alcohol consumption would put at risk the safety of others. The Office of the Data Protection Commissioner has said that testing should be proportionate to the risks identified. (Importantly, the principle of proportionality underpins intoxicant testing in the Act of 2005.)

The protections offered to workers in Ireland are further strengthened by a recent Equality Officer's decision that a worker was discriminated against on the grounds of a disability[52] (within the meaning of Section 6(2)g of the Employment Equality Act, 1998). The claimant had been passed over for promotion in a government department on the grounds of being an alcoholic (albeit recovering), but the Equality Officer decided that the claimant should have been promoted, and also awarded €6000 as compensation for distress caused by the discrimination. This decision follows *A Complainant* v. *Café Kylemore*,[53] where the Equality Officer held that alcoholism was a disability for the purposes of the Equal Status Act, 2000.

The fundamental importance of data protection in the context of workplace drug testing can also be seen in Finland, where the Act on the Protection of Privacy in Working Life (759/2004) delineates the circumstances whereby workplace drug testing is allowed. It defines a 'drug test certificate' and the occasions in which an employer 'may receive' or 'process information entered in a drug test certificate'. It goes on to delineate in what circumstances a certificates information (i.e. a drug test) can be used for (a) recruitment and (b) reasonable suspicion. The Finnish Ministry of Labour has also brought out a decree on workplace drug testing which will have in appendix form the Finnish workplace drug testing guidelines (not yet available in English) that are based on the EWDTS Guidelines.[34]

In France, the Department of Transport published a departmental order (24 August 2004) on foot of a Government Directive of July 2003 which allows for testing of drivers in safety critical jobs by employer SNCF (French State Railway Co.). (Note: In France, workplace drug testing can only be carried out by occupational health physicians.) SNCF has approximately 165 000 employees. Of 92 250 tests carried out thus far, 1845 have tested positive, the majority for cannabis. Other major companies in France are now developing intoxicant testing programmes as part of a corporate drug and alcohol policy.[54]

In the UK, there have been a number of employment tribunal and employment appeals tribunal cases taken under unfair dismissals legislation arising from drug testing at work. In *Booth* v. *Southampton Airport Ltd*[55] an air traffic controller was dismissed for cannabis use, notwithstanding the fact that he was off-duty when using the drug. The tribunal found that the requirement to maintain public confidence from a health and safety perspective justified the action taken by the employer. This pre-empts the thinking of the European Convention on Human Rights in *Wretlund* v. *Sweden* by more than 20 years, and raises once more the important issue of whether testing is one of measuring impairment or risk of impairment?

In *Racal Services* v. *Flockhart*,[38] the dismissal of a safety-critical railway worker for testing positive for cannabis was held to be fair.

In the Employment Appeal Tribunal case, *O'Flynn* v. *Airlinks Ltd*,[56] the appellant, a coach company customer care assistant, had brought a case for unfair dismissal or wrongful dismissal arising from a failed random drug test. She had been dismissed for 'gross misconduct and failure to comply with the drug and alcohol policy' (gross misconduct was defined as including reporting for work with drugs in the system). She appealed on the grounds that the decision to dismiss her was not reasonable and that a lesser sanction was more appropriate. It was also averred that the implementation of the random drug and alcohol screening was not part of her contract and also that the process amounted to an infringement of her rights under Article 8 of the Human Rights Act.

Among the submissions, it was heard that the appellant as part of her duties could at times be required to assist drivers in the manoeuvring of coaches or serve hot drinks to customers on-board. It was agreed that she was at all times aware of the company drug and alcohol policy, part of which was the provision for randomly screening 10% of the company workforce each year. It was also agreed that the appellant, prior to the giving of the sample for analysis, admitted that she had been smoking cannabis at the weekend, but she denied that she was 'under the influence of cannabis whilst carrying out her work for the Respondent' and that the 'mere existence of cannabis in her system did not amount to misconduct'. The tribunal, in dismissing the appellant's appeal, held that

> the introduction by the Respondent of a drug/alcohol policy in the introduction of random testing were necessary in the interests of public safety and that it was reasonable for the Respondent to introduce this policy and make it applicable to all its employees policy was necessary for the protection of the Respondents customers and for the protection of the Respondents employees, including the Applicant herself.

Another UK Employment Appeal Tribunal case,[57] concerned an appeal by a railway undertaking that an employment tribunal had found that a worker had been unfairly dismissed following a random drugs test. The respondent employee, having previously undergone and passed a number of random drugs tests from time to time during the course of his employment, was subjected to an unannounced drug test which was prompted by a tip off from police that the residence where the employee lived was under surveillance for drugs activity. This urine sample was positive and the worker was given a certificate of analysis that showed traces of cannabis and benzodiazepines. There was also a medical officer's report which stated that the worker was 'unfit for work' due to a 'positive for cause drug screen'. The company drug policy set out inter alia that 'traces of drugs can be detected days and even weeks after use. A trace of an illegal drug found during screening will lead to dismissal.'

The original tribunal found that 'the decision to dismiss the Applicant on the basis of his positive test for drugs was, in the circumstances of this particular case, unreasonable, and the dismissal unfair.' They reasoned that there was 'a lack of any evidence or link between the substances in the applicant's bloodstream and the ability for him to perform his job safely and satisfactorily.' But this finding was overturned by the Employment Appeal Tribunal, which found that the worker had been certified as unfit for duty by a medical practitioner.

In 2002, the Irish Labour Court, in *Irish Ferries* v. *SIPTU*[58] issued a recommendation on foot of a dispute re the company's proposal to introduce a new drug and alcohol testing policy, allowing for 'with cause' testing. The court held that an 'effective system of ensuring compliance . . . will inevitably involve mandatory testing in appropriate situations.'

Two important decisions of the European Court of Human Rights (4th Section) addressed the issue of the definition of 'safety-critical' occupation in the context of workplace drug testing. In *Madsen* v. *Denmark*[36] the applicant, a Danish national, was employed as a passenger assistant in a Danish shipping company. It was a fact that Madsen had 'no responsibility for the primary operation of the ship' but did have responsibility for passenger safety as a crew member. The shipping company did have a drug and alcohol testing policy in place whereby 'all employees are under an obligation to submit to tests for alcohol, drugs or any other intoxicating substances. The employees can expect to undergo such a test without notice at least once a year.' Madsen underwent an unannounced random drug and alcohol test in September 1999. The result was negative. Following this, his trade union issued civil proceedings against the shipping company before a Court of Arbitration, arguing among other things, that random urine tests were in breach of Article 8 of the European Convention on Human Rights. In a decision of February 2000, the Court found in favour of the company. The Court (although not a majority decision) said: 'the management have a right to introduce measures of control justified by operational considerations if such measures have a reasonable purpose, do not offend the employee's dignity, and do not cause any loss or appreciable inconvenience for the employees.' It went on to say that the provision of a urine sample 'is a possible measure of control'. Madsen applied to the European Court of Human Rights claiming that his rights under Article 8 of the Convention were infringed, stating that the shipping company's requirement that employee undergo 'random control measures by means of providing a urine sample', interfered with his right to respect for private life and 'was not in accordance with law or necessary in a democratic society.' (Note: The complaint was against the general testing regime, not the specific test itself.) The Court looked at employer control measures, the Act on Use of Health Data, the 1991 ILO Joint Maritime Commission resolution on drugs and alcohol in the maritime industry and The Seamen's Act 1995, all of which had relevance to the within proceedings. The Court, in holding that the testing regime was 'in accordance with law', looked to the company regulations on testing as part of the employer's right to manage and control work, which is given effect by the September agreement of 1899, thus giving the testing measures sufficient basis in Danish law. The Court also held that the legitimate aims are covered under Article 8.2 by the terms 'public safety' or 'protection of the rights and freedoms of others' (e.g. passengers). On the issue of intoxicant testing being 'necessary in a democratic society', the Court looked at the proportionality of the measures complained of and held that the control measures were not disproportionate with regard to the protection of public safety and the rights of others.

In *Wretlund* v. *Sweden*,[10] the applicant, an office cleaner at a Swedish nuclear plant, complained that 'her obligation to undergo drug testing as laid down in the judgment of the Labour Court, interfered with her right to respect for her private life under Article 8 of the Convention' (European Convention on Human Rights and Fundamental Freedoms). In this case, the applicant's trade union had resisted the implementation of a drug policy programme for existing employees in which workers would be subject to drug and alcohol testing. The testing programme was relatively 'benign' in that testing was to take place every third year, Cannabis was the sole drug to be tested for, and workers were given one week's advance warning that testing would be taking place. Further, an employee would not be dismissed for refusing to give a sample if there was no signs of drug and if they could give principled reasons. The applicant's trade union issued proceedings against the company in the Swedish Labour Court (Arbetsdomstolen) seeking a declaration that the applicant should not have to undergo drug and alcohol tests, arguing, inter alia, that testing was in breach of Article 8 of the Convention and the Swedish Secrecy Act.[59] The union also contended that testing was not justified given the nature of the applicant's duties at the nuclear plant. In August of 1998, the Labour Court decided that the applicant was liable to testing for cannabis but not for alcohol. It found that the company running the nuclear plant had a strong interest in testing to ensure a drug-free environment, given that such testing was carried out at all nuclear power plants and given that the National Nuclear Power Inspectorate (Statens Kärnkraftsinspektion) had stated the necessity of testing as part of ensuring a drug-free environment at plants. Further, the Labour Court stated that, under the Swedish Work Environment Act[60] the company had obligation to ensure measures were taken to prevent workplace accidents and illnesses. The applicant's complaint to the European Court of Human Rights had three strands:

1. the interference to the right to respect for her private life (Article 8.1)
2. that the introduction of the drug testing was 'not in accordance with law' as there was no Swedish legislation on drug testing, and therefore the Article 8.2 derogation from Article 8.1 cannot apply
3. compulsory drug testing not justifiable given her duties as an office cleaner, with no safety-critical role within the company.

The Court, in holding that there was no interference with the exercise of a right under Article 8.1 above, looked at the various limbs of Article 8.2, finding that although the obligation to submit to testing did not arise from specific legislation, an employer's right to manage and organise work has been given the effect of a general legal principle by the Labour Court. 'According to the Labour Court's case-law, the employer may have a right to carry out control measures as part of the right to manage and organise the work' and 'such control measures could include drug and alcohol tests.' Thus the Court held that the challenged measures were 'in accordance with law' for the purposes of Article 8.2. The Court further held that, notwithstanding the job description of the applicant (not safety-critical on its face), the operational considerations at the nuclear plant 'relating to the public safety and the rights and freedoms' of other employees, justified the testing. Finally, in looking at whether the challenged measures were 'necessary in a democratic society', the established case law of the Court has shown that the concept of necessity implies that the 'interference corresponds to a pressing social need', and, in particular, that it is proportionate to the legitimate aim pursued. It found here that the drug testing procedure and its operation were not disproportionate and thus the applicant's case was declared inadmissible. On the issue of consent to test, it is interesting that there was a triple mechanism employed whereby there was an initial consent to allow testing by laboratory to proceed, and on the same form a consent allowing results to be sent to the occupational health department. But there was also a 'special form' allowing consent for results to be given to the worker's immediate supervisor. From a procedural point of view, it is of vital importance that companies obtain proper advice before instigating certain causes of action.

Of most recent note in the same jurisdiction are two cases arising from dismissal of employees pursuant to a company drug and alcohol testing procedure. In *Kennedy* v. *Veolia Transport Ireland Ltd*[61] taken under the Unfair Dismissals Acts (1977–2001), the claimant was a tram driver with the respondent company since February 2004. In August 2005, the employee was part of a morning shift that was selected to be screened for drugs and alcohol as part of the company drug and alcohol policy. The tests were conducted by an independent testing contractor. The claimant expressed his dissatisfaction about being tested but nonetheless agreed to be tested. He subsequently screened positive for alcohol with a blood alcohol of three times the company's limit as set out in their policy. However, he did not wait to provide a urine sample to be sent for confirmatory testing and drove away from the depot.

Following this, the claimant was suspended without pay pending further investigation into the matter. At the disciplinary hearing, the claimant denied that he refused to provide the urine sample, but stated that he was unable to provide it due to sickness. He claimed that the testing procedure was not truly random. Evidence was also heard that a large proportion of the workforce, including the claimant, had not been given a copy of the company drugs and alcohol policy.

The claimant was dismissed from his employment on 5 September 2005.

The tribunal, having accepted that the employee had not received a copy of the drug and alcohol policy, examined the case under the claimant's contract of employment, and the union agreement with the company, both of which stated that employees must comply with the company's procedures for drug and alcohol testing.

The tribunal stated that it was 'satisfied that the breath sample provided by the claimant was clear evidence that the claimant was in excess of the limit for driving a tram' and that it was 'reasonable for the claimant to be required to submit to a urine test' having screened positive by breathalyser. The tribunal was satisfied that the claimant deliberately set out to avoid giving confirmatory urine and thus was in breach of the procedure. The tribunal held that it was thus reasonable for the company to 'conclude that the claimant was guilty of gross misconduct' under the terms of the employment contract and to dismiss him. Thus the tribunal found that the dismissal of the claimant was not unfair and the claim under the Unfair Dismissals Acts, 1977 to 2001 failed.

This case raised a number of interesting issues for companies with employees who are designated as 'safety-sensitive' who need to implement testing procedures as part of an overall drug and alcohol policy.

- First and importantly, if a company draws up a policy, it should be distributed to all affected employees.
- The method of selection for testing should be robust and truly random so as to minimise potential allegations of bias. (In this case, although the tribunal found that the claimant had not been deliberately targeted for testing by the company, the company subsequently changed its selection method upon objections from the claimant's trade union.)

The recent Irish Labour Court decision in *Alstom (Ireland) Ltd.* and *A worker*,[62] concerned a dispute over the dismissal of an employee who tested positive for an illicit drug as part of a random test, pursuant to the company's drug and alcohol policy. This policy was provided for by a collective agreement between Alstom Ltd and the TEEU (trade union), contingent upon implementation of the provisions of the Railway Safety Act 2005. Having undergone a random drugs test, the employee in question tested positive at the screening stage and this sample underwent confirmatory testing in a reference laboratory. The result of this test, which was below the defined threshold, but which showed the presence of a drug, was considered as gross misconduct by the company and in contravention of their 'zero tolerance' policy towards drug use in the workplace, with the subsequent dismissal of the employee.

The net question was whether the result of this test should be considered as positive given that it was approximately 50% of the threshold value internationally accepted for this drug as per the EWDTS Guidelines. Toxicology experts for both sides differed in their respective interpretations of the drug test result. In its opinion, the Labour Court broadly accepted the *raison d'être* for testing by stating 'The Court is conscious that drug and alcohol testing is becoming an increasingly common feature of many employments, particularly in safety critical areas. Changed societal factors, including increased drug abuse, has heightened the need, *and the justification* [italics added], for such testing.' It went on to say

> The Court has consistently supported the use of drug and alcohol testing in safety critical areas. However, given the inevitable consequences for employees who test positive it is crucial that the modalities of all aspects of the testing conform to predetermined standards, which as far as possible, are agreed between the employer and the trade unions.

In its decision, the Labour Court directed that 'the guidelines covering the testing procedure, including the processing of results, be put in place without delay.' It went on to say that there was a doubt as to whether the result should have been reported as positive or negative and because of this the dismissal of the work should be overturned and the worker re-engaged, with effect from the date of the decision.

This case highlights the importance for company policies of adherence to defined drug cut-off concentrations for screening and confirmatory analysis in order to prevent legal challenge to disciplinary action arising from testing. (Note: The EWDTS Guidelines can be instructive for companies embarking on testing as part of a substance abuse policy.[34]) Confirmatory testing cut-offs have been challenged in other spheres of drug testing. In *USA* v. *Frank Klimek*[63] the defendant, who had previously been sentenced to two years imprisonment followed by three years supervised release for possession of cocaine, was appealing a decision of the US District Court after he was found to have violated the terms of the supervised release. That Court held that he had ingested cocaine notwithstanding the result of the GC-MS was below the defined cut-off threshold used by the laboratory (cocaine metabolite detected at level of 118 ng/mL; laboratory cut-off was 150 ng/mL). Testimony was given that the urine sample was 'dilute', and when 'normalised' for dilution (creatinine levels in urine would normally be measured in laboratory to check if urine submitted is dilute or substituted, see EWDTS Guidelines[34]) would yield a cocaine metabolite of well above the accepted cut-off. The defendant argued in the appeal court that the original result 'could not be the basis of a violation' as the cut-off for cocaine is a 'standard' or 'guideline' which is promoted by statute regarding the drug testing of prisoners on supervised release.

The Appeal Court upheld the decision of the District Court and by taking into account the normalisation of the dilute urine sample, previous supervised release violations and other evidence, looked beyond the fact that the original result was below the cut-off concentration. It is unlikely that a set of circumstances like this could arise in a workplace drug testing scenario, but as in the Irish Labour Court case, expert testimony either way may influence the final outcome, but adherence to international accepted guidelines is preferable.[64]

A further contentious issue may arise with respect to testing of second or 'B' samples or aliquots (see EWDTS Guidelines, Section 2.4[34]). A donor who is dissatisfied with the screen and/or confirmatory positive result from the 'A' sample or aliquot is in the normal course of events entitled to have the 'B' sample analysed. But the storage time and conditions of the sample may cause problems. Under the SAMHSA Guidelines, the 'Drug Presence' Criteria,[65] it is stated that 'because some drugs or drug metabolites may deteriorate during storage, the retest of an aliquot of a single specimen or the test of a split (Bottle B) specimen is not subject to a specific drug cut-off requirement, but must provide data sufficient to confirm the presence of the drug or metabolite.' This approach, while being laudable from a technical perspective, could cast enough doubt on the efficacy of the testing process (because of potential disparity of results between 'A' and 'B' samples, the analysis of which may take place many months apart) in a tribunal or court of law, as to lead to different judgments or decisions depending on jurisdiction, or even between individual judges.

Further recent case law in Ireland has reinforced the view that challenges to drug and alcohol testing policies and procedures would seem to focus more on the procedures themselves than challenges to the efficacy or otherwise of the analyses and results themselves and/or testing apparatus used. This can be seen in three Irish High Court cases whereby members of the Irish Defence Forces (Army, Navy and Air Corps personnel) challenged their administrative discharges on foot of alleged positive drug tests as part of the Defence Forces Mandatory Drug Testing procedure. The challenges were by way of judicial review in the High Court. In *Rawson* v. *Minister for Defence*,[66] the applicant, who tested positive for cannabis in urine (confirmed by GC-MS), argued that the positive result was as a result of passive smoking. In *White* v. *Minister for Defence*[67] it was argued on behalf of the applicant that the Defence Forces failed to properly apply provisions and instructions relating to the mandatory drug testing procedure and that it had acted unfairly and disproportionately in discharging him. Here, the applicant had tested positive for cannabis on screening of a random urine sample. The test was confirmed by GC-MS, as indeed was the result of the B sample. It was acknowledged in court that there was no dispute as to the accuracy of the tests carried out by both screening apparatus and by both laboratories involved. The applicant did claim, however, that a pizza he had been cooking was 'spiked with cannabis' by some housemates, one of whom subsequently 'owned up' to the deed, stating it was a 'prank' or practical joke. This was not taken into consideration by the Defence Forces in deciding to discharge Private White. The Court held that fair procedures had not been adhered to, and the decision to discharge in the face of the evidence was 'fundamentally flawed'.

In *Heffernan* v. *Minister for Defence*,[68] a soldier said he had involuntarily ingested cannabis, which was allegedly put into a drink. A temporary injunction restraining his discharge was granted by the Court. The case has since been heard but the judgment is unreported.

In the *Rawson* case, the Air Corps member said his positive result came from being in a car with two friends who were smoking cannabis. He said he had been given no opportunity to call evidence on the possibility of a false positive test from passive smoking. The High Court restrained the military authorities from discharging Rawson, pending the outcome of the case. Mr Justice John Hedigan said compulsory random drug testing was introduced in the Defence Forces in January 2002. On 27 November 2006, he underwent a random drug test and provided a urine sample. He was notified he had tested positive on 11 December and was subsequently advised he was liable for discharge on 10 January 2007. On 26 January 2007, the general officer commanding decided he should be discharged with immediate effect. The judge said the Minister for Defence was dealing with a situation where members of the Defence Forces were likely to be in control of lethal weaponry and it was incumbent upon the armed forces to set the highest standards for such members. He said the Army could have chosen a zero tolerance level but chose a certain level in order to make allowance for the possibility of entirely innocent and unintended passive smoking.

It did this because it believed the use of cannabis or any other controlled drug was entirely incompatible with membership of the Defence Forces. The judge said the Army, correctly in his view, allowed a low level cut-off to provide for the possibility of some level of passive smoking. In Mr Rawson's case, the test reading was more than double the cut-off point. Mr Rawson said this was due to the presence in his car of friends smoking cannabis. Subsequently Rawson lost the High Court challenge to his discharge from the Army.

Conclusion

In common law jurisdictions in Europe, such as Ireland and the UK, employers have had a common law duty of care to employees to provide a safe place of work and not expose them to reasonably foresee harm arising out of the work duties they undertake.

Many European countries allow testing when there is a health, safety or security risk, or when it is deemed 'necessary' or 'proportionate', or is 'justified' or 'reasonable', or when there is a 'reasonable suspicion' that an employee is under the influence of an intoxicant (whether legal or illegal).

Three countries (Finland, Ireland and Norway) have specific or direct legislation on drug testing in the workplace. In Italy, the main drug law contains an article addressing specifically drug testing in the workplace. In all other countries, there is indirect legislation in the areas of privacy and data protection that regulate to some extent the type of testing that can take place.

In many European countries the occupational health physician can only inform the employer whether an employee is 'fit for work' or 'unfit for work' rather than revealing the full results of a particular test.

There are wide differences in practice between countries on the issue of pre-employment testing in comparison with the testing of existing members of the workforce.

Several court cases examined different aspects of workplace drug testing in Europe and in general the outcome was favourable to the practice of workplace drug testing. In nearly all cases, employees dismissed because of positive drugs test lost their case.

References

1. Shehandeh B, Caborn J. Ethical issues in workplace drug testing in Europe. Seminar on Ethics, Professional Standards and Drug Addiction, Strasbourg, 6–7 February 2003.
2. Tetley W. Mixed jurisdictions: common law vs. civil law (codified and uncodified). *Uniform L Rev* 1999; 3: 591–619.
3. See 'Danish Model' of 1899. In 1899, Danish Employers' Organisation (DA) and the Danish Confederation of Trade Unions (LO) signed the 'September compromise', the first basic agreement regulating Danish industrial relations.
4. Craig JDR. *Privacy and Employment Law*. Oxford: Hart Publishing, 1999: 174.
5. Ferguson G. Drug Testing at Work: A Legal Perspective. Report prepared for the Independent Inquiry into Drug Testing at Work, UK. Matrix Research Panel. March 2003.
6. European Monitoring Centre for Drugs and Drug Addiction (EMCDDA). European Legal Database on Drugs (ELDD). http://eldd.emcdda.europa.eu/ (accessed December 2010).
7. See *Wretlund* v. *Sweden*. There were three levels of consent: consent to test, consent to release results and further consent required to release results to human resources department.
8. Osman C. An ocean apart: US and EU employment law compared. Clifford Chance LLP, 23 January 2001. http;//crossborder.practicallaw.com/7-101-3606 (accessed December 2010).
9. Although a number of challenges to workplace drug testing on the grounds of infringement of Article 8.1 are evident in the last number of years; see *Madsen* v. *Denmark*, *Wretlund* v. *Sweden*, in European Court of Human Rights.
10. *Wretlund* v. *Sweden*: 1. The European Court of Human Rights (Fourth Section), sitting on 9 March 2004.
11. *Walton* v. *TAC Construction Materials* [1981] IRLR 357.
12. *Mathewson* v. *Wilson Dental Laboratory* [1988] IRLR 512.
13. International Labour Organization (ILO). Appendix V: Guiding principles on drug and alcohol testing. In: *Management of Alcohol- and Drug-related Issues in the Workplace*. Geneva: ILO, 1996.
14. Midford R, Heale P, eds. Under the influence? Issues and practicalities of alcohol and other drug testing in the workplace. Proceedings of a Forum held in Perth, Western Australia. 8 October 1996. National Centre for Research into the Prevention of Drug Abuse, Division of Health Sciences, Curtin University of Technology, Perth, Western Australia.
15. EU Directive 2002/14/EC of 11 March 2002. Establishing a general framework for informing and consulting employees in the European Community. http://eur-lex.europa.eu/LexUriServ/LexUriServ.do?uri=OJ:L:2002 : 080 : 0029 : 0033:en:PDF. (accessed December 2010).
16. Joseph Rowntree Foundation. Drug testing in the workplace: Summary conclusions of the Independent Inquiry into Drug Testing at Work. 2004.
17. *Ministre du Travail* v. *Société Peintures Corona* (1980) 6 Dr. Soc. 317.
18. *Whitefield* v. *General Medical Council* [2003] IRLR 62.
19. Information Commissioner's Office. Employment Practices Data Protection Code Part IV. www.ico.gov.uk (accessed December 2010).

20. Equality Officer's Decision No: Dec-E/2005/034.
21. For a useful analysis of reasonable accommodation see *Milazzo* v. *Autocar Connaisseur Inc. Motor Coach Canada*, 2003 CHRT 37.
22. European Monitoring Centre for Drugs and Drug Addiction (EMCDDA). Legal status if drug testing in the workplace. http://eldd.emcdda.europa.eu/html.cfm/index16901EN.html (accessed December 2010).
23. *X* v. *The European Commission* [1995] IRLR 320.
24. *Kapfunde* v. *Abbey National* [1998] IRLR 583.
25. Faculty of Occupational Medicine. *Guidance on Alcohol and Drug Misuse in the Workplace*. London: Royal College of Physicians, 2006. www.facoccmed.ac.uk/pubspol/pubs.jsp.
26. *A complainant* v. *Café Kylemore* (DEC-52003-024); Decision of the Irish Equality Tribunal under the Equal Status Act 2000. This decision was reaffirmed in *A Worker* v. *A Government Dept*.
27. International Code of Ethics for Occupational Health Professionals. Adopted by the Board of International Commission of Occupational Health (ICOH)/Commission Internationale de la Santé au Travail (CIST), March 2002. http:// www.icohweb.org/core_docs/code_ethics_eng.pdf (accessed December 2010).
28. Mills S. Clinical practice and the law. Haywards Health: Tottel Publishing, 2nd edition, 2007: 212.
29. US Department of Justice. Drug Enforcement Administration guidelines. www.usdoj.gov/dea/demand/dfmanual/09df.htm.
30. Lillsunde P, Haavanlammi K, Partinen R, Mukala K, Lamberg M. National Public Health Institute, Helsinki, Finland.
31. Playing safe. *Law Society Gazette*, pp. 22–26.
32. *Maher* v. *Jabil Global Services Ltd.* [2005] IEHC 130. (12 May 2005).
33. Bolster M. Stress, bullying and harassment in the workplace. Paper delivered at Legal Island Annual Review of Irish Law.
34. European Workplace Drug Testing Society (EWDTS). Guidelines for legally defensible drug testing. www.eapinstitute.com/documents/EWDTSGuidelines.pdf (accessed December 2010).
35. Breitstadt R, Kauert G. *The Worker – risk factor and reliability*. Germany: Shaker, 2004.
36. *Madsen* v. *Denmark*: The European Court of Human Rights, 2002.
37. For a comprehensive treatment of the interface of workplace drug testing and UK Legislation, see 'In the Matter of The Independent Inquiry into Drug Testing at Work,' Advice by Michael Ford, Barrister; 'Drug Testing at Work: Legal and Ethical Issues' Round Table Discussion, Ruth Evans, Yolande Burgin, Simon Deakin and Michael Ford; plenary session, Industrial Law Society, 12th Sept 2003.
38. *Racal Services* v. *Flockhart*. EAT 701/00.
39. Information Commissioner's Office (2000) Draft Code of Practice on the Use of Personal Data in Employer/Employee Relationships. www.ico.gov.uk.
40. Information Commissioner's Office. Employment Practices Data Protection Code Part IV. www.ico.gov.uk (accessed 15 February 2011).
41. *EEOC* v. *Exxon*. US Court of Appeals, Fifth Circuit 2000.
42. *Entrop* v. *Imperial Oil Co.* Ontario Court of Appeal, 2000.
43. *PF Worden* v. *Diamond Offshore Mining Co.* AIRC 1255/99.
44. *BHP Iron Ore*. WAIRC 130/98.
45. *Ishikawa* v. *Delta Air Lines, and LabOne Inc.*, Federal District Court, Oregon. (3 July 2001).
46. *Pioneer Construction*. 2003 WAIRC 10049.
47. *Milazzo* v. *Autocar Connoisseur Inc. Motor Coach Canada*, 2003 CHRT 37.
48. *Eastern Associated Coal Corp.* U.S. Court of Appeals, Fourth Circuit, 99–1038.
49. *Luedtke* v. *Nabors Alaska Drilling Inc.* 768 P 2d 1123. (Alaska SC).
50. *National Treasury Employees Union* v. *Von Raab*. US Supreme Court, 21st March 1989 (See also the issue of drug testing as a 'search' within the meaning of the 4th Amendment in *Skinner* v. *Railway Labor Executive Association*, 109 S.Ct. 1402. (1989)).

51. Poteet D (1996) Employee privacy in the public sector. Texas Board of Legal Specialization. http://akingump.com/docs/publication/279.html (accessed December 2010).
52. *An Employee* v. *A Government Dept.* DEC-E/2005/34.
53. *A Complainant* v. *Café Kylemore.* DEC-S/2004/24.
54. Archange J-C. Paper presented at EWDTS Symposium, Dublin, 2005.
55. *Booth* v. *Southampton Airport Ltd.* ET 39214/81.
56. *O'Flynn* v. *Airlinks Ltd.* EAT/0269/01.
57. *Southwest Trains Ltd.* v. *SA Ireland.* EAT/0873/01.
58. *Irish Ferries* v. *SIPTU.* CD/02/646 Recommendation no. 17371.
59. Convention and the Swedish Secrecy Act. Sekretesslagen, 1980: 100.
60. Swedish Work Environment Act. Arbetsmiljölagen, 1977: 1160.
61. *Kennedy* v. *Veolia Transport Ireland Ltd.* Employment Appeals Tribunal Case (no. UD240/2006).
62. *Alstom (Ireland) Ltd.* and *A worker.* Irish Labour Court: CD/07/413.
63. *USA* v. *Frank Klimek.* United States Court of Appeals (Second Circuit); 8 June 2005.
64. SAMHSA Guidelines for Federal Workplace Drug Testing Programs, 69 FR 19644, 13 April 2004.
65. Kadehjian L. Workplace drug testing: science supports society. Presentation to the EWDTS Symposium, Stockholm, Sweden, 25 May 2007.
66. *Rawson* v. *Minister for Defence.* 2007/88/JR.
67. *White* v. *Minister for Defence.* 2008/205/JR.
68. *Heffernan* v. *Minister for Defence.* Heard also in 2008.

5

Policies for drugs and alcohol

Lindsay Hadfield

Key points

- The workplace mirrors drug and alcohol use in society at large.
- The inappropriate use of drugs and alcohol can create a workplace risk, either through individual impairment or the longer term risk of dependency.
- A workplace policy has to provide rules and solutions that address both impairment and dependency. The key elements are:
  - a clearly worded policy, developed through consultation
  - education around the issues of drugs and alcohol
  - support for those who may need it
  - monitoring compliance with the policy, including the use of testing.
- Testing should not be the starting point of the policy, but it has a valuable role in making people take notice of the policy.
- Testing decisions include who and when to test, the test method and the consequences of a positive result.
- Testing should always be carried out to the highest scientific and ethical standards.

Introduction

This chapter looks at the practicalities of implementing a drug and alcohol policy that includes testing. The emphasis is on establishing the policy objectives, using testing as a support. Key elements of the approach are education and the provision of an Employee Assistance Programme (EAP).

Elsewhere in this book (see Chapter 4) there is information on the responses of different European countries to drugs, alcohol and work. The legality of workplace testing will vary from country to country, but the underlying principles of the policy remain the same. The purpose of the policy should be established first, with testing used as a support for the objectives.

Background

Alcohol and drug use is common throughout the world, and has a long history. Drugs and alcohol have had, and continue to have, medicinal and mystical uses, as well as their social function of providing pleasure, relaxation and enjoyment.

From the workplace perspective the problem is that social use can sometimes encourage irresponsible use, such as excessive consumption, or use immediately before or during working hours. Drugs and alcohol can also be used as a form of self-medication, to escape from the pressures of life. Use may then become a habit, with the danger that habit could become dependency.

The workplace is a mirror of society. It will include people who use drugs and alcohol occasionally as well as some regular social users who may from time to time over-indulge. Additionally there may be some who try a variety of substances but never become addicted, while others who are less fortunate may develop problems. A workplace policy must acknowledge the social use and the problem use of drugs and alcohol.

The inappropriate use of drugs and alcohol in the workplace context can affect the safety and security of co-workers, the organisation and the public. Drugs and alcohol can reduce the user's ability for logical judgement and sensible assessment. They can accentuate tiredness and other conditions that may already be reducing the individual's capabilities. As shown elsewhere in this book, there is a wealth of evidence to support the observation that the use of drugs and alcohol can cause impairment and lead to human error. Accidents are usually caused by a sequence of events, with one trigger. The risk is that the trigger could, for example, be an individual impaired by cannabis smoked some 12 hours previously, or suffering the ecstasy user's 'suicide Tuesday' hangover from the previous weekend's use.

Another consequence is that excessive use of drugs and alcohol can affect the health of individual users, making them more susceptible to minor illnesses and increasing sickness absence rates. These individuals also run the risk of dependency on a particular drug, and dependency in itself is considered an illness.

With the growth and normalisation of drug use, organisations are realising that doing nothing is no longer an option. There is a danger that because drug use is less understood and less visible than alcohol use management may assume it is not a problem. Ignoring the possibility can appear to condone it, leading drug users to believe their activity is tolerated, thus allowing the problem to grow.

Workplace policies

A workplace policy on drugs and alcohol has to provide rules and solutions for the two main problems associated with alcohol and drug use: impairment and dependency. Impairment creates an issue for any workplace in terms of safety and business critical risks and the resources required to manage the impaired individual. Dependency will probably only affect a few employees but the indicators of developing problems may only slowly become apparent, creating a gradual drain on productivity, with occasional acute incidents that start to highlight the problem use.

As a consequence, most workplace drug and alcohol policies have three objectives. These are to:

- deter the inappropriate use of alcohol and drugs
- provide positive intervention for problem users
- comply with legislative, regulatory and contractual requirements.

If an employee decides to challenge the validity of the policy, it will be judged on whether, in the context of your own country's employment culture:

- it is fair and reasonable, and a proportionate response to the issue
- there was proper consultation with employee representatives
- it is clearly stated, fully explained and understood
- it is being applied in a reasonable and consistent manner.

These are good criteria against which to measure your own policy. The remainder of this chapter looks at ways of achieving the objectives and creating a robust and effective drug and alcohol policy.

Where do you start?

The starting point is to be clear about why you want a policy and what you hope it will achieve. The motivator might be a straightforward commercial decision to keep up with standards and expectations for a particular industry or it may be because an issue has arisen at work, and it is apparent that there is no structure in place to handle it. Testing is a valuable tool within a policy, but it should not be a policy objective in itself.

A simple 'risk assessment' approach can help set out the need for the policy. On the basis that the inappropriate use of drugs and alcohol can constitute a hazard for the workplace, each organisation needs to consider the consequences for their working environment and the likelihood that they will occur.

Any occupation has associated risks. These can be compounded by other factors, for example poor training or tiredness. The use of drugs and alcohol can in turn make these factors worse and increase the risk of inattention or risk-taking behaviour. Although safety critical risks get most attention, business critical outcomes could also be considered. Employees who have direct contact with customers can damage your reputation, and within an office poor performance can reduce morale. A hidden danger may lie in the many functions that are now computer controlled, as errors of judgement might not become apparent for some time. The impact will vary from business to business, but each organisation has to assess the potential damage to:

- people
- property
- productivity
- public image
- profitability.

The consequences have to be matched with the probability of the inappropriate use of alcohol and drugs occurring among people working on the company's premises, or in the company's name. The likelihood can be linked to various factors:

- Availability. The European Monitoring Centre for Drugs and Drug Addiction (EMCDDA) annual reports indicate the widespread use of drugs throughout Europe.[1] The British Crime Survey occasionally asks questions about access to drugs, and in 2001/2002 65% of the 16- to 24-year-old age group acknowledged that it was very or fairly easy to obtain cannabis.[2] A Eurobarometer poll in 2002 again showed that the majority of people questioned would find it easy to purchase drugs[3] (see also Chapter 1).
- Acceptability. Alcohol is a socially acceptable drug when used in moderation. Recreational drug use is usually taken to mean use of drugs such as cannabis and ecstasy, and the word 'recreational' suggests that use is acceptable. As the current younger age group who see little wrong with cannabis use move into the workplace, acceptability will increase.
- Age. Younger people are more likely to be involved in illegal drug use. The 2007/2008 British Crime Survey reveals that 21.4% of 16- to 24-year-olds have used illegal drugs in the past year, compared with 9.3% of the population aged 16–59, and similar data are reflected each year in the EMCDDA annual reports.[1,4]
- Pressures. People with stressful and/or boring jobs are more likely to seek the relaxation and diversion that alcohol and drugs can provide.
- Independence and lack of immediate supervision gives people opportunities to break any rules in an organisation, including those on drugs and alcohol.

This assessment of consequences of the hazard occurring and the probability that it might occur can provide the rationale for policy development, since the logical 'hazard control' is a corporate approach to alcohol and drugs.

The organisation must be able to demonstrate to auditors, insurance assessors, customers, the public, the media, shareholders and their own employees that they have effective procedures in place to minimise the safety and business critical risks created by drugs and alcohol. This is where testing has an important role, which will be discussed later.

Who do you involve?

A policy often starts on the initiative of one individual, but steps must be taken to ensure that it reflect the needs of the whole organisation. European legislation promotes the consultation of workers and their involvement through Works Councils, seeing this as an important element of anticipating and managing change.

In every organisation there will be many people and groups who can make a useful and constructive contribution to policy development. Depending on the size of the company, a working party should consider including representatives from the following areas:

- directors/senior management
- human resources/occupational health/health and safety/security
- line management and employee representatives
- company lawyers/public relations
- drug testing service providers.

Directors/senior management

As with any workplace policy you need buy-in at the highest level, with acceptance that the policy will apply from top management down. Many an alcohol policy has foundered because senior management have assumed that the 'social' need for alcohol within business merits exemption from company rules, and a similar bias may apply to drug use. Senior managers' attitudes to drugs may be lenient and relaxed or harsh and intolerant, and these views will influence and may even distort the structure of the policy. If the commitment of this group to the overall tenor of the policy is not obtained at an early stage the efforts of the working party could be wasted. A manager who is not in agreement with the policy, or testing, can be obstructive, for example by refusing to release people for education or finding excuses for them not to be available for testing.

Human resources/occupational health/health and safety/security

People with these responsibilities are likely to have ownership of the policy in part or whole. Their shared knowledge will contribute to a robust foundation for the policy, and ensure that it is fairly balanced between the different interest groups.

Health and safety is a serious responsibility for companies, and in the context of a risk assessment approach might be expected to dominate policy development, particularly in industries with a poor accident record. Similarly, security staff may see their involvement with drug-related problems as critical, and may be pushing for a policy that helps them deal with issues such as fraud, drug dealing or impaired employees.

However, if the concept of a policy on drugs and alcohol involves a cultural change for the organisation, the human resources department is likely to be tasked with leading this. They will also be aware of the balance that has to be kept between the needs of the organisation and the rights of the employees. Human resources will have to handle the disciplinary consequences of policy breaches and will also be concerned about the implications of testing, and what impact that might have on industrial relations within their organisation. On a more practical side, human resources is the function that often holds the evidence of absences, work performance and disciplinary issues that may give a clue to an individual developing the type of problems that the policy is trying to prevent.

Occupational health is primarily concerned with the preventative element of the policy, and in helping people with dependency problems. There is consensus on this across most countries, but there is a difference in approach towards occupational health's involvement in testing. In some countries testing may need to be part of the occupational health remit (e.g. Finland, France, Ireland, see Chapter 4). However, where this is not prescribed, the occupational health department will have views on how closely they will want to be involved in the testing regime. Some may have the view that occupational health should only be concerned with the individual's health, not with policing a safety policy. However, personal medical information may be obtained during the testing process, and storing this would normally be within the remit of the occupational health department. These different views highlight the need for involving all departments in the policy development.

Line management and employee representatives

These are the people who will have closest involvement with the application of the policy on a day-to-day basis. They will be able to identify and resolve many of the operational issues that will arise. Their input will be an essential contribution to a practical and effective policy. They will be the people who have to spend most time explaining the policy and responding to queries so their understanding of the purpose of the policy, and the reasoning behind the words and phrases used within the policy document will smooth its introduction and ongoing implementation. It is critical that their views and concerns are listened to and addressed, as they will have prime responsibility for policy implementation.

Company lawyers/public relations

Although these two functions may not be specifically represented in the working group, their overview and input into the final version of the policy and its implementation is important because they are the people who are likely to be called on if things go wrong. If the company is too small to merit a specific PR function, then whoever would normally respond to external questions about the company's attitudes and working practices should be fully informed about the progress of the policy.

Drug testing service providers

If the decision is taken to include testing, then remember that your service provider should be a good source of information on the practicalities of implementing a drug testing programme, and if involved early on in the process can give valuable help. The working party could invite several service providers to make presentations, which would give them the opportunity to learn, compare and evaluate the common themes.

Working group activities

The working group (which could comprise anything from 2 to over 20 people, depending on the size of the company) has the responsibility for developing the policy along the lines of the agreed objectives.

To demonstrate commitment to the policy, it is important to start by agreeing a schedule of regular meetings, with a target date for completion. Built into this schedule should be plans for communicating the policy and its progress to the remainder of the workforce. The communication need not start immediately; it can wait until the policy is taking shape, at which point useful and constructive feedback can be obtained.

Some research may be necessary – for example looking for references to drugs and alcohol in existing company policies and also looking at how other policies that raise issues of personal rights (mobile phones, dress code, smoking) have been managed. The working group may also have to consider how company-sponsored social events will be managed in the context of their proposed policy.

Information can be sought from local, national and international sources, although it is always wise to consider the ethos of the source and balance this against the company's own values. For example, the United States is a good source of information on the practicalities of drug testing, but the cultural response to drug issues is substantially different to that in much of Europe.

In the UK the national sources of information are the Health and Safety Executive, the TUC (Trade Unions Congress) and the CBI (Confederation of British Industry), as well as the charities DrugScope and Alcohol Concern. Similar safety, union and employer organisations in other countries should be a source of information or opinion. A very useful source of international information is the ILO (International Labour Organization) SafeWork workplace drug and alcohol abuse prevention programmes.[5]

Other companies in the local area or similar industry may have policies available for comparison. The working group must consider carefully whether elements of other organisations' policies will work within their own company.

The working group members are the people who will have to answer questions on the policy so they should agree on wording that is meaningful and understandable, and they should check that they all put the same interpretation on it. Within the constraints of company policy templates, simple explanations should be used, and contentious issues should not be hidden in over-elaborate language as this will increase the risk of ambiguity and the suspicion that the organisation has a hidden agenda.

Inevitably questions will be asked, and it is arguable that the more detail that is provided, the more questions that will be provoked. Box 5.1 shows a list of the sort of questions that have been asked of policies within the UK. This questioning process should be viewed constructively, and where genuine anomalies or impractical steps are identified, amendments should be made.

The formal communication of the policy and the date from which it, and testing, becomes effective should be done in accordance with the organisation's normal process for the introduction or amendment of company policies. Sometimes there is a requirement for signed acceptance of changes to terms and conditions of employment, or it may be sufficient for the principle of testing to be accepted by the employee representatives.

Key elements of a policy

There are four key elements of a successful drug and alcohol policy:

- policy document
- education
- help
- monitoring compliance.

Policy document

The actual format of the policy document will have to conform to the template for other policies within a particular organisation, but there are some standard features that need to be covered.

Box 5.1 *Drug and alcohol testing programmes – questions asked*

- Why does the company see the need to test?
- Why are you testing for drug use, not impaired work performance?
- If an employee feels capable of working, is it fair to catch them out with random tests?
- What are the consequences of refusing to take a test?

About the tests

- How long will someone be kept if they are suffering from 'shy bladder'?
- What are the cut-off levels for the drug tests? Who sets them?
- What is the risk of a false positive result?
- What protection does the chain of custody give?
- Why aren't steroids and solvents included?

Follow-up to positive results

- What if the individual refuses help? Isn't dismissal then the only option?
- Can the individual go straight to HR with problem if manager is unsympathetic?
- If an individual is re-deployed, won't it be obvious that they have a drug/alcohol problem?
- How will you treat someone who tests positive for methadone?
- Will someone who opts for treatment avoid disciplinary consequences – is it the 'easy option'?
- What data on drug testing is available for comparison with the company's results?
- Will job applicants who have positive results be offered help?
- How is 'help' made available? How do managers direct people to help?

Random selection

- How was the random rate decided? Will it be changed? When will it stop?
- Will the selection process be published?
- How will shift workers and people frequently away from site (i.e. sales) be dealt with?

- If you get a positive result from random testing, will this person be targeted next time?
- How many times will a person be tested each year?
- Who will make the decision about 'unavailability' for random tests? Managers will have greater opportunity to avoid tests.

Contractors

- Will contractors have pre-access tests?
- Will you tell other companies if a contractor tests positive?
- Are temporary staff treated as contractors?
- Will visitors be subject to the policy?
- Will company employees from other divisions be subject to the policy?
- How will contractors be made aware of the policy?
- How will self-employed contractors be made aware of the policy?
- Continental contractors may have different attitude to drugs – is it fair to impose a policy on them – their own company may tolerate drug/alcohol use?
- Has the company considered that there may be a risk of excess charges from contractors if their employees are delayed because of drug tests?

General

- Will accident investigation reports identify if person is undergoing treatment?
- Will testing lead to under-reporting and/or misleading investigations to justify not testing?
- Who would you test if an incident occurs because individual was varying procedures on manager's instructions?
- How will the company respond to anonymous phone calls alleging drug misuse?
- What would the company do if cannabis were legalised?
- How do you intend to achieve consistency in drug testing 'for cause' decisions?
- What is the cost of testing? Couldn't the money be better spent elsewhere?
- Why don't you test for drugs at routine medicals?
- What do you do while waiting for the results to come through?

Source: © Concateno plc

The opening statement needs to summarise the purpose of the policy. Sample introductory paragraphs are shown in Box 5.2.

The statement should continue with the rules concerning the possession and consumption of alcohol, illegal drugs and medicines. This summary should briefly detail the consequences if the rules are broken and make clear the measures that will be taken to ensure compliance with the policy.

The policy statement is expressing the principles of the policy. Some organisations may prefer to include the detail in their policy document – others may provide the detailed guidelines in separate supporting documents. The advantage of this latter approach is that changes to practical details can be made more easily, while the principles underlying the policy remain intact.

Either way, covering the following points will contribute to the understanding, acceptance and effectiveness of the policy.

- Information to support the need for the drug and alcohol policy (i.e. the justification built up from your 'risk assessment').
- The detail of the rules governing the use of drugs and alcohol. The policy should distinguish between impairment due to the inappropriate use of drugs and/or alcohol, and dependency or personal problems resulting from their use.
- The disciplinary process that will apply if the rules are broken. The seriousness of the response will reflect the company culture and the nature of its business.
- Explanation of the measures to ensure compliance with the policy, which should include education on drug and alcohol issues.
- Information about the help available for employees, and how to access this.
- The drug testing programme, detailing who is eligible, and on what occasions. Drug testing protocols should be available for inspection.

Definitions of key terms such as 'misuse', 'drugs', 'positive result' are needed to avoid ambiguity. In the case of a word like 'misuse' the definition will help to avoid disputes arising from subjective opinions. 'Drugs' could mean illegal drugs, prescription drugs and over-the-counter medicines – it should be clear which of these are included. If the term 'substance' abuse is preferred, a definition will be required to identify which types of substances are subject to the policy.

Education

Communication is an essential part of building confidence in the policy. If employees understand the purpose of the policy, can see that it has clear and unthreatening objectives, and that they have the opportunity to give feedback, on the whole they will feel more comfortable with what they may otherwise see as an intrusion into their private life.

Box 5.2 *Sample opening statements for drug and alcohol policies*

- The abuse and misuse of alcohol and drugs is a significant and growing problem in today's society, and unfortunately the company cannot expect to be exempt. Management has a prime responsibility to take reasonable measures to ensure employee well-being and that any use of alcohol or drugs by employees or third parties involved in the company's operations does not jeopardise safety, performance or otherwise adversely affect the company.
- The company hold the health and safety of its employees to be of paramount importance and is committed to ensuring the highest possible safety standards. The purpose of the drug and alcohol policy is to maintain safe and efficient operational standards, to promote the health and well-being of the company's employees, and to ensure that their interests are protected in any accident investigation. Drug testing will be used to help us achieve this aim, to provide both a deterrent to use and a reminder of the company's expectations.
- The company recognises the generally responsible attitude of its employees, and believes that its Drug and Alcohol Policy should be primarily based on training, advice, recommendations and guidance. However the company also recognises its international and regulatory responsibility to implement a formal policy. Some rules, including testing for drugs and alcohol on a random and 'for cause' basis, must be implemented to protect the well being and safety of the vast majority from the occasional imprudence of a small minority.
- The company is committed to providing a safe, productive and healthy workplace for its employees, and acknowledges and appreciates a responsible attitude shown by all employees towards safety issues. The company recognises that alcohol, drug, or other substance misuse by individuals can have an adverse effect on their ability to perform work and consequently put the company and others as well as themselves at significant risk. The company has identified a need to respond to public concerns about the nature of its operation, its contractual obligations and its compliance with legislation. This policy aims to demonstrate that all possible steps are being taken to eliminate risk to individuals, the public and the environment.

- The company has a responsibility towards employees to provide a safe and healthy working environment and recognises that this may be jeopardised by those who misuse alcohol and drugs. The company also has to protect its business and commercial interests from the consequences of any such misuse. The company will, therefore, take appropriate action to protect all employees' health, safety and welfare, company property and the efficiency and success of our business against substance abuse.
- For reasons of health and safety, efficiency and effectiveness, and responsibilities towards customers and the public, the company is committed to a workplace free of substance misuse. The company recognises the importance of balancing respect for individual privacy with the need to maintain a safe, secure, and productive working environment free of alcohol and drug misuse. The policy encourages those employees who are experiencing difficulties with drugs, alcohol, or any other substance to seek help. Evidence of breach of this policy may be treated as serious misconduct that may lead to termination of employment.
- The company expects employees to be fit to carry out their work duties at all times without any risk of their performance being impaired or their efficiency reduced by drugs or alcohol. This applies equally to work in an office, on a site, or while travelling on company business. Any breach is regarded as gross misconduct. Nevertheless the company is anxious to help employees before a dependency on alcohol or drugs impairs their performance at work. The aim of the company's rehabilitation policy is to help the employee achieve successful treatment and return to productive employment with the minimum disruption to work, personal and social life.
- The company is committed to maintaining a healthy and productive workplace through the highest standards of safety and employment practice. The company recognises that the use of illegal drugs, misuse of legal drugs and the abuse of alcohol can impair job performance and can be a serious threat to safety, health, productivity and the environment. The company will minimize the risks involved by ensuring that all employees, subcontractors and other providers of services to this company are made aware of this policy as part of its induction and communication procedures.

There are four strands to the education process associated with a drug and alcohol policy. The first three are essential if the policy is to benefit both the organisation and individual employees. Education leads to understanding, and understanding to acceptance of the need for the policy. If the policy is accepted, most people will work towards ensuring that it is effective.

The first strand is the basic communication about the policy itself, so that employees cannot claim ignorance of its content. This process may start with the information released by the working group as the policy develops, but the completed policy must have some formal acknowledgement of inclusion into the company's procedures. If this step is neglected, employees could argue that although they are aware of the discussion phase, they did not realise that the policy had become 'live' and that they were now subject to its rules. The basic information about the policy must also be integrated into new employee and site visitor induction programmes. Depending on the size and resources of the organisation, newsletters, payslips, toolbox talks, etc. can be used to get the information about the policy circulated, discussed, amended and approved.

The second strand is general education on the effects and consequences of drug and alcohol use. With the exception of messages about safe driving, the adult population tends to be neglected by drug and alcohol awareness campaigns, which are usually designed either for schoolchildren or problem users. The general adult population remains uninformed and left to make assumptions based on information published in the media, which may present an alarmist and distorted version of the truth. However, within the workplace the problems associated with the inappropriate use of drugs and alcohol can be brought to employees' attention either directly linked to the policy, or aligned with other education campaigns on personal health, or as part of a workplace safety campaign. This information will help employees understand how they may need to moderate their drug use to comply with the policy requirements. Education can be provided by whatever means is appropriate to the organisation – it could be simple leaflets, on-line computer-based interactive learning, videos or visiting speakers – and it needs to be ongoing, planned to be repeated on a regular basis.

The first two types of education are company wide. Between them they should raise awareness of the issues, and show how the policy seeks to address them, for the benefit of the organisation and the employees. It is important to have commitment from all management to release people to attend education sessions or complete on-line training, if this is the chosen route.

Within the company there will be people who are likely to be directly involved in the application of the policy – line managers, supervisors, human resources, employee representatives. These people need to have confidence in their ability to handle situations that the policy might generate, and need to become aware of the signs to look out for. This is especially important if they are expected to take decisions about whether to ask someone to take a 'for cause' test. Without confidence in their own judgement, and the knowledge that they have the support of the company, the easy option would be to do nothing, and as a result the policy would gradually be undermined. The education should make them appreciate the importance of accurate recording of absence and accident statistics and other information which could be the first indicator of a developing problem. If these are ignored this could be a lost opportunity to encourage someone to seek help before the need for testing or disciplinary action.

The final strand is the requirement for specific training which may be necessary if some parts of the alcohol and drug testing programme are to be operated by the company. If alcohol breath test equipment is purchased for use on site, then the operators must have training in the operation, calibration and maintenance of the devices. Some occupational health departments may opt to collect the samples for laboratory drug analysis, which will require training to ensure that full 'chain of custody' procedures are understood and followed. And if the company's medical officer intends to receive the results from the laboratory, then training in the medical review officer role will be necessary to get a full understanding of how to interpret the results. As with all technical training, this should be subject to regular competency assessment and planned refresher training.

Employee Assistance Programme

Broadly, the aim of an Employee Assistance Programme (EAP) is to prevent an employee with problems becoming a problem employee.

The remit of the EAP should be much wider than just drug and alcohol issues. An EAP should function as a resource which employees can turn to for help in resolving work or personal matters. Such concerns may affect work performance, and in some cases, where the employee 'self-medicates' with alcohol or drugs, become the start of 'problem use'.

An EAP provider should be able to offer help across a wide range of topics, covering work-related issues such as relationships with colleagues, work/life balance, harassment, bullying and stress as well as personal issues that might distract the individual from their work, for example family problems, the need to care for relatives, problems with neighbours, consumer issues, medical advice and so on.

Ideally, access to the EAP would be via a telephone helpline available round the clock. Calls can be made from work or home, using an agreed means of identification – company name, password, PIN. The people answering the phone are likely to be from the caring professions (e.g. nurses, doctors, psychologists) as they will be in a position to deal with a caller's immediate emotional crises. If the caller is seeking advice on less pressured legal, financial or other issues, then the EAP service should be able to arrange for them to speak to an appropriate professional adviser. Most EAP services will give access to assessment and counselling sessions, with all the appropriate safeguards for confidentiality.

The EAP service provider should be able to provide management reports at agreed periods. These should show anonymous statistical data about the usage of the service, which could help the organisation understand the type of problems their employees are facing. Beyond that, the service should be completely confidential.

The benefit an EAP brings to the company's objectives for its drug and alcohol policy is firstly preventative. Too often the individual will use the 'oblivion' qualities of alcohol and drugs as a way of temporarily forgetting about the problem that they need to confront, but this temporary solution may become permanent unless the problem itself is solved – and that is what the EAP is there for.

The second benefit is having access to support for people with drug or alcohol problems. This may start with a supervisor or line manager ringing the helpline for advice on how to manage a particular situation, how to raise the issue with the individual, how to encourage the individual to seek help. Drug and alcohol problems are personal to each individual and require an initial assessment meeting before any decision can be taken on treatment. The treatment needs to be matched, not imposed, so an EAP service should be able to provide access to a wide range of treatment options.

Where EAP services are not available, local resources should be identified where people can turn to for help. The policy should be clear that 'help' is a genuine option for people who acknowledge that their use of alcohol and/or drugs is becoming a problem.

Whatever is provided, there should be regular reminders that the services are available and how they can be accessed. This should help all employees to move away from the belief that the best approach is to hide problems with drugs and alcohol and cover up for colleagues even when it is clear they have problems. Although this is a natural protective instinct, the individual concerned will benefit more from being encouraged to seek help while they still have a job.

Treatment for employees with problems

This encouragement for employees to seek help does not necessarily require a commitment from the company to pay for treatment. Help given to people with drug and alcohol problems can sometimes be perceived by co-workers as unfairly generous, so time off and funding for treatment should be dealt with in accordance with the company's policy on health matters.

To ensure the employee's participation in the chosen treatment option the company might agree a contract with the individual, which could stipulate regular attendance at counselling sessions, may make allowances for the fact that relapses are a common feature of giving up an addiction, and could include regular testing as a way of demonstrating that the problem use has been overcome.

Monitoring compliance with the drug and alcohol policy

Compliance with the policy can be recorded in various ways. Training records should be maintained to show the pro-active and ongoing approach to drug and alcohol education. Absence, accident and work performance records should be reviewed regularly to spot problems before they become entrenched. Usage of the EAP is an indicator that problems are being solved, and that employees have responded to the idea that help is available.

Testing is a valuable monitoring tool, because over time it provides statistics. The focus tends to be on positive results, but negative results are the marker of a successful policy. The American Civil Liberties Union (ACLU) circulated a report in 1999 which questioned the cost effectiveness of drug testing. By totalling all the costs associated with the federal drug testing programme, and then dividing by the number of positive results, ACLU quoted a figure of US$77 000 to find one drug user.[6] Where the objective of a drug testing programme is to deter drug use, then the higher the cost per single positive result, the more effective the programme.

What does testing bring to a policy?

Testing for drugs and alcohol within a policy is seen by some as an unnecessary step, one that intrudes into a person's private life and breaches their right to privacy under Article 8 of the European Human Rights Act.

Article 8 may give the right to privacy in private life but this right is balanced by the requirement not to affect other people's rights. As always, European laws get interpreted in the context of national cultures but the key is that the response must be proportional. Chapter 4 explores these aspects in more detail.

It is also argued that testing can destroy trust and undermine employee relations, which indeed it could if introduced without the explanation, discussion or justification described in this chapter.

A drug and alcohol policy does not have to include testing – however doing so can bring benefits, providing the policy development has followed the steps outlined above.

The principal benefit is that testing makes people notice the policy. Without testing the policy will be one paper policy among others – how many employees will (a) be aware of any rules and (b) consider they have to comply with them? Tell them that testing is about to be introduced and they will study the policy in detail to find out how they might be affected. And if unannounced testing based on random selection is included they will be constantly aware of the fact that they might be tested while at work, so will modify their social behaviour to make sure that their drug or alcohol consumption will not breach the policy. So testing helps with the first policy objective identified above by providing a deterrent to drug use, especially if random testing is used. This can help reduce the risks to the workplace and can benefit individuals by making them think about their own consumption, so possibly stopping a slow slide into problem use.

Testing raises concerns and prompts questions, so introducing testing encourages a company to invest more in education and supervisory support than they might do otherwise. Supervisors who may have to request 'with suspicion' tests will be particularly keen to learn the signs to look out for, and this increased knowledge can help with the positive intervention for problem users.

Testing helps to identify individuals who need help in two ways. Obviously a positive test result will prompt an investigation, and this may be the stimulus the individual needs to acknowledge that they do indeed have a problem. Many companies also find that as the policy gets discussed during its development stage and people become aware of the implications of testing, those who recognise that they will have difficulty complying with the testing programme will come forward to seek help – but only if they are aware of the help available, which takes us back to the importance of education, information and communication.

In these days of measurement as proof of management, testing provides statistics. Reduction in positivity levels or continuous negative results can demonstrate effective management of drug and alcohol issues, and provide the evidence necessary for compliance with legislative, regulatory and contractual requirements.

Testing – the practicalities

There are several decisions that have to be made if testing is to be integrated into a policy on drugs and alcohol. In some countries the options may be limited by local legislation. The list of questions below will have different answers according to the size, location and business activity of the organisation, but can be used as a basic checklist.

The issues to some extent reflect the various conventions that have become associated with the process of workplace drug testing. In some countries these may be mandatory, but where they are not the subjects need to be addressed to reduce the fear and uncertainty often associated with testing. Typical concerns relate to the accuracy of the testing, the risk of 'false positive' results, the degree of privacy and confidentiality surrounding the testing process, how the results are disclosed to the individual, and who within the organisation gets to see the results. There is also a perception that there are opportunities to cheat the test process, which can make people question whether any credence can be put on the results. The reliability and robustness of the test procedures is addressed elsewhere in this book, and these are fundamental to the success of a testing programme.

The policy, in either its main or supporting documents, needs to make sure that the following questions are answered:

1. What will be the consequences of a positive result?
2. Who will be eligible for testing?
3. Why and when will people be tested?
4. What drugs will be included in the tests?
5. Who will carry out the testing? (collection and analysis)
6. What is a 'positive' result for drugs, and alcohol?
7. Who will interpret the results?
8. What records will be kept, and who will have access to them?
9. What will be the consequences if someone refuses to take a test, or is clearly trying to defeat the test process?
10. How will the disclosure of illegal or problem drug use once a test is under way be handled?

What will be the consequences of a positive result?

An obvious first question is what will be the consequences of a positive result? There is an important distinction between 'drugs' and 'alcohol' which should be reflected in the wording of the policy. International drink/driving laws mean there is an accepted relationship between blood alcohol levels and impairment, and the time over which alcohol is eliminated from the body; however a positive drug test result merely provides evidence of use. It is not possible to say whether the individual was impaired at the time of the test, or when or where the drug was taken. This means that dismissal for an offence worded as 'impaired by the use of illegal drugs' or 'using drugs on company premises' might be challenged if the only evidence is a positive drug test result.

The disciplinary consequences of breaking the company rules will already have been specified but consideration must be given as to how test results fit into this process. It must be clear that a positive test result is a breach of the policy, irrespective of impairment or when the drug was used. However refusal to take a test, or deliberate interference with the test procedures should not be assumed as evidence of guilt, but should be dealt with under disciplinary procedures as refusal to comply with a company policy (unless national laws give entitlement to refuse to be tested).

There is an assumption that employees who test positive must lose their jobs. This may be appropriate for some organisations, but generally companies treat a positive result as a warning sign of developing problem use, not as a dismissal issue. However, the consequences of a positive result are always significant for the individual concerned, and this must be reflected in the standard of analysis. Employees must have confidence that they cannot be wrongly accused of alcohol or drug misuse, so using a drug testing organisation that follows the European Workplace Drug Testing Society Guidelines is essential (see Chapter 11).

Who will be eligible for testing?

'Safety critical' posts head the list of acceptable eligible job functions. The problem can come when defining which jobs should be considered as safety critical. In some businesses the decision can be made by looking at other identifiers, such as 'unescorted access' within a particular area – this may then include some people whose work may be administrative. Other approaches are to include those people with responsibility for people in safety critical posts, since they may take decisions that affect the working conditions, for example by increasing time pressures.

Some organisations may consider business critical factors to be as important as safety critical. In others the working group developing the policy may get feedback that all employees from directors down should be subject to testing. A decision also has to be taken on whether temporary staff, agency staff, contractors and visitors be subject to all or part of the testing programme, and, if so, how will this will be communicated to them.

Why and when will people be tested?

The typical occasions for testing are outlined in Box 5.3. They fall broadly into those used to detect drug use, and those that will be helpful in deterring drug use. It has to be remembered that a drug test is a snapshot in time, merely indicating whether drugs are absent or present at the time of the test.

Pre-employment testing is often described as an intelligence test, as most employable drug users would be able to abstain for long enough to achieve a negative result. In countries where pre-employment testing is permitted, the applicant must be fully aware that testing will be part of the recruitment process. To minimise the need for testing, it should be carried out as the last step in the recruitment process, as a condition of the job offer. However, if the applicant starts work before the result of the test is known, this may negate the condition, as the individual would then be subject to the organisation's terms and conditions of employment.

'For cause' testing is investigative, but is after the event (an accident, or behaviour giving rise to concern) has happened. Defining the category of incident that would automatically trigger a 'with cause' test causes much

Box 5.3 Opportunities for testing

Opportunity	Advantages	Disadvantages
Pre-employment	Establishes company's attitude to drugs and alcohol Deters drug users joining company Does not require changes to terms and conditions of employment Helps to introduce concept of testing to other employees	Result is only true for the day of the test No deterrent factor May create 'blacklist' of applicants in some sectors Needs record keeping to avoid repeat testing
Pre-access	Variation on pre-employment, where companies insist that all contractors must have a negative drug test result before being allowed on site. If an individual fails the test, they would not be allowed on to the site, although they may still retain their employment with the subcontracting company	
Routine medicals	Can be integrated into medical	Advance notice of dates means alcohol/illegal drug use can be adjusted to avoid detection Association with 'policing policy' compromises health benefit aspects
Post accident/post incident	Indicates whether drugs or alcohol might have contributed to incident Demonstrates that drugs/alcohol did not contribute to incident which brings PR benefits and reassurance to individual concerned	Unless integral part of any accident/incident investigation, testing may not be used If drug or alcohol related this is identified after event (i.e. too late)
'Reasonable cause' (i.e. behavioural indicators)	May confirm suspicion of drug/alcohol consumption contributing to impairment and/or deteriorating work performance If negative, may direct attention to some medical condition or other cause	Perception of victimisation If behaviour is drug or alcohol related then problem use has probably already developed
Unannounced, random selection	Constant possibility of selection means constant threat of detection Impartial selection method – can be made available for inspection by employee representatives Deterrent effect encourages people to examine and amend drug/alcohol habits, and recognise problem use at an earlier stage	Need to guard against risk that administrative convenience can lead to bias in selection process Need to closely define and monitor reasons for 'unavailability' for test

Box 5.3 (continued)

Opportunity	Advantages	Disadvantages
	Nil or below-average positive rate is positive image for company Demonstrates company's pro-active approach to safety etc.	
Monitoring	Used as disciplinary option after a positive result Useful to help individual demonstrate recovery from problem use	Regular testing needs management

Source: © Concateno plc

debate, but can be justified by looking at past data on accidents, and by being clear on whether the tests are to be used to show that drugs and alcohol did or did not play a part in the accident. In this way it becomes merely a process and does not carry any implication about the behaviour of the individuals being tested. Where there is a suspicion of drugs as a cause for unusual behaviour the decision to test needs to be based on clear criteria agreed within the organisation, and typically based on work performance, absence and accident records, and knowledge of the individual. Testing on the basis of behaviour can cause great anxiety, and as a result can be under-used unless the training and support for supervisors is maintained. Consistency for 'with cause' tests is essential if accusations of victimisation are to be avoided, so it needs to be reviewed regularly. This review needs to cover occasions when tests did not take place, as well as the occasions when they did. The policy also needs to specify what happens to the individual while waiting for the results, which if positive may not be available for some days. Reliable on-site screening tests can reduce the cost of personnel downtime, since only 'not negative' results would have to go for laboratory analysis.

Unannounced random testing provides the best deterrent, but needs safeguards for it to be recognised as a deterrent to the inappropriate use of drugs and alcohol. For random testing to be accepted, the basis for selection needs to be perceived as fair, and removed from the influence of management. If this cannot be achieved within the organisation, an external agency can be used. The selection can be as simple as a draw from the names of people present, or at the opposite extreme an elaborate computer-based tracking and selection process. Statisticians can debate the relative chance of detection at varying rates of random selection, but frequency and visibility (i.e. the knowledge that random testing is occurring) are more important factors in making sure that employees are aware that testing does take place. Eligible employees should understand that any time they are at work they may be selected for testing without warning. Random testing should not be predictable (i.e. not always on Mondays) and should not have 'blind spots' where it is known that testing will not take place. The proposed random selection process should be carefully reviewed for bias against particular groups (e.g. day workers more likely to be selected than shift workers).

Thought needs to be given as to who within the organisation will be given notice of a scheduled test, and penalties need to be applied if this information is circulated. The notification to the individuals selected for testing should be kept to a minimum, subject to the operational constraints of the business.

The essence of random selection is that every eligible employee has an equal chance of being chosen on every occasion that the selection is made. Further, the pattern of selection – the frequency interval between tests, the days and times of day – must be unpredictable. The method of selection should be demonstrably random and open to inspection by employee representatives. It is particularly important that the random selection method cannot be influenced, as suspicion that it is being used to target individuals will quickly reduce confidence in the programme and devalue the deterrent effect.

The distinction between random and 'for cause' testing must be maintained. Those selected must be confident that no assumptions will be made about their fitness to work at the time of the test, so they should return to work after the specimen for analysis has been collected. The use of on-site screening tests does not contribute anything useful to random testing.

What drugs will be included in the tests?

The best advice on drugs to include in the testing panel will come from your chosen analytical service provider. Alcohol, cannabis, amphetamines and cocaine are widely used recreational drugs, while the depressant drugs that have both medicinal use and abuse potential can be included. See Chapter 8 on the analytical process.

Who will carry out the testing? (collection and analysis)

Employees will be concerned about the testing process, because whichever matrix is used, urine, oral fluid, hair, there is an element of intrusiveness and loss of dignity. In some jurisdictions testing has to be carried out in a medical environment, but whether this should be the company's own medical department or an external one is a decision that has to be made. The use of independent collectors can avoid internal disquiet about occupational health in a 'policing' role, or security officers having access to personal information. Whoever collects the sample, they need to have guidance on what do to if problems arise during the collection, examples of which are given in Chapter 6.

Chapter 6 details the 'chain of custody' requirements that contribute to the 'informed consent' of the individual to the testing process. There are two stages of consent to testing. The first is the informed acceptance of the inclusion of testing within the drug and alcohol policy, which can be achieved by following the steps outlined in the earlier part of this chapter. The expectation will be that the employee will agree to take a drug/alcohol test whenever they are asked.

Thereafter each time they are asked to provide a sample (breath, urine, oral fluid, hair, blood) they should give their consent for that sample to be analysed. For such consent to be 'informed', the individual must be aware that it is a drug/alcohol test and they must be satisfied that it is their sample appropriately identified for testing.

The European Workplace Drug Testing Society (EWDTS) guidelines specify acceptable and reliable analytical methods, supported by appropriate quality control and assurance. Accepted by European accreditation agencies, laboratories that work to these standards will provide robust support for the testing programme within the drug and alcohol policy.

It is accepted good practice to allow the individual the right to challenge positive test results. In Europe this has evolved into a process where the individual witnesses the specimen (oral fluid, urine, hair) they have provided split into two portions, each of which is sealed. Only one of these portions is used for the analysis, with the second portion retained for independent analysis if requested. The policy should make it clear that such challenges will be allowed, but make it clear at whose expense – the company's or the individual's.

What is a 'positive' result for drugs and alcohol?

The policy must make clear what is meant by a positive result for drugs and for alcohol. A typical definition of a positive drug test result is 'a laboratory-positive result that has no legitimate medical explanation'.

There are one or two areas where the jargon associated with testing in some languages can conflict with the layman's use of the word. For example as described elsewhere (Chapter 8) the analysis that results in a positive result is a two-stage process whereby the samples are first 'screened', and those that are not negative are then 'confirmed'. If 'drug screening' is used within the policy as the generic term for drug testing, this can cause confusion – would 'positive drug screen' mean a positive screening test in the laboratory context, or a confirmed positive result?

This becomes especially relevant when on-site screening tests are used. With on-site tests the knowledge of a 'not negative' (i.e. presumptive positive) result has to be managed within the workplace, as it quickly becomes apparent when someone has not been allowed to return to work pending laboratory confirmation analysis.

For alcohol a level in blood, breath and urine is usually quoted, and is typically linked to the drink driving laws of the country (although in the UK, which has a high drink driving cut-off, many companies have opted for a cut-off lower than the drink driving legislation). Breath testing is considered the most appropriate way of testing for alcohol. A urine alcohol test may be considered a useful way of confirming a positive breath test result, but the levels of alcohol in the urine could be substantially different to the breath test result. Will you allow a urine test result to override a breath test result? These issues need the input of your medical adviser or the organisation chosen to provide the testing services.

The relationship of the result to impairment, and the conclusions that can be drawn are covered in Chapter 10, and as already recommended must be dealt with carefully in the policy.

Who will interpret the results?

Unqualified personnel must not be able to make judgements about positive results, and disciplinary proceedings should not be started on the basis of a laboratory-positive result that has not been through a medical review process, or on the basis of an on-site test result which has yet to be confirmed. The concept of medical review is essentially to make sure that a test result is interpreted correctly, and that the legitimate use of medication does not get confused with drug abuse. The importance of the medical review process merits a separate chapter, as it is an integral part of the acceptability of workplace drug testing (see Chapter 10). As a consequence of this review process the individual may be aware of the medical review officer outcome (i.e. positive or negative) before the company, and in some organisations this may not be acceptable, so alternative procedures would have to be developed.

What records will be kept, by whom, and where? Who will have access to them?

Testing generates records, and care needs to be taken that information is not obtained or stored unnecessarily or passed to third parties in breach of data protection laws.

People will question how the results will be handled. They need assurance that they will remain confidential, irrespective of whether they are negative or positive. If problem use is diagnosed, how much information will be passed to line management, bearing in mind that the individual may need support on returning to work.

Information on recent medication is taken into account if the test result is positive. How this information is obtained and recorded will again be affected by cultural variations, but it is important that individuals have confidence in the process, and disclosure of sensitive personal information is treated with care and respect for data protection legislation.

If job applicants are refused employment because of a positive result, will your policy have a rule that such individuals cannot re-apply within a certain time frame? How will this be managed? Similarly, if contractors are expected to have a negative drug test result before they come on site, how will this be monitored?

What will be the consequences if someone refuses to take a test, or is clearly trying to defeat the test process?

The policy must cover as a separate disciplinary issue what will happen if a person refuses to be tested. The penalty must be at least equal to that for a positive result, but it must not be assumed that the individual is refusing because they anticipate a positive result. The offence is refusing the request to be tested.

Similarly there must be a disciplinary consequence if someone is discovered trying to cheat the test process, by substituting, adulterating or otherwise tampering with the specimen to be tested. The organisation should agree with the service provider about how information on 'cheating' is communicated back to the company. It may be identified during the collection process, or during the analysis.

How will you handle 'late' disclosure of illegal or problem drug use during the test procedures?

The relationship of the drug testing programme to the policy as a whole must be clearly defined. Will the access to help, in whatever form it takes, be given to anyone who admits to problem use, even if this is at the time they are asked to take a drug test? Will the reason for the test make a difference? For example, if there are concerns about an individual's performance that result in a request for a test to establish whether drug use is contributing to the performance issue, and this prompts an admission from the individual, that is a demonstration that testing can help an individual confront the problem. However, if an admission of problem drug use is made when an individual is asked to take a random test, this might be viewed as the individual trying to mitigate the consequences of a positive result. Employment legislation, national laws and your own company culture will determine your company policy for these situations.

There may be occasions when an individual admits to the person collecting the sample that they have taken illegal drugs recently. The collector needs to know what to do with this information, as they have a duty of care to your company, as well as the need to respect the confidentiality of the individual. If your expectation is that you should be told, what will you do with this information? There is no guarantee that the drug test result will be positive, so does your policy cover an admission of drug use that took place in the individual's own time?

Conclusion

Drug and alcohol policies touch on employees' private lives, but there is growing recognition that the consequences of inappropriate use can impact on the workplace. The issues cannot be ignored, but they can be handled constructively, if the policy is based on considered judgement of the risk that drugs and alcohol create. The policy should be considered as part of a package that will deliver a positive message to employees – and education and support for employees' problems are necessary parts of this package.

When added as the final element in the drug and alcohol policy, testing helps bring the objectives of the company's drug and alcohol policy into focus. The policy is not simply another chapter in the company's protocols, but becomes something that affects all employees. It makes employees react to the policy, and listen to the education messages. It demonstrates to outsiders that the company is serious in its policy objectives, and over time it provides statistics.

Pre-employment testing establishes the organisation's attitude to drugs and alcohol. Testing after incidents is investigative rather than preventative, and has value in identifying and eliminating possible causes. Testing in the workplace context is best considered as a deterrent to drug use, not a way of detecting drug users, and this is where the benefit of a properly administered random programme lies. The selection method must be impartial and available for inspection by employee representatives. The possibility of selection must always be there, to encourage people to amend their drug/alcohol habits. It can also help individuals to acknowledge their problem use at an early stage.

Testing is becoming an expected, even accepted, part of workplace life, but it should never be the starting point of an organisation's drug and alcohol policy.

Sources of information

International Labour Organization 'SafeWork' – comprehensive advice and information on the management of drug and alcohol issues within the workplace.

European Monitoring Centre for Drugs and Drug Addiction (EMCDDA) – source of information on drugs in Europe, including new member states and Norway. Includes the European Legal Database on Drugs which contains information on the status of drug testing.

References

1. European Monitoring Centre for Drugs and Drug Addiction (EMCDDA) Annual reports. The state of the drugs problem in Europe – analysis and statistics. www.emcdda.europa.eu (accessed November 2010).
2. Research Development and Statistics Directorate, Home Office. Prevalence of drug use: Key findings from the 2001/2002 British Crime Survey British Crime Survey 2001/2002. www.homeoffice.gov.uk/rds/index (accessed November 2010).
3. European Opinion and Research Group (EORG) (2002) Attitudes and opinions of young people in the European Union on drugs. Eurobarometer 57.2. http://ec.europa.eu/public_opinion/archives/ebs/ebs_172_en.pdf (accessed November 2010).
4. Research Development and Statistics Directorate, Home Office. Drug Misuse Declared: Findings from the British Crime Survey 2007/2008.
5. International Labour Organization (ILO). SafeWork. Workplace drug and alcohol abuse prevention programmes. www.ilo.org/public/english/protection/safework/drug/index (accessed November 2010).
6. American Civil Liberties Union (ACLU) (1999) Drug Testing: A Bad Investment – Executive Summary (9/30/1999). www.aclu.org/drugpolicy/testing (accessed November 2010).

6

Urine sample collection process

Per Björklöv

Key points

- The collection of donor specimens involves some of the most difficult and sensitive areas of the workplace drug testing process.
- The following steps must be documented: verification of the identity of the donor, proper identification of the specimen with its donor, ensuring that no adulteration or tampering took place and that no unauthorised access to the specimen was possible and the secure transfer of the specimen to each person handling it.
- A collector is a trained individual who instructs and assists the donor at a collection site.
- A specimen collection kit contains two specimen bottles, a collection container, a temperature strip (separate from or incorporated onto the specimen bottle), a custody and control form, bluing (colouring) agent to add to the toilet bowl and tank and tamper-evident tape for securing taps and toilet tank tops.
- Urine collections are not routinely observed in workplace drug testing programmes, but there are cases where workplace specimen collections are directly observed (e.g. if the specimen temperature is outside the acceptable range or if the collector suspects that the donor may have tampered with the specimen).
- For saliva or oral fluid collection a number of specially designed 'oral fluid collection devices' are used.
- Hair is best collected from the area at the back of the head. The sample size varies considerably among laboratories and depends on the drug to be analysed and the test methodology.

Introduction

The collection of donor specimens involves some of the most difficult and sensitive areas of the workplace drug testing process. Despite the reliability of highly sophisticated laboratory analysis, an error by the urine specimen collector at the urine collection site can cause a laboratory-confirmed positive test to be cancelled due to clerical or procedural error. In addition, there are enormous challenges with ensuring specimens sent to the laboratory have not been tampered with. Individuals who use drugs will go to extreme measures to 'beat' the drug positive test. The proliferation of adulterants and substitutes available for purchase on the Internet and elsewhere cannot be understated. This fact increases the complexities associated with collection site security and specimen integrity. Therefore, drug test collectors must be thoroughly trained in basic custody and control procedures, and in how to circumvent (to the best of their ability) specimen tampering and substitution. Training must include security of the collection site and the specimens collected.

While the collector must ensure the integrity of the collection process, the collector must also be sensitive to each employee's privacy, and must respect the dignity of the donor, while at the same time ensuring that the sample is accurately collected and has not been tampered with.

To ensure a balance between the privacy of the donor and need to ensure the proper identification and integrity of the specimen, the following steps must be documented:

- the verification of the identity of the donor
- the proper identification of the specimen with its donor
- that no adulteration or tampering took place
- that no unauthorised access to the specimen was possible
- the secure transfer of the specimen to each person handling it.

This documentation process is the first link in what is referred to as the 'chain-of-custody' process. This process follows a data trail that, when reconstructed at a later date, can be used to prove that the final result properly matches the sample to the donor.

Urine collection

The procedures for collection of urine specimens for workplace drug testing are very specific. It is essential for each collection site to have written standard operating procedures and for collectors to comply with those procedures in order to minimize the possibility of procedural or administrative errors.

Personnel

A collector is a trained individual who instructs and assists the donor at a collection site, who receives and makes an initial inspection of the specimen provided by the donor, and who initiates and completes appropriate sections of the custody and control form (CCF).

Collector qualifications

No certification or medical education is usually required but a training course is necessary. On successful completion of collector training a person may begin performing collections. However, there are a few instances in which a collector may not perform a collection:

- A collector may not perform a collection if he or she is the immediate supervisor of the donor (unless no other collector is available), or if he or she is a co-worker, a relative or a close friend of the employee.
- An individual working for a drug testing laboratory may not act as a collector if that individual can link the donor with the specimen drug test result.

Collector training

Collectors can be trained by various methods (video, classroom, Internet, etc.). However, the training must include, at a minimum, instruction on:

- the collection process
- the chain-of-custody process
- the process involved with 'problem' collections (e.g. shy bladder, temperature out of range)
- the responsibility of the collector for maintaining donor privacy, confidentiality of information, and specimen integrity.

It is highly recommended that, upon completion of the training, each collector is tested on all subject matter covered in the training course to verify their understanding of the topics. It is also highly recommended that each training course include mock collections to assess collector proficiency.

Collection site

A collection site is a facility (permanent or temporary) selected by the employer where donors present themselves for the purpose of providing a urine specimen.

Access to the facility must be limited. Procedures for collection of urine specimens should allow for individual privacy. Preferably, there should be a sign outside prohibiting entry while a collection is occurring.

During the collection, there should be no access to water or other substances that could be used by the donor to substitute or adulterate the specimen. The collector should block areas and remove items that could be used to hide adulterants. There should be a suitable clean surface for the collector to use as a work area and for completing the required paperwork.

Custody and control form (CCF)

Chain of custody is the term used for the process of documenting the handling and storage of the urine specimen from the time the donor gives it to the collector until it is destroyed. A CCF is used to document the collection procedure and the chain of custody of the specimen. In Europe, there are many different types of CCFs (Figure 6.1). Almost every laboratory that performs workplace drug testing has its own version of this form which may also include different numbers of copies for each form.

The CCF is numbered with a unique specimen identification number and includes two bottle labels (i.e. for the primary and split specimens) that are printed with the same specimen identification number as the CCF. The tamper-evident labels also serve to seal the specimen bottles and are applied across the lid of each specimen bottle.

The minimum information required on the CCF is:

- unique specimen identification number
- name, address, e-mail address, and phone number of the testing laboratory
- information identifying the donor (e.g. birth date (YYMMDD) and name)
- information on how to reach the donor during daytime (i.e. telephone number)
- information on how to reach a representative of the employer (i.e. name and telephone number)
- medical review officer (MRO)/physician information (i.e. name, address, telephone phone, e-mail and fax numbers)
- collection site information (i.e. collector name, telephone number)
- date and time of the collection
- names and signatures of all individuals who had custody of the specimen during the collection process.

There should be at least three copies of the CCF to be distributed by the collector as follows:

- the original to the testing laboratory (with the specimen)
- one copy to the donor
- one copy retained by the collector.

There may be some CCF versions with additional copies for the employer and the MRO/physician.

The development of new 'drug testing' software and methods may change how many copies will be needed in the future. Everything that makes the process easier is welcomed as long as it still makes it legally defensible.

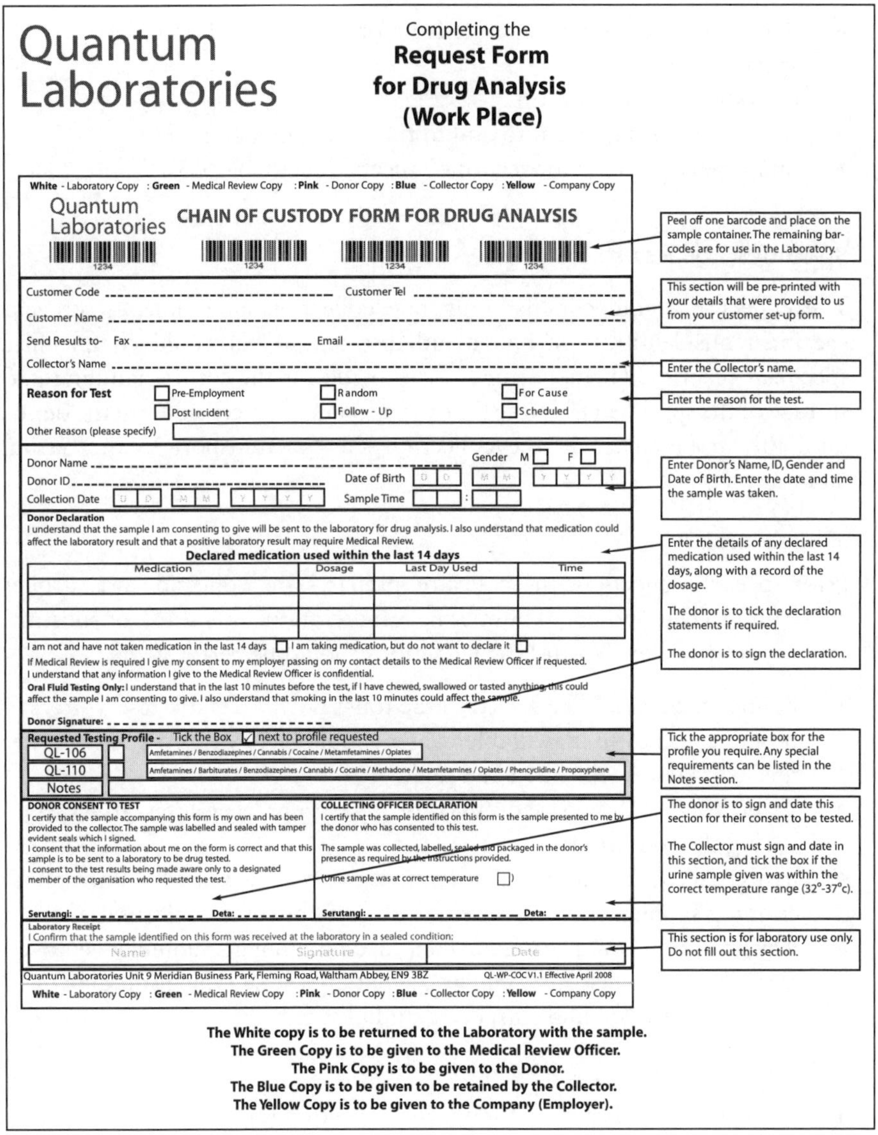

Quantum Laboratories

Completing the **Request Form for Drug Analysis (Work Place)**

White - Laboratory Copy : **Green** - Medical Review Copy : **Pink** - Donor Copy : **Blue** - Collector Copy : **Yellow** - Company Copy

Quantum Laboratories **CHAIN OF CUSTODY FORM FOR DRUG ANALYSIS**

1234 1234 1234 1234

Peel off one barcode and place on the sample container. The remaining barcodes are for use in the Laboratory.

Customer Code ______ Customer Tel ______

Customer Name ______

Send Results to- Fax ______ Email ______

Collector's Name ______

This section will be pre-printed with your details that were provided to us from your customer set-up form.

Enter the Collector's name.

Reason for Test ☐ Pre-Employment ☐ Random ☐ For Cause ☐ Post Incident ☐ Follow - Up ☐ Scheduled

Other Reason (please specify)

Enter the reason for the test.

Donor Name ______ Gender M ☐ F ☐

Donor ID ______ Date of Birth D D M M Y Y Y Y

Collection Date D D M M Y Y Y Y Sample Time ___ : ___

Enter Donor's Name, ID, Gender and Date of Birth. Enter the date and time the sample was taken.

Donor Declaration

I understand that the sample I am consenting to give will be sent to the laboratory for drug analysis. I also understand that medication could affect the laboratory result and that a positive laboratory result may require Medical Review.

Declared medication used within the last 14 days

Medication	Dosage	Last Day Used	Time

I am not and have not taken medication in the last 14 days ☐ I am taking medication, but do not want to declare it ☐

If Medical Review is required I give my consent to my employer passing on my contact details to the Medical Review Officer if requested.

I understand that any information I give to the Medical Review Officer is confidential.

Oral Fluid Testing Only: I understand that in the last 10 minutes before the test, if I have chewed, swallowed or tasted anything, this could affect the sample I am consenting to give. I also understand that smoking in the last 10 minutes could affect the sample.

Donor Signature: ______

Enter the details of any declared medication used within the last 14 days, along with a record of the dosage.

The donor is to tick the declaration statements if required.

The donor is to sign the declaration.

Requested Testing Profile - Tick the Box ☑ next to profile requested

QL-106	☐	Amfetamines / Benzodiazepines / Cannabis / Cocaine / Metamfetamines / Opiates
QL-110	☐	Amfetamines / Barbiturates / Benzodiazepines / Cannabis / Cocaine / Methadone / Metamfetamines / Opiates / Phencyclidine / Propoxyphene
Notes		

Tick the appropriate box for the profile you require. Any special requirements can be listed in the Notes section.

DONOR CONSENT TO TEST

I certify that the sample accompanying this form is my own and has been provided to the collector. The sample was labelled and sealed with tamper evident seals which I signed.

I consent that the information about me on the form is correct and that this sample is to be sent to a laboratory to be drug tested.

I consent to the test results being made aware only to a designated member of the organisation who requested the test.

Serutangi: ______ **Deta:** ______

COLLECTING OFFICER DECLARATION

I certify that the sample identified on this form is the sample presented to me by the donor who has consented to this test.

The sample was collected, labelled, sealed and packaged in the donor's presence as required by the instructions provided.

(Urine sample was at correct temperature ☐)

Serutangi: ______ **Deta:** ______

The donor is to sign and date this section for their consent to be tested.

The Collector must sign and date in this section, and tick the box if the urine sample given was within the correct temperature range (32°-37°c).

Laboratory Receipt

I Confirm that the sample identified on this form was received at the laboratory in a sealed condition:

Name	Signature	Date

This section is for laboratory use only. Do not fill out this section.

Quantum Laboratories Unit 9 Meridian Business Park, Fleming Road, Waltham Abbey, EN9 3BZ QL-WP-COC V1.1 Effective April 2008

White - Laboratory Copy : **Green** - Medical Review Copy : **Pink** - Donor Copy : **Blue** - Collector Copy : **Yellow** - Company Copy

The White copy is to be returned to the Laboratory with the sample.
The Green Copy is to be given to the Medical Review Officer.
The Pink Copy is to be given to the Donor.
The Blue Copy is to be given to be retained by the Collector.
The Yellow Copy is to be given to the Company (Employer).

Figure 6.1 Example of a custody and control form (CCF).

Specimen collection kit

The specimen collection kit is usually provided by the testing laboratory and includes:

- two specimen bottles
- one collection container

- one temperature strip (separate from or incorporated onto the specimen bottle)
- custody and control form
- bluing (colouring) agent to add to the toilet bowl and tank
- tamper-evident tape for securing faucets, toilet tank tops.

Specimen collection

The collector should conduct only one collection at a time, to prevent specimen misidentification and avoid distraction that could compromise specimen security. The collector must provide for the secure handling and storage of the specimen from the time the specimen is received from the donor until the specimen leaves the collection site for transport to the testing laboratory.

Site preparation

Prior to each collection, the collector prepares the collection area (toilet enclosure) to deter potential tampering, adulteration, alteration, or substitution of the specimen. The following actions should be performed:

- Bluing agent should be added to the toilet bowl and tank reservoir. If bluing agent is not available, water should be turned off and the toilet flushed to empty the bowl and tank.
- Water sources should be disabled or taped to prevent access to water during the collection.
- Items that could be used to adulterate a specimen (e.g. soap, disinfectants, cleaning supplies) should be removed from the toilet enclosure.
- Any items that could be used to conceal contaminants should be removed from the toilet enclosure, and areas that appear suitable for hiding contaminants should be inspected and blocked.

Collection process

The following describes steps for a urine collection (Figure 6.2):

1. Verify donor identity. When the donor arrives at the collection site, the collector should request photo identification to verify donor identity. If a photo ID is not available, it is acceptable for the donor's supervisor or other employer representative to identify the donor. If the individual's identity cannot be established without a doubt, the collector should not proceed with the collection.
2. Inspect and secure personal items, clean hands. The collector asks the donor to empty the contents of his or her pockets, to identify items that could be used to adulterate or substitute the urine specimen. The collector instructs the donor to leave all outer clothing, bags, briefcases,

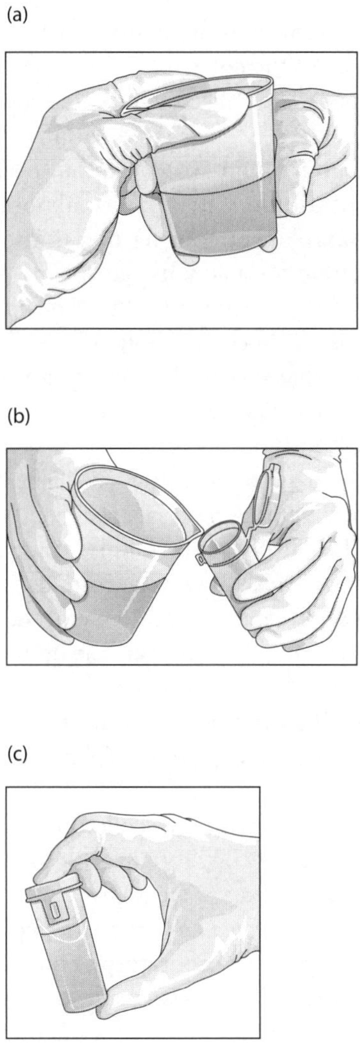

Figure 6.2 Urine sample collection: (a) the donor gives the urine to the collector; (b) the collector pours at least 25 mL into one of two specimen bottles; (c) the specimen bottle is closed and later sealed and initialled.

purses and other belongings outside of the collection area (toilet enclosure). The donor then is instructed by the collector to wash and dry his or her hands while under the supervision of the collector.

3 Provide collection kit. The collector instructs the donor to select a collection container from those available.

4 Instruct the donor to provide the specimen. The collector instructs the donor to take his or her selected specimen collection container into the toilet enclosure and fill the container to a minimum of 50 mL. The donor is instructed not to flush the toilet or the collection process will stop.

The donor will be allowed to wash his or her hands after giving the specimen container to the collector.

5 Check the specimen. The collector should check the temperature (acceptable range 32–38°C, measured within 4 minutes of voiding), check the volume (minimum 50 mL), and inspect the specimen for adulteration or substitution (e.g. objects, abnormal colour or odour). The use of a disposable thermometer that is inserted into the specimen introduces a potential for a contamination and is discouraged.

6 Pour the urine into the specimen bottles. The collector pours at least 25 mL into each of two specimen bottles. One will be the primary 'A-bottle' and the other will be the split 'B-bottle'.

7 Seal each bottle. The collector places the tamper-evident label/seal over the lid/cap of each bottle.

8 Instruct the donor to annotate bottle seals. The collector instructs the donor to initial and date each of the specimen bottle seals.

9 Annotate the CCF. The collector completes appropriate sections of the CCF with donor information (e.g. birth date, telephone numbers), collection information (e.g. date and time of the collection), and chain-of-custody entries, and instructs the donor to sign the CCF.

10 Check the CCF. The collector checks all copies of the CCF for legibility and completeness. If all copies are legible and complete, the collector then provides the donor a copy of the CCF and allows the donor to leave.

11 Prepare specimen for shipment. The collector places the specimen bottles along with the laboratory copy (original) of the CCF in a leak-resistant bag, and then places the bag in the appropriate shipping container. It is important that the collector ensures each specimen collected is shipped (or picked up by the laboratory's courier) in a timely fashion. This should not exceed 24 hours or the next business day.

Directly observed collections

Drug users often seek ways to beat the drug tests. Because of that, urine collections are directly observed in many rehabilitation or criminal justice testing programmes. To address individual privacy concerns and increase the acceptance of drug testing in the workplace, urine collections are not routinely observed in workplace drug testing programmes. The proper collection protocol described above includes many features that discourage and/or prevent tampering with the specimen (e.g. preventing access to water in the toilet enclosure, adding a bluing agent to the toilet water).

There are cases where workplace specimen collections are directly observed. An employer may require a directly observed collection for certain employees (e.g. when the reason for the test is return-to-duty or follow-up, or the donor has a verified past test result that was adulterated or substituted).

In addition, a directly observed collection may be necessary due to circumstances that arise during a collection. These include, but are not limited to:

- The specimen temperature is outside the acceptable range (32–38°C).
- The collector suspects that the donor may have tampered with the specimen.

Regardless of the reasons for an observed collection, the collector must always report to the MRO and the donor's employer that a collection was directly observed and the reason for the observation. This is documented on the CCF.

Problem collections

Occasionally, problems may arise during a specimen collection. The collector's standard operating procedures should describe common problems and the proper responses. The collector may also contact the employer for guidance on resolving problems specific to their employees.

Shy bladder

The collector allows a time period of up to 3 hours for the donor to provide a sufficient urine specimen (i.e. minimum volume 50 mL). After this time, if the donor claims that he or she is still unable to provide a sufficient specimen, the collector reports a 'shy bladder' to the MRO, along with the donor's explanation.

Refusal to test

When the donor's actions interfere with or prevent the specimen collection, the collector reports the 'refusal to test' to the donor's employer. Some examples of what constitutes a 'refusal to test' are as follows.

- The potential donor fails to appear for a test within the employer's stipulated time frame (it may be different if it is a pre-employment test).
- The potential donor fails to remain at the collection site after the collection process has begun.
- The potential donor fails to provide a sufficient amount of urine (unless there is a verifiable medical reason that they cannot accommodate this requirement).
- The potential donor fails to permit an observed collection when required.
- The potential donor fails to submit to a second test after being directed to do so by the employer or the collector.
- The potential donor fails to cooperate during the testing process (e.g. not signing the CCF, not initialling the specimen seals).

Other matrices

The following methods are not so common yet in Europe in workplace drug testing. However, they have increased lately so they are included, albeit in less detail than urine collection. To be legally defensible the collection, of course, needs to follow chain of custody and include a control and custody form (CCF) as described above.

Oral fluid collection

The traditional methods of saliva or oral fluid collection have involved techniques such as direct expectoration (spitting or dribbling) and stimulation using items including paraffin-based products, Teflon, pastilles, etc.

More recent years have seen the introduction of a number of specially designed 'oral fluid collection devices'. Some people think the use of an oral fluid collection device offers a more dignified and hygienic approach to the collection of a sample.

The devices differ in the type of oral fluid they collect, the method of collection and in some instances the user-friendliness both for the specimen donor and for the laboratory that will receive the specimen for analysis. Most of the devices use an absorbent material attached to a handle for ease of use. The specimen can be collected in only a few minutes. After the pad is saturated with oral fluid or a specific amount has been absorbed, the pad is placed in a tube of buffer for shipment to the laboratory.

The use of a buffer helps reduce any degradation of the specimen before it is analysed as it is known that some drugs and metabolites are unstable in the specimen.

On-site test methods may collect the specimen in the same way with an absorbent pad from which the specimen is applied to a non-instrumented or instrumented immunoassay device.

Hair collection

Collection procedures for hair analysis for drugs have not been standardised. In most published studies, the samples are obtained from random locations on the scalp, but hair is best collected from the area at the back of the head, called the vertex posterior. Compared with other areas of the head, this area has less variability in the hair growth rate, the number of hairs in the growing phase is more constant and the hair is less subject to age- and sex-related influences. The sample size varies considerably among laboratories and depends on the drug to be analysed and the test methodology. Sample sizes reported in the literature range from a single hair to 200 mg. When sectional analysis is performed, the hair is cut into segments of about 1, 2 or 3 cm, which corresponds approximately to about 1, 2 or 3 months' growth. When scalp hair is not available, other types of hair (pubic hair, arm hair or axillary hair) can be suggested as an alternative source for drug detection.

Conclusion

The collection of donor specimens is one of the most sensitive areas of the workplace drug testing process. Despite the reliability of highly sophisticated laboratory analysis, an error by the urine specimen collector at the urine collection site can cause a laboratory-confirmed positive test to be cancelled due to clerical or procedural error. Adulteration increases the complexities associated with collection site security and specimen integrity.

Drug test collectors must be thoroughly trained in basic custody and control procedures, and in how to circumvent (to the best of their ability) specimen tampering and substitution. Training must include security of the collection site and the specimens collected.

While the collector must ensure the integrity of the collection process, he or she must also be sensitive to the employee's privacy, and must respect the dignity of the donor.

The collection process consists of: verification of the identity of the donor, proper matching of the specimen with its donor, ensuring that no adulteration or tampering took place and that no unauthorised access to the specimen was possible and the secure transfer of the specimen to each person handling it.

Specimen collection kits are often used; they contain two specimen bottles, a collection container, a temperature strip, a custody and control form, bluing (colouring) agent to add to the toilet bowl and tank and tamper-evident tape.

Urine collections are not routinely observed in workplace drug testing programmes, but there are cases where workplace specimen collections are directly observed (e.g. if the specimen temperature is outside the acceptable range or if the collector suspects that the donor may have tampered with the specimen).

For saliva or oral fluid collection a number of specially designed 'oral fluid collection devices' are used.

Hair is best collected from the area at the back of the head. The sample size varies considerably among laboratories.

Further reading

1. Australian and New Zealand Standard. Procedures for the collection, detection and quantitation of drugs of abuse in urine. AS/NZS 4308:2008.
2. European Workplace Drug Testing Society. Guidelines for workplace drug testing. www.eapinstitute.com/documents/EWDTSGuidelines.pdf (accessed December 2010).
3. Swotinsky RB, Smith DR. *The Medical Review Officer's Manual*, 4th edn. Beverly Farms, MA: OEM Press, 2010.

4. US Department of Health and Human Services (HHS), Substance Abuse and Mental Health Services Administration (SAMHSA). HHS Specimen Collection Handbook for Federal Agency Workplace Drug Testing Programs. November 2004.
5. US Department of Transportation. Urine Specimen Collection Guidelines. Washington, DC, August 2001.

7

Alternative matrices to urine

Pascal Kintz

Key points

- Since 1979, hair has been used to document chronic drug exposure.
- Drug detection in hair has a longer detection window, which is weeks to months, depending on the length of hair shaft analysed (hair grows ±1 cm/month)
- Collection of oral fluid or sweat is almost non-invasive, relatively easy to perform and in forensic situations can be achieved under close supervision to prevent adulteration or substitution of the samples.
- The concentrations of many drugs in oral fluid correlate relatively well with blood concentrations. For basic drugs, the oral fluid concentrations are higher than in blood.
- With sweat-patch technology, sweat will saturate the pad, located in the centre of the patch over a period of several days and will slowly concentrate, and drugs present in sweat will be retained. With a sweat patch, one obtains a cumulative estimate of drug exposure over one week.
- In oral fluid and sweat, the parent drug is present in higher concentrations than the metabolites. This facilitates detection of heroin use, because the specific metabolite 6-acetylmorphine can be easily detected in oral fluid.
- Sweat is not used routinely for workplace drug testing.
- Repeated shampooing has no significant action on the drug content of hair. After cosmetic treatments, drug concentrations decline dramatically by decreasing from 50 to 80% of the original concentration.
- There is a weak relationship between the dose of the drug that was taken and the concentration of the drug in hair.

- The possibility of racial bias due to differences in melanin concentrations or in hair porosity is still in discussion.
- Markers of ethanol consumption in hair are ethylglucuronide, phosphatidylethanol or fatty acid ethyl esters (FAEE).

Introduction

It is generally accepted that chemical testing of biological fluids is the most objective means of detecting drug use. The presence of a drug analyte in a biological specimen can be used as evidence of recent exposure. The standard in drug testing is immunoassay screening, followed by gas chromatographic–mass spectrometric (GC-MS) confirmation conducted on a urine sample. More recently, a variety of body specimens other than urine, such as oral fluid, sweat or hair, have been proposed to document drug exposure.

Since 1979,[1] hair has been used to document chronic drug exposure. To date, more than 500 articles concerning hair analysis have been published reporting applications in forensic toxicology,[2] clinical toxicology,[3] occupational medicine[4] and doping control.[5] The major practical advantage of hair testing compared with urine and blood testing for drugs is its longer detection window, which is weeks to months, depending on the length of hair shaft analysed, against a few hours or days for blood and urine, respectively. In practice, detection windows offered by urine and hair testing are complementary: urinalysis provides short-term information of an individual's drug use, whereas long-term histories are accessible through hair analysis. Although there is a reasonable agreement that the qualitative results from hair analysis are valid, the interpretation of the results is still under debate, due to unresolved questions, such as the influence of external contamination[6] or cosmetic treatment[7] and a possible racial bias.[8]

The advantages of oral fluid or sweat over traditional fluids are that collection is almost non-invasive, relatively easy to perform and in forensic situations can be achieved under close supervision to prevent adulteration or substitution of the samples.

Oral fluid has been increasingly used as an analytical tool in pharmacokinetic studies,[9] therapeutic drug monitoring[10] and the detection of illicit drugs.[11] More recently, particular interest in oral fluid has been expressed by law enforcement agencies for roadside testing of intoxicated drivers.[12] The presence of metabolites of drugs in urine of potentially impaired drivers can be interpreted as evidence of relatively recent exposure, except for cannabis. However, this does not necessarily mean that the subject was under influence at the time of sampling. This is also obviously true for workplace drug testing. It has been claimed by some authors[13,14] that the concentrations of many drugs in saliva correlate well with blood concentrations, which suggests that qualitative measurements in oral fluid may be a valuable technique to determine the current degree of exposure to a definite drug at the time of sampling.

Researchers have known since 1911[15] that drugs are excreted by the body in sweat, but significant advances in sweat analyses have been made during the past years with the development of the sweat-patch technology.[16] Over a period of several days, sweat will saturate the pad, located in the centre of the patch and will slowly concentrate, and drugs present in sweat will be retained. Sweat appears to offer the advantage of being a non-invasive means of obtaining a cumulative estimate of drug exposure over one week. Sweat testing has found applications in monitoring of substance abusers, for example in detoxification centres[17] or for evaluating drug exposure of prisoners after a furlough. At this time, there is no application of sweat in workplace drug testing.

After a short review on the physiology of each specimen, this chapter will focus on sampling methods, preparative applications and analytical applications.

Oral fluid

Physiology

The most important functions of human saliva are: (1) to moisten the mucous membranes of the upper aerodigestive tract in order to facilitate speech and solubilise food to ease swallowing; (2) to control the bacterial flora of the mouth and establish defence; and (3) to supply enzymes for food digestion. Most of the oral fluid is produced by the major salivary glands (parotid, submandibular and sublingual). Saliva contains the usual electrolytes of the body fluids.

In addition to water (99%) and mineral salts, oral fluid also contains proteins such as mucins and some enzymes for digestion. The resting pH is about 6.8. Increasing the salivary flow will result in a higher osmolarity and a pH that approaches the pH of plasma or is even slightly higher (pH 7.8).

The total volume of oral fluid produced each day in adults is 500–1500 mL.

Salivary glands have a high blood flow. Before any drug circulating in plasma can be secreted into the salivary duct, it must pass through the capillary wall, the basal membrane, and the membrane of the glandular epithelial cells, which is the rate-determining step. Since saliva is not a simple ultrafiltrate of plasma, different mechanisms are thought to occur: (1) passive diffusion through the membrane; (2) active processes against a concentration gradient; (3) filtration through pores in the membrane; and (4) pinocytosis.[18] Small polar molecules, like ethanol, can be transported via the ultrafiltration route. An active transport mechanism has been suggested for some drugs, such as penicillin, metoprolol or methotrexate.

Most drugs appear to enter saliva by a simple passive diffusion process depending on their physicochemical properties (pK_a, liposolubility, molecular weight and spatial configuration), the degree of plasma protein binding and the pH of both media. Thus, lipophilic drugs with a low degree of ionisation can easily cross the barrier between plasma and saliva, the salivary concentration being a reflection of the non-protein bound plasma concentration. However, for weakly basic drugs, the pH of saliva is of paramount importance for the concentrations found in saliva. Especially for those drugs with a pK_a close to the salivary pH, the degree of ionisation will drastically change with small changes in pH, which will be reflected in the saliva-to-plasma ratio (S/P). The enormous influence of salivary pH on the S/P ratio of many drugs is perhaps the reason why experimentally determined S/P ratios are different from the theoretical values calculated from the Henderson–Hasselbach equation.[19]

The protocol for the collection of saliva differs depending on the study (with or without stimulation) and is probably of prime importance for the determination of S/P ratios.

Collection

Two main limitations of saliva are apparent: (1) the amount of matrix collected is smaller when compared to urine and (2) the concentrations of drugs in urine are higher than in saliva.

Saliva is usually collected by spitting into a collection vial, wiping the oral cavity with a cotton swab or by stimulation of saliva flow with sour candy, citric acid crystals or a chewing gum, or by chewing strips of Teflon. Substances such as Parafilm should be avoided because they may absorb highly lipophilic drugs.

One should note that the S/P ratios are sensitive to pH variations (at least when using citric acid) and that drug concentrations may be decreased when increasing the salivary flow.

With the exception of 'dry mouth' observed in case of stress (control by medical staff with a potential risk of positive identification, arrest by a police officer), it might be advantageous to use unstimulated saliva. The salivary flow can be decreased after intake of certain drugs (e.g. some tricyclic antidepressants and amphetamines). Individuals often collect more froth than actual liquid, providing a viscous sample with a small sample size, which complicates the analysis.

The donor should allow saliva to accumulate in the mouth and then expectorate into a suitable container. Some special devices have been designed to facilitate the sampling of saliva. The use of a dental cotton roll to collect saliva has been improved and is nowadays available as the Salivette (Sarstedt, Germany). Other commercialised devices are/were

Figure 7.1 Collection of oral fluid using the Intercept® device.

Omni-Sal, OraSure, Accu-sorb, Saliva Sampler, Intercept, Saliva Lollipop or SalivaSac. As an example, collection of oral fluid with the Intercept is illustrated in Figure 7.1.

The effect of collection methods on drug concentrations in oral fluid is not well described in the scientific literature. A controlled clinical study designed to determine the effects of selected collection protocols on oral fluid codeine concentrations was published in 2000.[20] Concentrations at different time points averaged 3.6 times higher after spitting without stimulation (control) than after acidic stimulation. The control method resulted in 1.3–2.0 times higher concentrations than concentrations obtained in specimens collected by chewing a sugarless gum, or using the Salivette or the Finger Collector containing Accu-Sorb (Avitar Technologies Inc., USA).

Analytical procedures

Oral fluid can be extracted and analysed like other biological fluids such as blood. In general, there will be less interference from endogenous compounds with saliva than with blood or urine. However, one should ensure that all necessary validation of drug-free and drug-spiked oral fluid is carried out prior to conducting casework.

An oral fluid sample collected with a special device usually provides the analyst with a clean specimen. However, a sample collected by spitting contains cell debris, food particles and strings of mucus; centrifugation is difficult because of the high viscosity. The specimen has to be stored at –4°C and measured as soon as possible because of possible bacterial and fungal growth. The cocaine concentration in saliva stored in a plastic receptacle without addition of citric acid or other stabilisers remains unaltered at +4°C for one week. Freezing and thawing of the sample lowers the viscosity substantially, so that centrifugation can be performed after thawing. This ensures better handling of the sample and a high stability for most analytes for a long period of time, except for tetrahydrocannabinol (THC). Sometimes, the addition of sodium fluoride is reported (e.g. for cannabis and benzodiazepine measurement).

Before oral fluid can be used for rapid screening, especially for on-site testing, the following criteria should be met: (a) a fast, simple, and validated sampling procedure; (b) a test that needs a small sample volume (100 microlitres); (c) an antibody targeted to the parent molecules rather than the metabolites; (d) an assay sensitivity adapted to the expected concentrations in oral fluid; (e) screening cut-off values that meet the requirements for high sensitivity and specificity; (f) an electronic reader.

Some prototypes of on-site tests have been investigated during the course of the ROSITA project.[21] Several problems with sampling have been reported. Unfortunately, none of the present devices is satisfactory in terms of sensitivity and reliability. However, many developments are under way and the companies involved are improving the ease of use and the accuracy of their tests.

The screening cut-offs will depend on the specificity of the antibodies, and the presence of other cross-reacting metabolites in oral fluid. In 2004 the Substance Abuse and Mental Health Services Administration (SAMHSA) cut-off values have been proposed for the screening and confirmation of most illicit drugs in oral fluid. Efforts to organise the provision of quality control samples are only just starting.

A selection of various chromatographic procedures for drugs of abuse in saliva has been published.[22] Quantitation is usually performed with the common GC-MS procedures for drugs of abuse in blood, using electron impact mode and the appropriate deuterated standards. Since oral fluid contains the parent drugs, it is important to add internal standards for the quantification of THC, cocaine and 6-acetylmorphine (6-AM). Because of the smaller sample volume of an oral fluid specimen in comparison to a blood sample, analytical procedures using MS in chemical ionisation mode, liquid chromatography-mass spectrometry (LC-MS) and tandem MS/MS confirmation are being developed.

The following is a selection of various procedures that are used by the active investigators.

Cocaine

Numerous reports have documented the excretion of cocaine and its metabolites in oral fluid. Cocaine appears in saliva rapidly following intravenous injection, inhalation and intranasal administration to volunteers.[23] Contamination of the oral cavity after smoking and sniffing was variable but significant during the first 2 hours after dosing. Anhydroecgonine methyl ester was detectable in oral fluid after smoking, but it was quickly cleared. Benzoylecgonine and ecgonine methyl ester levels were only comparable with cocaine concentrations at times when these had declined to below 100 ng/mL. However, the concentrations of the metabolites would be expected to be higher in chronic users. Proposed SAMHSA screening cut-off values are 20 ng/mL for benzoylecgonine as the target analyte and 8 ng/mL for the confirmation.

In general, cocaine and its metabolites can be detected in saliva using a simple solid-phase extraction procedure: the sample is diluted with acetate buffer pH 4.0 and applied to a conditioned Bond Elut Certify column; washing is performed with water, buffer pH 4.0 and acetonitrile and elution occurs with dichloromethane/isopropanol/ammonia (80/20/2) (v/v/v). Replacing the buffer with 0.1 N HCl allows a washing step with methanol instead of acetonitrile because of the ionic binding of benzoylecgonine to the column. Derivatisation is often performed with *N-O*,-bis-(trimethylsilyl)trifluoroacetamide (BSTFA) but pentafluoropropionic anhydride in combination with pentafluoropropanol improves the sensitivity for benzoylecgonine. Limits of detection are in the range 1–5 ng/mL.

The most complete study on cocaine excretion in saliva was published in 1997 by Cone *et al.*[24] Saliva specimens (1 mL) were mixed with a solution of deuterated internal standard (IS), followed by pH adjustment to 4.0 with acetate buffer. Specimens were submitted to solid-phase extraction columns, previously conditioned with methanol (2 × 2 mL), water (2 × 2 mL) and acetate buffer. The columns were washed with water (2 × 1 mL) and acetate buffer (1 mL), then aspirated for 5 min, washed with acetonitrile (2 × 1 mL), dried for 5 min and eluted with 3 × 2 mL of freshly prepared elution solvent (methylene chloride-2-propanol-ammonium hydroxide, 80 : 20 : 2, v/v). The eluate was evaporated to dryness and derivatised with 20 microlitres BSTFA + 1% TMCS (trimethylchlorosilane) at 60°C for 30 min. A 1-microlitre aliquot was injected into an HP-1 fused-silica capillary column (12 m × 0.2 mm i.d., 0.33 micrometre film thickness). Injection port temperature was 250°C. The mass selective detector was a HP 5970B, operated in the selected ion-monitoring mode. The range of the standard curve was 1.1–500 ng/mL for each analyte. The limits of detection by this method for cocaine, benzoylecgonine and ecgonine methylester were approximately 1 ng/mL. Between-run coefficients of variation were in the range 1.0 to 10.1%.

As an alternative,[25] we described a liquid–liquid extraction that can be summarised as follows: saliva and 200 ng of deuterated IS were extracted with 10 mL chloroform–isopropanol–*n*-heptane (50 : 17 : 33, v/v) under alkaline conditions (2 mL of phosphate buffer at 1 mol/L, pH 8.4). After agitation and centrifugation, the organic phase was purified by an additional acid extraction (5 mL of 0.2 mol/L HCl) and the aqueous layer was re-extracted with 2 mL phosphate buffer, 1 mL 1 mol/L NaOH and 5 mL chloroform. After agitation and centrifugation, the organic phase was removed and evaporated to dryness. BSTFA + 1% TMCS (30 microlitres) was added to the dry extract, which was sealed and heated at 70°C for 20 min. A 1.5-microlitre portion was then injected into a HP5-MS column (30 m × 0.25 mm i.d.). Limits of detection (LOD) were in the range 1 to 5 ng/mL for all the compounds. This procedure can also be used for the simultaneous monitoring of opiates.

Cannabis

The main psychoactive compound of cannabis is Δ9-tetrahydrocannabinol (THC), which is first biotransformed to an active metabolite, 11-hydroxy-THC (11-OH-THC), which in turn is rapidly converted to an inactive metabolite, 11-nor-9-carboxy-THC (THC-COOH), the latter being the principal urinary metabolite excreted as glucuronide conjugate.

As detecting THC-COOH in urine does not necessarily indicate impairment, since the window of detection is very large (at least several days), oral fluid has been proposed as a non-invasive specimen to document recent cannabis exposure. At this time, all the immunoassays and particularly the on-site devices that were used to detect cannabis in oral fluid failed to detect the drug, probably because they were specific for the urinary THC-COOH and not the parent THC, which is present in oral fluid.[26–28]

SAMHSA proposes a screening cut-off of 4 ng/mL for THC as the target analyte for the initial screen and 2 ng/mL of THC in the confirmation analysis.

In several recent studies performed using hyphenated chromatography,[29–32] THC was identified as the major component in oral fluid, with a detection time in the range from 2–10 hours. In a presentation from 2000,[33] the authors reported a highly significant correlation ($P < 0.01$) between mean saliva THC concentrations and several subjective, performance and physiological measures of drug effect. However, when individual saliva data were correlated with concurrent measures, the correlations were not significant, leading the authors to conclude that predictions of performance effects from a single THC saliva test would be unreliable as a result of high individual variability. More recently,[32] the same authors concluded that a positive oral fluid test provides credible evidence of active cannabis use.

The procedure used in this laboratory is as follows.[34] To 0.5 mL (minimum 0.25 mL) of mixed buffer and oral fluid (collected with the Intercept device) in a silanised Pyrex tube, 20 ng of THC-d3 and 5 mL hexane/ethyl acetate (90/10, v/v) were added. The mixture was shaken for 30 min at ambient temperature. A maximum of organic phase was removed, then 0.2 mL 10% acetic acid was added to the organic phase. After agitation for 20 min and centrifugation, the organic phase was evaporated to dryness. THC was then derivatised by methylation, by adding 200 microlitres tetrabutyl-ammonium hydroxide (55–60% in water)/dimethyl sulfoxide (1 : 20, v/v) reagent, freshly prepared. After 2 min at room temperature, 50 microlitres of iodomethane were added. After 15 min at room temperature, the reaction was stopped by adding 200 microlitres 0.1N HCl. Drugs were then extracted into 1 mL of isooctane. After centrifugation, the top organic layer was removed and evaporated to dryness. The residue was dissolved in 25 microlitres isooctane.

A 1.5-microlitre aliquot of the derivatised extract was injected into the column of a Hewlett Packard (Palo Alto, CA, USA) gas chromatograph (6890 Series) via a Hewlett Packard (7673) autosampler. The flow of carrier gas (helium, purity grade N 55) through the column (HP5-MS capillary column, 5% phenyl–95% methylsiloxane, 30 m × 0.25 mm i.d. × 0.25 mm film thickness) was 1.0 mL/min. The injector temperature was 270°C and splitless injection was employed with a split valve off-time of 1.0 min. The column oven temperature was programmed to rise from an initial temperature of 60°C, maintained for 1 min, to 295°C at 30°C/min and maintained at 295°C for the final 6 min. The detector was a Hewlett Packard 5973 operated in the electron impact mode. The electron multiplier voltage was set at 600 V above the EI-tune voltage. Retention times and ions were as follows: THC: 9.87 min, *m/z* 285, 313 and 328; and THC-d3: 9.86 min, *m/z* 316 and 331. THC was identified based on the relative abundance of its three ions and quantified using the underlined ions, versus the deuterated standard.

From this study,[34] it appears clearly that the Drugwipe device was not sensitive enough to be used routinely by the enforcement agencies. High concentrations of THC were not detected. Too many subjects will pass the test, with negative consequences for public safety.

In the process of smoking cannabis, THC is deposited in the oral cavity, and it appears that this depot is the primary source of THC that is collected and analysed during oral fluid testing. From results of passive and active cannabis studies,[32,35] it is suggested that initial oral fluid contamination by THC occurs immediately after exposure, but that the majority of drug is cleared from oral fluid within 60 min. Investigations with radiolabelled THC have shown, in humans, that little THC is secreted in saliva.[36] This is the reason why a very sensitive test is needed, with antibodies targeted against THC and not its metabolite THC-COOH.

Opiates

Heroin is rapidly metabolised to 6-AM in blood, which is, in turn, converted to morphine. After intravenous injection, the saliva/plasma ratio for heroin and 6-AM can be lower than 1, depending on the salivary pH. After smoking or sniffing heroin, the concentrations of the analytes in saliva remain higher than in plasma for 2–3 hours due to contamination of the buccal cavity.

In many cases, 6-AM has been detected in oral fluid in high concentrations but not in the corresponding blood sample.[37] SAMHSA proposed cut-off values are 40 ng/mL morphine for the initial screen and 40 ng/mL of morphine and 4 ng/mL of 6-AM for the confirmation. Detection of morphine, codeine and 6-AM in saliva is based upon similar analytical procedures as for cocaine. However, a washing step with a strong acid will result in the hydrolysis of 6-AM, so acetate buffer pH 4.0 is preferred for opioids. GC-MS data after silylation show similar results as for the pentafluoropropionic (PFP) derivatives.

Codeine was detected in oral fluid for 12–24 hours after oral intake of 30 mg of liquid codeine phosphate, depending on the individual and on the collection protocol.[20] After solid-phase extraction, derivatisation occurred with trifluoroacetic anhydride (TFAA) and GC-MS analysis was performed using positive-ion chemical ionisation. The limit of quantification was 5 ng/mL and the limit of detection 1.0 ng/mL. Substantially different pharmacokinetic parameters were detected after spitting, with or without stimulation, using a Salivette or the Finger collector containing Accu-Sorb. Moreover, *in vitro* studies showed that more than 90% of codeine and morphine could be recovered from the Salivette after centrifugation but only 60% from the Finger collector after milking the foam.

Amphetamines

It has been shown recently[30,37] that the concentrations of amphetamine and methylenedioxymethylamphetamine (MDMA) in oral fluid, either obtained by spitting or with a Salivette, exceed the corresponding plasma concentrations 10- to 100-fold. After oral administration of 100 mg 1-(1,3-benzodioxol-5-yl)-*N*-methylbutan-2-amine (MBDB) to one volunteer, the parent drug was detectable in saliva for 17 hours after intake. The samples, collected by spitting, were extracted with ethyl acetate after the addition of 1 mol/L sodium hydroxide. Derivatisation was performed using heptafluorobutyric anhydride (HFBA) before analysis on the GC-MS in EI mode. The limit of detection was 2 ng/mL. Oral fluid samples can also be extracted using the common solid-phase extraction procedures for amphetamines in blood. Proposed SAMHSA screening cut-off values are 160 ng/mL for d-methamphetamine as the target analyte and confirmation cut-off values are 160 ng/mL for d-amphetamine and 160 ng/mL for d-methamphetamine.

An innovative approach to the problem of low sample volumes is the use of LC-MS with a minimum sample work-up. Detection limits are 10 ng/mL for amphetamine and 5 ng/mL for methamphetamine and the designer amphetamines, using only 100 microlitres of oral fluid.[38] Although Clauwaert *et al.* used a liquid extraction procedure for sample preparation, a simple precipitation of the proteins with methanol, followed by centrifugation or even dilution of the saliva sample and direct injection, should allow the analyst to process large numbers of low-volume oral fluid samples.

Sweat

Physiology of sweat

Sweat is a liquid secreted from sweat glands, which are derivatives of the epidermis. Sweat glands occur in almost every part of the skin and are classified into two types: eccrine and apocrine. The apocrine glands are larger than the eccrine glands (most numerous) and secrete a more viscous substance. As sweat glands are associated with hair, it is thought to be a major contributor to drugs appearing in hair.[39] Sweat aids in controlling body temperature via surface evaporation of sweat. Moisture may be lost from the skin by both insensible sweat (sweat not visible), and sensitive sweat, which is actively excreted during stress and exercise. The amount of sweat that is excreted is affected by body location, ambient temperature, body temperature and relative humidity of the environment (insensible sweat) and by emotional, physical and thermal stress (sensitive sweat).[40] The variability of these factors and the uneven distribution of the sweat glands make it difficult to obtain specimens of sweat systematically.

Between 300 and 700 mL/day of insensible sweat is produced over the whole body, whereas 2–4 L/h of sensible sweat may be produced by extensive exercise.

Sweat is a hypotonic solution of weak acid pH, between 5.2 and 6.9. Water (99%) is the major component. Na^+ is the major ion, present in variable concentrations, ranging from 5 to 140 mmol/L. Glucose, lactic acid, pyruvic acid and urea are the essential organic elements. Proteins are generally not identified in sweat.

Sweat collection

The analysis of drugs in sweat is rarely performed because it is extremely difficult to estimate sweat volume and evaluate drug concentrations.

When sweat is to be tested for drugs, the first problem is to collect an adequate specimen. Thermal[41] or pharmacological stimulations, such as with pilocarpine,[42] were proposed to secrete an unusually large amount of sweat. An occlusive bandage consisting of one to three layers of filter paper[43] or pieces of cotton, gauze or towel[44] were proposed to collect sweat. By using these homemade collectors, it was possible to identify various drugs, including quinine, salicylic acid, antipyrine, methadone, phenobarbital, morphine, cocaine, cannabis, methamphetamine and phencyclidine.

Significant advances have been made in recent years to develop a sweat patch technology, which was proposed by PharmChem Labs (Menlo Park,

CA, USA). The sweat patch acts as a specimen container for non-volatile and liquid components of sweat, including drugs. Sweat components are collected on a special absorbent pad, located in the centre of the patch. Non-volatile substances from the environment cannot penetrate the transparent film, which is a semi-permeable membrane over the pad that allows oxygen, water and carbon dioxide to pass through the patch, leaving the skin underneath healthy. Over a period of several days, sweat saturates the pad and slowly concentrates it; drugs present in sweat are retained. A unique number is imprinted on each patch to aid with chain of custody and identification.

Kidwell *et al.*[45] investigated an alternative collection of sweat to detect cocaine in a university population by wiping the skin with a cotton pad moistened with 500 microlitres of 90% isopropanol. This procedure allows rapid collection of drugs that may arise both from sweat evaporating on the surface of the skin and from external contamination. Three additions of 2 mL of 0.1 mol/L HCl were added to the pad in presence of 20 ng of deuterated IS, and the extraction solvent removed by centrifugation after each addition. The aqueous extract was applied to a C18 AR/MPI solid-phase extraction column (Ansys), which had been conditioned with methanol and 0.1 mol/L HCl. After sample application, the column was washed with 0.1 mol/L HCl and 20% aqueous acetone. The column was dried under a vacuum and the drugs eluted with 5 : 1 methylene chloride:isopropanol + 1% ammonium hydroxide. The eluate was concentrated to dryness under a stream of nitrogen and derivatised with pentafluoropropanol and propionic anhydride containing 0.1% dimethylaminopyridine.

The excess derivatisation reagents were removed, the residue reconstituted with 20 microlitres of ethyl acetate, and 2 microlitres were injected into a Saturn 4 GC-MS/MS. The samples were injected onto a 30-m DB-5MS column. The GC parameters were as follows: initial temperature 100°C for 0.2 min, ramped to 280°C at 18°C/min, than to 300°C at 5°C/min and held for 2.9 min. Samples were run using chemical ionisation using isobutane. LOD for both cocaine and benzoylecgonine were 1 ng/swab.

All but one[45] recent reports have demonstrated the ability of the sweat patch to collect enough specimen that can be submitted to immunoassays or GC-MS. Although it is still under evaluation for routine applications, at least in Europe, testing of individuals for drugs with sweat patches increases the window of drug detection to one week. Low doses of cocaine (about 1–5 mg) produce detectable amounts in sweat.[16]

Subjects can wear one patch with minimal discomfort for at least one week, although a few individuals developed slight irritation from the patches, especially after exposure to the sun. Normal hygiene practices can be used.

It was observed that the parent drug, which is more apolar, tends to be found in higher concentrations in sweat than the metabolites. For example, Kintz *et al.*[46] detected heroin in sweat at concentrations 2–4 times higher than those of 6-AM and 5–20 times higher than morphine. Cocaine is also the major analyte excreted in sweat following its administration.[16]

The first published paper documenting the use of the sweat patch was by Cone *et al.*[16] Sweat patches were applied to the back and abdomen of subjects prior to and periodically after drug administration. Before affixing the patches, the skin area was cleaned with an isopropyl alcohol (70%) swab. Patches were removed by pulling an edge of the adhesive backing. For storage, the patch was frozen at −30°C. The absorbent pad was extracted with 2.5 mL of a mixture of 0.1% Triton X-100 in 0.2 mol/L acetate buffer in presence of deuterated IS. After agitation and centrifugation, the filtered extract solution was mixed with 2 ml of 2 mol/L sodium acetate buffer (pH 4.0). The extracts were purified by solid phase extraction (SPE) and submitted to GC-MS. LOD for cocaine, heroin and metabolites were approximately 1 ng/patch. Within- and between-run coefficients of variation were less than or equal to 10%.

From a study conducted in a detoxification centre,[17] all the urine tests were consistent with the sweat findings, but to identify the same drugs (with the same rate of positivity), it was necessary to test two urine specimens along with only one sweat specimen. It was concluded that sweat testing appears to offer the advantage of being a relatively non-invasive means of obtaining a cumulative estimate of drug exposure over a period of several days.

Sweat analysis has been proposed recently for identifying drug abusers. Specimens can be collected under close supervision without embarrassment and are not subject to evasive manoeuvres. Testing individuals for illicit drugs with sweat patches worn continually would provide effective coverage for a week. Studies conducted in a detoxification centre have shown that sweat analysis is more sensitive for detecting illicit drug use than urine screening. However, sweat is not used in routine workplace drug testing.

Hair

Physiology of hair

In 1979, Baumgartner *et al.*[1] published the first report of the detection of morphine in the hair of heroin abusers. They found that differences in the concentration of morphine along the hair shaft correlated with the time of drug use. This paper was followed by a large number of studies, mostly using radioimmunoassay (RIA) and/or GC-MS. Today chromatographic procedures, especially those coupled to mass spectrometry, represent the gold standard for the identification and quantification of drugs in hair, because of their high sensitivity and selectivity.

Technically, testing of hair for drugs is no more difficult or challenging than testing in any other matrix. In fact, the application of analytical methods and instrumental approaches are in most cases quite similar, regardless of the initial sample preparation. Today, hair analysis is routinely used as a tool for detection of xenobiotics (drugs of abuse, pharmaceuticals, environmental contaminants, hormones, etc.) in forensic science, traffic medicine, occupational medicine and clinical toxicology.

Hair is a product of differentiated organs in the skin of mammals and is composed of protein (65–95%, keratin essentially), water (15–35%), lipids (1–9%) and minerals (<1%). The hair shaft consists of an outer cuticle surrounding a cortex and, in some types of hair, a central medulla. It begins in a follicle closely associated with glands (sebaceous and apocrine), and grows in cycles, alternating between periods of growth (anagen phase) and periods of quiescence (catagen and telogen phases). Of the about one million hair follicles of the adult scalp, approximately 85% is in the growing phase and the remaining 15% is in a quiescent stage. Hair is produced during 4–8 years for head hair (<6 months for non-head hair) at a rate of approximately 0.22–0.52 mm/day or 0.6–1.42 cm/month[47] for head hair (growth rate depending on hair type and anatomical location).

The exact mechanism by which chemicals are bound into hair is not known, but it is generally proposed that xenobiotics can enter hair during at least three stages: from the blood during hair formation, from sweat and sebum, and from the external environment.

Collection of hair

Collection procedures for hair analysis for drugs have not been standardised. In most published studies, the samples are obtained from random locations on the scalp, but hair is best collected from the area at the back of the head, called the vertex posterior. Compared with other areas of the head, this area has less variability in the hair growth rate, the number of hairs in the growing phase is more constant and the hair is less subject to age- and sex-related influences. The sample size varies considerably among laboratories and depends on the drug to be analysed and the test methodology. Sample sizes reported in the literature range from a single hair to 200 mg. When sectional analysis is performed, the hair is cut into segments of about 1, 2 or 3 cm, which corresponds approximately to about 1, 2 or 3 months' growth. When scalp hair is not available, other types of hair (pubic hair, arm hair or axillary hair) can been used as an alternative source for drug detection. To illustrate, the hair collection procedure at X-Pertise Consulting is shown in Figure 7.2.

After incorporation in the hair shaft, organic substances are capable of surviving for hundreds of years under favourable conditions (protected from light and humidity). For example, the cocaine metabolite benzoylecgonine has been detected in hair from ancient, spontaneously mummified human remains of 163 individual samples, obtained from populations living in northern Chile during the past 4000 years.[48]

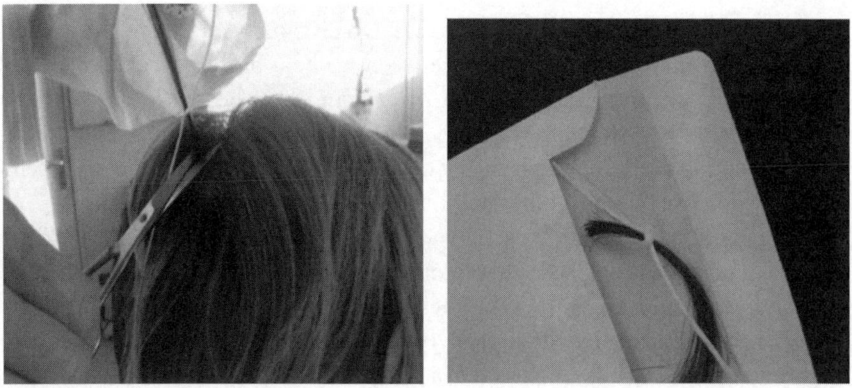

Figure 7.2 Collection procedure for hair at X-Pertise Consulting for testing for drugs of abuse. When?: 3–5 weeks after the control in the case of challenging a urinary result; upon request in other cases. How much?: four samples of about 100 hairs. Where?: in vertex posterior. How?: root and tip ends must be distinguished, using a string 1 cm from the root; hair must be cut by scissors as close as possible to the scalp. Do not pull out. Do not use adhesive. Store in an envelope at ambient temperature or ask for a hair collection kit.

An important issue of concern for drug analysis in hair is the change in the drug concentration induced by cosmetic treatment of hair. Hair is continuously subjected to natural factors, such as sunlight, weather, water, pollution, etc., which affect and damage the cuticle, but hair cosmetic treatments enhance that damage. Particular attention has been focused on the effects of repeated shampooing, perming, relaxing and dyeing of hair. Repeated shampooing was found to have no significant action on the drug content of hair, but after cosmetic treatments, such as bleaching, permanent waving, dyeing or relaxing, drug concentrations decline dramatically from 50% to 80% of the original concentration. The products used for these cosmetic treatments are strong bases. They will cause hair damage and reduce drug content or directly affect drug stability.

Analytical procedures

The most important issue facing hair analysis is the avoidance of false positive results caused by passive exposure to the drug.[49] In most laboratories, hair analysis starts with a wash step to remove external contamination. After decontamination, the hair sample can be pulverised in a ball-mill or cut into segments before the hydrolysis step, or dissolved whole to enhance drug solubilisation. Finally, the xenobiotics are extracted or purified from the incubation medium before the analysis.

The first publication dealing with the analysis of morphine in hair for determining opiate abuse histories reported on analysis with RIA.[1] This paper was followed by a large number of studies, which mostly included RIA and/or GC-MS. Chromatographic procedures seem to be a more powerful tool for the identification and quantification of drugs in hair because of their high sensitivity and selectivity. Nowadays, chromatographic techniques (GC or HPLC) coupled to mass spectrometry or tandem mass spectrometry represent the gold standard in hair analysis for xenobiotics.

Drug solubilisation can be achieved by chemical (acid or alkaline) hydrolysis, enzymatic hydrolysis, direct solvent extraction or supercritical fluid extraction. Solubilisation must be such that analytes are not altered or lost. Care is necessary to prevent hydrolytic conversion. The preparation of the hair specimen is the most important factor that can influence the quantitative result.

The development of methods in the past ten years is combined with the development of screening methods by GC-MS for opiates, cocaine, cannabinoids and amphetamine (including its derivatives) simultaneously. Three methods dominate in the literature, as briefly described in Table 7.1. Liquid–liquid extraction after HCl hydrolysis as introduced by Kintz and Mangin[50] and solid-phase extraction[51] after enzymatic hydrolysis with β-glucuronidase/sulfatase led to similar results, both with the disadvantage that heroin and 6-AM might be hydrolysed to morphine. The methanol method, published in detail by Kauert and Röhrich,[52] is undoubtedly the simplest method with high sensitivity for heroin and cocaine itself, but a poor sensitivity for their metabolites morphine and benzoylecgonine, high sensitivity for THC, but no sensitivity for THC-COOH.

Positive cut-offs of these drugs have been proposed by the Society of Hair Testing[53] and are given in Table 7.2.

Cocaine

In the case of cocaine, the fact that the parent drug shows higher concentrations in hair of drug users has been well known since 1991. In Table 7.1 routine test methods for cocaine are listed, to which the procedure of Cone *et al.*[54] can be added. In this method the hair sample is cut into approximately 1-mm segments. After a washing procedure with methanol the specimens are incubated overnight at 37°C in 0.05 mol/L sulfuric acid. The acid extracts are neutralised with 1.0 mol/L NaOH and then adjusted to pH 4.0 with 1 mL sodium acetate. SPE extraction with methylene chloride and 2-propanol (8 : 2) containing 2% ammonium hydroxide is followed by evaporation and derivatisation with BSTFA (with 1% TMCS). Cocaine, benzyolecgonine, ecgonine methyl ester, norcocaine, cocaethylene and norcocaethylene can be quantified in the same run.

In contrast to heroin, cocaine consumption can be detected by measurable metabolites (norcocaine, cocaethylene) that cannot be caused by cocaine contamination.

Table 7.1 Screening procedures for the detection of illegal drugs in hair

Reference	Kauert[52]	Moeller[51]	Kintz[50]
Analytes	Heroin, 6-AM, dihydrocodeine, codeine, methadone, THC, cocaine, amphetamine, MDMA, MDEA, MDA	6-AM, dihydrocodeine, codeine, methadone, THC, cocaine, amphetamine, MDMA, MDEA, MDA	6-AM, codeine, methadone, cocaine, amphetamine, MDMA, MDEA, MDA, most pharmaceuticals
Decontamination step	Ultrasonic 5 min each 5 mL H_2O 5 mL acetone 5 mL petrolether	20 mL H_2O (2×) 20 mL acetone	5 mL $C_{12}CH_2$ (2 × 5 min)
Homogenization	100 mg hair cut into small sections in a 30 mL vial	Ball mill	Ball mill
Extraction	4 mL methanol ultrasonic 5 hours, 50°C	20–30 mg powdered hair, 2 mL acetate buffer + β-glucuronidase/aryl-sulfatase, 90 min/40°C	50 mg powdered hair, 1 mL 0.1N HCl, 16 h/56°C
Clean-up	None	$NaHCO_3$; SPE (C18), elution with 2 mL acetone/CH_2C1_2 (3 : 1)	$(NH_4)_2HPO_4$; extraction 10 mL CHC_{13}/2-propanol/*n*-heptane (50 : 17 : 33); organic phase purified with 0.2N HCl; HCl phase to pH 8.4; re-extraction with CHC_{13}
Derivatisation	Propionic acid anhydride	100 microlitres PFPA/75 microlitres PF-*n*-propanol; 30 min/60°C; N_2/60°C; 50 microlitres ethyl acetate	40 microlitres BSTFA/1% TMS; 20 min/70°C

6-AM, 6-acetylmorphine; BSTFA, *N-O*,-bis-(trimethylsilyl)trifluoroacetamide; MDEA, methyldiethanolamine; MDMA, methylenedioxymethamphetamine; PFPA, pentafluoropropionic anhydride; SPE, solid phase extraction; THC, tetrahydrocannabinol

The determination of the pyrolysis product of cocaine, androhydroecgonine methylester (AEME), is helpful to distinguish cocaine and crack users. Kintz *et al.*[55] found AEME in a range of 0.2–2.4 ng/mg in samples from seven crack users.

The literature and the scientific meetings concerning cocaine are dominated by discussion surrounding whether decontamination procedures can remove external contamination completely and whether there is a racial bias. This is important when hair analysis is used as 'stand-alone' evidence for workplace testing. Baumgartner *et al.* solve the problem by a washing procedure that leaves the drugs in an 'inaccessible domain' that cannot be reached

Table 7.2 Cut-offs proposed by the Society of Hair Testing

Analytes	Screening by ELISA	Confirmation by MS
Opiates	0.2 ng/mg	0.2 ng/mg for morphine, codeine, 6-AM
Cocaine	0.5 ng/mg	0.5 ng/mg for cocaine 0.05 ng/mg for benzoylecgonine and cocaethylene
Amphetamines	0.2 ng/mg	0.2 ng/mg for amphetamine, methamphetamine, MDA, MDMA, MDEA
Cannabis	0.1 ng/mg	0.1 ng/mg for THC 1 pg/mg for THC-COOH

6-AM, 6-acetylmorphine; MS, mass spectrometry.

by external contamination but only enzymatic disintegration of the hair. They argue that the drug found in this area can only have been incorporated by consumption when it exceeds a certain value, the used cut-off.[56]

Kidwell and Blank[6] state that after contamination of the hair with certain drugs, small amounts will pierce the hair matrix. During cosmetic treatment over weeks the contamination will be washed away but not the small amounts that have passed the cuticula. The determination of those samples will lead to positive hair tests.

An important study with controlled doses of cocaine-d5 was published by Henderson *et al.* in 1996.[57] The deuterium-labelled cocaine was administered intravenously and/or intranasally in doses of 0.6–4.2 mg/kg under controlled conditions. A single dose could be detected for 2–6 months, the minimum detectable dose appeared to be between 22 and 35 mg, but within the range of the doses used in the study, the hair test did not provide an accurate record of either the amount, time or duration of drug use.

Opiates

In 1995 Rothe and Pragst[58] confirmed by systematic extraction studies that methanol and water had the best extraction capability for opiates, but using hydrophobic solvents such as dioxane and acetonitrile, a low extraction rate was found. With toluene, almost no extraction occurred.

As heroin samples always contain codeine, codeine is also detected in cases of heroin abuse. Morphine is a metabolite of codeine and can be detected when codeine is abused. The quantification of both drugs was proposed several years ago to differentiate between codeine and heroin abuse. If the morphine level is clearly higher than the codeine level in the examined hair sample, heroin or morphine abuse is highly probable. If the codeine concentration is largely higher than the morphine level, then it may be assumed that codeine has been ingested. This is no longer acceptable today as discrimination of heroin users from individuals exposed to other sources of morphine alkaloids can be achieved by identifying heroin or 6-AM directly. In this case, no alkaline hydrolysis can be performed to avoid hydrolysis. In most samples, it was demonstrated that 6-AM exceeds morphine, which is a less lipophilic compound.

Pubic hair shows higher drug levels than scalp hair.[59] This may be due to the slightly lower growth speed of pubic hair than of scalp hair. In addition, pubic and scalp hair have totally different telogen/anagen ratios so the concentrations cannot be compared directly.

In order to take differing growth speeds and the problem of telogen/anagen ratios into consideration, dose/concentration relation studies should only be performed with hair samples grown from the shaved skin before drug administration and under control of the growth speed of the hair.

Cannabis

In 1995 two groups (Cirimele *et al.*[60] and Jurado *et al.*[61]) reported the first results using GC-MS to test for cannabis. Both determined THC and THC-COOH in the same run. The first procedure was specifically devoted to cannabis, while the second was included in a general screening for opiates, cocaine and cannabis. The measured concentrations were low, particularly in comparison with other drugs. Some authors have suggested the use of negative chemical ionisation to target the drugs[62] or the application of tandem mass spectrometry.[63] More recently, Cirimele *et al.*[64] have developed a simpler method, based on the simultaneous identification of cannabinol (CBN), cannabidiol (CBD) and THC. This procedure appears to be a screening method that is rapid, economic and does not require derivatisation prior to analysis. Since THC, CBD and CBN are present in smoke, to avoid potential external contamination, THC-COOH, the endogenous metabolite, should be tested to confirm drug use.

After decontamination with various mixtures (organic solvents, aqueous solvents, alone or with combination), hair specimens are generally hydrolysed in a strong alkaline medium to obtain complete dissolution of the matrix.

The concentrations measured are very low, particularly for THC-COOH, which is only seldom identified as being present in the low pg/mg range.

Amphetamines

Almost all of literature dealing with amphetamines in hair has been written by Japanese researchers. In most cases, amphetamine and methamphetamine have been the target drugs. More recently, particular attention has been focused on methylenedioxy-amphetamine derivatives, such as methylene-dioxymethamphetamine (MDMA). The screening procedures listed in Table 7.1 are also used for amphetamine and its derivatives.

In all cases, a decontamination step was included in the entire procedure. When comparing four different procedures for hair preparation (methanol sonication, acid hydrolysis, alkaline hydrolysis and enzymatic hydrolysis) Kintz and Cirimele[65] found that best recoveries were observed after alkaline hydrolysis. However, it was not possible to determine which method performed best, based on recoveries, precision and practicability. Lower concentrations were observed after methanol sonication together with heavy-laden chromatograms.

Although sometimes proposed for urine, chiral analysis of amphetamine-related substances has not been extensively studied in hair. Tagliaro *et al.*[66] proposed a procedure applicable to hair using capillary electrophoresis with native β-cyclodextrin (15 mmol/L) as the chiral selector. The optimised conditions were: pH 2.5 phosphate, uncoated capillary (45 cm × 50 micrometres inner diameter), potential 10 kV. To improve the concentration sensitivity, the authors adopted a field-amplified sample stacking procedure. Good resolution with excellent chiral selectivity and efficiency was obtained for all the analytes.

Liquid chromatography is probably not a useful tool for the analysis of methylenedioxyamphetamine derivatives present in hair at trace concentrations.

Hair applications

Although there are still controversies on how to interpret the results, particularly concerning external contamination, cosmetic treatments, ethnic bias or drug incorporation, the investigations into hair analysis have reached a plateau, having solved almost all the analytical problems. Various conferences on hair analysis around the world since 1992 have indicated the increasingly important role of this method for the investigation of drug abuse.

Although GC-MS is the method of choice in practice, GC-MS/MS or LC-MS are today used in several laboratories, even for routine cases, particularly to target low dosage compounds, such as THC-COOH, fentanyl, flunitrazepam, zolpidem or buprenorphine.

Today, quality assurance is a major issue for drug testing in hair. Since 1990, the National Institute of Standards and Technology (Gaithersburg, MD, USA) has developed inter-laboratory comparisons, followed by the Society of Hair Testing (Strasbourg, France).

Sectional analysis

Multisectional analysis involves taking a length of hair and cutting it into sections to measure drug use over periods of time. The hair must be cut as close as possible to the scalp. Particular care is also required to ensure that each individual hair in the strand retains the position it originally had in relation to other hairs. The further away from the hair root, the more cautious the interpretation of the quantitative findings of the individual hair sections has to be. It has been claimed that this technique can be applied to provide a retrospective calendar of an individual's drug use. For example, multisection analysis can be performed for people who test positive on an initial screen. This information can then be used to validate an individual's claim of prior drug use but abstinence during more recent months. Another use of such information is to compare the results with the individual's self-reported drug use history, to establish the level of denial prior to referring the individual to rehabilitation.

The most extensive study on sectional analysis for drugs of abuse involved patients in rehabilitation centres. Segmental hair analysis was used to verify both their previous drug history and their recent enforced abstinence. In case of well observance, the lowest drug concentrations must be found in the segments nearest the root, thus confirming decreased drug use or recent abstinence. Abstinence from tobacco can be demonstrated by sectional analysis. The switch from heroin to another drug (codeine, ethylmorphine, dihydrocodeine) can be established with accuracy. Given the variation of hair growth rates and the long half-life of particular drugs (cannabinoids) that can be retained in the body for weeks or months after last use, results from a multisectional analysis should not be used to determine a precise period of drug abuse or to compare individuals.

Dose–concentration relationship

A critical question about hair analysis that remains controversial is the relationship between intake dose and concentration in hair. In cases of chronic abuse, daily doses vary significantly from day to day and the establishment of a dose–response relationship requires a large amount of data to take individual differences into consideration. Weak dose–concentration relationships can be explained by the following points: the drug dose of abusers is uncertain, the purity of illicit compounds is unknown and the uptake of the drug from blood to hair varies with the individual. On the other hand, some papers report that there is a significant dose–concentration relationship for digoxin, cocaine, phencyclidine, cannabinoids, morphine, meprobamate, haloperidol and amitriptyline. These results strongly suggest that a dose–response relationship exists between drug levels in hair and the administered dose and this seems particularly true in controlled studies, in which a drug was taken for the first time or under close supervision.[67]

The possibility of racial bias due to differences in melanin concentrations or in hair porosity is still under discussion. Melanins are responsible for the colour of hair. Two types of melanin are present, eumelanin (with low sulfur content) and pheomelanin (with high sulfur content). Black and brown hair contains more eumelanin than red and blond hair. It appears that it is not simply the concentration of drugs in blood that determines the concentration in hair. Numerous factors may influence the incorporation of drugs into hair, such as the nature of the compounds (pK_a, lipid solubility, metabolism pattern) and variation in hair growth cycles. Until these mechanisms are elucidated, the quantitative results and extrapolation to the amount of drug intake of such a hair analysis should be considered with extreme caution.[68] However, in 1995 Kintz and Mangin[50] proposed some approaches (distribution along a histogram) to estimate the level of cocaine and heroin consumption.

Comparison with urine testing

There are essentially three types of problem with urinalysis drug testing: false positives when not confirmed with GC-MS, embarrassment of observed urine collection and evasive manoeuvres, including adulteration. These problems can be greatly mitigated or eliminated through hair analysis. It is always possible to obtain a fresh, identical hair sample if there is any claim of a specimen mix-up or breach in the chain of custody. This makes hair analysis essentially fail-safe, in contrast to urinalysis, since an identical urine specimen cannot be obtained at a later date.

Another potential use of hair analysis is to verify accidental or unintentional ingestion of drinks or food that has been laced with drugs. In case of a single use, the hair will not test positive. Ingestion of poppy seeds appears to be sufficient for the creation of a positive urine result, while ingestion of up to 30 g of poppy seeds did not result in positive hair identification (Sachs, personal communication, 1994). Its greatest use, however, may be in identifying false negatives, since neither abstaining from a drug for a few days nor trying to 'beat the test' by diluting urine will alter the concentration in hair. Urine does not indicate the frequency of drug intake in subjects who might deliberately abstain for several days before biomedical screenings. While analysis of urine specimens cannot distinguish between chronic use and single exposure, hair analysis can make this distinction. Table 7.3 summarises the differences between hair and urine.

Verification of history of drug use

By providing information on exposure to drugs over time, hair analysis may be useful in verifying self-reported histories of drug use in any situation in which a history of past rather than recent drug use is desired, as in pre-employment and employee drug testing. In addition, hair analysis may be especially useful when a history of drug use is difficult or impossible to obtain, such as from psychiatric patients. During control tests of hair fragments, a drug addict is not able to hide the fact of drug abuse. In the case of an addict who takes drugs every few days, this fact cannot be proved by means of urine and blood tests even when the tests are repeated.

Table 7.3 Comparison between urine and hair

Parameters	Urine	Hair
Major compound	Metabolites	Parent drug
Detection period	2–5 days	Weeks, months
Type of measure	Incremental	Cumulative
Screening	Yes	Difficult
Invasiveness	High	Low
Storage	–20°C	Ambient temperature
Risk of false negative	High	Low
Risk of false positive	Low	Undetermined
Risk of adulteration	High	Low
Control material	Yes	Needed

Alcohol abuse

Considering the extent of alcohol-associated problems, the diagnosis of excessive alcohol consumption is an important task from a medical point of view. The methods used for this purpose are based on indirect alcohol markers such as increased liver enzyme activity (γGT or GPT), increased erythrocyte mean cell volume or presence of carbohydrate-deficient transferrins, which can also originate from other pathological causes. Markers of ethanol consumption are ethylglucuronide, phosphatidylethanol or fatty acid ethyl esters (FAEEs). The first investigations of a marker of alcohol consumption in hair were reported by Sachs and colleagues and focused on ethylglucuronide,[69] but recent examination of the presence of this ethanol metabolite in hair were rather discouraging.[70] Detection of ethylglucuronide in hair is always associated with alcohol consumption, whereas a negative result does not unambiguously exclude the alcohol abuse.

More recently, new investigations on FAEEs have been proposed by Pragst and colleagues[71] to monitor alcohol consumption. FAEEs are formed in the presence of ethanol and free fatty acids, triglycerides, lipoproteins or phospholipids by a FAEE synthase found in liver but also in hair roots. FAEE determination is of interest, as they appear responsive to alcohol-induced organ damage. In blood, FAEEs can be used as markers of an actual or recent alcohol intake at lest 24 hours after completion of alcohol intake. Hair concentrations of four FAEEs (ethyl myristate, ethyl palmitate, ethyl oleate and ethyl stearate) found in the hair of children, adult teetotallers and social drinkers in comparison with FAEE concentrations found in the hair of alcoholics led the authors to conclude that FAEEs are suitable markers for the detection of heavy alcohol consumption.

Segmental hair analysis in a case of alcohol withdrawal treatment showed a decrease in FAEE content from the distal to the proximal root segment. Further investigations are in progress to examine the applicability of the FAEE determination in clinical practice.

Recent trends in the use of alternative specimens for workplace drug testing

In a paper from 2006, Musshoff *et al.*[72] have compared data obtained from hair versus urine and self-report. Hair test results demonstrated that methadone abuse in general was under-reported by people who did not participate in a substitution programme. Comparing self-reports and the results of hair analyses, drug use was dramatically under-reported, especially cocaine. Cocaine hair tests appeared to be highly sensitive and specific in identifying past cocaine use even in settings of negative urine tests. In contrast to cocaine, hair lacks sensitivity as a detection agent for cannabinoids and a proof of cannabis use by means of hair analysis should include the sensitive detection of the metabolite THC-COOH in the lower picogram range.

This was also confirmed by Tsanaclis and Wicks,[73] as they demonstrated that 1 in 10 workplace hair tests detected the presence of at least one drug, which is twice the rate of detection using urine (1 in 20 urine samples). This means that the chance of identifying people on drugs in the workplace by testing hair samples is twice that by using urine samples. In the same study, the positive rate for the workplace sector was 10%, and the most common drugs detected in the workplace samples in each group were: THC (4%), codeine (2%), cocaine (2%), MDMA (0.5%) and diazepam (0.1%). The concentration levels of drugs found in samples from the workplace were lower than in the medico-legal sector.

As a consequence of the increase of the use of hair as a matrix of interest in workplace drug testing, analytical improvements to reduce the turnaround time are of interest. Today, major companies are using ELISA tests for screening, followed by gas or liquid chromatography confirmation.[74] In a paper presenting their methodology, the authors concluded that the ELISA tests could be useful in workplace drug testing or driving licence regranting, especially when many samples need to be tested and when the number of expected negative results is high, because ELISA is an easy and high-throughput method.

Another topic under debate among active researchers has been the best ethyl glucuronide cut-off in hair to discriminate heavy chronic alcohol drinkers. The Society of Hair Testing, on 16 June 2009, published a consensus[75] proposing 30 pg/mg as positive threshold.

Although described as a promising approach, sweat testing has no practical application in drug testing.

In contrast, there is a growing interest in oral fluid on-site tests. An important feature of urine testing is the accuracy of the on-site tests to detect drugs of abuse in fresh samples. Unfortunately, this is not always the situation for oral fluid testing. The application of the immunochemistry-based devices for screening of oral fluid has not produced satisfactory results to date, particularly for cannabis.[76,77] Most devices that were used to detect cannabis in oral fluid failed to identify the drug, probably because they were specific for THC-COOH and not for the parent THC that is present in oral fluid. Today, the detection limits are improving for cannabinoids,[78] but there is a need to detect cannabis more accurately. It appears that the most sensitive devices on the market can detect cannabis for 2–3 hours after smoking, which corresponds to the period of severe impairment. Is this enough to be used routinely? If too many subjects pass the test this will have negative consequences for safety. This is also the case if the time window of detection in oral fluid is too short when compared to urine testing.

In order to propose on-site tests for cannabis in oral fluid, manufacturers, will have to target the parent THC in their device. The ultimate goal for these devices is to be able to give a positive response for THC in concentrations equivalent to 2 ng/mL, ideally extending the time window of detection to 6–8 hours after the last cannabis exposure.

Conclusion

It appears that the value of alternative specimen analysis for the identification of drug users is steadily gaining recognition. This can be seen from its growing use in pre-employment screening, in forensic sciences and in clinical applications.

Oral fluid will probably be used in the near future in on-site testing both for epidemiological and screening purposes.

Hair analysis may be a useful adjunct to conventional drug testing in toxicology. Methods for evading urinalysis do not affect hair analysis.

Specimens of oral fluid or sweat can be more easily obtained with less embarrassment than urine, and hair can provide a more accurate history of drug use. However, costs are too expensive for routine use but the generated data are extremely helpful to document positive urine cases. These new technologies may find useful applications in the near future, for example in doping control or law enforcement agencies to document illicit drug use.

References

1. Baumgartner AM, Jones PF, Baumgartner WA, Black CT. Radioimmunoassay of hair for determining opiate-abuse histories. *J Nucl Med* 1979; 20: 748–752.
2. Sachs H. Forensic applications of hair analysis. In: Kintz P, ed. *Drug Testing in Hair*. Boca Raton: CRC Press, 1996: 211–222.
3. Kintz P. Clinical applications of hair analysis. In: Kintz P, ed. *Drug Testing in Hair*. Boca Raton: CRC Press, 1996: 267–277.
4. DuPont RL, Baumgartner WA. Drug testing by urine and hair analysis: complementary features and scientific issues. *Forensic Sci Int* 1995; 70: 63–76.
5. Kintz P. Hair testing and doping control in hair. *Toxicol Lett* 1998; 102103: 109–113.
6. Kidwell DA. Blank DL. Environmental exposure – the stumbling block of hair testing. In: Kintz P, ed. *Drug Testing in Hair*. Boca Raton: CRC Press, 1996: 17–68.
7. Jurado C, Kintz P, Menendez M, Repetto M. Influence of cosmetic treatment of hair on drug testing. *Int J Legal Med* 1997; 110: 159–163.
8. Cone EJ, Joseph R. The potential for bias in hair testing for drugs of abuse. In: Kintz P, ed. *Drug Testing in Hair*. Boca Raton: CRC Press, 1996: 69–93.
9. Haeckel R, Hänecke P. Application of saliva for drug monitoring. *Eur J Clin Chem Clin Biochem* 1996; 34: 171–191.
10. Mucklow JC. The use of saliva in therapeutic drug monitoring. *Ther Drug Monit* 1982; 4: 229–248.
11. Samyn N, Verstraete A, van Haeren C, Kintz P. Analysis of drugs of abuse in saliva. *Forensic Sci Rev* 1999; 11: 1–19.
12. Verstraete A. Oral fluid testing for driving under the influence of drugs: history, recent progress and remaining challenges. *Forensic Sci Int* 2005; 150: 143–150.
13. Cone EJ, Kumor K, Thompson LK, Sheren M. Correlation of saliva cocaine levels with plasma levels and with pharmacologic effects after intraveous administration in human subject. *J Anal Toxicol* 1988; 12: 200–206.
14. Menkes DB, Howard RC, Spears GSF, Cairns ER. Salivary THC following cannabis smoking correlates with subjective intoxication and heart rate. *Psychopharmacology* 1991; 103: 277–279.
15. Tachau H. Uber den Ubergang von Arneimitteln in der schweiss. *Arch Exp Pathol Pharmacol* 1911; 66: 224–246.
16. Cone EJ, Hillsgrove MJ, Jenkins AJ, Keenan RM, Darwin WD. Sweat testing for heroin, cocaine and metabolites. *J Anal Toxicol* 1994; 18: 298–305.
17. Kintz P, Tracqui A, Mangin P, Edel Y. Sweat testing in opioid users with a sweat patch. *J Anal Toxicol* 1996; 20: 393–397.
18. Höld KM, de Boer D, Zuidema J, Maes RAA. Saliva as an analytical tool in toxicology. *Int J Drug Testing* 1996; 1: 1–36.
19. Matin SB, Wan SH, Karam JH. Pharmacokinetics of tolbutamide: prediction by concentration in saliva. *Clin Pharmacol Ther* 1974; 16: 1052–1058.
20. O'Neal CL, Crouch DJ, Rollins DE, Fatah AA. The effects of collection methods on oral fluid codeine concentrations. *J Anal Toxicol* 2000; 24: 536–542.
21. EU Project ROSITA Roadside Testing Assessment. www.Rosita.org (accessed February 2006).
22. Kintz P, Samyn N. Unconventional samples and alternative matrices. In: Bogusz M, ed. *Handbook of Analytical Separations*, Vol. VI: *Forensic Science*. Amsterdam: Elsevier, 2000: 459–488.
23. Drummer OH. Review: Pharmacokinetics of illicit drugs in oral fluid. *Forensic Sci Int* 2005; 150: 133–142.
24. Cone EJ, Oyler J, Darwin WD. Cocaine disposition in saliva following intravenous, intranasal and smoked administration. *J Anal Toxicol* 1997; 21: 465–475.
25. Kintz P, Sengler C, Cirimele V, Mangin P. Evidence of crack use by anhydroecgonine methylester identification. *Hum Exp Toxicol* 1997; 16: 123–127.

26. Grönholm M, Lillsunde PA. Comparison between on-site immunoassay drug-testing devices and laboratory results. *Forensic Sci Int* 2001; 121: 37–46.
27. Mura P, Kintz P, Papet Y, Ruesch G, Piriou A. Evaluation de 6 tests rapides pour le dépistage du cannabis dans la sueur, la salive et les urines. *Acta Clin Belg Suppl* 1999; 1: 35–38.
28. Samyn N, van Haeren C. On-site testing of saliva and sweat with Drugwipe and determination of concentrations of drugs of abuse in saliva, plasma and urine of suspected users. *Int J Legal Med* 2000; 113: 150–154.
29. Kintz P, Cirimele V, Ludes B. Detection of cannabis in oral fluid (saliva) and forehead wipes (sweat) from impaired drivers. *J Anal Toxicol* 2000; 24: 557–561.
30. Kauert GF. Drogennachweis in Speichel vs. Serum. *Blutalkohol* 2000; 37(suppl1): 76–83.
31. Niedbala S, Kardos KW, Fritch DF *et al.* Detection of marijuana use by oral fluid and urine analysis following single-dose administration of smoked and oral marijuana. *J Anal Toxicol* 2001; 25: 289–303.
32. Huestis MA, Cone EJ. Relationship of delta 9-tetrahydrocannabinol concentrations in oral fluid and plasma after controlled administration of smoked cannabis. *J Anal Toxicol* 2004; 28: 394–399.
33. Huestis MA, Dickerson S, Cone EJ. Can saliva THC levels be correlated to behavior? American Academy of Forensic Sciences, Abstract, AAFS Publication 92-2, Fittje Brothers Printing, Colorado Springs, 190 (1992).
34. Kintz P, Bernhard W, Villain M *et al.* Detection of cannabis use in drivers with the Drugwipe device and by GC-MS after Intercept device collection. *J Anal Toxicol* 2005; 29: 724–727.
35. Niedbala S, Kardos K, Salamone S *et al.* Passive cannabis smoke exposure and oral fluid testing. *J Anal Toxicol* 2004; 28: 546–552.
36. Hawks RL. The constituents of cannabis and the disposition and metabolism of cannabinoids. In: Hawks RL, ed. *NIDA Research Monograph* no. 42, Rockville, MD: NIDA, 1982: 125–137.
37. Verstraete A, Puddu M. Deliverable D4: Evaluation of different roadside drug tests. ROSITA Contract DG VII RO 98-SC.3032, 2000. www.rosita.org (accessed 2001).
38. Clauwaert K, Van Boxlaer J, Willems A *et al.* Quantitation of amphetamine, methamphetamine, MDA, MDMA and MDEA in saliva with a Q-TOF LC/MS/MS system. In: *Proceedings of the 38thTIAFT-Meeting*, 13–17 August 2000, Helsinki, Finland.
39. Henderson GL. Mechanisms of drug incorporation into hair. *Forensic Sci Int* 1993; 63: 19–29.
40. Sunshine I, Sutliff JP. Sweat it out. In: Wong SH, Sunshine I, eds. *Handbook of Analytical Therapeutic Drug Monitoring and Toxicology*. Boca Raton: CRC Press, 1997: 253–264.
41. Fox RH, Goldsmith R, Hampto IFG, Lewis HE. The nature of the increase in sweating capacity produced by heat acclimatization. *J Physiol* 1964; 171: 368–374.
42. Balabanova S, Schneider E, Wepler R *et al.* Significance of drug determination in pilocarpine sweat for detection of past drug abuse. *Beitr Gerichtl Med* 1992; 50: 111–115.
43. Parnas J, Flachs H, Gram L, Würtz-Jorgensen A. Excretion of antiepileptic drugs in sweat. *Acta Neurol Scand* 1978; 58: 197–204.
44. Ishiyama I, Nagai T, Komuro B, Momose T, Akimori N. The significance of drug analysis of sweat in respect to rapid screening for drug abuse. *Z Rechtsmed* 1979; 82: 251–256.
45. Kidwell DA, Blanco MA, Smith FP. Cocaine detection in a university population by hair analysis and skin swab testing. *Forensic Sci Int* 1997; 84: 75–86.
46. Kintz P, Brenneisen R, Bundeli P, Mangin P. Sweat testing for heroin and metabolites in a heroin maintenance program. *Clin Chem* 1997; 43: 736–739.
47. Saitoh M, Uzaka M, Sakamoto M, Kobori T. Rate of hair growth. In: Montana and Dobson, eds. *Advances in Biology of Skin*, Vol. IX: *Hair Growth*. Oxford: Pergamon Press, 1969: 183–194.
48. Cartmell LW, Aufdemide AC, Spinfield A, Weems C, Arriaza B. The frequency and antiquity of prehistoric coca-leaf-chewing practices in northen Chile: radioimmunoassay of a cocaine metabolite in hair. *Latin Am Antiquity* 1991; 2: 260–268.

49. Baumgartner WA, Hill VA. Hair analysis for drugs of abuse: decontamination issues. In: Sunshine I, ed. *Recent Development in Therapeutic Drug Monitoring and Clinical Toxicology*. New 0York: Marcel Dekker, 1992: 577–597.
50. Kintz P, Mangin P. What constitutes a positive result in hair analysis: proposal for the establishment of cut-off values. *Forensic Sci Int* 1995; 70: 3–11.
51. Moeller MR, Fey P, Wennig R. Hair analysis as evidence in forensic cases. *Forensic Sci Int* 1993; 63: 43–53.
52. Kauert G, Röhrich J. Concentrations of delta9-tetrahydrocannabinol, cocaine and 6-monoacetylmorphine in hair of drug abusers. *Int J Legal Med* 1996; 108: 294–299.
53. Recommendations of the Society of Hair Testing. *Forensic Sci Int* 2004; 145: 83–84.
54. Cone EJ, Yousefnajed D, Darwin WD, Maguire T. Testing human hair for drugs of abuse II. Identification of unique cocaine metabolites in hair of drug abusers and evaluation of decontamination procedures. *J Anal Toxicol* 1991; 15: 250–255.
55. Kintz P, Cirimele V, Sengler C, Mangin P. Testing human hair and urine for anhydroecgonine methylester, a pyrolysis product of cocaine. *J Anal Toxicol* 1995; 19: 479–482.
56. Baumgartner WA, Hill VA. Hair analysis for drugs of abuse. In: Sunshine I, ed. *Recent Development in Therapeutic Drug Monitoring and Clinical Toxicology*. New York: Marcel Dekker, 1992: 577–597.
57. Henderson GL, Harkey MR, Zhou C, Jones RT, Jacob P. III. Incorporation of isotopically labeled cocaine and metabolites into human hair: 1. dose-response relationship. *J Anal Toxicol* 1996; 20: 1–12.
58. Rothe M, Pragst F. Solvent optimization for the direct extraction of opiates from hair samples. *J Anal Toxicol* 1995; 19: 236–240.
59. Kintz P, Tracqui A, Mangin P. Opiate concentrations in human hair of the head, axillary and pubic regions. *J Forensic Sci* 1993; 38: 657–662.
60. Cirimele V, Kintz P, Mangin P. Testing human hair for cannabis. *Forensic Sci Int* 1995; 70: 175–182.
61. Jurado C, Giménez MP, Ménendez M, Repetto M. Simultaneous quantification of opiates, cocaine and cannabinoids in hair. *Forensic Sci Int* 1995; 70: 165–174.
62. Kintz P, Cirimele V, Mangin P. Testing human hair for cannabis II. Identification of THC-COOH by GC/MS/NCI as an unique proof. *J Forensic Sci* 1995; 40: 619–623.
63. Uhl M. Determination of drugs in hair using GC/MS/MS. *Forensic Sci Int* 1997; 84: 281–294.
64. Cirimele V, Sachs H, Kintz P, Mangin P. Testing human hair for cannabis. III. Rapid screening procedure for simultaneous identification of THC, cannabinol and cannabidiol. *J Anal Toxicol* 1996; 20: 13–16.
65. Kintz P, Cirimele V. Interlaboratory comparison of quantitative determination of amphetamine and related compounds in hair samples. *Forensic Sci Int* 1997; 84: 151–156.
66. Tagliaro F, Manetto G, Bellini S, Scarcella D, Smith FP, Marigo M. Simultaneous chiral separation of MDMA, MDA, MDEA, ephedrine, amphetamine and methamphetamine by capillary electrophoresis in uncoated and coated capillaries with native beta-cyclodextrin as the chiral selector. *Preliminary application to the analysis of urine and hair. Electrophoresis* 1998; 19: 42–50.
67. Beumer JH, Bosman IJ, Maes RA. Hair as a biological marker for therapeutic drug monitoring. *Int J Clin Pract* 2001; 55: 353–357.
68. Harkey MR, Henderson GL, Zhou *et al.* Simultaneous quantitation of cocaine and its major metabolites in human hair by gas chromatography chemical ionization mass spectrometry. *J Anal Toxicol* 1991; 15: 260–265.
69. Sachs H. Drogennachweis in Haaren. In: Kijewski H, ed. *Proceedings of the Symposium on Das Haar als Spur-Spur de Haare*. Lübeck: Schmidt-Römhild, 1997: 119–133.
70. Skopp G, Schmitt G, Poetsch L, Droenner P, Aderjan R, Mattern R. Ethyl glucuronide in human hair. *Alcohol Alcohol* 2000; 35: 283–285.
71. Pragst F, Auwaerter V, Sporkert F, Spiegel K. Analysis of fatty acid ethyl esters in hair as possible markers of chronically elevated alcohol consumption by headspace solid-phase

microextraction (HS-SPME) and gas chromatography-mass spectrometry (GC-MS). *Forensic Sci Int* 2001; 121: 76–88.

72. Musshoff F, Driever F, Lachenmeier K, Lachenmeier DW, Banger M, Madea B. Results of hair analyses for drugs of abuse and comparison with self-reports and urine tests. *Forensic Sci Int* 2006; 156: 118–123.
73. Tsanaclis L, Wicks JF. Patterns in drug use in the United Kingdom as revealed through analysis of hair in a large population sample. *Forensic Sci Int* 2007; 170: 121–128.
74. Pujol ML, Cirimele V, Tritsch PJ, Villain M, Kintz P. Evaluation of the IDS One-Step ELISA kits for the detection of illicit drugs in hair. *Forensic Sci Int* 2007; 170: 189–192.
75. Kintz P. Consensus of the Society of Hair Testing on hair testing for chronic excessive alcohol consumption 2009. *Forensic Sci Int* 2010; 196(1–3): 2.
76. Raes E, Verstraete A. Evaluation of rapid point-of-collection oral fluid testing devices. In: Verstrate A, Raes E, eds. *Rosita-2 Project: Final Report*. Ghent: Academia Press, 2006: 227–257.
77. Drummer OH. Introduction and review of collection techniques and applications of drug testing of oral fluid. *Ther Drug Monit* 2008; 30: 203–206.
78. Kintz P, Brunet B, Muller JF *et al.* Evaluation of the Cozart DDSV test for cannabis in oral fluid. *Ther Drug Monit* 2009; 31: 131–134.

8

Analytical techniques

Daniëlle Borrey

Key points

- The analysis of a workplace drug test is performed in three steps: (1) When the sample is received at the laboratory, screening tests are carried out to look for the presence of drugs. (2) If the screening results are all negative (results below a predefined cut-off level) no further analysis is necessary. In samples which test positive (above a predefined cut-off level) the presence of the drug is confirmed using a chromatographic technique, preferably in combination with mass spectrometry. (3) A medical review officer interprets the results.
- Different screening techniques exist. Most of them are based on immunoassays.
- Chromatography is a physical method of separation in which the components to be separated are distributed between two phases, one of which is stationary (stationary phase) while the other (mobile phase) moves in a definite direction.
- A suitable sample preparation is essential for chromatographic analysis and it involves, if required, cleavage of conjugates followed by isolation and eventually derivatisation of the compounds.
- Different detectors exist for liquid or gas chromatography, but by far the most important for workplace drug testing is (tandem) mass spectrometry.
- Mass spectrometry is a microanalytical destructive technique with which characteristic information about the structure and molecular weight of very small amounts of a component can be obtained.
- In order to increase throughput one can automate sample preparation, use shorter and smaller internal diameter columns with fast temperature programming in gas chromatography or use ultra performance liquid chromatography.

- All methods must be thoroughly validated as only validation can demonstrate that minimum acceptance criteria are fulfilled and that the method is suitable for a certain purpose. Different validation parameters need to be assessed for qualitative or quantitative analytical procedures.

Introduction

The analytical techniques used for workplace drug testing must give accurate and reliable information about a person's drug use. The most common specimen used for drug analysis is urine as sample collection is not invasive and the intake of a drug can be demonstrated for a longer time. Alternative matrices such as hair can also be used for toxicological analyses but external contamination, cosmetic treatment or racial bias must be considered for interpretation (see Chapter 7). Detection of the parent component is less important in urine analysis as most drugs are extensively metabolised and the concentrations of the metabolites are often much higher in urine than those of the parent drug.[1] When the sample is received at the laboratory, screening tests are carried out to look for the presence of drugs. If the screening results are all negative (results below a predefined cut-off level) no further analysis is

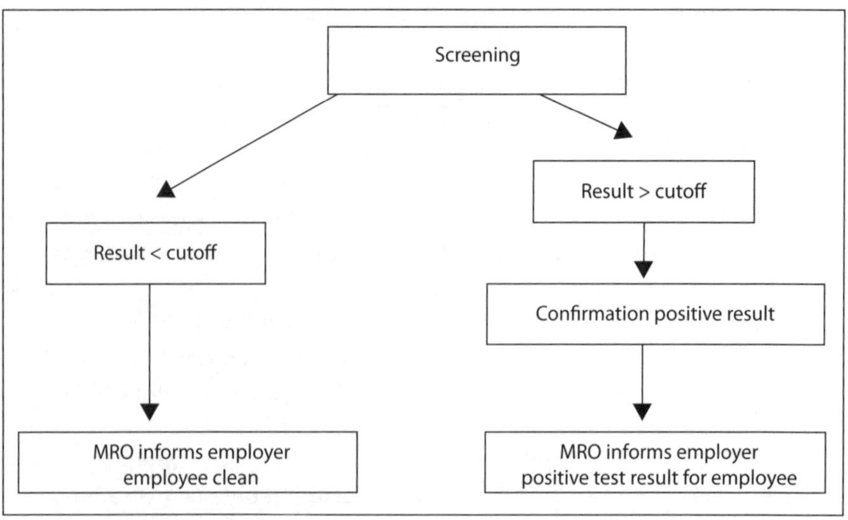

Figure 8.1 Schematic representation of analyses performed from screening to reporting of results. MRO, medical review officer.

necessary. Samples that test positive (result above a predefined cut-off level) must have the presence of the drug confirmed using a chromatographic technique, preferably in combination with mass spectrometry. Results are interpreted by a medical review officer who informs the employer (Figure 8.1).

Screening tests

Before the screening process is started it needs to be demonstrated that the sample received for analysis is really urine. For this purpose creatinine must always be measured. Complementary tests could be pH, nitrite or other adulterants (see Chapter 9). Currently accepted screening techniques include immunoassays and chromatographic techniques.[2]

Immunoassay screening techniques

Immunoassays are designed to separate the negative samples from the positives, yielding an increased efficiency and reduced turnaround time. In immunoassays the reaction of an antibody to its antigen is used to measure the concentration of a class of components. An advantage of these tests is that the target analyte does not need to be extracted from the matrix, yielding easy operation and rapidity. The specificity of immunoassays depends on the capacity of the antibodies to generate a measurable signal for the target analytes only. Endogenous components that enhance or suppress the signal and substances with similar chemical structures can interfere in immunoassays. Evaluation of cross-reactivity is therefore essential during the optimisation of an assay.[3] For drug analysis different homogeneous and heterogeneous immunoassay techniques are available, depending on whether the assay includes a separation step of the bound and unbound tracer.

Enzyme multiplied immunoassay technique

The enzyme multiplied immunoassay technique (EMIT) (Figure 8.2) is a homogeneous immunoassay based on the competition for antibody-binding sites between the drug in the sample and drug labelled with the enzyme glucose-6-phosphate dehydrogenase (G6P-DH) from the bacterium *Leuconostoc mesenteroides*. This bacterial G6P-DH converts nicotinamide adenine dinucleotide (NAD) to NADH, which can be measured spectrophotometrically at 340 nm (Figure 8.2a). Endogenous G6P-DH does not interfere as this enzyme converts NADP, and not NAD. G6P-DH–drug conjugates and specific anti-drug antibodies are added to the sample. The antibodies either bind to the enzyme–drug conjugate when no drug is present in the sample (Figure 8.2b) or to the drug, if present in the sample (Figure 8.2c). Binding of the drug–enzyme complex to the antibody yields a decrease in enzyme activity. With increasing drug concentrations in the sample the amount of free,

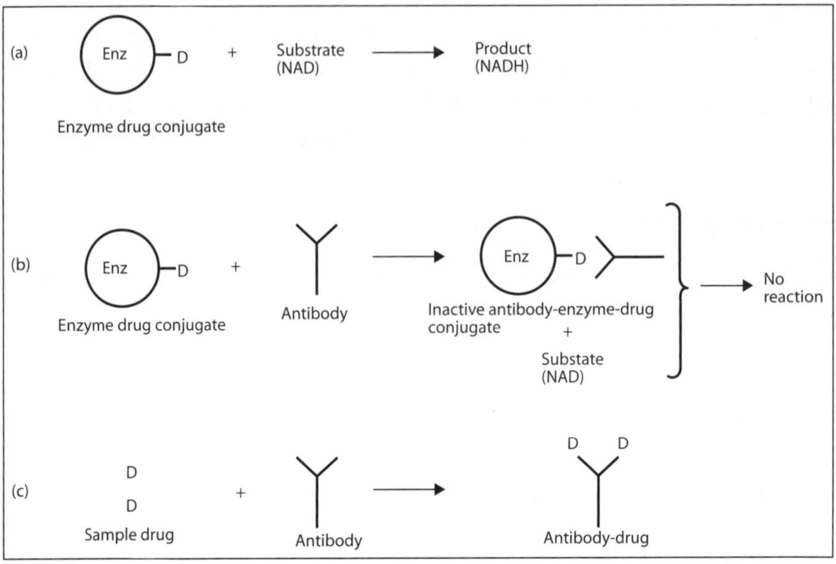

Figure 8.2 Schematic representation of enzyme multiplied immunoassay technique (EMIT).

active drug–enzyme complex increases, so the drug concentration in the sample is proportional to the enzyme activity.

EMIT can differentiate concentrations over a wide range and there are only few interfering substances. The enzyme activity, however, can be disturbed not only by cross-reactivity with structurally similar compounds but by matrix components as well. Adulterants often produce false negative results in EMIT which will not be confirmed (see Chapter 9).

Fluorescence polarisation immunoassays

Fluorescence polarisation immunoassays (FPIA) (Figure 8.3) are based on the difference in the rotation speed of a small antigen labelled with fluorescein that is free or bound to an antibody. The drug in the sample and drug labelled with fluorescein (tracer) compete for the binding sites on the antibody molecules. The tracer is excited with polarised blue light (481–489 nm) and returns to its steady state by emitting green light (525–550 nm). If the tracer is bound to the antibody it will not rotate freely in the solution and the emitted light will be polarised as well. In a sample that contains little or no drug, a high concentration of the tracer will be bound, yielding a high polarisation or response. In this assay the drug concentration is thus inversely proportional to the signal. FPIA is a homogeneous immunoassay with low limits of detection that is more stable than enzyme-linked immunoassays. The reagents can be preserved longer than those for enzyme-linked assays but only a few analysers are adapted for this method.

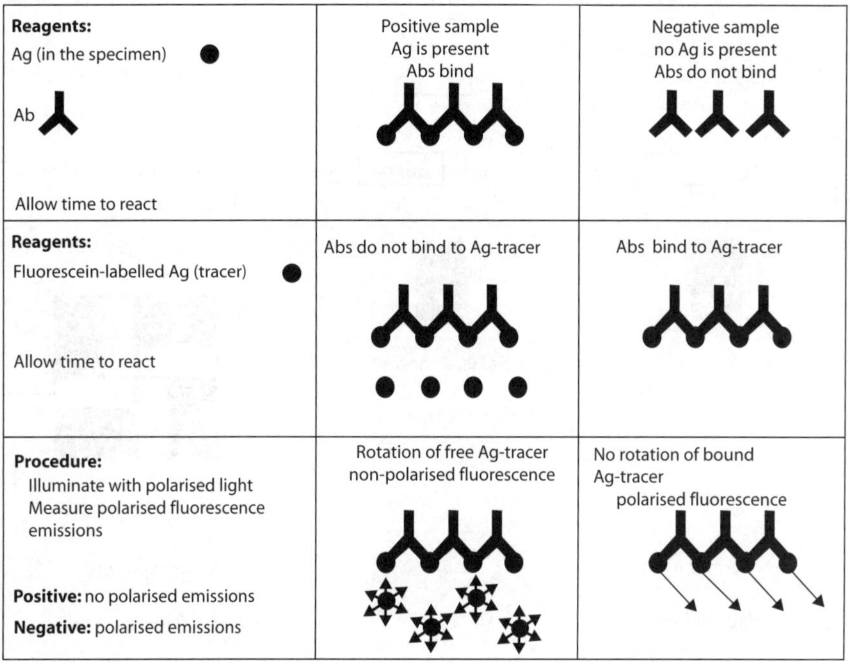

Figure 8.3 Schematic representation of fluorescence polarisation immunoassays (FPIA). Ab, antibody; Ag, antigen.

Cloned enzyme donor immunoassay

Some enzymes are composed of inactive fragments that associate spontaneously to form an active enzyme. Cloned enzyme donor immunoassay (CEDIA®) (Figure 8.4) is a homogeneous assay based on this principle and uses the bacterial enzyme β-galactosidase (< *E. coli*) that cleaves a substrate and generates a colour change. Substrates used are *o*-nitrophenyl-β-D-galactopyranoside (ONPG) or chlorophenol red-β-D-galactopyranoside (CPRG). The drug present in the sample and drug conjugated with an inactive fragment of the enzyme compete for the antibody-binding sites. If the drug conjugate is bound to the antibody the active enzyme cannot be assembled. If drug is present in the sample it binds to the antibody, leaving the inactive fragments free to form the active enzyme and generate an absorbance change. The obtained signal is proportional to the concentration of the drug in the sample. CEDIA has only a few problems with interfering substances and false positive results are obtained if *E. coli* is present in the sample.

Kinetic interaction of microparticles in solution

Kinetic interaction of microparticles in solution (KIMS) (Figure 8.5) is an assay where the antibodies are bound to microparticles. When the drug is absent in the sample, soluble drug conjugates bind to antibodies bound on

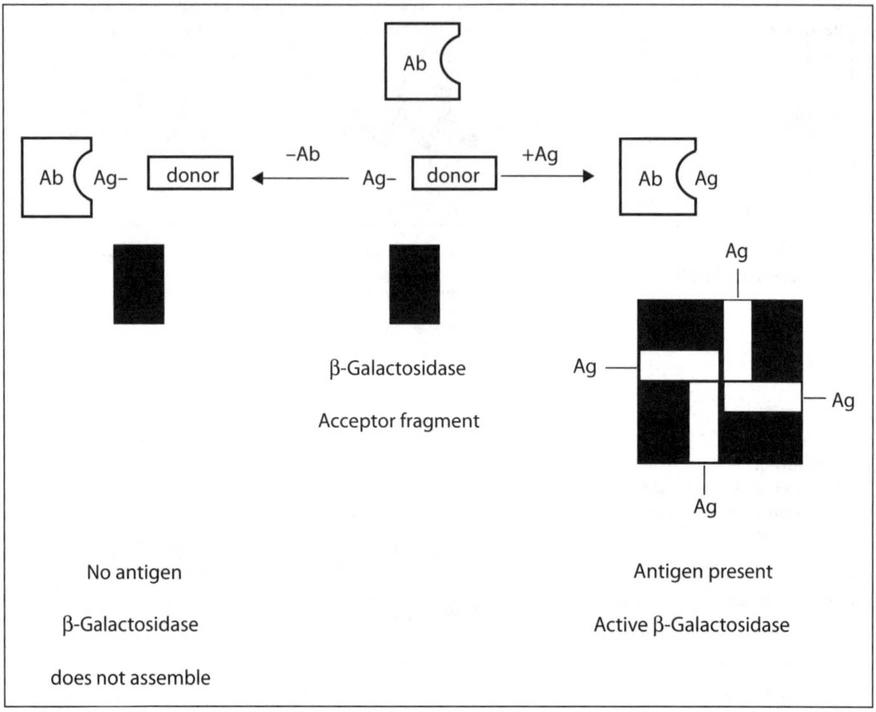

Figure 8.4 Schematic representation of cloned enzyme donor immunoassay (CEDIA). Ab, antibody; Ag, antigen.

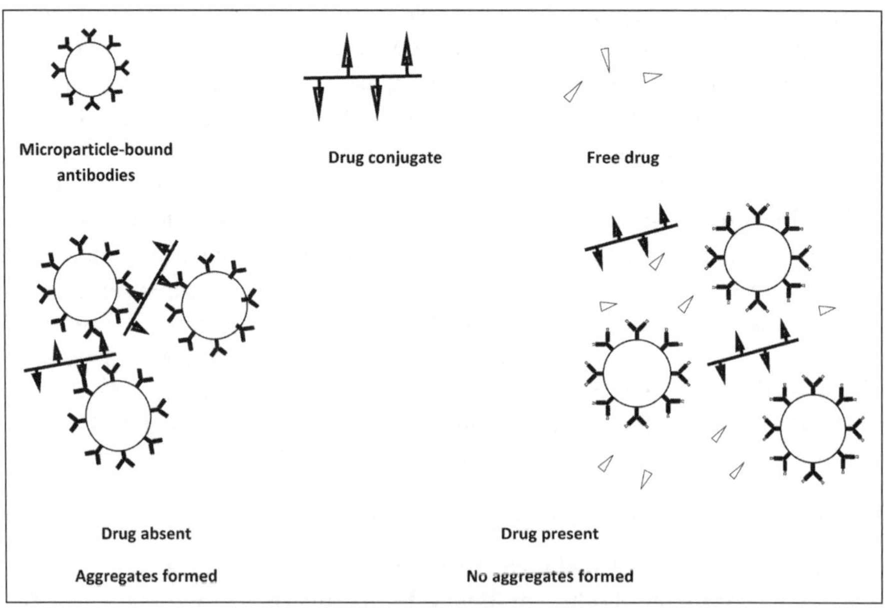

Figure 8.5 Schematic representation of kinetic interaction of microparticles in solution (KIMS).

microparticles yielding the formation of particle aggregates and an increase in absorption. Presence of the drug leads to a competitive reaction between the drug in the sample and the drug conjugates for microparticle-bound antibodies. Antibodies bound to the drug are no longer available to form aggregates, yielding a decreased absorption proportional to the drug concentration in the sample. The aggregates formed are more stable than enzyme conjugates and there are only few interferences. Substances that interfere with the agglutination process will usually produce false positive results that will not be confirmed by more specific testing. A disadvantage of KIMS is the small linear concentration range.

Enzyme-linked immunosorbent assay

The enzyme-linked immunosorbent assay (ELISA) (Figure 8.6) is a heterogeneous immunoassay using a microplate as solid phase. The wells of the plate are coated with antibody for the target drug. After addition of the sample and a drug–enzyme conjugate the well is incubated and competition for the binding sites on the microplate is taking place (Figure 8.6a). Excess reagents are then washed (Figure 8.6b) and a substrate (S, Figure 8.6c) is added. At the end of the enzyme–substrate incubation a stop reagent is added and the developed

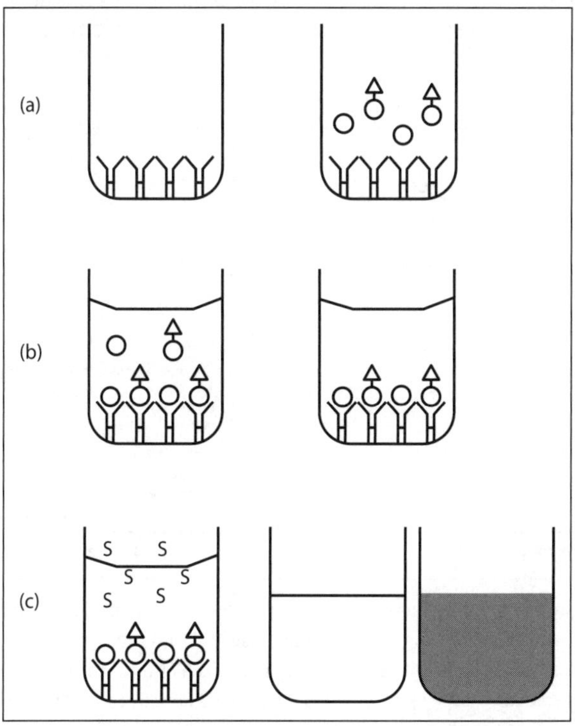

Figure 8.6 Schematic representation of enzyme-linked immunosorbent assay (ELISA).

colour is measured with an ELISA plate reader (Figure 8.6c). With increasing drug concentrations the absorbance measured in the well will decrease. Important advantages of ELISA are the possibility to analyse drugs in blood and other matrices with little or no sample pre-treatment as is needed with EMIT and FPIA, and the sensitivity and specificity of the assay which are comparable to radioimmunoassays.[4–6]

In Figure 8.7 the signal versus drug concentration graphs for the different immunoassays discussed are illustrated.

Point-of-collection drug testing devices

Besides these laboratory assays, point-of-collection drug testing (POCT) devices for urine and oral fluid testing are commercially available.[7] These devices are useful in situations that require immediate testing and results for drugs of abuse. They utilise the same immunoassay technologies and the response is read visually. Most of these tests have built-in quality control zones ensuring reagent integrity and test validity. In kits based on the use of Ascend Multiimmunoassay (AMIA) technology, chemically labelled drugs (drug conjugate) compete with drugs that may be present in the urine for antibody-binding sites. After transfer of the mixture to the detection area, which contains immobilised antibodies in discrete drug class-specific zones, and a washing step, each zone is visually inspected for the presence of a coloured bar. The response is proportional to the concentration of the

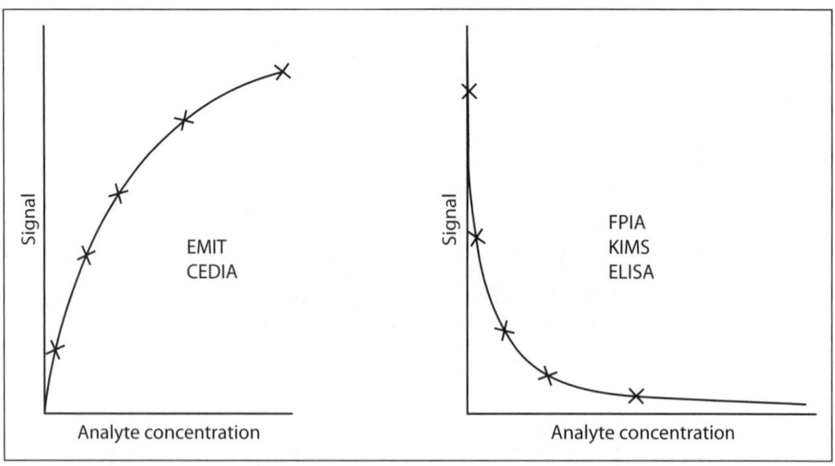

Figure 8.7 Signal versus drug concentration graphs. For enzyme multiplied immunoassay technique (EMIT) or cloned enzyme donor immunoassay (CEDIA) the signal is proportional to drug concentration. For fluorescence polarisation immunoassays (FPIA), kinetic interaction of microparticles in solution (KIMS) or enzyme-linked immunosorbent assay (ELISA) the signal is inversely proportional to drug concentration.

unbound drug conjugate so that no signal is observed for a negative specimen while a positive urine sample produces a distinct coloured bar.

A screening device based on the principle of microparticle capture inhibition is the OnTrak Testcup Collection/Urinalysis Panel (Roche Diagnostic Systems, Inc., Somerville, NJ, USA). This relies on the competition between drug (which may be present in the urine) and drug conjugate (immobilised on a membrane in the test chamber) to interact with antibody-coated microparticles. In the absence of drug in the urine, the antibody is free to interact with the drug conjugate yielding a coloured band as a negative sign. When drug is present in the specimen it binds to the antibody-binding sites and no signal is generated.

Non-technical personnel usually perform these tests and therefore extensive training and quality assurance procedures are required in order to guarantee correct operation and interpretation of results. Furthermore, it must be stressed that, just like the laboratory immunoassays, these kits only provide preliminary results, which need to be confirmed by a more specific confirmation method.

Drugs for which no immunoassays are available need a more extensive screening procedure to be detected and for this purpose different chromatographic techniques have been described.

Chromatographic screening techniques

Chromatography: introductory theory

The International Union of Pure and Applied Chemistry (IUPAC) defines chromatography as a physical method of separation in which the components to be separated are distributed between two phases, one of which is stationary (stationary phase) while the other (mobile phase) moves in a definite direction. Several combinations of mobile and stationary phases can be used, yielding different chromatographic techniques which can be classified according to the shape of the chromatographic bed, the physical state of the mobile phase or the mechanism of separation. The stationary phase can be within a tube (column chromatography) or can be present as or on a plane (planar chromatography). The mobile phase can be a gas (gas chromatography), a liquid (liquid chromatography) or a supercritical fluid (supercritical fluid chromatography). The stationary phase can be a solid, a gel or a liquid. If a liquid it may be chemically bonded to a solid (bonded phase) or immobilised onto it (immobilised phase). The mobile phase containing the sample moves through the stationary phase where the sample interacts.

Separation of components can be achieved by differences in adsorption (adsorption chromatography), solubility (partition chromatography), ligand interaction (affinity chromatography), ion exchange affinity (ion exchange chromatography) or molecules can be separated according to their size (exclusion chromatography).

The visual output of the chromatographic separation is the chromatogram (Figure 8.8). The retention time is plotted on the x-axis and the signal generated by the detector is plotted on the y-axis. If separation is optimal different peaks in the chromatogram correspond to different components of the separated mixture as they move with a different velocity through the column. Identification of components in a chromatogram can be performed based on retention time while peak height or peak area can be used for quantification.

From the chromatogram different theoretical parameters can be derived which reflect the quality of the chromatographic system. The retention of an analyte on the chromatographic column can be measured by the retention (or capacity) factor k. The retention factor is the ratio of the retention time t_x of the analyte to the retention time of a non-retained component. A non-retained component elutes with the solvent front at the so-called dead time t_0. A high k-value indicates that the component has a strong interaction with the stationary phase and thus is highly retained.

The separation factor α is the ratio of the capacity factors and indicates the ability of the chromatographic system to distinguish between sample components. However α only indicates the separation between the apex of peaks as the peak width is not taken into account. The separation of peaks is therefore

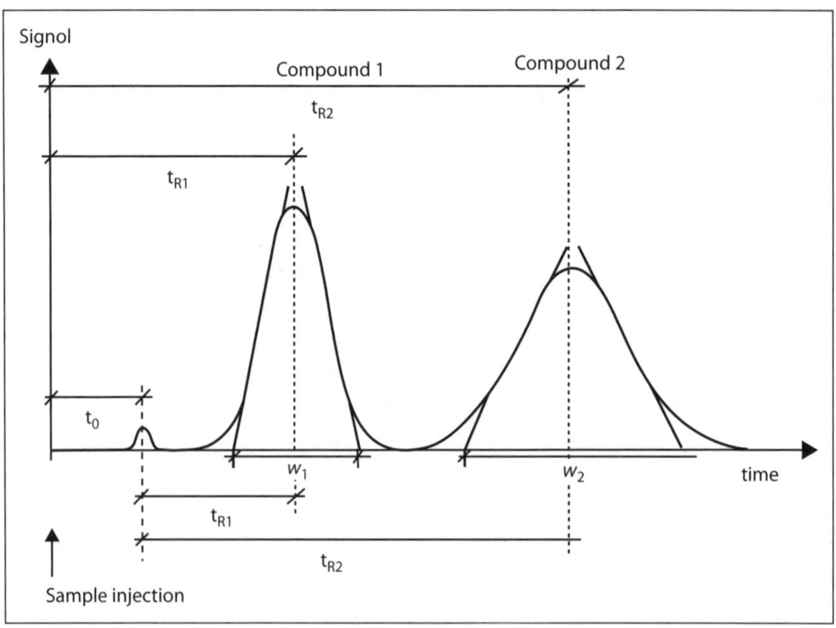

Figure 8.8 Example of a chromatogram.

better estimated by the resolution which is calculated using the retention time and the peak width.

Peak or band broadening increases with the retention time and is a measure of the column efficiency. Van Deemter introduced an equation which combines the three sources of band broadening and represents them as the dependence of the theoretical plate height (H) on the mobile phase velocity (u):

$$H = \mathrm{A} + \mathrm{B}/u + Cu$$

A theoretical plate is a hypothetical zone or segment of the column in which the mobile phase is in equilibrium with the stationary phase. Band broadening originates from the multiple paths followed by the analyte molecules through the column packing (A term), the molecular diffusion (B term) and the effect of mass transfer between phases (C term).

- A term: the molecules of a component follow a different pathway around the particles of the stationary phase. The covered distance and residence time in the column can differ significantly and is dependent on the particle diameter and the structure of the sorbent bed. The linear velocity of the mobile phase has no influence on this process.
- B term: molecules are transported from a region of higher concentration to one of lower concentration by random molecular motion. In the stationary phase longitudinal diffusion is negligible but it becomes important in the mobile phase especially in gas chromatography. As the diffusion increases with the residence time of the molecules in the column, the effect on band broadening will decrease with increasing mobile phase velocity.
- C term: the mass transfer term combines band broadening effects caused by a lack of equilibrium between the stationary phase and the mobile phase. Mass transfer is hampered by pools of immobilised mobile phase in the pores of the stationary phase particles. Molecules need to migrate through this immobilised mobile phase before mass transfer to the mobile phase or the stationary phase can occur. The equilibration time is also influenced by the type of stationary phase and the diffusion coefficient of the molecule in the stationary phase. The deviation from equilibrium increases with increasing mobile phase velocities as less time is provided for equilibration yielding band broadening.

The three processes occur in gas and liquid chromatography but the relative importance of the processes is different for both techniques due to the difference in physical properties between a gas and a liquid.

The van Deemter equation is graphically represented in the van Deemter curve, which is a plot of the plate height H as a function of the mobile phase

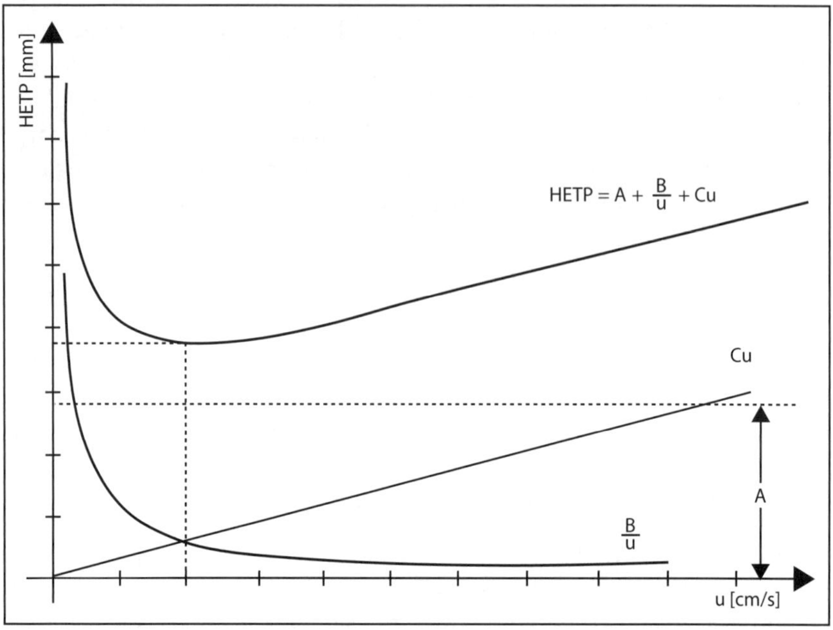

Figure 8.9 van Deemter curve (see text).

velocity *u* (Figure 8.9). This curve is very useful to determine the optimum mobile phase velocity at which the smallest plate height and thus the highest column efficiency is attained.

Sample preparation

For screening purposes several classes of toxicants need to be analysed simultaneously. A good understanding of the pharmacokinetics and metabolism of the drugs is important to apply the correct sample pre-treatment. Metabolism is an integral part of drug elimination and generally can be divided in two types: phase I and phase II reactions. Phase I reactions include oxidation, hydroxylation, reduction, hydrolysis, *N*- and *O*-dealkylation and sulfoxide formation. Phase II reactions remove or mask functional groups by the addition of an endogenous substrate. The conjugation reactions include acetylation, methylation and conjugation with sulfate and glucuronic acid. The different metabolic pathways that are possible can yield a complex mixture of metabolites in urine (Figure 8.10).

A suitable sample preparation is essential for chromatographic analysis and it involves, if required, cleavage of conjugates followed by isolation and eventually derivatisation of the compounds. Cleavage of conjugates can be performed by rapid acid or alkaline hydrolysis or by a more gentle but time-consuming enzymatic hydrolysis. After hydrolysis of urine samples some form of extraction procedure is usually required for chromatographic analysis.

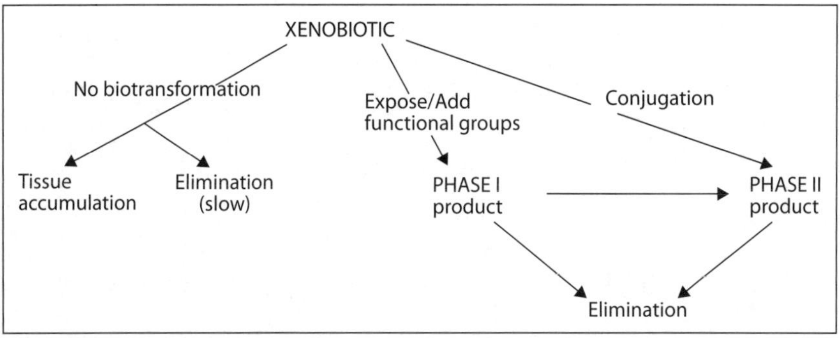

Figure 8.10 Phase I and phase II biotransformation reactions.

Sample clean-up procedures generally used are liquid–liquid and solid-phase extraction. However solid-phase microextraction (SPME) and liquid-phase microextraction (LPME) are also gaining popularity. Solvent and sorbent selection are dependent on the properties of the analytes to be extracted but as the substances present are not known in advance, the extraction procedure chosen needs to be capable to isolate a broad range of substances.[9–11] The analyst should keep in mind that variation can occur between different batches of SPE-sorbents and that the same sorbent from different manufacturers can give different results. For quantitative analyses use of a suitable internal standard, a compound that matches as closely as possible the chemical properties of the analyte of interest is, therefore, highly recommended.

The internal standard is added in a constant amount to all samples. The effects of sample preparation should, relative to the amount of each compound, be the same for the internal standard and the component of interest. To correct for the loss of analyte during sample preparation, the ratio of the analyte signal to the internal standard signal is plotted as a function of the analyte concentration.

An alternative procedure for sample clean-up is direct injection of the sample onto a precolumn and elution of the components in back-flush mode to the analytical column. These techniques are restricted to high-performance liquid chromatography (HPLC) and require an extra pump compared to conventional instrumentation, but avoiding an extraction step can lead to significant improvements in throughput (Figure 8.11).

Chromatographic separation

The components in the extracts can be separated by gas chromatography (GC) or HPLC (Figure 8.12). Methods reliant on GC separation often use single or multiple derivatisation procedures as polar components with carboxylic, hydroxy, primary or secondary amino groups chromatograph poorly and all analytes need to have the prerequisite volatility. Commonly used derivatisation procedures are acetylation, trimethylsilylation, trifluoroacetylation

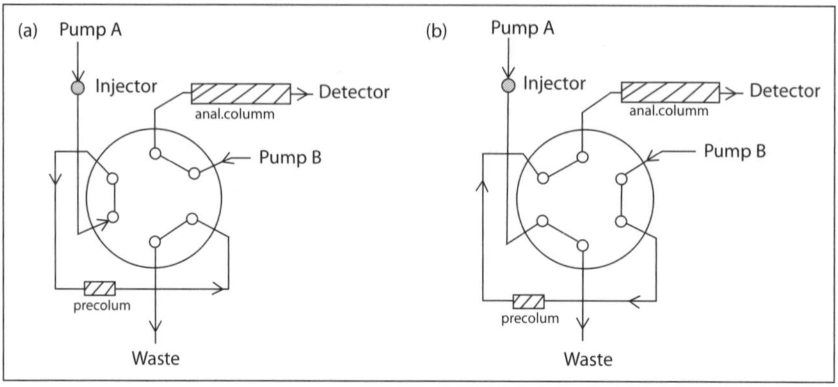

Figure 8.11 Column-switching set-up for sample clean-up. (a) The sample is injected onto a precolumn that is flushed with mobile phase I (pump A) to remove matrix components. In the mean time the analytical column is equilibrated with mobile phase II (pump B). (b) After valve switching, the analytes are eluted from the precolumn in backflush mode onto the analytical column.

and methylation. For reason of universality, stationary phases containing methylsilicone and 2–5% phenylsilicone are generally used. In this way the range of substances to be detected in one chromatographic system can be enlarged.

HPLC is a more versatile technique and offers the capability to quantify simultaneously several drugs and their metabolites even those too large or polar to be volatilised in GC. Reversed-phase (C8 or C18) stationary phases are most often used with mobile phases composed of buffers at different pH values mixed with different organic solvents at different percentages. The composition of the mobile phase can remain unchanged during the entire elution process (isocratic elution) or the solvent strength of the mobile phase can be increased continuously or stepwise during the analysis (gradient

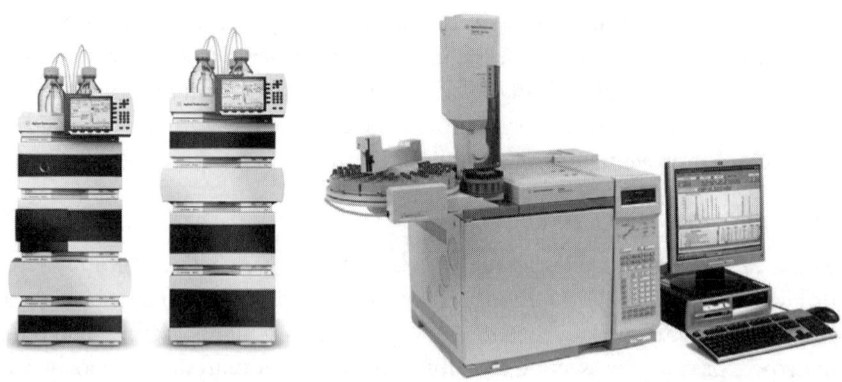

Figure 8.12 Liquid chromatography (left) and gas chromatography (right) configurations. Copyright 2010 Agilent Technologies, Inc. Reproduced with permission (courtesy of Agilent Technologies).

elution). Isocratic elution is preferred as it gives reproducible retention times, a constant baseline signal during the analytical run-time and the possibility to run the mobile phase in recycling mode. With gradient elution components with very different polarity can be separated in the same analysis but time-consuming equilibration times are needed between consecutive analyses. The separation power of HPLC remains inferior to that of capillary GC.

Detection

Detection after liquid chromatography (LC) separation is often performed with a diode-array detector (DAD) as modern DADs provide a high sensitivity, a high wavelength resolution and accuracy yielding reproducible spectra. Only the conjugated system of π-electrons and free electron pairs of heteroatoms are normally responsible for UV absorption. The obtained spectra can be influenced by the pH and polarity of the mobile phase. If the basic or acidic group is part of the chromophore, the spectrum can be completely different at different pH. Concentration effects on the spectra can occur at very high concentrations but can be overcome by using the front or the tail of the HPLC peak for substance identification or by the analysis of a diluted sample.

Metabolites predominate in urine samples and their presence can be suspected if several peaks with similar UV spectra are seen in a chromatogram. Similarity of the spectra of parent compound and metabolite will occur if the metabolisation does not occur at or near the chromophore as is illustrated in Figure 8.13 for diazepam and its main metabolite nordiazepam. As metabolisation usually leads to the formation of more hydrophilic components the metabolite retention times will be shorter than those of the parent drugs on a reversed-phase column. The detection of several metabolites can help to confirm the identification of the parent drug. A disadvantage of DAD is that the limits of detection are rather high (10–50 ng/mL) and that components with poor UV absorption can be overlooked.

No chromatographic technique is capable of detecting all substances with acidic, basic or neutral properties and different stability, polarity or detector sensitivity.[8] Moreover, the nature of toxicologically relevant substances is also changing constantly. Several drugs can be detected in general chromatographic screening assays but others, such as THC and its metabolites, morphine and its metabolites, benzoylecgonine and LSD, are more difficult to analyse without resorting to specific testing. For newer designer drugs like pyrrolidinophenones e.g. 4′-methyl-α-pyrrolidinopropiophenone (MPPP), 4′-methyl-α-pyrrolidinohexanophenone (MPHP), 3′,4′-methylenedioxy-α-pyrrolidinopropiophenone (MDPPP) and α-pyrrolidinovalerophenone (PVP) general screening procedures using GC separation are not applicable due to the zwitterionic properties of these components and their metabolites.

LC coupled to a single-stage or tandem mass spectrometer has several limitations for screening applications. Not only the spectral information is

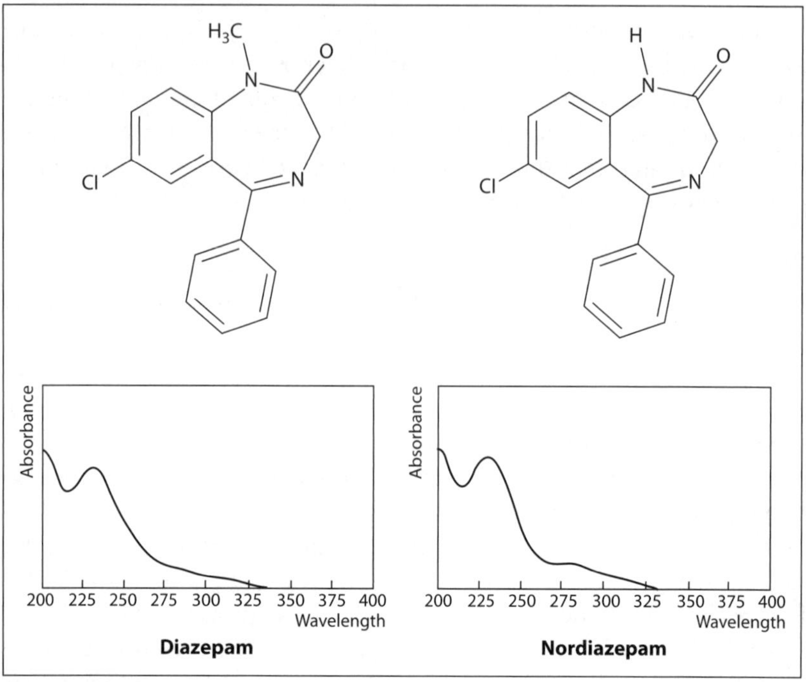

Figure 8.13 Chemical structures and UV spectra of diazepam and its metabolite nordiazepam.

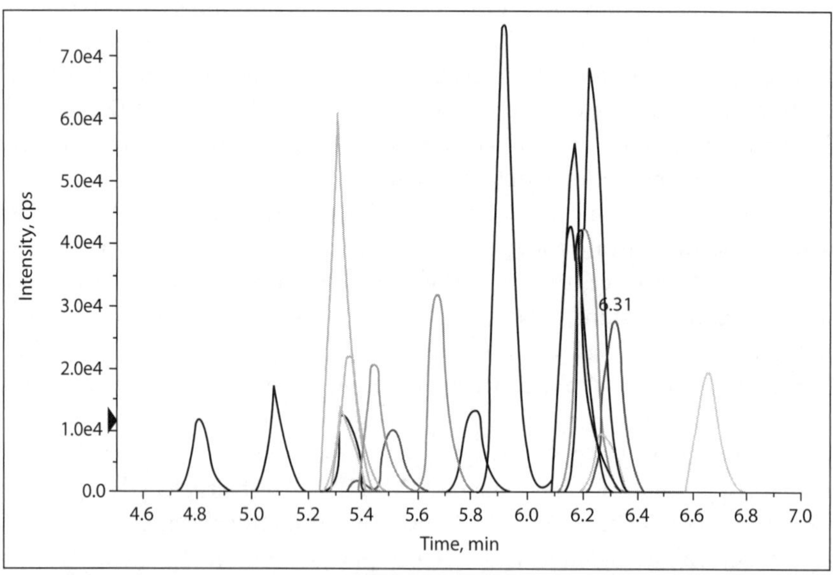

Figure 8.14 LC-MS/MS chromatogram of drugs (of abuse) (alprazolam, cocaine, codeine, diazepam, estazolam, flunitrazepam, flurazepam, heroin, ketamine, MDMA, methadone, methamphetamine, methaqualone, midazolam, morphine, nitrazepam, pethidine, pholcodine and triazolam).

limited but the fragmentation patterns also differ substantially between different apparatus. Due to ion suppression effects toxic components might even be overlooked. However recently liquid chromatography-tandem mass spectrometry (LC-MS/MS) techniques have been described that can detect and quantify more than 30 drugs, including all the relevant drugs for workplace drug testing[9–11] (Figure 8.14). LC-MS/MS can also be very helpful for further confirmation of drugs identified with DAD.[8,12–15]

Confirmation tests

Confirmation techniques must provide a higher degree of specificity for the analyte tested and the sensitivity (limit of quantification and detection) must be well below the cut-off value used for the screening. Positive screening results are confirmed by a suitable sample pre-treatment, a chromatographic separation of the extract and preferably mass spectrometric detection.

Mass spectrometry

Mass spectrometry is a microanalytical destructive technique. With very small amounts of a component, characteristic information about its structure and molecular weight can be obtained. In a mass spectrometer the components are ionised by some form of energy transfer. This produces a molecular ion representing the intact molecule that can be stable or unstable. Unstable molecular ions will decompose almost completely and produce fragment ions. The ions are separated under high-vacuum conditions and detected based on their mass-to-charge ratio (*m/z*-value). The graphical presentation of the intensity or abundance of the fragment ions (*y*-axis) to the *m/z*-value of the ions (*x*-axis) is the mass spectrum (Figure 8.15).

The relative abundance of the ions formed is characteristic for a compound, and the absolute abundance is a function of the amount of the analyte present. Interpretation of the mass spectrum allows identification and even quantification of the analytes detected. Quantification is usually performed

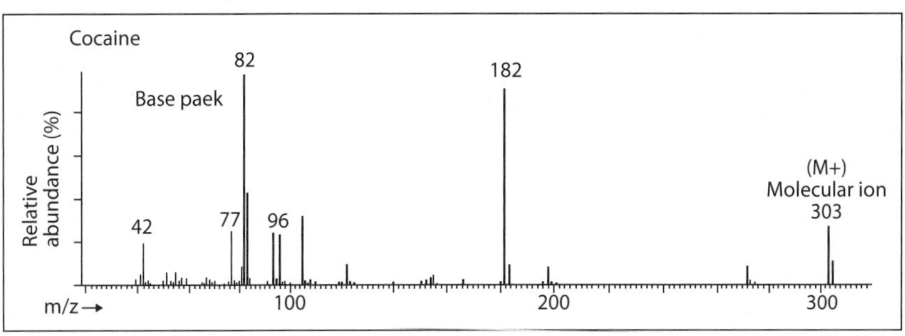

Figure 8.15 Example of a mass spectrum: cocaine.

by internal standardisation and the internal standards need to be chemically similar to the analyte of interest but must be distinguished by the mass spectrometric detector (MSD).[16]

Ionisation in GC-MS

In recent decades GC with capillary columns combined with mass spectrometric detection has been widely used to analyse licit pharmaceuticals and drugs of abuse. The column effluent enters the ionisation chamber through the interface and the molecules are ionised as they sequentially enter the ion source.

The oldest but most frequently used ionisation technique is electron impact (EI) ionisation (Figure 8.16a). The molecules that enter the ion source are bombarded with a beam of electrons with a high energy of 70 eV, which are emitted from a filament. The electrons are attracted to the anode, which is located on the opposite side of the ionisation chamber from the filament (the cathode). In this way the emitted electrons are forced through the centre of the ionisation chamber and transfer energy to the neutral molecules in the vapour state. The components get sufficient energy to emit one of their own electrons and become charged with a positive charge. The molecular ions formed still have excess energy, which can be dissipated by fragmentation of chemical bonds, yielding the formation of more stable fragment ions. The positively charged ions are subsequently transferred into the mass analyser and separated according to their mass-to-charge ratio.

The energy of the electrons in electron impact ionisation is determined by the potential difference between the filament and the anode and is expressed in electron volts (eV). By traversing an electric field maintained by a potential difference of 1 V an electron gains 1 eV of energy. Most data are generated at 70 eV as reproducible fragmentation patterns are obtained at that energy level and the obtained spectra can be compared with reference spectra, which are

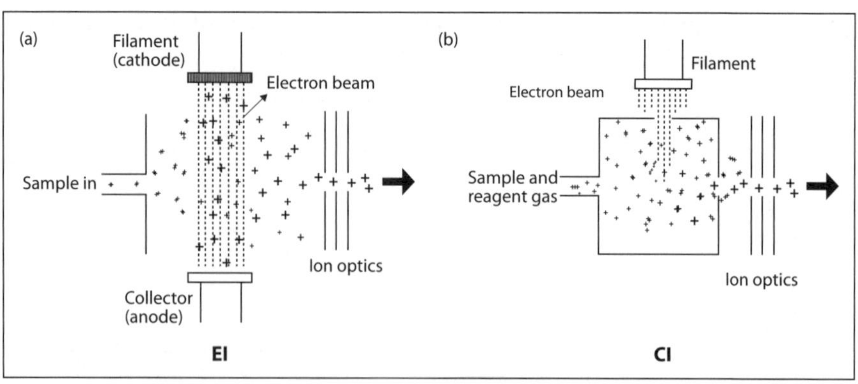

Figure 8.16 Schematic representation of (a) electron impact ionisation (EI) and (b) chemical ionisation (CI) ionisation sources.

available in libraries. The excessive fragmentation seen with electron impact ionisation can be unfavourable for molecule identification (e.g. tricyclic antidepressants fracture into the low mass ion *m/z* 58, which cannot be considered as specific).

Chemical ionisation (CI), often referred to as a soft ionisation can be applied to prevent this extensive fragmentation (Figure 8.16b). The ion source is comparable to the one used in electron impact ionisation but it is more enclosed. The ionisation chamber is filled with a reagent gas that is bombarded with high-energy electrons of up to several hundred electron volts to guarantee effective penetration of the electrons into the reagent gas. The reagent gas ions transfer their charge to the molecules in the column effluent by interaction or collision. Instead of a molecular ion, a pseudomolecular ion [$(M+1)^+$ or $(M-1)^+$] is formed. Using methane as a reagent gas, adduct ions of $(M+C_2H_5)^+$ and $(M+C_3H_5)^+$ are formed as well, yielding a sequence of peaks for M+1, M+29 and M+41 (Figure 8.17).

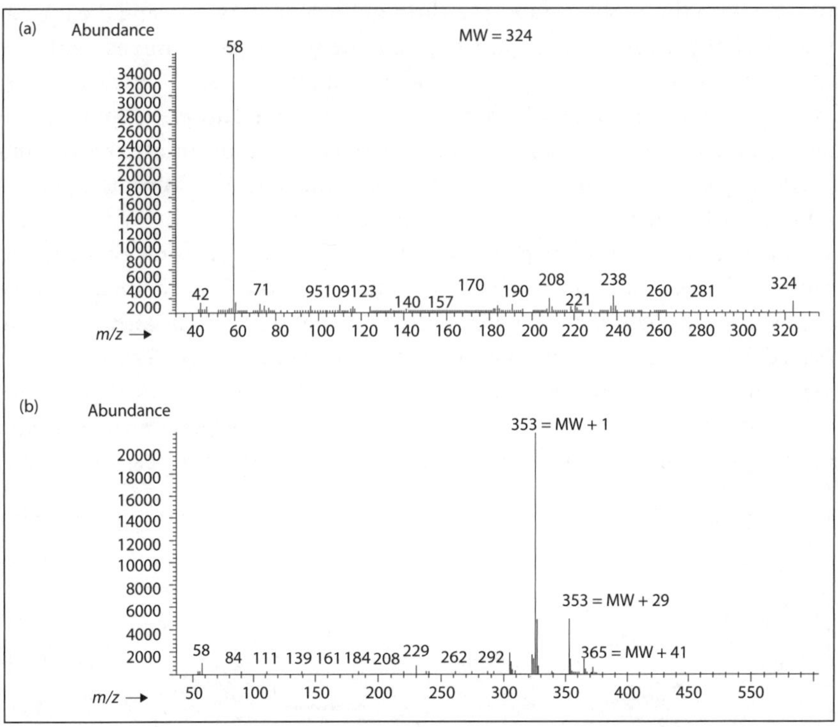

Figure 8.17 (a) Electron impact (EI) and (b) positive chemical ionisation (PCI) spectrum of citalopram (molecular mass = 324). EI yields excessive fragmentation to the non-specific ion *m/z* 58. After PCI using methane as reagent gas, the major peak in the mass spectrum corresponds to MH^+ (*m/z* 325). Adduct ions M+29 (*m/z* 353) and M+41 (*m/z* 365) are formed as well.

The reagent gas and the pressure can be chosen to influence the degree of fragmentation. Selective ionisation can be achieved by selecting a reagent gas that has a proton affinity slightly below the proton affinity of the analyte of interest. The fragmentation of the ions formed is influenced by many factors and less predictable than with EI ionisation.

The analysis of negative ions also became possible with CI as the high number of collisions in the source yields the production of a large flux of low-energy electrons including thermal electrons. Thermal electrons have an energy of 0.1 eV or less and can produce a negative molecular ion by resonance electron capture. In EI sources the energies of the available electrons are so great that the molecules are completely fragmented, leaving no high-mass negative ions.

Ionisation in LC-MS

Until the early 1990s the combination of mass spectrometry with LC was problematic but the development of atmospheric pressure ionisation sources greatly expanded and improved LC-MS applications.

In electrospray ionisation (ESI) a high voltage is put onto the probe and a solution with the analyte is sprayed through the capillary, causing the formation of charged droplets (Figure 8.18). A nebuliser gas is mixed with the solvent to produce a stable flow and to allow the use of higher flows. Solvent evaporates from each charged droplet until the droplet explodes into many smaller droplets. Finally the ions are freed and appropriate charges and gas flows direct the ions into the mass spectrometer. The solvent vapour is removed from the ion source through the exhaust.

ESI is a soft ionisation process and permits the formation of single or multiple charged molecular ions. If the capillary is positively charged, positive ions will be formed, if the capillary is negatively charged, negative ions are formed. The possibility to put multiple charges on large molecules yields lower *m/z*-values within the range of the analyser and allows the analysis of molecules in the molecular weight range >100 000 Da. ESI works well with aqueous and polar solvents and thus can be used in combination with reversed-phase HPLC

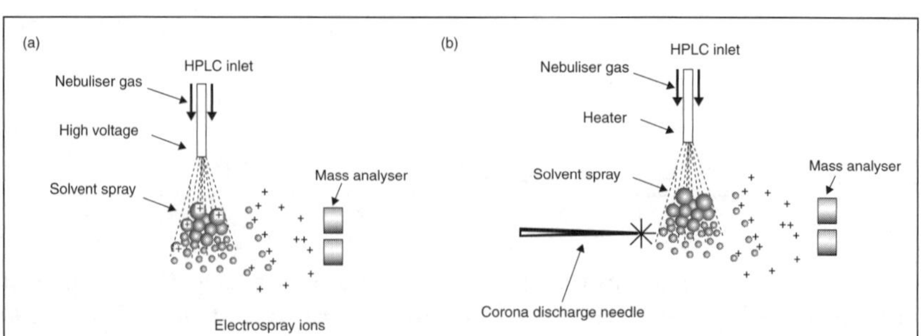

Figure 8.18 Schematic representation of (a) electrospray and (b) atmospheric pressure ionisation (APCI) sources.

and capillary electrophoresis. Disadvantages are the formation of adduct ions, especially Na- and K-adducts, and the possibility of ionisation suppression or enhancement due to interference with matrix components. Use of a nano-electrospray interface can decrease these matrix effects substantially. Specificity and sensitivity for an analyte can also be increased by the use of derivatisation and the spectra produced can yield more structural information.

Atmospheric pressure chemical ionisation (APCI) is an alternate ionisation mode and is based on the flow of the solvent through a heated probe and the creation of a plasma with a corona-discharge needle (Figure 8.18). In this plasma the solvent molecules are ionised and the resulting solvent ions then transfer their charges to the analytes by collisions. Early fragmentation in the ion source and matrix effects are less common than with ESI. APCI permits less polar and more volatile analytes to be converted to gas-phase ions that can be introduced into a mass spectrometer.

Atmospheric pressure photo-ionisation (APPI) is complementary to APCI and ESI and typically produces protonated ions. For molecules with low proton affinity M^+ is observed as is the case with electron impact ionisation. The APPI source usually has an APCI design that creates the aerosol. A lamp filled with krypton gas is positioned to transmit 10 eV photons at the cross-section of the aerosol. APPI is used to analyse components that are not easily amenable to APCI or ESI, such as steroids and polycyclic aromatic hydrocarbons (PAHs).

Mass analysis

Several types of mass spectrometers are available but for drug analysis most often quadrupole or ion-trap mass spectrometers are used. A quadrupole mass spectrometer (QMS) consists of two pairs of metal rods which are placed in a square (Figure 8.19). DC and AC currents are placed on

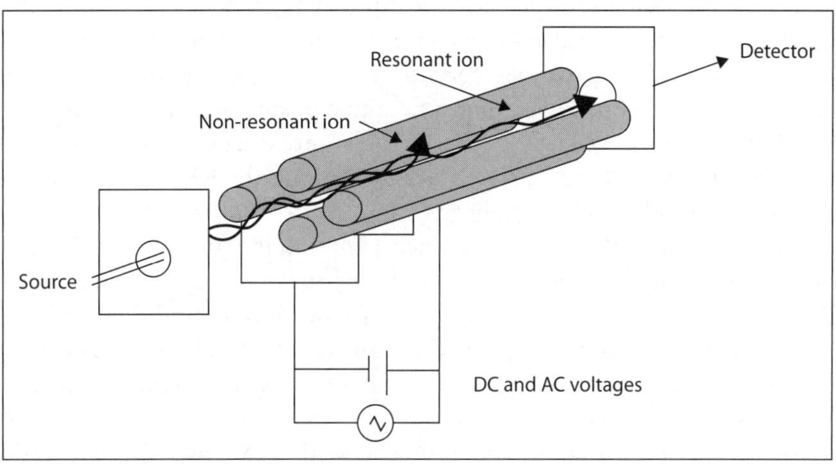

Figure 8.19 Schematic representation of a quadrupole mass spectrometer.

these rods and are ramped at a constant ratio, allowing only ions with a specific mass-to-charge ratio to pass through the rods and reach the detector. All other ions will deflect and be neutralised on the rods. Programming the QMS allows either all *m/z*-ratios within the instrument's mass range to be measured (scan mode, usually 50–800 Da) or particular ions to be monitored (SIM mode). The voltages that control the mass scale in a quadrupole analyser can be adjusted very rapidly and several mass scans can be monitored per minute, yielding full mass spectra of the components analysed. The more ion currents monitored in a mass spectrum, the more confidence that the corresponding compound is present in the sample. The efficiency of this process, however, is very small as the largest part of the ions formed never reaches the detector. Selected ion monitoring (SIM) refers to the use of a mass spectrometer to acquire the ion current of certain selected mass-to-charge values. High sensitivity is one of the major features of SIM and usually only two or three ion currents are monitored when high sensitivity is required. Identification of the compound of interest is performed based on the correct intensity ratio of the measured ion currents at the appropriate retention times. A chromatographic run can be divided into several acquisition groups depending on the retention time of the target components and per group the ion current of several ions can be measured.

An ion-trap mass spectrometer (ITMS) consists of one ring electrode and two endcap electrodes. In contrast to the quadrupole mass spectrometer the ion-trap experiment can be divided into two steps: ion accumulation and mass analysis. In the first step the ions formed are trapped in the three-dimensional chamber between the electrodes until the trap is full. The ions are cooled to the centre of the ion-trap by collisions with helium which removes kinetic energy from the ions. A radiofrequency (RF) voltage applied to the ring electrode causes a rapid change in field polarities and by fluctuating the electric field ions are alternatively accelerated and decelerated in an oscillating manner, forming a stable trajectory within the trap. Automatic gain control is a gating system that ensures that the trap is filled in an optimum manner. In the second step ions are ejected out of the endcap at specific mass-to-charge ratio values by varying the RF voltage and are detected by the electron multiplier.

The recovery of this process is much higher than with QMS as 50% of the ions formed reach the detector and SIM measurements are no longer advantageous. The sensitivity of the SCAN mode has the additional advantage that per component a full spectrum can be recorded. However, because of the long residence time of the ions in the trap, space-charge effects can occur, causing the generated spectra to be less reproducible. In general, higher sensitivity is obtained in full scan with ITMS whereas ion ratio stability is better for QMS.

Tandem mass spectrometry

Another method to increase the signal-to-noise (S/N) ratio and thus enhance sensitivity is to use tandem mass spectrometry. A tandem mass spectrometer has two mass filters, which are arranged in series. Both mass selective devices are separated by a quadrupole reaction chamber, the collision cell. Ions with a certain *m/z*-value are selected in the first mass analyser (parent or precursor ions) and enter the collision cell, which is filled with an inert gas, most often nitrogen. As the parent ions drift through this chamber, fragment ions are formed. The process using a gas to fragment ions is called collision-activated dissociation (CAD) or collision-induced dissociation (CID). The fragmentation process can be controlled by the applied accelerating voltages and the gas density in the chamber. The ions formed in the collision cell (daughter or product ions) are then separated in the second mass analyser and detected by the electron multiplier. Both mass analysers can be used in scan or SIM mode yielding different analytical strategies:

- Single reaction monitoring (SRM) or multiple reaction monitoring (MRM): mass filter 1 SIM, mass filter 2 SIM (Figure 8.20). With these settings a certain fragmentation process or mass transition is followed. SRM is used for each pair of ions that is measured. As most instruments are capable of following different transitions the term MRM is usually applied.
- Product ion scanning: mass filter 1 SIM, mass filter 2 scan. In this case one precursor ion is fragmented, all product ions formed are monitored and a spectrum is created.

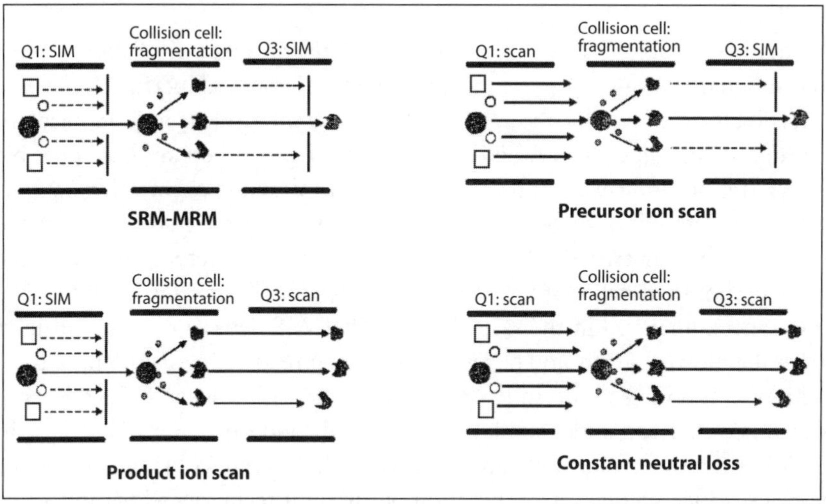

Figure 8.20 Different analytical strategies applicable in tandem mass spectrometry.

- Precursor ion scanning: mass filter 1 scan, mass filter 2 SIM. The instrument will measure all precursor ions that fragment to a certain product ion. As several components from a certain class of substances can form common product ions this technique can be applied to search for certain classes of molecules.
- Neutral loss scanning: mass filter 1 scan, mass filter 2 scan. Both mass filters are set in a way that the mass difference or offset between them is constant. Precursor ions of certain groups of components can produce identical neutral fragments. As a mass spectrometer can only analyse ions, the presence of the neutral fragments must be confirmed by the measurement of the respective precursor and product ions and by subtracting their masses.

Precursor/product ion pair measurements (MRM) provide the highest sensitivity in target analysis of known drugs or metabolites but the analytical result is reduced to a limited number of compounds. As the core chemical structure of many drugs is retained by their metabolites and often produces a common fragment, precursor ion scanning or constant neutral loss can be applied to detect metabolites of a particular drug. Unknown drugs or components with unknown dissociation pathways under conventional CID remain undetected.

Knowledge of the chemical characteristics of the different interfaces has increased over the last few years and will probably result in methods requiring no or minimal sample pre-treatment. However several drawbacks still need to be overcome before LC-MS/MS can be applied as a standard procedure for drug screening. As the fragmentation patterns depend on the instrument configuration used, commercial libraries with MS/MS spectra are not available.

In order to obtain unequivocal evidence of the presence of a substance in a certain matrix, rules concerning the analytical method performance and interpretation of results are required.[17] Each analytical technique needs to be able to distinguish between the compound of interest and all possible interfering substances from the matrix. The physical and chemical behaviour of the analyte needs to be identical to that of a reference substance in the corresponding matrix. For GC and LC applications, the retention time of the analyte should match that of the reference standard (GC $<1\%$, HPLC $<2\%$ difference), analysed in the same batch. When MS detection is used at least three diagnostic ions should be monitored. Their relative intensities need to be within $\leq 20\%$ in CI mode and $\leq 10\%$ in EI mode with respect to the reference substance analysed under similar experimental conditions. For LC-MS applications many spectra usually are recorded with different collision energies or various orifice voltages. Combination of different techniques for the correct identification of compounds increases the confidence in the analytical results.

Increase throughput

Automation in sample preparation is essential when discussing high throughput because sample preparation occupies about 60% of the time a sample is handled. Fast sample preparation can be done with SPE, SPME or microwave-assisted extraction (MAE).[18] Microwave extraction is based on the interaction between microwaves and the permanent dipoles of molecules. The rate of sample heating is dependent on several factors: the dielectric constant, the dielectric loss factor and the dissipation factor. The dielectric constant is the ability of a molecule to be polarised by an electric field, the dielectric loss factor describes how electromagnetic energy can be converted into heat by the sample material and the dissipation factor is a measure of the ability to convert electromagnetic energy into other forms of energy. A final parameter is the penetration depth, which is different for different materials and this affects the heating of the sample. The degree of heating is only dependent on the dielectric properties of the material so that it is possible to target specific analytes. Using microwave energy there is an increased speed of extraction and efficiency compared to conventional heating methods. Possible explanations are that in a closed vessel higher temperatures than the normal boiling points of the solvents can be reached or that the increased extraction rates are due to localised superheating. In general, the analytes diffuse faster into the extraction solvent as the mass transport of the analytes is increased at the higher temperatures. Parameters to be optimised and controlled are the power, the maximum temperature reached and the extraction time. Uneven heating can occur in the microwave and due to degradation or adsorption recovery may decrease with increasing extraction times.

The introduction of capillary columns offered higher resolution than packed columns due to the longer lengths, thinner films and smaller internal diameters. Before high-speed separations could be fully exploited, injection speed, injection port design and detector response times needed to be optimised.

Peak broadening that occurs in the injector is due to the injection speed, the rate of evaporation and transfer from the inlet to the column. Headspace is a possible mode of sample introduction that minimises the solvent peak and allows for a faster analysis. Choosing the correct inlet liner dimensions is important to minimise band broadening in fast GC. Smaller internal diameter liners used with the same volumetric flow rate (mL/min) cause a faster carrier gas flow rate and sweep the analytes faster onto the column.[19] The columns used for fast GC applications are generally much shorter, have a smaller internal diameter, are coated with a thinner film and therefore require smaller amounts of sample to be injected to prevent overloading of the column. This in turn causes the detection limits to be higher.

Fast temperature programming is a means of doing fast GC as the temperature affects the analysis time much more than the flow rate or the column length. An increase in the temperature programming rate will cause a decrease in analysis time but at the same time peak heights are increased and resolution can be lost. The increase in peak height indicates that it would be possible to inject less sample maintaining the same signal-to-noise ratio. To maintain low detection limits, the detector has to be in good working condition with a low noise level and high sensitivity. To prevent band broadening of the peaks in the detector it needs to have a low volume and a fast time constant in order to rapidly sample the narrow peaks and obtain 10–12 data points per peak.

A novel approach to perform fast LC analyses that still separate closely related compounds is the use of ultra-performance liquid chromatography (UPLC). In UPLC very small particles (<2.5 micrometres) are used as column packing material, providing increased efficiency and the ability to work at higher linear velocities. The particles are packed in rugged columns with a very smooth interior surface and have special end-frits to retain the small particles and resist clogging. As backpressure is proportional to flow rate these small particles require much higher operating pressures than those that can be achieved by classical HPLC instrumentation. Therefore a pump that can deliver solvents reproducibly at these high pressures is required. To resist these high pressures the particles also need enhanced mechanical stability (Figure 8.21).

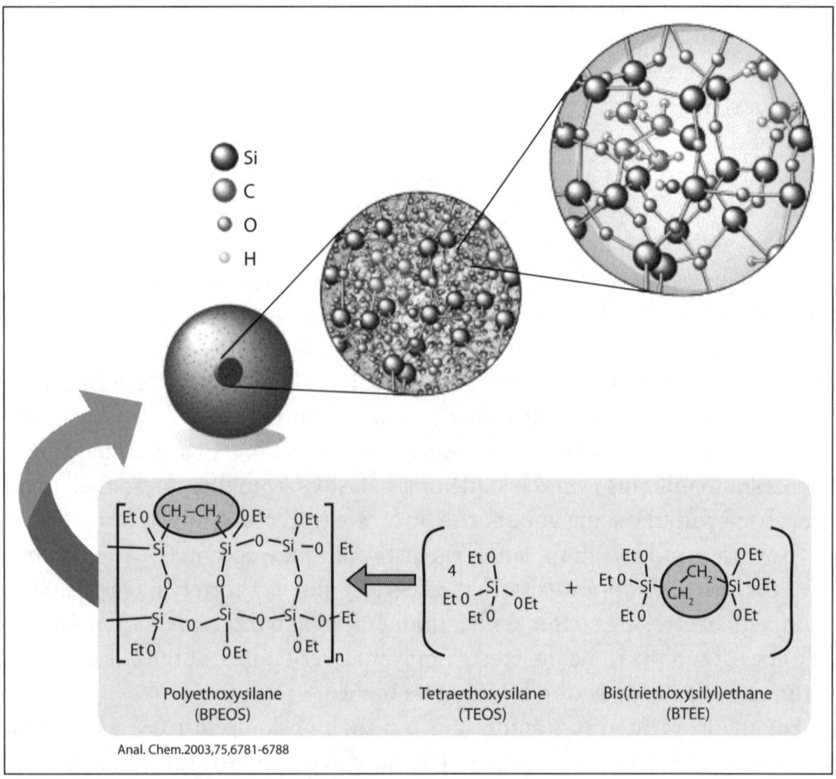

Figure 8.21 Ethylene bridged hybrid (BEH) particle used in Acquity UPLC.[20]

Sample introduction must be pulse-free and fast with minimal dispersion. Also the detection process is critical as the detector sampling rate must be high enough to capture enough data points across the peak and minimal dispersion in the detector cell is required to preserve the separation efficiency.

Method validation

Before a new method is implemented in daily routine, it must be thoroughly validated as only validation can demonstrate that minimum acceptance criteria are fulfilled and that the method is suitable for a certain purpose. Different validation parameters need to be assessed for qualitative or quantitative analytical procedures. For qualitative analyses (immunoassay screening procedures) at least selectivity and the limit of detection (LOD) need to be evaluated. Precision, recovery and robustness might also be important. For quantitative analyses (chromatographic techniques) selectivity, linearity, stability, accuracy, precision and the limit of quantification (LOQ) should be evaluated. LOD, recovery, reproducibility and robustness may also be included. When ESI-MS is used for detection, experiments to assess matrix effects need to be performed.[21]

Selectivity

This is the ability of the bioanalytical method to measure unequivocally and to differentiate the analyte(s) in the presence of other components that may be expected to be present. Typically these might include metabolites, impurities, degradation products and matrix components. Selectivity can be established by the analysis of at least 10–20 different sources of blank matrix, showing that there are no signals interfering with the signal of the analyte(s) or the internal standard. Interferences from other xenobiotics can be examined by the analysis of spiked blank samples or authentic samples containing the possible interfering substance but not the analyte of interest.

Linearity

This is the choice of a mathematical model that adequately describes the relationship between the analyte concentration in the sample and the response. The appropriateness of the chosen model needs to be confirmed by statistical tests for model fit.

Accuracy (bias)

This is the difference between the expectation of the test results and an accepted reference value. Accuracy is usually expressed as a percentage deviation from the accepted reference value and can be assessed by the analysis of quality control (QC) samples. Acceptance criteria for accuracy are bias within ±15% of the accepted reference value and within ±20% near limit of quantification (LOQ).

Precision

This is the closeness of agreement between a series of measurements obtained from multiple sampling of the same homogeneous sample. Precision can be assessed by the analysis of QC samples. It is usually expressed as an absolute or relative standard deviation (RSD) and does not relate to reference values. Acceptance criteria for precision are 15% RSD and 20% RSD near LOQ. Precision can be considered at three levels:

- Repeatability: Within-run or within-day precision, expresses the precision under the same operating conditions over a short interval of time.
- Intermediate precision: Between-run or between-day precision expresses the precision under varied conditions: different days, different analysts or different equipment.
- Reproducibility: This expresses the precision between laboratories. It only has to be studied if a method is supposed to be used in different laboratories.

Limit of quantification (LOQ)

The LOQ is the lowest amount of an analyte in a sample that can be quantitatively determined with suitable precision and accuracy. Quantification below the LOQ is not acceptable.

Limit of detection (LOD)

The LOD is the lowest concentration of an analyte in a sample that can be reliably differentiated from background noise but not necessarily quantified as an exact value. Of course the specific identification criteria still need to be fulfilled.

Stability

This is the chemical stability of an analyte in a given matrix under specific conditions for given time intervals. Stability needs to be evaluated during the whole analytical procedure: storage before analysis, freeze–thaw stability if samples are frozen, in-process stability under the conditions of sample pre-treatment and stability in prepared samples under autosampler conditions for the expected maximum time of analysing a batch.

Recovery

This is calculated as the percentage of the analyte response after sample workup compared to that of a solution containing the analyte at a concentration corresponding to 100% recovery.

Robustness

This is a measure for the susceptibility of a method to small changes that might occur during routine analysis.

Matrix effects

A well-known phenomenon in LC-MS/MS analysis is the suppression or enhancement of analyte ionisation by co-eluting compounds. These effects are dependent on the sample matrix, the sample preparation, the chromatographic separation, the mobile phase and the ionisation type. Electrospray ionisation is more prone to such effects but they may also occur with atmospheric pressure chemical ionisation.

The complete validation of a new method is obviously associated with a high workload but this is justified when the method has to be used for routine applications. A fully validated method also assures sufficient quality of the results.

Quality of results

Quality assurance is defined as a 'total integrated management programme for assuring the reliability of data' and should be the prime goal of any laboratory.[22] The implementation of a quality assurance (QA) programme with internal and external quality controls is therefore very important and needs to be performed for the initial screening and the confirmation tests. Internal quality controls need to monitor every part of the analytical procedure and detect changes in the performance of routine operations. The control samples can be 'blinded' to ensure that they are treated in the same way as routine samples.

An effective QA system also implies participation in proficiency testing programmes (PTP) or external quality assessment schemes (EQAS) to assess the reliability of the methods used and the accuracy of the analytical data produced. The advantage of these schemes is that the impact of metabolites on the overall accuracy of the method can be evaluated.

Of course quality control doesn't imply quality. A control can inform about the current quality of the procedure if the QC samples are treated as real samples and do not get more care and attention. If improvement of the quality is needed, better methods, equipment and/or training need to be introduced.

Conclusion

To determine the identity of a compound ingested a combination of different analyses needs to be performed. Most important toxicants are basic or neutral, however some classes of acidic drugs need to be screened for as well. Immunological assays were developed to facilitate the rapid screening of samples and identify those that need further analysis. Undoubtedly GC-MS with electron impact ionisation remains the method of choice for confirmation of positive screening tests in urine. The separation power and specificity are better than those achieved with LC. Modification in the column bore size and stationary phases, heating rate of the oven and carrier-gas control has led to the development of fast GC. Combined with microwave extraction, much more samples can be processed a day as sample preparation is very rapid and chromatographic analyses can be performed up to ten times faster than with standard GC. HPLC-DAD and LC-MS/MS cover compounds not volatile in GC and can give more information on the identity of the drug ingested. Reduced run times, better resolution and sensitivity can be obtained by UPLC. Of course, knowledge of the limitation of every analysis performed is essential to provide a correct interpretation of the obtained results.

References

1. Verstraete AG, Pierce A. Workplace drug testing in Europe. *Forensic Sci Int* 2001; 121: 2–6.
2. Langman LJ, Kapur BM. Toxicology: then and now. *Clin Biochem* 2006; 39: 498–510.
3. George S. Position of immunological techniques in screening in clinical toxicology. *Clin Chem Lab Med* 2004; 42: 1288–1309.
4. Hino Y, Ojanperä I, Rasanen I, Vuori E. Performance of immunoassays in screening for opiates, cannabinoids and amphetamines in post-mortem blood. *Forensic Sci Int* 2003; 131: 148–55.
5. Keller T, Schneider A, Dirnhofer R, Jungo R, Meyer W. Fluorescence polarization immunoassay for the detection of drugs of abuse in human whole blood. *Med Sci Law* 2000; 40: 258–262.
6. Pujol M-L, Cirimele V, Tritsch PJ, Villain M, Kintz P. Evaluation of the IDS One-Step ELISA kits for the detection of illicit drugs in hair. *Forensic Sci Int* 2007; 170: 189–192.
7. Walsh JM. New technology and new initiatives in US workplace testing. *Forensic Sci Int* 2008; 174: 120–124.
8. Maurer HH. Position of chromatographic techniques in screening for detection of drugs or poisons in clinical and forensic toxicology and/or doping control. *Clin Chem Lab Med* 2004; 42: 1310–1324.

9. Simões SS, Ajenjo AC, Franco JM, Vieira DN, Dias MJ. Liquid chromatography/tandem mass spectrometry for the qualitative and quantitative analysis of illicit drugs and medicines in preserved oral fluid. *Rapid Commun Mass Spectrom* 2009; 23(10): 1451–1460.
10. Øiestad EL, Johansen U, Christophersen AS. Drug screening of preserved oral fluid by liquid chromatography-tandem mass spectrometry. *Clin Chem* 2007; 53(2): 300–309.
11. Concheiro M, de Castro A, Quintela O, Cruz A, López-Rivadulla M. Determination of illicit and medicinal drugs and their metabolites in oral fluid and preserved oral fluid by liquid chromatography-tandem mass spectrometry. *Anal Bioanal Chem* 2008; 391(6): 2329–2338.
12. Wille SMR, Lambert WEE. Recent developments in extraction procedures relevant to analytical toxicology. *Anal Bioanal Chem* 2007; 388: 1381–1391.
13. Pragst F. Application of solid-phase microextraction in analytical toxicology. *Anal Bioanal Chem* 2007; 388: 1393–1414.
14. Smith ML, Vorce SP, Holler JM, Shimomura E, Magluilo J, Jacobs AJ, Huestis MA. Modern instrumental methods in forensic toxicology. *J Anal Toxicol* 2007; 31: 237–253.
15. Pragst F, Herzler M, Erxleben B-T. Systematic toxicological analysis by high-performance liquid chromatography with diode array detection (HPLC-DAD). *Clin Chem Lab Med* 2004; 42: 1325–1340.
16. Drummer OH. Chromatographic screening techniques in systematic toxicological analysis. *J Chromatogr B* 1999; 733: 27–45.
17. Rivier L. Criteria for the identification of compounds by liquid chromatography-mass spectrometry and liquid chromatography-multiple mass spectrometry in forensic toxicology and doping analysis. *Anal Chim Acta* 2003; 492: 69–82.
18. Fernández P, Lago M, Lorenzo RA, Carro AM, Bermejo AM, Tabernero MJ. Microwave assisted extraction of drugs of abuse from human urine. *J Appl Toxicol* 2007; 27: 373–379.
19. van Lieshout M, van Deursen M, Derks R, Janssen H, Cramers CA. The influence of liner dimensions on injector band broadening in split injections in fast capillary gas chromatography. *J High Resolut Chromatogr* 1999; 22: 116–118.
20. Wyndham KD, O'Gara JE, Walter TH, Glose KH, Lawrence NL, Alden BA, Izzo GS, Hudalla CJ, Iraneta PC. Characterization and evaluation of C18 HPLC stationary phases based on ethyl-bridged hybrid organic/inorganic particles. *Anal Chem* 2003; 75: 6781–6788.
21. Peters FT, Drummer OH, Musshoff F. Validation of new methods. *Forensic Sci Int* 2007; 165: 216–224.
22. Ferrara DS, Tedeschi L, Frison G, Brusini G. Quality control in toxicological analysis. *J Chromatogr B* 1998; 713: 227–243.

9

Specimen adulteration

Claire George

Key points

- Specimen adulteration is increasingly being recognised as an important issue affecting workplace drug testing programmes.
- Specimen adulteration can occur through *in vivo* and *in vitro* methods or through specimen substitution, with a recent estimate suggesting that around 400 different products are currently available.
- The effect of an adulterant is dependent on its concentration and the analytical methodology used. Adulterants may affect screening assays, point-of-care testing devices and confirmatory techniques.
- Assays capable of identifying the active constituents of adulterant formulations, including chromate, nitrite and peroxidase, are becoming increasingly available.
- The generation of an accurate workplace drug testing result is increasingly being dictated by the ability of the testing laboratory to stay one step ahead of the adulterant manufacturers.

Introduction

Workplace drug testing programmes, originally introduced in the safety critical industries such as the nuclear and transportation sectors, are now becoming increasingly common within other industries. A MORI poll of UK businesses conducted in 2003 revealed that 9% of companies were planning to introduce a drug testing policy within the next year. Of the 204 respondents, 78% said they would consider introducing a testing programme if they thought that drug and alcohol use was affecting the company's productivity. This increased to 89% when questioned about the impact of drug and alcohol use on health and safety at work.[1] Published data suggest that workplace drug testing programmes are also increasing in popularity in other European countries.[2]

The increasing use of testing programmes, together with the grave ramifications of a positive test result, suggests that specimen adulteration will become an increasing problem for drug testing laboratories. A large American provider of workplace drug testing services estimated that it sees approximately 360 000 adulterated specimens per year. This equates to around one in every hundred specimens processed.[3] In addition, recent statistics suggest that the frequency of specimen substitution in American Federally mandated testing programmes could be as high as 2.4%.

A recent European study to determine the frequency of specimen adulteration concluded that 10.2% of subjects submitting samples for analysis were adulterating their specimens.[4] In contrast, detection of oxidant adulterants in the American Federally mandated testing schemes has shown a steady decline in recent years, reducing from 0.82% in 2001 to 0.42% in 2004.[5] This decline is almost certainly linked to an increase in laboratory staff awareness of the availability of chemical adulterants and other commercial products specifically designed to 'beat' the drug testing process.

The Substance Abuse and Mental Health Services Administration (SAMHSA), the body which regulates Federally mandated drug testing programmes in the United States, the United Kingdom Workplace Drug Testing Forum (UKWDTF) and the European Workplace Drug Testing Society (EWDTS) have all produced guidelines for legally defensible workplace drug testing which include criteria to minimise specimen adulteration or substitution during the collection process.[6–8] These criteria include the removal of unnecessary outer clothing and luggage such as handbags prior to specimen collection, the removal of water sources, soap, toilet cleaners and other products that could be used to adulterate the specimen from the collection area and the use of blue dye in the toilet cistern to prevent specimen dilution or substitution. In addition, collection officers are also asked to note the specimen temperature and report any unusual observations which may suggest specimen adulteration, including the presence of precipitate or unusual sample colour, to the testing laboratory.

Historically the guidelines issued by SAMHSA made provision for specimens to be tested for the presence of adulterants at the discretion of the drug testing laboratory. However, due to the increased prevalence of products specifically designed to help individuals conceal their drug use the 2004 revision of these guidelines requires validity testing to be performed on all specimens collected as part of the Federal workplace drug testing programme.[6] Provision for specimen validity testing is also made within the EU and UK guidelines for legally defensible drug testing.

For many years, urine has been the only matrix accepted by workplace drug testing programmes. It is only recently that the potential of alternative matrices such as oral fluid and hair has been recognised. The UKWDTF has begun drafting a set of guidelines for the use of oral fluid in legally defensible workplace drug testing. Similarly, the EWDTS are currently developing guidelines to enable the use of oral fluid and hair as testing matrices. SAMHSA are also reviewing the use of alternative matrices, including hair and oral fluid, however they are not currently recognised as acceptable specimens in federal workplace drug testing programmes. The majority of literature regarding adulterants and their potential impact on the drug screening process therefore focuses on urinary adulterants. For this reason a large part of this chapter will be devoted to the impact of adulterants on urinary immunoassay screening and confirmatory procedures for drugs of abuse and their detection.

Mechanisms of specimen adulteration

Even though the specimen collection procedure is strictly regulated, specimen substitution and/or adulteration still occur. Adulteration can be achieved in several ways, including the addition of a substance/product to a specimen which affects the test being performed (*in vitro* adulteration), the use of diuretics, detoxifying/cleansing products or water to provide an overly dilute specimen (*in vivo* adulteration) or the substitution of the test specimen with an artificial or 'clean' specimen.

In vitro adulteration

Household products, including bleach, detergent and vinegar, were among the first reported chemical adulterants since they are readily accessible. However, the marked growth in drug screening has resulted in the development of a large market for relatively cheap commercial products specifically designed to 'beat the test'. A recent estimate suggests that around 400 different products are currently available or known about.[9] The increased use of the Internet as a marketing resource means that these products are readily availably in many countries, making specimen adulteration a global issue for laboratories involved in drug testing. In addition, many products marketed are undergoing continual re-formulation to evade detection by drug testing laboratories.

One of the first commercially available products purposely designed to 'beat the test' was marketed as 'UrinAid'. Each UrinAid kit contained a 5-mL vial of glutaraldehyde solution, which was sold for between US$20 and US$30 per kit. This was later followed by the introduction of products such as 'Klear' and 'Whizzies' which appeared on the market in the mid 1990s. The constituents of 'Klear' and 'Whizzies' were identified as potassium nitrite and sodium nitrite, respectively. More recently, other products including 'Urine Luck', a product known to contain pyridinium chlorochromate or potassium dichromate, and 'Stealth', a formulation containing both peroxide and peroxidase, have been introduced.[10–12]

The presence of a chemical adulterant is difficult to identify when the only criteria used to determine specimen validity are parameters such as pH, specific gravity and creatinine concentration. Therefore there is an increasing requirement to use specific testing procedures which target the active constituents of products such as nitrite or chromate.

In vivo adulteration

In vivo adulteration is the term commonly used to refer to the consumption of large quantities of water and/or the use of products to 'detoxify' or 'flush' the system to achieve specimen dilution. There are a number of commercially available products, for example 'Naturally Klean Herbal Tea' and 'Green Clean Drug Detox', which claim to 'cleanse' or 'detoxify' the body, thereby producing a negative drug test. The instructions supplied with many of these products specify that the product should be consumed with large quantities of water. It is therefore likely that the consumption of large volumes of water is in part responsible for the success of these particular types of products in reducing the likelihood of drug detection.[13]

The consumption of large volumes of fluid causes the creatinine concentration and specific gravity (parameters commonly used to identify dilute specimens) to decrease below the levels accepted in workplace drug testing programmes. Cone *et al.*[13] demonstrated that both creatinine concentrations below 1.77 mmol/L (20 mg/dL) and specific gravity measurements below 1.003 were achieved following the consumption of 2 L water. Lafolie *et al.*[14] reported creatinine results of less than 0.7 mmol/L (8 mg/dL) following the consumption of 1 L water. Furthermore, the consumption of large volumes of fluid several hours prior to undergoing a drugs test has been shown to result in the production of false negative drug screening results, where people known to be using illicit drugs avoided detection.[13]

The European Guidelines for Legally Defensible Workplace Drug Testing[8] stipulate that where the creatinine result is determined to be between 0.5 and 2.0 mmol/L (5.6–22.6 mg/dL) and the specific gravity is determined to be within the acceptable range of 1.001–1.020, the sample must be identified as dilute. Similar guidance is given in the United Kingdom Guidelines for Legally Defensible Workplace testing and the American mandatory guidelines for federal workplace drug testing programmes issued by SAMHSA.[6,7] However, it is important when applying such guidelines to consider the impact of medical conditions such as diabetes mellitus, diabetes insipidus or psychogenic polydipsia, as well as other causes of polyuria. Both diabetes mellitus and diabetes insipidus cause polyuria, the passing of excessive volumes of dilute urine, and polydipsia, the consumption of large volumes of fluid due to excessive thirst.[15]

Creatinine concentrations as low as 1.1 mmol/L (13 mg/dL) and specific gravity measurements ranging between 1.003 and 1.007 have been reported in individuals diagnosed with diabetes insipidus. A review of creatinine concentrations and specific gravity measurements in urine specimens collected from 10 subjects with psychogenic polydipsia, the consumption of excessive volumes of fluid due to a personality disorder, were reported to range between 0.35 mmol/L (4 mg/dL) and 16 mmol/L (185 mg/dL) and 1.000–1.017, respectively.[16]

Polyuria may also occur because of the use of diuretics, a group of drugs which enhance the clearance of water and electrolytes. Potent diuretic formulations including bendroflumethiazide and frusemide are used clinically in the treatment of hypertension and oedema and will cause significant urine dilution. Other compounds, including caffeine and alcohol also have some diuretic effect, however their impact on urine dilution is less significant.[17,18]

Some of the herbal preparations advertised as 'cleansing' or 'detoxifying solutions' contain high concentrations of carbohydrates as well as 'natural' diuretics such as dandelion or marshmallow root. It is suggested that this type of product produces the desired effect (i.e. a negative drug screening result), by functioning as a potent osmotic diuretic. Compounds such as glucose, if taken in large enough quantities, can also act as osmotic diuretics. Glucose is reabsorbed in the proximal tubule via a saturable sodium-coupled receptor. When this absorption mechanism becomes saturated an osmotic gradient is produced, facilitating the elimination of water and sodium chloride. Interestingly, the literature provided with many of the products also states that to be effective they should be consumed with large quantities of water.

Substitution

Substitution of a specimen may be difficult to achieve when specimen collection is observed, however it is sometimes still attempted. There are several devices available on the Internet which are supplied as complete 'substitution kits' containing certified drug-free urine, a battery-operated heater or chemically reactive heat pads and a concealable container complete with adhesive temperature strips to ensure that the specimen provided is within the temperature range deemed acceptable by many workplace drug testing programmes. Certified drug-free lyophilised human urine and synthetic urine are also available separately to allow devices to be re-used. The authorities are beginning to crack down on the availability of these products, with a successful legal case recently being bought against the manufacturer of one such device.

To minimise the possibility of adulteration or substitution, collection officers are required to measure and record the temperature of a specimen within 4 minutes of voiding. The measured temperature should fall within the range 32–38°C.[8] Drury *et al.*[19] used specimen temperature as a criterion to evaluate the extent to which substituted specimens are likely to be accepted for drug testing. Condoms filled with water were either inserted into the anterior region of the subject's underpants or strapped under the arm using an elastic band for a minimum of 2 hours prior to testing. Specimens were collected into sterile specimen cups, and the temperature measured using a temperature strip attached to the side of the cup. Analysis of the data revealed that 90% of the specimens fell within the range 32–38°C and would therefore have been accepted for testing. The mean temperature recorded for specimens concealed in the underpants was 32.8°C, with the mean temperature for those concealed under the arm being recorded as 33.7°C. The authors conclude that the substitution of a specimen for a synthetic or 'clean' urine specimen is feasible and is only avoidable if specimens are collected under direct observation.[19]

Effect of adulterants on immunoassays

The validity of immunoassay screening results is of particular concern to drug testing laboratories, since a negative screening result usually negates the requirement to perform further confirmatory analyses using a more sensitive and specific technique such as gas chromatography-mass spectrometry (GC-MS). The determination of specimen integrity is therefore becoming an increasing priority in drug testing because of the advent of a large number of commercially available adulterant products which have been specifically designed to produce false negative screening results.

Numerous studies have revealed the effect of chemical adulterants upon immunoassay screening procedures.[20–31] Their effect appears to be concentration dependent and will vary according to the drug/drug class being screened as well as the methodology used. However, irrespective of the methodology employed, the cannabinoid assays appear to be the most sensitive to the majority of adulteration agents.

The variation in effect of adulterants upon the various immunoassay methodologies may in part be explained by the different mechanisms used for drug detection.

Various enzyme immunoassays (EIAs) including the enzyme multiplied immunoassay technique (EMIT®) and the cloned enzyme donor immunoassay (CEDIA®) together with the fluorescence polarisation immunoassay (FPIA) and the Roche kinetic interaction of microparticles in solution (KIMS) assay all rely on spectrophotometric detection for the determination of drug concentration. However, all of these techniques utilise different wavelengths. The EMIT assay relies upon the conversion of oxidised nicotinamide adenine dinucleotide (NAD) to NADH which results in an absorbance change that can be measured spectrophotometrically at 340 nm. CEDIA, however, relies upon the formation of the active bacterial enzyme β-galactosidase to cleave a substrate (chlorophenol red-β-galactopyranoside) generating a colour change that can be measured at 570 nm.

The determination of drug concentration in an FPIA assay is determined by measuring the emission of polarised light in the region of 525–550 nm whereas the overall change in absorbance (i.e. an endpoint measurement), at 505 nm is utilised in the turbidometric KIMS assay. Therefore, the presence of an adulterant which absorbs at 570 nm will cause interference in the CEDIA assay but is less likely to impact on the results obtained in FPIA or KIMS assays due to the different wavelength used in drug detection.

The radioimmunoassay (RIA) drugs of abuse assays appear to be least affected by adulterants. This technique does not rely upon spectrophotometric detection. Instead the drug concentration is determined by measuring the number of counts per specimen following the addition of a radiolabelled (^{125}I) tracer.[17,18,32] However, this is a relatively labour-intensive technique in comparison with other homogeneous immunoassays and is no longer commonly used for routine drugs of abuse screening.

In addition to adulterants affecting method-specific detection parameters enzyme immunoassays may also be adversely affected by any adulterant which causes a dramatic shift in pH. A very acidic or very alkali pH will result in the loss of enzyme activity. The extent to which specimen pH affects an immunoassay is dependent upon the buffering capacity of the urine specimen and assay reagents.[18]

The effects of the readily available adulterants on immunoassay drug screening methodologies have in the main been extensively researched and well described in the literature. A review of the data currently available are collated in alphabetical order below.

Ammonia

EIA

There is currently no information available regarding the impact of ammonia on the CEDIA or EMIT technologies.

FPIA

A 10% ammonia solution was found to have no impact on the Abbott amphetamine/methamphetamine II, cannabinoid, cocaine metabolite, opiate and phencyclidine II assays. However, an increase in the apparent concentration of barbiturates was observed in both the positive and negative samples although no false positive results were reported.[26]

KIMS

There is currently no information available regarding the impact of ammonia on the KIMS drugs of abuse assays.

RIA

Analysis of 5% and 10% ammonia solutions produced false negative results in the Roche Abuscreen High Specificity cocaine metabolite assay. In addition, an increase in the apparent cannabinoid concentration was observed in both positive and negative samples although no false positive results were reported. No effect was observed in the Roche Abuscreen High Specificity amphetamine, barbiturate, phencyclidine and specific morphine assays at ammonia concentrations ranging between 1% and 10%.[24]

Ascorbic acid

EIA

There is currently no information available regarding the impact of ascorbic acid on the CEDIA and EMIT drugs of abuse assays.

FPIA

The presence of 1%, 5% and 10% ascorbic acid was reported to have a detrimental effect on the Abbott cannabinoid assay, with false negative results being produced at all three concentrations. In addition, a slight decrease in apparent concentration was observed in the amphetamine and barbiturate assays at a concentration of 10%. No discernible effect was observed in the Abbott cocaine metabolite, opiate and phencyclidine assays in the presence of 10% ascorbic acid.[26]

KIMS

There is currently no information available regarding the impact of ascorbic acid on the KIMS drugs of abuse assays.

RIA

The presence of 1%, 5% and 10% ascorbic acid had no discernible effect on negative control specimens in the Roche Abuscreen High Specificity amphetamine/metamphetamine II and specific morphine assays. However, a decrease in the apparent morphine and amphetamine concentration in known positive specimens was reported, with a 10% solution producing results near the assay cut-off in both cases. Conversely, both 5% and 10% solutions produced an increase in the apparent cannabinoid concentration in negative control specimens in the Roche Abuscreen High Specificity cannabinoid assay. However, this finding was not reproduced in known 'cannabis' positive specimens at either ascorbic acid concentration. Instead, a decrease in the apparent cannabinoid concentration was observed. No effect was observed on the Roche Abuscreen High Specificity barbiturate, cocaine metabolite and phencyclidine assays at any of the concentrations studied.[24]

Bleach/hypochlorite

EIA

Concentrations of between 1.2% and 12.5% have been demonstrated to produce false negative results in the EMIT d.a.u.™ amphetamine, barbiturate, benzodiazepine, cannabinoid, cocaine metabolite and opiate assays.[22] These results are supported by the findings of Warner[23] who observed false negative results in the EMIT d.a.u. amphetamine, benzodiazepine, cannabinoid, opiate and phencyclidine assays at bleach concentrations of 5.2%.

A decrease in the apparent barbiturate, cannabinoid and cocaine metabolite concentrations was observed in the CEDIA assays in the presence of 1% bleach. Furthermore, it has been suggested that false negative results are likely to be obtained in the amphetamine, barbiturate, benzodiazepine, benzoylecgonine, cannabinoid, opiate and phencyclidine assays in the presence of 10% bleach.[28]

FPIA

Analysis of a 5.2% solution produced false negative results in the Abbott amphetamine, cannabinoid, opiate and phencyclidine assays. However, there was no visible effect on the negative control specimens at this concentration, with the exception of the Abbott benzodiazepine assay where a false positive benzodiazepine result was reported.[23]

These data are supported by the findings of Schwarzhoff and Cody[26] who reported false negative results in the Abbott cannabinoid and opiate assays at bleach concentrations of 5% and 10%.[26]

KIMS

There is currently no information available regarding the impact of bleach/hypochlorite on the KIMS drugs of abuse assays.

RIA

The Roche Abuscreen High Specificity amphetamine and cannabinoid assays were found to produce false negative results at bleach concentrations of both 5% and 10%. False negative cannabinoid results were also observed at 1%. However, the results produced were near the cut-off level of the assay.[24]

Blood

EIA

There are currently no data available regarding the influence of blood on the CEDIA and EMIT drugs of abuse assays.

FPIA

A 10% solution had no effect on the Abbott amphetamine/methamphetamine II, barbiturate II U, cocaine metabolite, opiate and phencyclidine II assays. However, a decrease in the apparent cannabinoid concentration was observed although no false negative results were reported.[26]

KIMS

There is currently no information available regarding the impact of blood on the KIMS drugs of abuse assays.

RIA

Analysis of specimens containing 0.1%, 1%, 5% and 10% blood had no discernible effect on the Roche amphetamine, barbiturate, cannabinoid, cocaine metabolite, specific morphine and phencyclidine assays.[24]

Chromate

EIA

A 1% solution of pyridinium chlorochromate decreased the apparent cannabinoid concentration in the EMIT II cannabinoid assay. When the concentration was increased to 5%, false negative results were obtained in the EMIT II cannabinoid assay. In addition, a decrease in the apparent opiate and phencyclidine concentrations in the EMIT II assays was also observed. An increase in the pyridinium chlorochromate concentration to 10% resulted in false negative results in the EMIT II amphetamine and opiate assays. A decrease in the apparent benzoylecgonine concentration was also observed in the EMIT II assay at this concentration although no false negative results were reported.[11]

FPIA

There are currently no data available regarding the influence of chromate on FPIA drugs of abuse assays.

KIMS

There is currently no information available regarding the impact of chromate on the KIMS drugs of abuse assays.

RIA

A 1% solution of pyridinium chlorochromate resulted in a decrease in the apparent cannabinoid concentration in the Roche Abuscreen High Specificity assay. This effect appears to be concentration dependent, with a concentration of 5% producing false negative cannabinoid results in the Roche assay.[11]

The presence of 10% pyridinium chlorochromate resulted in a decrease in the apparent benzoylecgonine concentration, a slight decrease in the apparent phencyclidine concentration and an increase in the apparent amphetamine concentration in the Roche Abuscreen High Specificity assays. In addition, false negative results were reported in the Roche Abuscreen High Specificity opiate assay at this concentration.[11]

Detergent

Ionic surfactants, such as Joy® dishwashing detergent, have been shown to have a significant impact on the EMIT, CEDIA, Roche RIA and Abbott FPIA drugs of abuse assays.

EIA

The analysis of a 10% detergent solution produced false negative results in the EMIT d.a.u. benzodiazepine, cannabinoid and phencyclidine assays. In addition, an increase in the apparent barbiturate concentration in known positive specimens was also observed, although this finding was not reproduced in negative control specimens.[23]

A 10% solution produced false negative results in the CEDIA amphetamine, barbiturate, cannabinoid, cocaine metabolite, opiate and phencyclidine assays. However, no effect on the CEDIA benzodiazepine assay has been reported.[28]

FPIA

False positive results were obtained from the negative control samples in the Abbott amphetamine, barbiturate, benzodiazepine and cannabinoid assays in the presence of 10% Joy.[23] However, a more recent study only reported false positive results in the Abbott barbiturate II U assay, although an increase in the apparent amphetamine concentration was also observed.[26]

KIMS

There are currently no data available regarding the influence of detergent on KIMS drugs of abuse assays.

RIA

It has been suggested that false positive results are likely to be obtained in the Roche benzodiazepine and cannabinoid assays in the presence of detergent.[23] However, it would appear that the impact of specimen adulteration with detergent is concentration and analyte dependent. Analysis of specimens containing 1%, 5% and 10% Joy had no impact on the results obtained in the Roche Abuscreen High Specificity amphetamine, barbiturate, specific morphine and phencyclidine assays. However, a 10% solution produced false negative results in the Roche Abuscreen High Specificity cocaine metabolite assay. In addition, an increase in the apparent cannabinoid concentration was observed in the positive specimens and negative controls at both 5% and 10%.[24]

Drano

Drano®, a solution of sodium hydroxide and sodium hypochlorite, was found to have a concentration-dependent effect on both EMIT and RIA drugs of abuse assays.

EIA

Wu *et al.*[28] reported that the addition of 0.1% Drano was likely to produce false negative results in the CEDIA cannabinoid assay. An increase in the Drano concentration to 2% resulted in a decreased response in the CEDIA amphetamines, barbiturate, benzodiazepine, cannabinoid, cocaine metabolite, opiate and phencyclidine assays, therefore increasing the likelihood of obtaining false negative results.

The presence of Drano also has a marked impact on the EMIT d.a.u. drugs of abuse assays. These are summarised in Table 9.1.

FPIA

The presence of Drano has little effect on the Abbott amphetamine/methamphetamine II, barbiturate II U, cannabinoid, opiate and phencyclidine II

Table 9.1 The effect of Drano® on EMIT d.a.u. drugs of abuse assays[22]

Analyte (concentration ng/mL)	Drano concentration (mL/L of specimen)	% Drano concentration	Screening result
Amphetamines (<520)	12	1.2	False negative
Amphetamines (<1800)	23	2.3	False negative
Barbiturates (<1450)	125	12.5	False negative
Benzodiazepine (<3000)	125	12.5	False negative
Cannabinoids (31–122)	12	12.0	False negative
Cocaine metabolite (1180)	42	4.2	False negative
Cocaine metabolite (1820)	125	12.5	False negative
Opiates (<2700)	125	12.5	False negative

assays. However, a 10% solution produced false negative results in the Abbott cocaine metabolite and phencyclidine assays.[26]

KIMS

There are currently no data available regarding the influence of Drano on KIMS drugs of abuse assays.

RIA

A 1% Drano solution produced false negative results in the Roche Abuscreen High Specificity cocaine metabolite assay. In addition, a slight increase in the apparent cannabinoid concentration in both the positive specimens and negative control samples was also observed. The Roche Abuscreen High Specificity amphetamine, barbiturate, specific morphine and phencyclidine assays were unaffected at this concentration.[24]

An increase in Drano concentration to 5% resulted in a more dramatic effect on the Abuscreen High Specificity assays. False positive results were obtained from negative control sample in the amphetamine, barbiturate, cannabinoid, specific morphine and phencyclidine assays. In addition, at this concentration a rise in the apparent cocaine metabolite concentration in the negative control specimen was also observed. In the presence of 10% Drano an increase in the apparent cocaine metabolite concentration was observed in negative control specimens, although no false positive results were reported.[24]

Glutaraldehyde (UrinAid)

EIA

A 0.75% solution produced false negative results in the EMIT II cannabinoid assay. A significant effect on the EMIT II amphetamine, benzodiazepines, cocaine metabolite and methadone assays was reported at a concentration of 1–2% with all of the above assays yielding false negative results.[29]

The presence of 10% glutaraldehyde resulted in a significant reduction in the rate of reaction in the CEDIA barbiturate, cannabinoid, cocaine metabolite and phencyclidine assays. This suggests that false negative results are likely to be obtained even in specimens containing relatively high drug concentrations. A less marked effect was observed in the CEDIA benzodiazepine assay at this concentration. The authors therefore concluded that false negative benzodiazepine results are only likely in specimens that contain concentrations near to the assay cut-off. A 10% solution had no discernible effect on the CEDIA amphetamine and opiate assays.[28]

FPIA

A 66% solution, equivalent to the use of one vial of the commercial product 'UrinAid', yielded false positive results in the Abbott phencyclidine assay.[27]

KIMS

The addition of one vial (4 mL) UrinAid to a 60-mL urine specimen yielded false positive results in the KIMS amphetamine and phencyclidine assays. In addition, an increased response in the Roche KIMS cannabinoid assay was also observed, although only one false positive result was reported.[27]

RIA

False positive results were obtained in the Roche phencyclidine assay in the presence of 66% glutaraldehyde.[27]

Lemon juice

EIA

Unlike ascorbic acid, citric acid (lemon juice) had no effect on the EMIT d.a.u. amphetamine, barbiturate, benzodiazepine, cannabinoid, cocaine metabolite and opiate assays when used to analyse urine specimens collected from known drug users. However, a 50% solution was determined to affect 'spiked' specimens.[22]

A 33% citric acid solution produced a decrease in the apparent drug concentration in the CEDIA amphetamine, barbiturate, benzodiazepine, cannabinoid, cocaine metabolite and opiate assays. The addition of lemon juice may therefore adversely affect the results obtained, especially from specimens containing drug concentrations near the assay cut-off. The CEDIA phencyclidine assay appeared not to be affected by the presence of citric acid.[28]

FPIA

A 10% citric acid solution had no effect on the Abbott amphetamine/methamphetamine II, barbiturate II U, cannabinoid, cocaine metabolite, opiate and phencyclidine II assays.[26]

KIMS

There are currently no data available regarding the influence of lemon juice on KIMS drugs of abuse assays.

RIA

A 10% citric acid solution had no effect on the Roche Abuscreen High Specificity amphetamine, barbiturate, cannabinoid, cocaine metabolite, opiate and phencyclidine assays.[24]

Lime-A-Way tile cleaner

EIA

There are currently no data available regarding the influence of 'Lime-A-Way' on the CEDIA and EMIT drugs of abuse assays.

FPIA

A 5% 'Lime-A-Way' solution produced a false negative result in the Abbott cannabinoid assay. In addition, a slight decrease in the apparent amphetamine and barbiturate concentrations were observed in negative control specimens at 10%. A 10% solution had no discernible effect on the Abbott cocaine metabolite, opiate and phencyclidine II assays.[26]

KIMS

There are currently no data available regarding the influence of 'Lime-A-Way' on KIMS drugs of abuse assays.

RIA

Analysis of 1%, 5% and 10% 'Lime-A-Way' solutions had no discernible effect on the Roche Abuscreen High Specificity barbiturate, cocaine metabolite and phencyclidine assays. However, both the 1% and 5% solutions produced a reduction in the apparent amphetamine and morphine concentration. Analysis of a 10% solution resulted in both amphetamine and morphine positive specimens producing readings equivalent to the assay cut-off concentration. An apparent increase in cannabinoid concentration was observed at concentrations of 5% and 10%. However, no false positive results were obtained.[24]

Liquid soap

EIA

Vu Duc[21] highlighted the potential for using liquid soap as an effective urine adulterant. He reported that a 10% liquid soap solution affected all EMIT drugs of abuse assays utilising lysozyme as the active enzyme and *M. lateus* as the substrate. However, assays utilising other substrates such as glucose 6-phosphate or malate did not appear to be affected until soap concentrations reached 30%.[21] These findings are supported by Mikkelsen and Ash[22] who described false negative results in the EMIT d.a.u. barbiturate, benzodiazepine and cannabinoid assays at concentrations of 2.3%, 4.2% and 1.2%, respectively. A 1.2% solution had no visible effect on the EMIT d.a.u. amphetamine, cocaine metabolite and opiate assays.[22]

FPIA

Analysis of a 10% solution produced false positive results in negative control specimens in the Abbott barbiturate II U assay. Increases in the response of negative control specimens were also observed in the Abbott amphetamine/methamphetamine II and cannabinoid assays although no positive results were obtained. However, the authors concluded that false positive results in these assays may be obtained in specimens adulterated with higher concentrations of soap.[26]

A 10% solution had no discernible effect on the cocaine metabolite, opiate and phencyclidine II assays.[26]

KIMS

A 10% soap solution resulted in false negative results being obtained in the Roche 'Agglutex' opiate assay.[21]

RIA

Both 1% and 5% soap solutions had a marked effect on the results obtained in the Roche Abuscreen High Specificity amphetamine and cannabinoid assays. The apparent concentration of amphetamine and cannabinoids increased in both known positive specimens and the negative control samples. An increase in the soap concentration to 10% resulted in the negative control giving a positive result in the Roche Abuscreen High Specificity cannabinoid assay. Although an apparent increase in the amphetamine concentration was also noted at this concentration, no positive results were recorded for any of the specimens tested.[24]

The Roche Abuscreen High Specificity barbiturate, cocaine metabolite, specific morphine and phencyclidine assays were not affected at concentrations of 1%, 5% and 10%.[24]

Nitrite

Nitrite is one of the few adulterants that is believed to decrease drug concentration rather than exerting a direct effect on the screening technique used to process the specimen. Nitrite produces a pH dependent decrease in the concentration of the cannabis metabolite, 11-nor-Δ-9-tetrahydrocannabinol-9-carboxylic acid (THC-COOH). Therefore adulteration with a nitrite-containing product such as 'Klear' or 'Whizzies' will have a detrimental effect on the detection of the cannabis metabolite. A noticeable decrease in the cannabinoid immunoassay response was observed in acidic specimens within 4 hours of adulteration with 0.3 mol/L and 0.15 mol/L nitrite. One day following adulteration, negative cannabinoid screening results were recorded for all acidic specimens. Specimens with pH values greater than 7 appeared to be less affected by nitrite adulteration, with the majority of specimens screening cannabinoid positive 72 hours following adulteration.[10] The presence of nitrite has also been shown to adversely effect the detection of other analytes including amphetamine, cocaine and opiates by a number of screening techniques (Table 9.2).

Table 9.2 The influence of 1.02 g/L nitrite on the apparent concentration of common drugs of abuse (Cardiff Bioanalytical Services, UK, private communication)

Analyte (concentration)	Abbott assays (inc. ADX, TDX, Axsym and FPIA)	CEDIA®	EMIT® d.a.u. and EMIT II	Roche KIMS assays (inc. On-Line and OnTrack)
d-Amphetamine (2 mg/L)	Decrease	Decrease	Decrease	Decrease
Cocaine metabolite (1 mg/L)	No effect	No effect	Decrease	No effect
Opiates (morphine 3 mg/L)	Decrease	Decrease	Decrease	Decrease
Heroin metabolite (6-AM 30 micrograms/L)	No assay available	Decrease	No assay available	No assay available
Buprenorphine (10 micrograms/L)	No assay available	Decrease	No assay available	No assay available

Papain

This is a recent addition to the list of more commonly available adulterants. Papain is a protease enzyme which is obtained from the dried latex of the papaya fruit. It is commonly used in the food processing industry for tenderising meat but is also available over the Internet as a health food supplement.[34] It has been suggested that this proteolytic enzyme is activated by the presence of urea and/or cysteine.[35] Although the mechanism of action of this adulterant has not yet been elucidated, papain appears to have an assay- and concentration-dependent effect on cannabis screening assays.

EIA

Burrows *et al.*[34] proposed papain as a novel urine adulterant due to its potential to interfere with cannabinoid immunoassays. False negative results were obtained in the EMIT d.a.u. cannabinoid assay following the addition of 10 mg/mL papain.[34]

The addition of 10 mg/mL latex papain has been shown to lead to a decrease in response in the EMIT II cannabis assay of between 16% and 43%. Similar findings were also observed in the CEDIA cannabis assay where the apparent cannabis assay response was found to decrease by between 7% and 16%.[35]

The addition of 10 mg/mL of meat tenderiser was found to have a varying effect dependent upon the assay. An increase in response of between 5% and 20% was observed in the EMIT II cannabis assay, however this effect was not observed in the CEDIA cannabis assay.[35]

FPIA

Using an unstated cannabinoid assay Burrows *et al.*[34] reported an average 50% reduction in the cannabinoid concentration and a 12% decrease in the apparent benzodiazepine concentration following the addition of 10 mg/mL papain. However, FPIA amphetamine, barbiturate, benzoylecgonine, opiate and phencyclidine assays appeared not to be affected at this concentration.

The response in the Abbott cannabinoids assay was found to decrease by 19–23% following the addition of latex papain (10 mg/mL). Assay response was also found to decrease by between 8% and 15% following the addition of meat tenderiser (10 mg/mL).[35]

KIMS

False positive results were observed in the KIMS cannabis assay following the latex papain (10 mg/mL), with assay responses increasing by between 123% and 197%. A slight increase (∼15%) in assay response was observed following sample adulteration with meat tenderiser (10 mg/mL). However, this effect decreased over time with an overall 12% decrease in assay response being reported 10 days following sample adulteration.[35]

RIA

There are currently no data available regarding the influence of papain on RIA drugs of abuse assays.

Peroxide/peroxidase

Hydrogen peroxide is a powerful oxidising agent. When added to a sample in combination with peroxidase oxidation of the target analyte may occur. However, its impact on drugs of abuse screening is dependent upon the target analyte and assay used for analysis as described below.

EIA

A 3% solution of hydrogen peroxide had no visible effect on the EMIT d.a.u. amphetamine, barbiturate, benzodiazepine, cannabinoid, cocaine metabolite, opiate and phencyclidine assays.[23]

'Stealth', a commercially available product containing two individual vials of peroxide and peroxidase, does not affect the CEDIA amphetamine barbiturate, cocaine metabolite and phencyclidine assays. However, specimens containing cannabinoids, lysergic acid diethylamide (LSD) and morphine at concentrations between 25% and 50% above the assay cut-off produced negative results in the CEDIA assays.[12]

FPIA

Analysis of a 3% solution of hydrogen peroxide produced an increase in the apparent drug concentration in both known positive specimens and negative control specimens in the Abbott benzodiazepine assay. Furthermore, at this concentration false positive benzodiazepine results were obtained from the negative control specimens. An increase in the apparent cannabinoid concentration in known positive specimens was also observed at a concentration of 3%. However, this effect was not reproduced in the negative control specimens.[23]

A 3% solution had no visible effect on the Abbott amphetamine, barbiturate, cocaine metabolite, opiate and phencyclidine assays.[23]

KIMS

The addition of Stealth does not appear to affect the Roche OnLine® amphetamine barbiturate, cocaine metabolite and phencyclidine assays. However, specimens containing cannabinoids, LSD and morphine at concentrations between 25% and 50% above the assay cut-off produced negative results.[12]

RIA

A 3% solution had no visible effect on the Roche amphetamine, barbiturate, benzodiazepine, cocaine metabolite, opiate and phencyclidine assays. However, an increase in the apparent cannabinoid concentration in known positive specimens was observed.[23]

Sodium bicarbonate

EIA

False negative results were obtained from known positive specimens in the EMIT d.a.u. opiate assay at a concentration of 20% sodium bicarbonate. In addition, an increase in the apparent barbiturate concentration was also observed in positive specimens at this concentration, although no effect on the negative control specimens was reported. A 20% solution had no discernible effect on the EMIT d.a.u. amphetamine, benzodiazepine, cannabinoid, cocaine metabolite and phencyclidine assays.[23]

A 5% solution had no visible effect on the CEDIA amphetamine, barbiturate, benzodiazepine, cannabinoid, cocaine metabolite, opiate and phencyclidine assays.[28]

FPIA

The presence of sodium bicarbonate had a detrimental effect on the Abbott phencyclidine assay with a 20% solution producing false negative phencyclidine results. However, a 20% solution had no discernible effect on the Abbott amphetamine, barbiturate, benzodiazepine, cannabinoid, cocaine metabolite and opiate assays.[23]

KIMS

There is currently no information available regarding the impact of sodium bicarbonate on the KIMS drugs of abuse assays.

RIA

A 25% solution produced an increase in the apparent drug concentration in the Roche amphetamine, barbiturate, cannabinoid and opiate assays in both known positive specimens and negative control specimens, with false positive results being reported in all of these assays with the exception of the cannabinoid assay. No effect on the benzodiazepine, opiate and phencyclidine assay was observed at this concentration.[23]

Sodium chloride

EIA

The interference in the EMIT drugs of abuse assays has been well described.[20,22–24,26] The presence of 7.5% sodium chloride produced false negative results in the EMIT d.a.u. amphetamine, barbiturate and cocaine metabolite assays. However, 5% was sufficient to cause false negative results in the EMIT d.a.u. cannabinoid and opiate assays. Interestingly, no effect on the EMIT d.a.u. benzodiazepine assay was reported.[22]

Analysis of a 25% solution produced false negative results in the EMIT d.a.u. amphetamine, barbiturate, benzodiazepine, cannabinoid, cocaine metabolite, opiate and phencyclidine assays. A decrease in the apparent drug concentration in the negative control specimens was also observed at this concentration in all assays with the exception of the barbiturate assay, where no effect on the apparent drug concentration was reported.[23]

A 5% solution had no discernible effect on the CEDIA amphetamine, barbiturate, benzodiazepine, cannabinoid, cocaine metabolite, opiate and phencyclidine assays.[28]

FPIA

A 10% solution produced a decrease in the apparent cannabinoid concentration in known positive specimens although no effect on the negative control specimens was recorded. A 10% solution had no discernible effect on the amphetamine/methamphetamine II, barbiturate II U, cocaine metabolite, opiate and phencyclidine assays.[26]

A 25% solution produced a decrease in the apparent benzodiazepine concentration in known positive specimens in the Abbott assay. However, this effect was not reproduced in the negative control specimens. No effects were observed at this concentration in the either the known positive or negative control specimens in the Abbott amphetamine, barbiturate, cannabinoid, cocaine metabolite, opiate and phencyclidine assays.[23]

KIMS

There is currently no information available regarding the impact of sodium chloride on the KIMS drugs of abuse assays.

RIA

A 10% solution produced a decrease in the apparent cannabinoid concentration in the Roche Abuscreen High Specificity cannabinoid assay. However, no discernible effect on the Roche Abuscreen High Specificity amphetamine, barbiturate, cocaine metabolite, morphine and phencyclidine assays was observed at this concentration.[24]

Sodium phosphate

EIA

There are currently no data available regarding the influence of sodium phosphate (Bondex®) on the CEDIA and EMIT drugs of abuse assays.

FPIA

There are currently no data available regarding the influence of sodium phosphate (Bondex) on the FPIA drugs of abuse assays.

KIMS

There is currently no information available regarding the impact of sodium phosphate on the KIMS drugs of abuse assays.

RIA

The effect on the Roche Abuscreen High Specificity assays appears to be analyte and concentration dependent. The presence of 5% and 10% sodium phosphate resulted in a decrease in the apparent cocaine metabolite concentration although no false negative results were reported. In addition an increase in the apparent cannabinoid concentration was also observed at both these concentrations, with false positive cannabinoid results being obtained for the negative control specimens at a concentration of 10%.[24]

Analysis of a 5% solution had no discernible effect on the Roche Abuscreen High Specificity amphetamine, barbiturate, specific morphine and phencyclidine assays. However, a 10% solution produced an increase in the apparent amphetamine, barbiturate, morphine and phencyclidine concentration in both the known positive samples and the negative control specimens. The increase in the apparent drug concentration was particularly significant in both the barbiturate and specific morphine assays, as results were obtained near the assay cut-off for the negative control specimens in both assays.[24]

Vanish

Vanish® is a commercially available toilet bowl disinfectant which lists hydrochloric acid and ammonium chloride among its ingredients. There is limited information available regarding its impact on drugs of abuse screening assays.

EIA

There are currently no data available regarding the influence of Vanish on the CEDIA and EMIT drugs of abuse assays.

FPIA

A 10% solution had no discernible effect on either the positive or negative control specimens in the Abbott amphetamine/methamphetamine II, barbiturate II U, cannabinoid, cocaine metabolite, opiate and phencyclidine II assays.[26]

KIMS

There is currently no information available regarding the impact of Vanish on the KIMS drugs of abuse assays.

RIA

The effects of Vanish on the Roche Abuscreen High Specificity drugs of abuse assays appears to be dependent upon the analyte under investigation as well as the adulterant concentration.

Vanish has been shown to produce a significant but varied effect on the Roche Abuscreen High Specificity cannabinoid assay. A 1% solution of Vanish resulted in a decrease in the apparent cannabinoid concentration but a 5% solution resulted in an increase in the apparent cannabinoid concentration in both known positive specimens and negative control specimens. A 10% solution produced false negative cannabinoid results in known positive specimens. However, an increase in the apparent cannabinoid concentration was observed in negative control specimens at this concentration, with results being obtained near the assay cut-off.[24]

A 10% solution also produced a decrease in the apparent drug concentration of known positive specimens in the Roche Abuscreen High Specificity amphetamine and specific morphine assays. However, no influence on the negative control specimens was observed.[24]

The Roche Abuscreen High Specificity barbiturate, cocaine metabolite and phencyclidine assays appeared to be unaffected in the presence of 1%, 5% and 10% Vanish solutions.[24]

Vinegar

EIA

Vinegar typically contains between 3% and 5% acetic acid. The addition of vinegar totalling 12.5% of sample volume had no observable effect on the EMIT d.a.u. amphetamine, barbiturate, benzodiazepine, cocaine metabolite and opiate assays. This concentration did, however, produce a false negative result in the EMIT cannabinoid d.a.u. assay.[22]

A 1.0% solution produced a decrease in response in the CEDIA cannabinoid and cocaine metabolite assays. This may result in false negative results being obtained in these assays where the drug concentration is near the assay cut-off.[28]

FPIA

A 5% solution produced a decrease in the apparent cannabinoid concentration in known positive specimens in the Abbott cannabinoid assay. This decrease in the apparent concentration was sufficient to produce a false negative result. No effects were observed in the Abbott amphetamine/methamphetamine II, barbiturate II U, cocaine metabolite, opiate and phencyclidine II assays at the 5% or 10% concentration.[26]

KIMS

There is currently no information available regarding the impact of vinegar on the KIMS drugs of abuse assays.

RIA

A 1%, 5% and 10% vinegar solution had no measurable effect on the analysis of known positive or negative specimens using the Roche Abuscreen High Specificity amphetamine, barbiturate, cannabinoids, cocaine metabolite, specific morphine and phencyclidine assays.[24]

Visine eye drops

EIA

Visine® concentrations ranging between 2% and 10% produced false negative results in the EMIT d.a.u. cannabinoid assay. However, these findings were not reproducible when analysing solutions containing concentrations in excess of 20%. A decreased response in the EMIT d.a.u. barbiturate assay was observed at concentrations ranging between 2% and 30%, although no false negative results were reported. Decreases in the apparent cocaine metabolite and phencyclidine concentrations were observed at concentrations ranging between 5% and 30%, with decreases in the apparent benzodiazepines and opiate concentration being observed at concentrations ranging between 10% and 30%. However, no false negative results were reported. Visine solutions of between 2% and 30% had no visible effect on the EMIT d.a.u. amphetamine assay.[25]

An additional study reported false negative results in the EMIT d.a.u. benzodiazepine assay in the presence of 10.7% Visine.[22]

A decrease in the apparent barbiturate, benzodiazepine and cocaine metabolite concentrations was observed in the CEDIA at a concentration of 33% although no false negative results were reported. A more dramatic effect was observed in the CEDIA cannabinoid assay, where a reduction in the rate of reaction equal to or greater than 100 ΔAbs/min was reported.[28]

FPIA

Concentrations ranging between 1% and 10% appeared to have little effect on the Abbott amphetamine/methamphetamine II, barbiturate II U, cocaine metabolite, specific morphine and phencyclidine II assays. However, a decrease in the apparent cannabinoid concentration in known positive samples was observed with results near the assay cut-off being reported.[24]

KIMS

There is currently no information available regarding the impact of Visine on the KIMS drugs of abuse assays.

RIA

A 10% solution had little observable effect on the Roche Abuscreen High Specificity amphetamine, barbiturate, benzoylecgonine, opiate and phencyclidine assays. However, the Roche Abuscreen High Specificity cannabinoid assay was susceptible to Visine adulteration. A reduction in the apparent cannabinoid concentration was observed in this assay in the presence of 1%, 5%, 10% and 25% Visine. However, no false negative results were reported.[26]

In summary, it is difficult to directly compare data regarding the impact of adulteration on different methodologies, since the experimental conditions used and the panel of assays investigated varies significantly between studies. Table 9.3 aims to summarise the data described above in relation to the effect of individual adulterants on the apparent drug concentration determined.

Table 9.3 A summary of the effects of adulterants on immunoassay screening techniques

Adulterant	EMIT	CEDIA	FPIA	KIMS	RIA	Refs
Ammonia	N/D	N/D	Increased: Barb	N/D	Increased: Can Decreased: Coc	24, 26
Ascorbic acid	N/D	N/D	Decreased: Amph, Barb, Can	N/D	Decreased: Amph, Can, Mor	24, 26
Bleach	Decreased: Amph, Barb, Benz, Can, Coc, Opia, PCP	Decreased: Amph, Barb, Benz, Can, Coc, Opia, PCP	Increased: Benz Decreased: Amph, Can, Opia, PCP	N/D	Decreased: Can, Amph	22, 23, 24, 26, 28
Blood	N/D	N/D	Decreased: Cann	N/D	No effect: Amph, Barb, Can, Coc, Mor, PCP	24, 26
Chromate	Decreased: Amph, Can, Coc, Opia, PCP	N/D	N/D	N/D	Increased: Amph Decreased: Can, Coc, Opia, PCP	11
Detergent	Increased: Barb Decreased: Can, Benz, PCP	Decreased: Amph, Barb, Can, Coc, Opia, PCP	Increased: Amph, Barb, Benz, Can	N/D	Increased: Benz, Can Decreased: Coc	23, 24, 26, 28
Drano	Decreased: Amph, Barb, Benz, Can, Coc, Opia	Decreased: Amph, Barb, Benz, Can, Coc, Opia, PCP	Decreased: Coc, PCP	N/D	Increased: Coc, Amph, Barb, Can, Mor, PCP Decreased: Coc	22, 24, 26, 28
Glutaraldehyde	Decreased: Amph, Benz, Can, Coc, Meth	Decreased: Barb, Can, Coc, PCP, Benz	Increased: PCP	Increased: Amph, Can, PCP	Increased: PCP	27, 28, 29

Table 9.3 *Continued*

Adulterant	EMIT	CEDIA	FPIA	KIMS	RIA	Refs
Lemon juice	No effect on Amph, Barb, Benz, Can, Coc, Opia	Decreased: Amph, Barb, Benz, Can, Coc, Opia	No effect on Amph, Barb, Can, Coc, Opia, PCP	N/D	No effect on Amph, Barb, Can, Coc, Opia, PCP	22, 24, 26, 28
Lime Away	N/D	N/D	Decreased: Can	N/D	Increased: Can Decreased: Amph, Mor	24, 26
Liquid soap	Decreased: Barb, Benz, Can	N/D	Increased: Amph, Barb, Can	N/D	Increased: Amph, Can	21, 22, 24, 26
Nitrite	Decreased: Amph, Can, Coc, Opia	Decreased: Amph, Can, Opia	Decreased: Amph, Can, Opia,	Decreased: Amph, Opia	Decreased: Can	10
Papain	Decreased: Can	N/D	Decreased: Benz, Can	Increased: Can	N/D	34, 35
Peroxide/ peroxidase	No effect on Amph, Barb, Benz, Can, Coc, Opia, PCP	Decreased: Can, LSD, Opia	Increased: Benz, Can	Decreased: Can, LSD, Opia	Increased: Can	12, 23
Sodium bicarbonate	Increased: Barb Decrease: Opia	No effect on Amph, Barb, Benz, Can, Coc, Opia, PCP	Decreased: PCP	N/D	Increased: Amph, Barb, Can, Opia	23, 28
Sodium chloride	Decreased: Amph, Barb, Benz, Cann, Coc, Opia, PCP	No effect on Amph, Barb, Benz, Can, Coc, Opia, PCP	Decreased: Can, Benz	N/D	Decreased: Can	20, 22, 23, 24, 26, 28
Sodium phosphate	N/D	N/D	N/D	N/D	Increased: Amph, Barb, Can, Mor, PCP Decreased: Coc	24

Vanish	N/D	N/D	No effect on Amph, Barb, Can, Coc, Opia, PCP	N/D	Increased: Can Decreased: Amph, Can, Mor	24, 26
Vinegar	Decreased: Can	Decreased: Can, Coc	Decreased: Can	N/D	No effect on Amph, Barb, Can, Coc, Mor, PCP	22, 24, 26, 28
Visine	Decreased: Benz, Barb, Can, Coc, Opia, PCP	Decreased: Barb, Benz, Can, Coc	Decreased: Can	N/D	Decreased: Can	22, 24, 25, 26, 28

N/D No data currently available.

EMIT, enzyme multiplied immunoassay technique; CEDIA, cloned enzyme donor immunoassay; FPIA, fluorescence polarisation immunoassay, KIMS, Roche kinetic interaction of microparticles in solution; RIA, radio-immunoassay.

Amph, amphetamines; Barb, barbiturates; Benz, benzodiazepines; Can, cannabinoids; Coc, cocaine metabolite; LSD, lysergic acid diethylamide; Mor, morphine; Opia, opiates; PCP, phencyclidine.

Effect of adulterants on confirmatory techniques

GC-MS is commonly used to confirm presumptive positive immunoassay results. Although other techniques incorporating mass spectrometry, for example liquid chromatography-mass spectrometry (LC-MS), can also be used, GC-MS has long been accepted as the 'gold standard' methodology. Therefore, the majority of the literature relates to the impact of adulterants on GC-MS procedures. A summary of the current data is given below.

As previously described, adulterants can have a significant impact on the outcome of the initial immunoassay screen. In the majority of cases erroneous results occur due to specific interference with the immunoassay methodology as opposed to the breakdown or loss of the specific analyte under investigation. However, a substantial decrease in the concentration of some analytes has been observed in specimens adulterated with oxidising agents such as nitrite, chromate and peroxide/peroxidase. There appears to be little impact on the GC-MS analysis of the cocaine metabolite (benzoylecgonine) or phencyclidine. However, several authors have reported a significant impact on the quantitation of opiates and the cannabis metabolite, 11-nor-9-carboxy Δ9-tetrahydrocannabinol (THC-COOH).[11,12,30,36]

It has been estimated that the resultant nitrite concentration in a specimen adulterated with either of the commercially available nitrite containing products, 'Klear' or 'Whizzies', is likely to be between 0.05 mol/L and 0.6 mol/L depending upon specimen volume.[10,37] Tsai *et al.*[10] demonstrated the total loss of THC-COOH and its deuterated analogue (commonly used as an internal standard) in specimens adulterated with between 0.15 mol/L and 1.0 mol/L nitrite. It has been suggested that the loss of THC-COOH in nitrite-adulterated specimens may be due to the formation of unstable nitroso-THC-COOH complexes which are 'lost' during the extraction process prior to GC-MS analysis.[36]

The presence of nitrite also appears to affect the quantitation of amphetamine, buprenorphine, morphine and the heroin metabolite 6-acetylmorphine, with the respective recoveries reduced considerably following the addition of nitrite. However, nitrite does not appear to significantly affect the GC-MS quantitation of benzoylecgonine (Figure 9.1).

Chromate has also been shown to detrimentally affect the quantitation of both THC-COOH and its deuterated analogue, with recoveries decreasing dramatically following the addition of as little as 10 g/L. Furthermore, the addition of 100 g/L pyridinium chlorochromate reportedly produced a 35-fold decrease in morphine concentration as well as a slight decrease in codeine concentration from 589 micrograms/L to 368 micrograms/L. However, no decrease in the recovery of either of the deuterated opiate analogues was reported.[11]

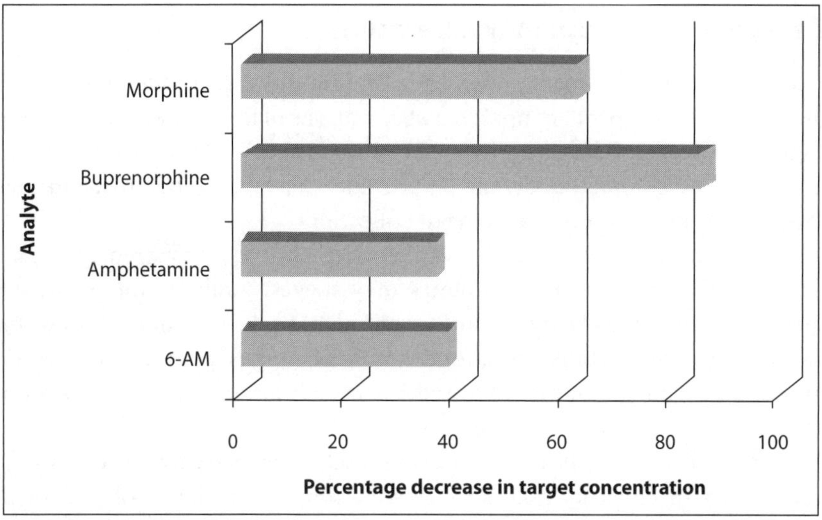

Figure 9.1 The percentage decrease in drug concentration following the addition of 1.02 g/L nitrite (Cardiff Bioanalytical Services, UK, private communication). 6-AM, 6-acetylmorphine.

The addition of peroxide/peroxidase, marketed commercially as 'Stealth', has also been shown to affect the GC-MS detection of both opiates, THC-COOH and their deuterated analogues. Quantitative analysis of specimens adulterated with Stealth revealed a 17% decrease in morphine concentration, a 30% decrease in codeine concentration and a total loss of THC-COOH.[12,30]

In order to reduce the impact of oxidising adulterants on the detection of opiates and THC-COOH several authors have proposed the use of a disulfite/bisulfite pre-treatment stage.[10,12,38] The addition of 250 mg sodium bisulfite 5 min prior to extraction resulted in an 89% recovery of THC-COOH in nitrite-adulterated specimens. However, even after the pre-treatment of specimens with sodium bisulfite, a decrease in the THC-COOH concentration was still apparent one hour after nitrite adulteration.[10,37] Similarly, the addition of 2.5 mg/mL sodium disulfite 15 min prior to extraction enabled the detection of morphine, codeine and their deuterated analogues in specimens that had previously screened negative in the presence of 'Stealth'.[12]

Several other adulterants including bleach and papain have also been shown to affect the detection and subsequent quantitation of THC-COOH by GC-MS. The addition of 0.8% bleach was demonstrated to decrease THC-COOH concentrations by up to 45%. A 66% decrease in THC-COOH concentration was observed following the addition of 10 mg/mL papain. In addition, a 24% decrease in nordiazepam concentration was also reported.[34,39]

Detection of specimen adulteration

The detection of specimen adulteration and the subsequent identification of the adulterant is dependent upon the observations of the specimen collector as well as the integrity checks performed by the laboratory. Specimen characteristics such as colour, odour and appearance may be useful in identifying 'suspicious' specimens at the point of collection.

A freshly voided specimen is usually odourless and transparent. A strong odour or the presence of precipitates may suggest adulteration. However, specimen odour and clarity are influenced by both the diet and health status of the individual. Certain foods, for example asparagus, produce a characteristic odour, while the presence of red blood cells and/or bacterial infections can cause the specimen to become cloudy.[16]

These parameters, however, are less useful when trying to identify an adulterated specimen in a laboratory situation. The majority of specimens are not received by a drug testing laboratory on the day of collection. As specimens age they develop a characteristic odour and may become cloudy or turbid due to crystal precipitation. The presence of precipitates is also common in specimens that have undergone several freeze–thaw cycles.[16,40]

Laboratory detection of adulterants

Laboratories have traditionally relied upon three basic parameters to determine whether a specimen is suitable for testing, namely creatinine, pH and specific gravity. All three parameters are subject to physiological variation. Creatinine is a breakdown product of creatine, a constituent of muscle. Its formation is dependent on muscle mass. As there is minimal fluctuation in muscle mass the production and subsequent elimination of creatinine is regarded as relatively constant providing kidney function is not impaired. However, urinary creatinine concentration is affected by fluid intake, the use of diuretic compounds and diurnal variations. Over the course of 24 hours urinary pH fluctuates. Early morning samples will have lower pH values than specimens collected later in the day. In addition, urinary pH measurements are also influenced by the bacterial content of the specimen. Urine specimens collected from individuals with a urinary tract infection are likely to have a raised pH due to bacterial formation of ammonia. Specific gravity can be defined as a measure of the amount of solutes dissolved in solution, and values increase accordingly. Specific gravity is known to vary according to fluid intake and degree of hydration.[16]

Acceptable values for these parameters in specimens collected for workplace drug testing purposes have been defined as follows:

- creatinine: greater than 2.0 mmol/L (22.6 mg/dL)
- pH: within the range 4–9
- specific gravity: within the range 1.001–1.020.[8]

The usefulness of creatinine, specific gravity and pH to distinguish between adulterated and 'normal' specimens was evaluated by Edwards *et al.*[41] The authors noted that 47.9% of the 144 'suspicious' specimens studied were not identified as adulterated if a creatinine concentration of less than 4 mmol/L (45 mg/dL) and a specific gravity measurement outside the range of 1.007–1.035 were used as the distinguishing criteria. When pH was added as a further parameter to assess sample integrity, only one additional specimen was identified as unsuitable for testing. The authors therefore concluded that the assessment of creatinine, pH and specific gravity is not sufficient to identify a potentially adulterated specimen. These findings are supported by other published studies, which are summarised in Table 9.4.

Table 9.4 The effect of various adulterants on urine pH and specific gravity measurements

Product	pH	Specific gravity/visual and olfactory observations	Refs
Ascorbic acid (1–10%)	3.0–4.5	1.025–1.035	24, 26, 40
Bleach (1–10%)	6.0–6.2	1.021–1.025 Aroma	23, 24, 26, 40
Chromate (Urine Luck)	3.7–8.0	No data available	11, 42
Detergent (1–10%)	6.1–10.0	1.021–1.022	23, 24, 26, 40
Drano (1–13%)	6.0–13.5	1.018–1.035	22, 24, 26, 40
Glutaraldehyde	No data available	No data available	27, 29, 31
Golden seal (0.009–3%)	6.0–7.0	1.021–1.024 Brown colour	22, 24, 26
Lemon juice (10%)	3.5–4.0	1.022	24, 26, 40
Lime Away (1–10%)	1.8–4.7	1.021–1.027	24, 26, 40
Liquid soap (1%–11%)	5.9–8.0	1.018–1.033 Cloudy, turbid	22, 40
Nitrite	Values within acceptable range	Values within the acceptable range	41, 37
Papain (10 mg/L)	5.7–5.9	1.001–1.045	34
Stealth	5.4–6.6	No data available	12, 30
Vinegar (1–13%)	3–5.8	1.018–1.020	22, 24, 26, 40
Visine (1–25%)	6.0–7.0	1.016–1.021	22, 24, 26, 40

This has led to the development of more specific assays that are targeted at the detection of the active constituents of common adulterant formulations.[41]

There are three general approaches used to identify adulterated specimens: (i) point-of-care adulterant test strips (POCAT), (ii) screening techniques (including spot tests and automated assays) and (iii) specific techniques, for example chromatography. The procedures used to detect commonly encountered adulterants are summarised below.

Chromate

Chromium is an essential nutrient which is required for fat and sugar metabolism. It is excreted renally predominantly as the trivalent form, Cr^{3+}. Urinary chromium concentrations are usually relatively low, with concentrations ranging between 0.1 and 1.0 micrograms/L being reported. Concentrations following overdose, dietary intake or occupational exposure are reported not to exceed 5.4 micrograms/mL.[43]

The chromium salts chlorochromate and dichromate have been identified as the active ingredients in the commercial product Urine Luck. These anions are not present in unadulterated specimens. Chromium concentrations in adulterated specimens far exceed physiological concentrations and have been reported to range between 20 and 7501 micrograms/mL.[11,43]

Point-of-care adulterant test strips (POCAT)

There are several devices currently available to determine the presence of chromate in a specimen. Both the AdultaCheck® 6 and Intect 7 devices have been shown to effectively identify the presence of chromate over the concentration range 500–50 000 micrograms/mL.[45]

Screening techniques

Chromate can be determined spectrophotometrically using a variety of indicators including diphenylcarbazide, hydrogen peroxide, potassium permanganate and potassium iodide. The addition of two drops of a solution of 10 g/L 1,5-diphenylcarbazide in methanol to 1 mL of urine will produce a reddish purple colour in the presence of chromate. The intensity of the colour produced can be determined spectrophotometrically between 540 and 550 nm. This reaction has been adapted for use with automated analysers, providing a rapid technique for the determination of chromate over the range 5–500 micrograms/mL.[11,43] Examples of automated chromate assays include 'SVT® Chromate Assay' produced by Sciteck® Inc, the DRI® Chromate-Detect™ produced by Thermo Scientific and the Syva® Chromium (VI) Validity Test marketed by Siemens.

Confirmatory techniques

The POCAT and screening methods described above can be used as qualitative or semi-quantitative assays for the determination of urinary chromate.

They are, however, subject to interferences from the presence of other analytes including mercury.[43] Positive results should therefore be confirmed using a more definitive technique to ensure that the results produced are defensible. Current methodologies utilised in the determination of chromium in biological fluids include atomic absorption spectrometry, inductively coupled plasma mass spectrometry and capillary ion electrophoresis.[43]

Glutaraldehyde

'UrinAid', a commercially available adulterant product containing glutaraldehyde, was withdrawn from the market in 1994. However, glutaraldehyde is still utilised as a cleaning solution in hospitals and clinics and is also available in some over the counter preparations used in the treatment of warts.[29,45] Another commercial product, 'Instant Clean ADD-it-ive', had previously been reported to contain glutaraldehyde. However, a recent evaluation of 'Instant Clean ADD-it-ive' suggests that this is no longer the case.[46]

Point-of-care adulterant test strips (POCAT)

There are several devices available for the detection of glutaraldehyde, including AdultaCheck 4, AdultaCheck 6 and Intect 7. These devices have been shown to be effective in the identification of adulterated specimens.[45–47]

Screening techniques

The commercially available 'SVT® Aldehyde Assay' produced by Sciteck® Inc utilises the conversion of glutaraldehyde to a fluorescent product, which can be monitored spectrophotometrically at 415 nm.[48]

Confirmatory techniques

There are currently no published data available regarding confirmatory techniques for the detection of glutaraldehyde in urine.

Nitrite

Guidelines for laboratories involved in workplace drug testing require the concentration of nitrite in a specimen to be determined. Results above 500 micrograms/mL are regarded as conclusive proof that the specimen has been adulterated.[8] A study of the urinary nitrite concentration in specimens collected from healthy volunteers concluded that nitrite represented only 0.4% of the total nitrate in urine, equivalent to 0.2 micrograms/mL. Although nitrite concentrations have been reported to increase slightly in individuals with urinary tract infections due to the presence of *Staphylococcus* and Enterobacteriaceae such as *Escherichia coli*, the increase observed is minimal, with concentrations between 0.7 and 35.5 micrograms/mL being reported. Similarly, the increase in urinary nitrite concentration observed in specimens collected from individuals receiving nitrate- or nitro-containing medications, for example nitroglycerin or isosorbide commonly used in the treatment of angina, is also minimal. In these cases the reported nitrite concentrations ranged between <0.6 and 5.9 micrograms/mL.[44] Such concentrations are in strict contrast to those reported following specimen adulteration with nitrite, where the concentrations have been found to range between 3275 and 12 466 micrograms/mL.[49]

Point-of-care adulterant test strips (POCAT)

The presence of nitrite in a specimen can be determined qualitatively at the point of specimen collection using rapid POCAT devices. Evaluation of the AdultaCheck 4, AdultaCheck 6 and Intect 7 revealed that all three products were effective at detecting the presence of nitrite in a specimen.[45,47] Dasgupta *et al.*[45] reported that there was a significant difference between the intensity of colour produced following the analysis of samples containing low nitrite concentrations (50 mg/L) and those containing high concentrations. The author therefore concluded that both the AdultaCheck 6 and Intect 7 were effective in distinguishing between specimens containing low nitrite concentrations due to bacterial infection and adulterated specimens. However, the determination of the intensity of colour produced is subjective and therefore the outcome of the test may vary between operators.

Screening techniques

Similarly, rapid spot tests performed in the laboratory can also be used to determine the presence of nitrite. One such example was described by Dasgupta *et al.*[50] Briefly, between 6 and 7 drops of a 2% aqueous potassium permanganate solution were placed into a glass tube. Approximately 4 drops of the adulterated urine specimen was then added, followed by the addition of 2–3 drops of 2 mol/L hydrochloric acid. The pink permanganate solution instantly turned colourless in the presence of nitrite. In addition, effervescence was also observed in adulterated specimens.

Automated assays for the determination of urinary nitrite concentration are also available. Examples include the include 'SVT Nitrite Assay' produced by Sciteck Inc, the DRI Nitrite-Detect™ produced by Thermo Scientific and the Syva Nitrite Validity Test marketed by Siemens.

Although POCAT, spot tests and automated screening assays are a rapid way of determining the presence of nitrite, they cannot be used to distinguish between the presence of nitrite in a specimen due to bacterial contamination and the addition of nitrite as an adulterant. Positive spot test results have been reported at both low (less than 50 micrograms/mL) and high (greater than 500 micrograms/mL) nitrite concentrations.[50]

Confirmatory techniques

All positive results from qualitative and semi-quantitative colourimetric screening techniques should be confirmed by a more specific technique to provide conclusive evidence of nitrite adulteration. Singh *et al.*[49] described a rapid isocratic high-performance ion chromatography method for the quantitative determination of nitrite in urine. Briefly, specimens were diluted 1 : 50 with mobile phase and filtered prior to injection. Separation was achieved using a Dionex IonPac AS 14 column. The limit of detection of this method was determined as 30 micrograms/mL.

Peroxide/peroxidase

Point-of-care adulterant test strips (POCAT)

There are no specific devices available for the detection of peroxide/peroxidase. However, adulterated samples can be identified using a general 'oxidant' test such as AdultaCheck 6. This device contains a pad impregnated with an oxidant indicator that turns green/blue in the presence of oxidants including peroxide/peroxidase, chromate and nitrite.[51]

Screening techniques

Microgenics developed an automated assay specifically designed to detect the presence of peroxide/peroxidase in a specimen. The 'Peroxidase-Detect Test' was calibrated using a 100 ng/mL peroxidase solution and had a limit of detection of 4.1 ng/mL. There were no documented assay interferences caused by endogenous compounds, with the exception of ascorbic acid which produced a positive result at 40 micrograms/mL.[52]

In addition, the automated 'SVT Oxidant Assay' produced by Sciteck Inc. also facilitates the detection of peroxide, peroxidase and other oxidants including bleach, chromate and nitrite.[48]

Confirmatory techniques

There are currently no published data available regarding confirmatory techniques for the detection of peroxide/peroxidase in urine.

Specimen adulteration and quality assurance

The impact of sample adulteration on a variety of urine drugs of abuse screening and confirmatory techniques as well as point-of-care testing devices was investigated by the organisers of the United Kingdom National External Quality Assurance Scheme (UKNEQAS) (Cardiff Bioanalytical Services, UK, private communication). Urine samples were spiked with a variety of analytes and then subsequently adulterated with acid, liquid detergent, nitrite or sodium hypochlorite. Samples were sent to scheme participants alongside unadulterated samples to determine the effect of sample adulteration on drug detection. A summary of the findings is given here.

The addition of 5.8% w/w sodium hypochlorite to mimic sample adulteration with bleach had a significant impact on the ability of the common screening techniques, namely EMIT, CEDIA, FPIA and KIMS, to detect the presence of amphetamine, buprenorphine, methadone, opiates (6-AM and

Table 9.5 Percentage of false negative results following analysis of a sample containing 5.8% w/w sodium hypochlorite (bleach)[a]

Target analyte and spiked concentration	POCT	EMIT	CEDIA	FPIA	KIMS
d-Amphetamine 2 mg/L	95 (19)	100 (34)	100 (62)	100 (13)	100 (37)
THC-COOH 250 micrograms/L	100 (24)	100 (33)	100 (57)	100 (14)	100 (38)
Benzoylecgonine 1 mg/L	5 (20)	3 (39)	53 (57)	0 (12)	2 (41)
Methadone 1 mg/L	100 (16)	100 (28)	100 (24)	100 (10)	100 (26)
6-AM 30 micrograms/L	N/D	N/D	100 (25)	N/D	N/D
Morphine 3 mg/L	96 (24)	100 (40)	100 (54)	100 (14)	100 (42)
Buprenorphine 10 micrograms/L	100 (7)	N/D	96 (27)	N/D	N/D

[a] Number of laboratories reporting results given in parenthesis.
N/D, no data currently available; 6-AM, 6-acetylmorphine; POCT, point-of-collection testing; EMIT, enzyme multiplied immunoassay technique; CEDIA, cloned enzyme donor immunoassay; FPIA, fluorescence polarisation immunoassay, KIMS, Roche kinetic interaction of microparticles in solution.

morphine) and THC-COOH. These results were reflected in the confirmatory assays with a high proportion of false negative results being reported by participants using GC-MS and LC-MS techniques. The detection of benzoylecgonine was less affected, with the percentage of false negative results reported ranging between 0% and 53% dependent upon the assay used to perform the analysis (Table 9.5). Interestingly, several of the scheme participants noted negative absorbance readings in the CEDIA assays, suggesting this may provide a useful mechanism of identifying an adulterated sample.

Sample adulteration with sulfuric acid resulted in a decrease in the number of scheme participants detecting the cannabis metabolite THC-COOH (Table 9.6). However, this effect was not observed in the results for confirmatory assays, suggesting that addition of acid affects the performance of the screening technique and does not result in the destruction of the drug itself.

The addition of liquid detergent appeared to have little effect on the detection of amphetamine, benzoylecgonine, opiates and THC-COOH using the EMIT, KIMS and FPIA assays. However, false positive results were observed in the KIMS methadone assay and the benzodiazepine FPIA assay. Conversely, the addition of liquid detergent appeared to have a marked effect on the performance of CEDIA assays (Table 9.7). Data collated from GC-MS and LC-MS assays identified a number of false positive results for both 6-monoacetylmorphine and buprenorphine.

Table 9.6 Percentage of false negative results following analysis of a sample containing 1.4 mL/L sulfuric acid (pH <3)[a]

Target analyte and spiked concentration	POCT	EMIT	CEDIA	FPIA	KIMS
d-Amphetamine 1.5 mg/L	70 (23)	32 (44)	41 (66)	13 (15)	35 (37)
THC-COOH 31 micrograms/L	100 (26)	100 (42)	91 (64)	100 (16)	87 (38)
Benzoylecgonine 0.45 mg/L	27 (22)	11 (47)	2 (62)	0 (15)	5 (40)
6-AM 15 micrograms/L	N/D	N/D	8 (36)	N/D	N/D
Morphine 2.5 mg/L	35 (26)	6 (48)	2 (61)	0 (16)	0 (42)
Buprenorphine 8 micrograms/L	71 (7)	N/D	10	N/D	N/D

[a] Number of laboratories reporting results given in parenthesis.
N/D, no data currently available; 6-AM, 6-acetylmorphine; POCT, point-of-collection testing; EMIT, enzyme multiplied immunoassay technique; CEDIA, cloned enzyme donor immunoassay; FPIA, fluorescence polarisation immunoassay, KIMS, Roche kinetic interaction of microparticles in solution.

Table 9.7 Percentage of false negative results following analysis of a sample containing 0.1 mL liquid detergent in 20 mL urine[a]

Target analyte and spiked concentration	POCT	EMIT	CEDIA	FPIA	KIMS
d-Amphetamine 1.9 mg/L	9 (23)	0 (47)	48 (65)	0 (14)	0 (35)
THC-COOH 238 micrograms/L	11 (27)	2 (47)	29 (62)	0 (14)	0 (35)
Benzoylecgonine 0.95 mg/L	0 (22)	2 (48)	68 (63)	0 (14)	3 (38)
6-AM 29 micrograms/L	N/D	N/D	0 (34)	N/D	N/D
Morphine 2.85 mg/L	0 (27)	0 (51)	2 (60)	0 (15)	0 (40)
Buprenorphine 9 micrograms/L	0 (4)	N/D	7 (28)	N/D	N/D

[a] Number of laboratories reporting results given in parenthesis.
N/D, no data currently available; 6-AM, 6-acetylmorphine; POCT, point-of-collection testing; EMIT, enzyme multiplied immunoassay technique; CEDIA, cloned enzyme donor immunoassay; FPIA, fluorescence polarisation immunoassay, KIMS, Roche kinetic interaction of microparticles in solution.

The addition of nitrite to a sample to mimic the use of the commercially available product Klear resulted in a decrease in the detection of amphetamine and morphine. However, it appeared to have little impact on the detection of oxazepam and methadone (Table 9.8). A similar trend was observed in both GC-MS and LC-MS assays.

Table 9.8 Percentage of false negative results following analysis of a sample containing 8.46 g/L nitrite[a]

Target analyte and spiked concentration	POCT	EMIT	CEDIA	FPIA	KIMS
d-Amphetamine 1.2 mg/L	83 (6)	62 (65)	60 (10)	49 (35)	88 (17)
Oxazepam 1.2 mg/L	0 (8)	1 (68)	0 (11)	0 (28)	0 (17)
Methadone 1.2 mg/L	0 (7)	0 (59)	0 (7)	0 (24)	0 (18)
Morphine 1.2 mg/L	57 (7)	97 (75)	55 (11)	81 (33)	100 (21)

[a] Number of laboratories reporting results given in parenthesis.
POCT, point-of-collection testing; EMIT, enzyme multiplied immunoassay technique; CEDIA, cloned enzyme donor immunoassay; FPIA, fluorescence polarisation immunoassay, KIMS, Roche kinetic interaction of microparticles in solution.

Alternative matrices and adulteration

Recently there have been several innovations in the drug testing field involving the greater use of alternative matrices such as hair and oral fluid specimens. As this is still a relatively new approach to drug screening, the market for adulterants is not as well developed as that for urine testing adulterants. However, despite the relative infancy of these methods of testing, there are already a few products that are marketed as 'aiding individuals to pass an oral fluid or hair drug test'.

There are several oral fluid adulterant products available including QCarbo Fixx Mouthwash, the Aqua Clean™ Effervescent Cleansing System and the Urine Luck Quick Fizz effervescent tablets produced by Spectrum Laboratories. The QCarbo Fixx Mouthwash contains yohimbe bark, peppermint leaf, stevia leaf, bark oil as well as water and propylene glycol. The product claims to be effective for up to one hour following use. However, the manufacturer recommends that 'unwanted toxins' should be avoided for between 24 and 48 hours preceding a test. The Aqua Clean product consists of two effervescent tablets which are promoted as a 'healthy solution' containing herbs and berries to 'flush the body of harmful pollutants'. Directions supplied with the Aqua Clean product state that each tablet should be dissolved in 10 ounces of water and the solution swilled around the mouth for 10 seconds before ingesting. This process should occur within 2 hours of an oral fluid test. In addition, the retailer recommends that a high fluid intake and healthy lifestyle should be maintained and that exposure to 'toxins' should be avoided for at least 4 hours prior to the test.

The Urine Luck Quick Fizz product is sold as an 'undetectable' method of 'holding toxins in the body so that they are not released during a drugs test'. The retailers suggest that this is accomplished by preventing the body burning fat cells. The product contains a combination of herbs, vitamin B2 and creatine. The directions for use supplied with the product are very similar to those supplied with Aqua Clean. Both Aqua Clean and Urine Luck Quick Fizz products claim to be effective for up to 2 hours.[51]

Adulterant products designed for use prior to a hair test include the Clear Choice Hair Follicle Shampoo and the Root Clean® hair cleansing system. Both products are marketed as being effective on any hair type and any hair length. The Clear Choice product claims to be effective within 15 min of application, with the effects of the treatment lasting for up to 8 hours. The directions supplied with Clear Choice shampoo require an entire bottle of shampoo to be used for washing the hair. Users are advised not to blow dry hair or use any other hair care products in conjunction with Clear Choice shampoo. The Root Clean hair cleansing system is provided as a bottle of shampoo and a bottle of root clean gel. Directions supplied with the product require the entire bottle of shampoo to be massaged into the scalp for 3 min prior to rinsing. The entire bottle of Root Clean gel should then be applied and left in the hair for 15 min prior to rinsing. Once again the manufacturers advise that no other hair care products are used in conjunction with the Root Clean system. This product claims to be effective within 1 hour of application with the effects of the treatment lasting for up to 8 hours.[54,55]

As with the urine adulterant products, formulations of both hair and oral fluid adulterants are also continually changing and/or being withdrawn from sale adding yet another dimension to the task of detecting specimen adulteration. Unfortunately, there are currently very few published studies which critically review whether products of this nature have a detrimental effect on oral fluid and/or hair drug testing.

Conclusion

Due to the impact that specimen adulteration may have on the identification of drug abuse, it is being increasingly recognised as an issue in workplace drug testing programmes. Because of this the UKWDTF, EWDTS and SAMHSA have all produced guidelines for legally defensible workplace drug testing which include criteria to minimise specimen adulteration or substitution. However, although the specimen collection procedure is strictly regulated, specimen adulteration and/or substitution may still occur.

Specimen adulteration can be achieved in one of three ways namely *in vitro* adulteration (the addition of a substance/product to a specimen), *in vivo* adulteration (the use of diuretics, detoxifying/cleansing products or water to provide a very dilute specimen) or the substitution of a test specimen with an artificial or 'clean' specimen.

The majority of the 'first generation' adulterants were readily available household products, including bleach and detergents. However, in recent years a large market for commercial products specifically designed to 'beat the test' has developed. A recent estimate suggests that around 400 different products are currently available. The ever increasing use of the Internet as a marketing resource means that these products are readily availably in many countries making specimen adulteration a global issue.

There are a number of 'popular' commercially available adulterants. Examples of *in vitro* adulterants include Stealth and Urine Luck. These products are known to affect both screening and confirmatory techniques. The *in vivo* products are usually sold as detoxifying or cleansing products, for example 'Naturally Klean Herbal Tea' and 'Green Clean Drug Detox'. The majority of these preparations contain osmotic diuretics as well as 'natural' diuretics such as dandelion or marshmallow root. Furthermore, the manufacturers suggest that the product should be consumed with large volumes of fluid. There are also several commercially available urine substitution kits which are known to contain certified drug-free urine, for example 'The Urinator'.

The effect of the various adulterants is both concentration dependent and variable according to the analyte under investigation and the methodology used. Adulteration agents affect the different types of screening assays in different ways. For example, an adulterant which causes a false negative result in a CEDIA assay may produce a false positive result in a FPIA assay. Confirmatory methods can also be affected by specimen adulteration, with substantial decreases in the concentration of amphetamine, buprenorphine, opiates and THC-COOH being observed in specimens adulterated with oxidising agents such as nitrite, chromate and peroxide/peroxidase.

Although observations made at the point of specimen collection are useful, the advent of more sophisticated adulterant formulations which have little or no effect on specimen characteristics such as odour, colour, pH or specific gravity means that the detection of specimen adulteration is increasingly dependent upon the use of targeted laboratory testing. Assays capable of identifying the active constituents of adulterant formulations, including chromate, nitrite and peroxidase, are therefore now becoming increasingly available and the use of such products is advocated in order to ensure invalid specimens are correctly identified.

It can therefore be seen that, with regard to workplace drug testing, the generation of an accurate result is dictated by the ability of the testing laboratory to stay one step ahead of the adulterant manufacturers who continue to reformulate their products in order to evade detection.

References

1. MORI (2003) Most uk employers are open-minded about drug and alcohol testing at work. www.ipsos-mori.com/researchpublications/researcharchive.aspx?keyword=Drug+testing+at+work (accessed 7 March 2010).

2. Verstraete AG, Pierce A. Workplace drug testing in Europe. *Forensic Sci Int* 2001; 121(1–2): 2–6.
3. Pass It (2000) Hair testing information. http://passitkit.com/testing.htm (accessed 7 March 2010).
4. Zaera A, Granados DE, Pérez A. Urine samples from drug addicts: a study of the rate of manipulation. *Dade Behring J* 2005; 3(1): 22–23.
5. Quest Diagnostics, Inc. The Drug Testing Index, 2005.
6. SAMHSA (2004) Federal Register Part III April 13 2004. http://ncadistore.samhsa.gov/catalog/ProductDetails.aspx?ProductID=16833 (accessed 7 March 2010).
7. UKWDTF guidelines (2001) http://ltg.uk.net/pages/monographs/guidelines.asp (accessed 7 March 2010).
8. EWDTS guidelines (2002) http://www.ewdts.org/guidelines/guidelines_form.html (accessed 7 March 2010).
9. United States Government Accountability Office (2005) Drug tests. Products to defraud drug use screening tests are widely available. http://gao.gov/new.items/d05653t.pdf (accessed 7 March 2010).
10. Tsai JSC, ElSohly MA, Tsai S *et al.* Investigation of nitrite adulteration on the immunoassay and GC-MS analysis of cannabinoids in urine specimens. *J Anal Toxicol* 2000; 24: 708–714.
11. Wu AHB, Bristol B, Sexton K *et al.* Adulteration of urine by 'Urine Luck'. *Clin Chem* 1999; 45(7): 1051–1057.
12. Cody JT, Valtier S, Kuhlman J. Analysis of morphine and codeine in samples adulterated with StealthTM. *J Anal Toxicol* 2001; 25: 572–575.
13. Cone EJ, Lange R, Darwin WD. *In vivo* adulteration: Excess fluid ingestion causes false-negative marijuana and cocaine urine test results. *J Anal Toxicol* 1998; 22: 460–473.
14. Lafolie P, Beck O, Blennow L *et al.* Importance of creatinine analyses of urine when screening for abused drugs. *Clin Chem* 1991; 37: 1927–1931.
15. The Diabetes Foundation, Inc (2003) What is diabetes insipidus? http://diabetesinsipidus.org/whatisdi.htm (accessed 7 March 2010).
16. Cook JD, Caplan YH, LoDico CP *et al.* The characterisation of human urine for specimen validity determination in workplace drug testing: A review. *J Anal Toxicol* 2000; 24: 579–588.
17. Wu AHB. Integrity of urine specimens for toxicologic analysis – adulteration, mechanisms of action, and laboratory detection. *Forensic Sci Rev* 1998; 10(47): 48–65.
18. Cody JT. Specimen adulteration in drug urinalysis. *Forensic Sci Rev* 1990; 2(1): 64–75.
19. Drury DL, Masci V, Jacobson JW *et al.* Urine drug screening: can counterfeit urine samples pass inspection. *J Occup Environ Med* 1999; 41(8): 622–624.
20. Kin HJ, Cerceo E. Interferences by NaCl with the EMIT method of analysis for drugs of abuse. *Clin Chem* 1976; 22: 1935–1936.
21. Vu Duc T. EMIT® tests for drugs of abuse: interference by liquid soap preparations. *Clin Chem* 1985; 31(4): 658–659.
22. Mikkelsen SL, Ash O. Adulterants causing false negatives in illicit drug testing. *Clin Chem* 1988; 34(11): 2333–2336.
23. Warner A. Interference of common household chemicals in immunoassay methods for drugs of abuse. *Clin Chem* 1989; 35(4): 648–651.
24. Cody JT, Schwarzhoff RH. Impact of adulterants on RIA analysis of urine for drugs of abuse. *J Anal Toxicol* 1989; 13: 277–284.
25. Pearson SD, Ash OK, Urry FM. Mechanism of false-negative urine cannabinoid immunoassay screens by VisineTM eyedrops. *Clin Chem* 1989; 35(4): 636–638.
26. Schwarzhoff R, Cody JT. The effects of adulterating agents on FPIA analysis of urine drugs of abuse. *J Anal Toxicol* 1993; 17: 14–17.
27. Goldberger BA, Caplan YH. Effect of glutaraldehyde (UrinAid) on detection of abused drugs in urine by immunoassay. *Clin Chem* 1994; 40(8): 1605–1606.
28. Wu AHB, Forte E, Casella G *et al.* CEDIA for screening drugs of abuse in urine and the effect of adulterants. *J Forensic Sci* 1995; 40(4): 614–618.

29. George S, Braithwaite RA. The effect of glutaraldehyde adulteration of urine specimens on Syva EMIT II drugs-of-abuse assays. *J Anal Toxicol* 1996; 20: 195–196.
30. Cody JT, Valtier S. Effects of StealthTM adulterant on immunoassay testing for drugs of abuse. *J Anal Toxicol* 2001; 25: 466–470.
31. Uebel RA, Wium CA. Toxicological screening for drugs of abuse in samples adulterated with household chemicals. *S Afr Med J* 2002; 92(7): 547–549.
32. Liu RH. Comparison of common immunoassay kits for effective application in workplace drug urinalysis. *Forensic Sci Rev* 1994; 6(1): 19–57.
33. PatentStorm. US (2004–2010). Immunoassay for the detection of amphetamines, methamphetamines and methylenedioxy designer amphetamines. http://patentstorm.us/patents/6534325/description.html (accessed 28 February 2010).
34. Burrows DL, Nicolaides A, Rice PJ *et al.* Papain: A novel urine adulterant. *J Anal Toxicol* 2005; 29: 275–295.
35. Larson SJ, Holler JM, Magluilo J *et al.* Papain adulteration in 11-nor-Δ9-tetrahydrocannabinol-9-carboxylic acid-positive urine samples. *J Anal Toxicol* 2008; 32: 438–443.
36. Lewis SA, Lewis LA, Tuinman A. Potassium nitrite reaction with 11-nor-delta9-tetrahydrocannabinol-9-carboxylic acid in urine in relation to the drug screening analysis. *J Forensic Sci* 1999; 44(5): 951–955.
37. Tsai SCJ, ElSohly MA, Dubrovsky T *et al.* Determination of five abused drugs in nitrite-adulterated urine by immunoassays and gas chromatography-mass spectrometry. *J Anal Toxicol* 1998; 22: 474–480.
38. ElSohly MA, Feng S, Kopycki WJ *et al.* A procedure to overcome interferences caused by the adulterant 'Klear' in the GC-MS analysis of 11-nor-Δ9-THC-9-COOH. *J Anal Toxicol* 1997; 21: 240–242.
39. Baiker C, Serrano L, Lindner B. Hypochlorite adulteration of urine causing decreased concentration of Δ9-THC-COOH by GC-MS. *J Anal Toxicol* 1994; 18(2): 101–103.
40. Cody JT. Adulteration of urine specimens. In: Liu RH, Goldberger BA, ed. *Handbook of Workplace Drug Testing*. Washington DC: AACC Press, 1995: 181–207.
41. Edwards C, Fyfe MJ, Liu RH *et al.* Evaluation of common urine specimen adulteration indicators. *J Anal Toxicol* 1993; 17: 251–252.
42. Coldbourne PD, Boisvert YM, Parent S *et al.* Chromate adulteration in employment-related drug screens. *J Anal Toxicol* 2001; 25 369.
43. Ferslew KE, Nicolaides AN, Robert TA. Determination of chromate adulteration of human urine by automated colourimetric and capillary ion electrophoretic analyses. *J Anal Toxicol* 2003; 27: 36–39.
44. Urry FM, Komaromy-Hiller G, Staley B *et al.* Nitrite adulteration of workplace drug testing specimens I. Sources and associated concentrations of nitrite in urine and distinction between natural sources and adulteration. *J Anal Toxicol* 1998; 22: 89–95.
45. Dasgupta A, Chughtai O, Hannah C *et al.* Comparison of spot tests with adultaCheck 6 and Intect 7 urine test strips for detecting the presence of adulterants in urine specimens. *Clin Chim Acta* 2004; 348: 19–25.
46. Peace MR, Tarni LD. Performance of three on-site adulterant detection devices for urine specimens. *J Anal Toxicol* 2002; 26: 464–470.
47. King EJ. Performance of AdultaCheck 4 test strips for the detection of adulteration at the point of collection of urine specimens used for drugs-of-abuse testing. *J Anal Toxicol* 1999; 23: 72.
48. Sciteck Inc (2004) SVT® automated adulteration reagent package insert. http://sciteck.org (accessed 7 March 2010).
49. Singh J, Elberling JA, Hemphill G *et al.* The measurement of nitrite in adulterated urine samples by high-performance ion chromatography. *J Anal Toxicol* 1999; 23: 137–140.
50. Dasgupta A, Wahed A, Wells A. Rapid spot tests for detecting the presence of adulterants in urine specimens submitted for drug testing. *Am J Clin Pathol* 2002; 117(2): 325–329.
51. Sciteck Inc (2004). AdultaCheck®6 package insert. http://sciteck.org (accessed 7 March 2010).

52. Luo W, Peapally A, Shama S *et al.* Development of peroxidase-DetectTM test for automated chemistry analysers to screen urine samples adulterated with StealthTM. *J Anal Toxicol* 2001; 25 368.
53. Jumora.net (2002–2005) Detox products for pass saliva drug test. http://pass-drug-test.jumora.net/pass-saliva (accessed 27 January 2006).
54. Drug-Testing-Solutions.net (2006) Hair follicle shampoo and hair purifier drug removal treatment pack by Clear Choice. http://drug-testing-solutions.net/hairfolshamb.html (accessed 7 March 2010).
55. Jumora.net (2002–2005) How to pass a drug test? http://pass-drug-test.jumora.net/ (accessed 7 March 2010).

10

Interpretation of urine drug test results by the medical review officer

Helen Vangikar

Key points

- Specialised training is needed in substance misuse and related clinical aspects, including alternative medical explanations for positive drug test reports.
- Knowledge of sample adulteration and substitution techniques plus collections errors are essential when reviewing results.
- Knowledge of in-country guidelines is needed along with an understanding of other internationally recognised guidelines, policies and procedures of companies for which the medical review officer provides services.
- The medical review officer is the last quality check on the laboratory and has a responsibility to develop excellent communications with the laboratory.

Introduction

An essential element of workplace drug testing is a process for a medical review of the results. This should be undertaken by a medical review officer (MRO), who provides an important safety net in the testing process. A positive laboratory result does not identify an employee or candidate with a substance misuse issue, whether legal or illegal drugs. Furthermore a laboratory result that indicates the sample may have been diluted, adulterated, substituted or is for other reasons invalid does not necessarily identify specimen tampering. A specialist with detailed knowledge in this field is required to interpret non-negative results in conjunction with information gathered at the donor interview.

The American Federal Regulations define the MRO as 'a licensed physician responsible for receiving laboratory results generated by an agency's drug testing program who has knowledge of substance abuse disorders and has appropriate medical training to interpret and evaluate an individual's positive test result with his or her medical history and any other relevant biomedical information'.[1]

US Department of Transportation (DOT) drug testing regulations issued on 1 August 2001 and updated 31 August 2009 affected more than eight million workers within the transportation industry. These regulations also affected MROs and defined their duties and responsibilities when serving this industry. The 49 CFR Part 40 rule requires specialised training for MROs and states 'following your completion of qualification training, you must satisfactorily complete an examination administered by a nationally-recognised MRO certification board or sub-speciality board for medical practitioners in the field of medical review of DOT-mandatory drug tests'. It also states that MROs must be re-trained every three years and recommends that to maintain competencies a minimum of 12 hours continuous professional development in topics relevant to the work of a MRO are undertaken over a three-year period.[2]

Thus the MRO is a required element of a Federally mandated drug testing programme, and is increasingly required in other testing programmes (e.g. private sector or other non-Federal testing, sport, rehabilitation, prison etc.). Each one of these categories has its own unique legal and technical requirements.

The UK Laboratory Guidelines for Legally Defensible Workplace Drug Testing (which were adopted by the European Workplace Drug testing Society (EWDTS)),[3,4] define the MRO as 'a medical physician responsible for receiving laboratory results from the drug testing laboratory who has knowledge of substance abuse and appropriate training or experience to interpret and evaluate an individual's positive test results, in light of declared information.'

Therefore both in the US and UK/EU MROs receive reports from drug testing laboratories which they interpret. This may, however, be an oversimplification of the role compared with that which clients/companies expect of their MROs.

The role of the MRO is primarily to interpret the results of laboratory testing, but differences exist between the US and UK/EU approach. In the United States, processes are well defined and affordable, so companies use MROs according to their true definition. In contrast, in the UK/EU workplace drug testing programmes are not as well developed and companies either do not have an MRO or use them only for cases that require detailed medical information. Companies that retain an occupational health (OH) service provider to undertake their workplace drug testing programme must ensure that the MRO associated with the OH service provider is trained and competent in the interpretation of drug results.

Every medical review must also consider job role; the declared use of a drug may explain a positive drug test, but the associated medical condition may be a risk for certain safety-sensitive job roles.

In the United States, the panel of drugs which must be included for testing is defined in the Federal Register, the so-called Substance Abuse and Mental Health Services Administration or SAMHSA-5, which consists of opiates, cannabinoids, cocaine metabolites, amphetamines and phencyclidine. The UK/EU does not have a set panel, but here the five most important drugs to monitor are opiates, cannabinoids, cocaine metabolites, amphetamines including ecstasy, and benzodiazepines.

Throughout the interpretive aspect of this chapter it must be remembered that workplace drug testing has been developed to rapidly eliminate samples that are negative for a limited range of drugs using automated analysers and immunoassay technology. Samples positive by immunoassay are subject to confirmation using a different analytical technique to identify specific drugs at agreed cut-offs. Workplace drug testing is not designed to find any drug that might be present regardless of the concentration. Immunoassays have been developed with high specificity and assays such as benzodiazepines and barbiturates will respond to most of the drugs in their group, however, the cross-reactivity to each drug is different and thus the sensitivity to each will vary. Confirmations may be undertaken for a few specified drugs in a group, for example the UK Guidelines do not list the barbiturates to confirm, so this must be agreed in advance between the laboratory and requestor; also for the benzodiazepine group only oxazepam, temazepam and desmethyldiazepam are named, any additional drugs should be agreed with the customer.

The MRO needs to have a reasonable grasp of the analytical techniques used and their limitations if they are to fulfil their duties.

Qualifications

The US Department of Health and Human Services (DHHS) Mandatory Guidelines (effective 1 November 2004)[5] define an MRO as a licensed physician holding either a Doctor of Medicine (M.D.) or Doctor of Osteopathy (D.O.) degree who has:

- knowledge about and clinical experience in controlled substance abuse disorders
- detailed knowledge of alternative medical explanations for laboratory positive drug testing results

- knowledge about issues relating to adulterated and substituted specimens
- knowledge about possible medical causes for specimens reported as having an invalid result.

Compliance with these criteria is a requirement for physicians who wish to serve as MROs for federally regulated programmes. Additional training in substance misuse, regulatory guidelines, current thinking on drug use and so on is beneficial in providing continued medical education for MROs.

It is vital to maintain the independence of the MRO in the process, and the DHHS Mandatory Guidelines state:

1 'The MRO must not be employed by or an agent of or have any financial interest in the laboratory for which the MRO is reviewing drug testing results.'
2 'The MRO must not derive any financial benefit by having an agency use a specific drug testing laboratory or have any agreement with the laboratory that may be construed as a potential conflict of interest.'

Along with many aspects of workplace drug testing, the role of the MRO in the UK/EU has developed somewhat differently from that in the United States. While many MROs are medically qualified, there are a significant number of nurse qualified occupational health advisers (OHA) who undertake this role. Some companies do not employ an MRO, leading to dependence on the toxicologist within the drug testing laboratory that provided the result. Although possible under the UK Guidelines, it may be viewed as unacceptable by the donor and the testing laboratory.

Whether physician or nursing trained, there is no compulsion in the UK/EU for the MRO to undertake appropriate training. Many MROs identify suitable training courses to maintain their competencies and as the world becomes more litigious, and donors more prepared to challenge findings, it is likely that bodies such as the Royal Colleges and Medical Practice Societies (e.g. the UK's Medical Defence Union) will insist on mandatory training.

A recent publication from the Faculty of Occupational Medicine states that the function of the MRO is to interpret the results of laboratory drug testing, however they see this within the broader one of the occupational physician, who may also be called upon to advise on suitable suppliers, quality assurance and chain-of-custody arrangements.[6] The faculty also acknowledges that the MRO is normally a physician, though may be a forensic toxicologist. This could compromise the independence of the MRO especially if the forensic toxicologist is responsible for the final authorisation of results (i.e. is employed by the testing laboratory).

Financial independence of the MRO from a testing laboratory is an essential element of American programmes. This permits the MRO to be not only impartial and neutral, but also the last quality control on the testing laboratory, since they are advocates for accuracy and integrity. Independence of the MRO is also a requirement elsewhere in the world, but this is not as well defined and it cannot be guaranteed that the MRO and testing laboratory do not have a financial relationship. Under IS017025 : 2005, a testing and calibration standard used by laboratories a service level agreement or contract is necessary between the laboratory and their clients. Within this accreditation standard the laboratory has to clearly identify when subcontractors are used (i.e. MRO services).

Urine has long been established as the biological sample of choice for analysis in workplace drug testing, however alternative matrices such as hair and oral fluid are now also being analysed and knowledge of substance misuse in relation to these samples must also be verified when appointing an MRO.

MROs need to document and be able to demonstrate a range of competencies. Country-specific requirements such as the US DOT Regulations must be followed and MROs will need training on these specific details to fulfil their tasks. In addition knowledge of drug use (therapeutic, recreational, misuse/abuse) must be understood and kept current. Many MROs do not undertake collections, but they must be familiar with the process and able to discuss collection issues and errors. MROs should also be familiar with the laboratory processes and have a good working relationship with the laboratory toxicologist.

The medical review process

This review process allows the MRO to quality check the testing laboratory, before making a final positive/fail or negative/pass determination. The final determination is then communicated to the company-appointed manager for action.

Ideally, the review process should be carried out face to face, and occupational health companies that offer healthcare screening together with workplace drug testing often undertake the review this way. However some companies that outsource their workplace drug testing programmes, where the MRO is a subcontracted service, initially undertake the MRO process over the telephone and follow with a face-to-face interview in more complex cases. Whichever mechanism is chosen, pressures of time and cost need to be considered.

Prior to review, a sample is collected from the donor and divided into two portions (A and B) under full chain of custody. It is then transported to the accredited laboratory for analysis and a report generated in a timely manner. This is sent to the MRO together with their copy of the documentation. Donor details are checked, as are the specimen validity tests (SVT) and drug results. If the SVTs are acceptable and results negative, the donor is not contacted and a negative/pass is communicated to the company manager by the MRO or their staff. Where supervised staff are used to communicate negative results the MRO must audit this process by reviewing at least 5% of them.

Reports that are either positive, or fail the SVT must be reviewed before communicating to the company. The MRO must contact the donor, if possible within 24 hours of receiving and reviewing the report. The key point here, as in all other aspects of workplace drug testing, is documentation and every attempt to contact the donor must be recorded. There is no agreement over what are 'reasonable efforts' when it comes to establishing contact with a donor and MROs are advised to set and document their own standards. One view is to make three reasonably spaced (3 hourly) attempts within 24 hours of receiving the laboratory results. The MRO should also be aware that when contact has been established, the donor may not be in a position to converse and an agreed time/date should be set for the discussion.

If the MRO is unable to establish contact with the donor the MRO should report this to the company, without revealing details of the test results or other confidential information and it then becomes the responsibility of the company to establish contact with the donor.

However, if the donor refuses to make contact with the MRO or will not discuss the results, the MRO should report this as their justification for a positive/fail report to the company.

When making telephone contact it is advisable for the MRO to develop a simple script to guide themselves through the conversation. In this script, the MRO should clearly identify themselves and on whose behalf they are calling, and the purpose of the call. To ensure the MRO is speaking with the donor, they must establish the identity of the donor using such mechanisms as National Insurance number (UK), Social Security Number (USA), date of birth, date of urine collection and so on. The same script can also be developed for face-to-face interviews.

Should a third party answer the telephone, it is important for the MRO to maintain confidentiality regarding the purpose of the call. A message can be left asking the donor to contact the MRO's office, but this should be done without causing alarm.

Once the MRO and donor are in contact, the donor should be reassured about the confidentiality of the conversation and the circumstances under which confidentiality is no longer valid (e.g. medical disqualification in the case of an epileptic working track-side on the rail network).

The substantial part of the conversation should be about possible medical explanations for the drug test result. The MROs may or may not tell the donor the content of the laboratory report. However, the key point is that the MRO must not influence the declarations of the donor; they should only enable what should be a neutral process.

The MRO should review all medical records that may explain the laboratory results and investigate any claims the donor makes. In the United States the donor is responsible for providing the medical information and the MRO should establish a deadline by which the donor must provide it. Failure to meet this deadline would result in a positive/fail report. In the UK/EU the onus for gathering medical information lies with the MRO, who, with consent from the donor, writes in medical confidence to the donor's physician or other healthcare professionals. This can impact greatly on the timeframe in which feedback can be provided to the employer. Non-medical staff acting as MROs must declare their interest and relationship to the donor (e.g. HR manager). However this is no guarantee that a healthcare professional will discuss any medical matters relating to the donor, further delaying the review.

The MRO is also responsible for processing a request for a challenge of the analytical result. This process provides the donor with the opportunity to have a duplicate sample re-tested using established procedures. The question of a challenge may not arise during the initial contact and time lines for a challenge vary between the United States and UK/EU. It is not uncommon in the UK/EU for donors to request a challenge once all other avenues have been exhausted (i.e. at the disciplinary hearing). Challenge analyses are usually undertaken to confirm/deny drug results, however MROs should also be prepared for a donor to challenge specimen validity tests where an adulterated or substituted result is reported by the testing laboratory.

There is no consensus regarding who is responsible for advising the donor about their rights and the associated procedures. Companies must liaise with their service provider to establish clear lines of responsibility and the required procedures, especially when it comes to identifying challenge laboratories. A challenge laboratory is a laboratory of equal standing to the one that initially tested the specimen. Both must be accredited to the same standard and scope with similar techniques as the aim is to replicate the initial analysis. Issues regarding the range of analytes, analytical techniques and assay sensitivity of the challenge laboratories need to be assessed before any challenges arise. The UK Guidelines[4] set minimum standards for challenge laboratories:

- All laboratories that undertake B sample testing must be able to demonstrate that they can accurately determine the concentration of a drug or metabolite at 50% of the recommended confirmation cut-off concentration.
- It is recommended that the laboratory that receives the B sample must perform a confirmation analysis only for those drugs identified to it within 10 working days of receipt.
- The final report on the B sample must say either that there was no drug found, or a named drug was found at a level that is either consistent or inconsistent with the level in the corresponding A sample. Cut-off levels must not be used, and the report must not state positive or negative.

After all investigations have been completed, the MRO makes their final decision and communicates this to the donor as well as the company representative.

The UK Guidelines has scope for a toxicology review officer (TRO). This role is defined as 'a person responsible for interpreting a positive analytical result for the customer or the customer's designated Medical Review Officer.' The definition allows companies to dispense with the services of an MRO, however this may limit the depth of investigation (e.g. access to medical records).

Throughout the whole process the MRO must make detailed notes of conversations and actions, and if in doubt, refer to the company policy and associated procedures.

MRO checklist

The processes detailed in this chapter go someway to describing what is expected of an MRO and also for various industries and/or countries the specific needs to be accommodated. A few key elements that make an effective MRO are summarised below:

- training and education on MRO processes
- documentation, even if one believes we are moving to a paperless society!
- obtain copies of the policy and procedures from each of the companies the MRO is serving, and ensure updates are obtained
- learn about sample collections and laboratory analysis, be prepared to audit them
- MROs can be audited too, be prepared
- develop good face-to-face and telephone interview skills
- get to know the toxicologists at the laboratories undertaking the analysis
- develop procedures and document them for failure to establish contact with donors, additional tests such as free morphine determinations, challenge analysis and so on
- remember, the MRO is the last quality control on the process, so have contacts to consult in unusual circumstances.

Additional roles of the MRO

Within American workplace drug testing programmes, MROs can assume additional duties provided they have appropriate qualifications (e.g. they serve as substance abuse professionals (SAPs) or provide rehabilitation/treatment services). These functions are not MRO responsibilities and if offered they must be in deference to the requirements of the employer's policies and procedures.

Although hiring and firing is a human resource role, sometimes the MRO has to advise on return-to-duty or decision-to-hire recommendations. These decisions are not based on the single laboratory test that an MRO usually reviews, but requires them to consider many factors (e.g. medical history, rehabilitation treatment and progress made, further treatment requirements, prognosis, type of safety-sensitive duties. etc.).

As part of the American DOT rules employers are responsible for managing a blind quality assurance programme, and many expect the MRO to undertake this duty. In regulated testing programmes employers are also responsible for the random selection process and many ask MROs to undertake this task.

In the UK/EU MROs may be asked to contribute towards developing a company's workplace drug testing written policy and procedures. This provides them with an opportunity to define their role and that of occupational health with respect to testing and how to test. In addition, the MRO may be responsible for education of employer and employees, however many will hand over this aspect of implementation of the policy and procedures to an experienced organisation that can deliver this training. Often the MRO is a focal point and through their resources find supporting services and contacts that can be of assistance.

Urine physiology

There are three main processes involved in the formation of urine. First, an ultrafiltrate of plasma is collected in the glomerular capsule; second, some of the solutes and water are partially or completely reabsorbed from various parts of the tubule; third, some solutes are secreted into the tubule by the epithelial cells. The normal range of pH is 5–7.[7]

The major component of urine is water, however another important constituent with respect to workplace drug testing is creatinine, which is eliminated from the body at a rate of 1–4 g daily, the amount being consistent for an individual since it is related to the total muscle mass. Creatinine is formed from creatine, an important constituent of skeletal muscle which is not normally excreted in urine.

Nitrite is not present in significant quantities in urine.

Specimen validity testing

Validity testing aims to establish that the submitted sample is physiologically normal urine that has not been tampered with. Validity is assessed before or during the screening tests prior to any confirmations. The minimum requirement to establish validity is creatinine and pH. In addition, tests for adulterants may be offered by some laboratories (e.g. nitrates, chromates).

UK Guidelines have established criteria for their set report comments. The MRO must be familiar with these comments and their underlying meaning and should verify that their testing laboratory follows these guidelines. Laboratory reports should summarise the specimen validity tests and classify the sample as either normal or abnormal. The MRO should check which validity tests the sample failed. Below are the current UK guidelines, however at the time of going to press, these guidelines are under review as they do not address the issue of samples with pH at 3.5 or 10.

pH should be reported as follows:

- pH 4–9 are within the normal range
- pH less than 3 or greater than 11 are adulterated
- Samples falling outside of the normal range should be reported as 'Sample adulterated – pH out of range'.

Creatinine concentration should be reported as follows:

- If the creatinine concentration is less than or equal to 20 mg/dL (1.77 mmol/L) the specific gravity must be determined. Acceptable values for specific gravity are 1.001–1.020.
- Samples with a creatinine concentration between 5 and 20 mg/dL (0.44–1.77 mmol/L) and a specific gravity within range 1.001–1.020 should be reported as 'Sample dilute'.
- Samples with creatinine concentration equal to or less than 5 mg/dL (0.44 mmol/L) OR a specific gravity result that is out of range are unsuitable for testing and should be reported as 'Sample is not consistent with normal human urine'.

In addition, the UK Guidelines provide an acceptance range for a nitrite test, as nitrites have been identified in a number of commercially available adulteration products:

- A nitrite level equal to or above 500 micrograms/mL is conclusive proof of an adulterated sample. The results should be reported as 'Sample adulterated, Nitrite is too high'.

The specimen validity tests in the UK Guidelines are similar to the US Federal Register, however the US guidelines use different interpretive comments (e.g. 'substituted' instead of 'Sample is not consistent with normal human urine'). All samples that fail the SVTs must be noted as invalid without reporting the drug test (if undertaken). Should the MRO decide to re-collect this must be under direct observation (i.e. a collector watches the urine flow from the body into a collection vessel).

In March 2007, the UK National External Quality Assessment Service (NEQAS) issued adulteration guidelines suitable for the clinical field. These were later revised and re-issued in February 2009, with the following criterion for unsatisfactory sample integrity:[8]

- creatinine of less than 2.0 mmol/L
- osmolality of less than 50 mmol/kg
- pH less than 4.0 or greater than 9.0.

The Steering Committee does not recommend specific gravity measurements as being suitable for use. If applied, values less than 1.0010 or greater than 1.0200 are unsatisfactory.

Negative drug testing reports with comments on the specimen validity must be subject to medical review. The MRO needs to be aware of the laboratories defined reporting procedures (e.g. is the sample analysed when the SVT is abnormal?).

Cannabis

Metabolism

The main psychoactive ingredient of cannabis is Δ9-tetrahydrocannabinol (THC) which is highly lipid soluble and accumulates in the fatty tissue of the body. The quantity stored by an individual depends on the amount of drug use and the THC content of the material. THC is slowly released from the fatty tissues and metabolised by the liver to a number of metabolites, some of which are pharmacologically active while others are not. Up to about 25% of a dose of THC is excreted in urine in three days, mainly as 11-nor-Δ9-THC-COOH glucuronide. Δ9-THC is primarily oxidised by cytochrome P450 enzymes to pharmacologically active 11-hydroxy-Δ9-THC and 8β-hydroxy-Δ9-THC; and also to 8α-hydroxy-Δ9THC and 8α,11-dihydroxy-Δ9-THC (which are pharmacologically inactive). Further oxidative metabolism of 11-hydroxy-Δ9-THC to 11-nor-Δ9-THC-9-carboxylic acid occurs which is then subject to phase 2 metabolism and elimination as the pharmacologically inactive glucuronide.

Passive exposure

The most common way that cannabis is used is by smoking, either on its own or combined with tobacco. Hand-rolled herbal cigarettes are often referred to as a 'reefer', and herbal or cannabis resin smoked with tobacco is often referred to as a 'joint' or a 'spliff'. As with any gas the exhaled smoke expands to fill the container (i.e. room). This smoke contains a quantity of THC, but the atmospheric concentration required for an individual to inhale sufficient smoke to test positive is so extreme that most individuals would vacate the room. Anyone remaining would by their presence be offering tacit consent to inhaling cannabis.

Several trials have been undertaken to study the passive inhalation of cannabis under extreme conditions.[9,10] In these studies the subjects wore goggles to protect their eyes, but those who removed their goggles during the sessions reported irritation to their eyes and nose. If individuals remain in a room under these unrealistic conditions it implies consent.

Realistic studies were undertaken by Mule *et al.*,[11] in which the exposure environment mimicked a real-life situation, such as a private party. In the second study, subjects were passively exposed to four cannabis cigarettes containing a total of 27 mg of Δ9-THC over a period of 1 hour in a room measuring 10 × 10 × 8 ft (3 × 3 × 2.4 m). The atmospheric Δ9-THC level was also measured and determined to be 5 micrograms/L, a high concentration, although Δ9-THC-acid levels in urine samples collected from the subjects 20–24 hours later were less than 6 ng/mL, as analysed by radioimmunoassay (RIA). This indicates that the cut-off level for cannabinoids (50 ng/mL) that is widely used, excludes donors who have been passively exposed, under realistic conditions.

Herbal teas

Available through reputable stores, these teas offer relaxation and health benefits to those who drink them. However a number of individuals have claimed the teas as a reason for their positive drug test. Not all herbal teas are purchased from reputable stores and some are purchased on market stalls where there is an opportunity for the tea to be manipulated either before or after purchase by the stall holder or the purchaser. This manipulation can take the form of adding herbal cannabis or shavings of cannabis resin. One tea, which originates within the West Indian heritage, is sometimes referred to as 'bush tea'. Users of this tea claim that its components are lemongrass, mint and other legal herbal components. However TLC analysis of a selection of these teas has indicated the presence of cannabis in a couple (DJ Berry, personal communication, 1996).

In their *DrugLink* magazine of July/August 2006, the British charity Drugscope commented on a commercially available cannabis tea, C-Ice Swiss Cannabis Ice Tea, with ingredients that included hemp bloom syrup (5%) and hemp bloom extract (0.0015%).[12] The makers claim although it gives a 'fantastic natural high', drinkers will not get a genuine high and that all the narcotic elements of the plant have been removed to make it legal. No comment was made regarding whether drinkers of the tea would test cannabis positive. The product was launched in Switzerland in 2003 and is readily available in Austria, Germany, The Netherlands, Portugal and Spain.[13] It has since been rebranded as Chronic Ice Tea offering a 'delicious drink bursting with flavour and a fantastic natural feeling'.[14]

The MROs role in such cases is not to investigate whether the ingestion was intentional or whether the tea was 'spiked' with cannabis. It is the company's role to provide clear guidance to all employees stating that herbal teas will not be accepted as a reason for a positive drug test.

Foods

In the United States, the Drug Enforcement Administration (DEA) issued its final rule clarifying control of natural and synthetic THC in April 2003 (21 CFR Part 1308). The rule states that it is illegal for anyone to manufacture, distribute or market products used, or intended for use, for human consumption that contain any amount of THC. Personal hygiene products such as shampoos are not included as they are not designed to be consumed, neither are clothes nor animal feed.

MROs may be inclined to consider any claims and ask for details of what was purchased and when consumed, however these rarely explain the laboratory findings. MROs faced with cases of food supplements as an explanation for testing positive must remember that their role is to verify the results. Whether the ingestion was intentional or unknowing is not a medical issue and therefore not within their role. The correct forum is the disciplinary hearing where mitigating circumstances can be considered.

Hemp foods such as bread, chocolate, oil and seeds are increasingly popular and available from health shops and Internet providers.[15] They contain products such as 'fresh cold pressed hemp oil (*Cannabis sativa*)' and 'shelled hemp'. Comments from the supplier include 'hemp seed has no intoxicating effect'.

Hemp has low levels of THC usually less than 1.0%, although other cannabinoids may be present in large amounts. Callaway *et al.*[16] reported on two experiments involving the controlled consumption of hemp products. In the first experiment a volunteer ingested 10 mL/day of hemp oil for 29 days. Urine was collected which tested positive by immunoassay (cut-off 20 ng/mL) and gas chromatography-mass spectrometry (GC-MS) confirmation determined the urine concentration to be 87 ng/mL after 29 days of oil consumption. This is above the 15 ng/mL workplace cut-off level. In the second experiment a volunteer consumed 24 1-g hemp oil gelatine capsules at one time. Eleven samples were collected on the first day starting with 2.3 hours after consumption, six on the second day and a single sample was collected on day 3. The immunoassay again tested positive, but the maximum GC-MS levels were 10 ng/mL achieved in the second sample of day 1. Concerns were raised whether other cannabinoids may also be present as a by-product of the manufacturing process which cross-react with the immunoassay (see Boxes 10.1 and 10.2).[16]

Self-medication

Cannabis has a long history as a folk remedy and for medicinal use. Introduced to Western medicine in the 1840s it is rumoured to have been

Box 10.1 Case study

A rail worker tested positive for cannabis ingestion. He maintained that he was positive as a result of eating a chocolate bar containing cannabis seed. Details were provided about the bar and manufacturer who was emailed under a pseudonym and questioned about the contents of the chocolate bar and implications for workplace drug testing. The manufacturer advised that the chocolate bars should not cause a positive urine test, however to be on the safe side, abstain for two weeks before urine collection.

The rail worker's explanation was not accepted and he was dismissed.

Box 10.2 Case study

A 16-year-old school boy was taking hemp oil capsules on a daily basis. He was subject to unannounced testing as part of the school drug testing programme and declared the capsules at the collection. On analysis his sample was positive by CEDIA immunoassay for cannabinoids. The sample was then subject to confirmation by GC-MS. The confirmation was negative at cut-off 15 ng/mL, achieving a value of less than 10 ng/mL. This was communicated to the school.

used as a pain killer by Queen Victoria in childbirth. More recently there has been clinical research and anecdotal reports of the therapeutic properties of cannabis for treatment of multiple sclerosis, epilepsy, muscle spasms, nausea, vomiting and some forms of pain. However as cannabis is illegal, self-medication cannot be viewed as a medical reason to accept a positive drug test.

Medicinal use

Marinol is a drug that has been approved both by the US Food and Drug Administration (FDA) and the Canadian authorities for treating nausea and vomiting associated with cancer chemotherapy in patients who have failed to respond to conventional medication. It is also approved to treat appetite and weight loss in people with AIDS.[17] The active ingredient is dronabinol,[18] a synthetic version of the naturally occurring Δ9-THC. To date there is no evidence of Marinol contributing to a positive drug test.

GW Pharmaceuticals, whose vision 'is to be the global leaders in cannabinoid and botanical medicines' have a cannabinoid product portfolio that contains Sativex® Oromucosal Spray.[19] Sativex has received regulatory approval in Canada for symptomatic relief of neuropathic pain in multiple sclerosis and adjunctive analgesic treatment in patients with advanced cancer and moderate to severe pain. It is currently in the latter stages of trials in Europe and the United States.

Another product that GW Pharmaceuticals have in Phase 1 development as a potential treatment for obesity, diabetes and related metabolic disorders is Δ9-tetrahydrocannabivarin (THCV).

All these medications are prescription-only drugs and can be traced to the prescribing physician. Furthermore, in many cases, the user would not be in employment or would be on long-term sick leave.

Opiates

Metabolism

The most widely abused drug within the opiate group of compounds is heroin (diacetylmorphine, or diamorphine). Following administration, heroin is rapidly deacetylated to produce the short-lived metabolite 6-acetylmorphine (6-AM), which is itself rapidly metabolised to morphine together with some other minor derivatives.

Morphine is also the major metabolite of codeine, a common drug in UK/EU over-the-counter medications. The ingestion of morphine-containing compounds results in morphine alone being detected, but morphine will also be detected as a result of ingesting codeine, heroin and poppy seed products. The related drug, dihydrocodeine (DF 118), is not metabolised to either codeine or morphine and is excreted in urine partly unchanged together with the minor metabolites dihydromorphine, nor-dihydrocodeine and glucuronide conjugates.

For correct interpretation of analysis, total codeine and total morphine must be accurately measured, which requires the laboratory to undertake pre-extraction hydrolysis to cleave the glucuronide conjugates. Following ingestion of morphine approximately 15% is excreted unchanged in urine, with 85% as a glucuronide conjugate. Following ingestion of codeine approximately 10% is excreted unchanged, 15% as morphine (mainly conjugated) and 60% as codeine glucuronide. During laboratory analysis, the glucuronide conjugate is cleaved with either an enzyme or by acid hydrolysis, ensuring that total morphine and total codeine are analysed.

A morphine-only drug test report should alert the MRO to the need for additional information from the drug testing laboratory, namely are there any findings sub cut-off that could assist in the interpretation and what was the concentration of morphine detected? This information is not automatically reported, unless defined in the contract between the MRO and testing laboratory, thus reiterating the quality role of the MRO.

On 1 December 1998, an amendment to the US Mandatory Guidelines for Federal Workplace Drug Testing Programmes came into effect, which raised the initial immunoassay cut-off and confirmatory concentration for codeine and morphine in urine from 300 to 2000 ng/mL. In addition, they established a new requirement to test for 6-AM, a metabolite that comes only from heroin, to a cut-off of 10 ng/mL for specimens that confirmed the presence of morphine at or above 2000 ng/mL. The purpose of the change was to eliminate individuals who had legitimately taken prescription medications including codeine or morphine and those who had ingested poppy seeds. A number of studies have demonstrated that it is possible to achieve morphine levels greater than 2000 ng/mL from poppy seed ingestion.[20,21]

However, unlike the other drug groups that form the DHHS mandatory testing panel, the burden of proof with opiates lies not with the donor, but with the MRO, who has to determine that there is 'clinical evidence' of unauthorised use. This evidence may consist of:

- recent needle track marks
- behavioural and psychological signs including those of withdrawal
- the presence of illnesses that are more common in injecting drug users
- past clinical history of unauthorised use.

In situations where donors may have attempted to disguise the source of the morphine, the MRO may request additional tests, such as free morphine (non-glucuronide conjugated morphine).

UK and EU guidelines acknowledge prescribing differences between the UK/EU and the United States. UK/EU laboratories analyse their urine samples for dihydrocodeine, in addition to codeine, morphine and 6-AM and follow the same testing rationale as the United States with respect to 6-AM.

Additional drugs within the opiates classification can be measured (e.g. hydrocodone, hydromorphone, oxycodone and oxymorphone). To date, these are more often requested when testing samples from specific professions such as healthcare workers. Access to these drugs as part of a daily routine and can result in substance misuse, however, these other opiates are now beginning to be more widely available and generally misused. MROs need to liaise with their clients should they require these additional drugs in order to establish cut-off levels and service expectations.

Passive exposure

With the improved quality of many smokable drugs and the concerns associated with needle use, such as hepatitis/HIV, there has been an increased preference to smoke rather than inject drugs. Of course, in parts of Asia smoking has long been the preferred delivery method (opium dens). To date, however, there have been no studies on the bioavailability of heroin from passive smoking.

Poppy seed tea

Poppy tea has been used for centuries as a folk remedy to combat diarrhoea, cure malaria, sedate troublesome children and calm anxieties. Within the baking and catering industry it is seen as an occupational hazard with the risk of addiction. King *et al.*[22] reported the case of a 26-year-old baker who had his first seizure and was hospitalised. While under medical investigation he admitted to drinking poppy seed tea at night, a practice to which he had been introduced while an apprentice and he subsequently become addicted to heroin. He successfully completed a methadone treatment programme, but several months later returned to drinking poppy seed tea, though not heroin use. His daily morphine intake from the tea was calculated to be 280 mg and his blood morphine concentration was approximately three times the level observed in heroin users that had overdosed.[22]

In 2007, Braye *et al.*[23] undertook a written questionnaire at the Community Alcohol and Drug Clinic, Wellington, New Zealand. Eleven of the 24 opiate-dependent patients attending the clinic reported using poppy seed tea, five of whom used it as their primary source of opiates and two patients had used it to withdraw from other opiates. Comment was made that this source of opiates is of low cost, legally available and easily administered orally. However concern was raised that the same rationale made poppy seed tea a 'gateway drug'.[23]

Poppy seed food

Hayes *et al.*[24] undertook two trials of poppy seed ingestion in volunteers and not only determined the quantity of codeine and morphine in their poppy seeds, but also measured the urine concentration in samples from volunteers who ingested known amounts of seeds. In trial 1 four volunteers ingested 25 g of seeds and urine samples were collected for up to four days after ingestion. In trial 2 two volunteers ingested 40 g of seed each and were subjected to more frequent sampling. Both doses were equivalent to one or two servings of poppy seed cake. Urine samples were collected over 48 hours and analysed by both immunoassay (EMIT and RIA) and GC-MS. In trial 1 the peak mean concentration of opiates in the urine was 1568 ng/mL (range 1158–2100) 3 hours after ingestion as measured by RIA with three of the four volunteers remaining positive by EMIT at 48 hours. In trial 2 peak urinary morphine concentration by GC-MS were 700 and 2635 ng/mL at 3 hours after ingestion, and it took 24 hours for the morphine concentration to decrease below 300 ng/mL (the UK/EU immunoassay and GC-MS cut-off levels). The study concluded that poppy seeds represent a potential source of positive morphine results.[24]

Poppy seeds contain both morphine and codeine, so individuals who consume poppy seeds can test positive for morphine with or without codeine.

This is because the concentration of codeine in poppy seeds is very low compared to morphine.[24] Morphine results greater than 2000 ng/mL, with or without codeine, must be subject to 6-AM analysis to try and establish whether heroin was the initially ingested substance. However, 6-AM has a very short plasma elimination half-life ($t\frac{1}{2}$ average 0.6 hours) and may thus be present in urine above 10 ng/mL for only a short time after heroin ingestion (detection time range 2–8 hours).[25] This can leave the MRO with a morphine-positive result and no assistance with resolving the issue of whether the morphine came from poppy seeds or another source.

An additional test that can assist the MRO is the analysis of free (unconjugated) morphine. In the metabolism of morphine, following ingestion approximately 15% of morphine is excreted unconjugated. Normally total morphine is assayed but free morphine can be determined by extracting the urine without the deconjugation step. The rules on interpretation are not firmly defined, but after the ingestion of poppy seeds a free morphine value of approximately 15% of the total morphine would be expected. After the ingestion of heroin or large doses of morphine, the proportion of free morphine increases. Free morphine analysis is most useful if the interval since ingestion and sample collection is no greater than 24 hours, after which interpretation becomes difficult. It is essential that an MRO requesting a test for free morphine has a good understanding of the limitations of this test.[26]

Medicinal use

Opiates are used primarily for pain relief and allow the individual to maintain reasonable functionality. Opiates can be purchased as medication from pharmacies and chemists in lower doses (e.g. Co-codamol (codeine phosphate/paracetamol) 8 mg/500 mg), but medications containing higher doses of opiates tend to be available only with a doctor's or dentist's prescription (e.g. Co-codamol 30 mg/500 mg).

A common claim is that the donor was taking a relative's medication, sometimes known as 'spousal user doctrine'. The US DOT and Federal programme view this as a verified positive and report it as such to the employer. However, in the UK/EU a more generous approach is usually taken, and the donor is advised against using another person's medication in the future. This allows the MRO to use professional discretion and judgement (see Box 10.3).

When medically reviewing an opiates-positive report, the concentrations of all relevant analytes measured are important, as substances quantified below the cut-off level may aid interpretation (although the testing laboratory cannot report these). These data are available from the testing laboratory and should be obtained by the MRO.

The presence of 6-AM with a morphine concentration above 2000 ng/mL of morphine does not require further investigation. 6-AM is a metabolite of

Box 10.3 Example

A donor provides a urine sample which is codeine and morphine positive. At medical review the donor admits to taking his wife's medication. The MRO advises against this in the future and at the medical review asks the donor to provide another sample. If that is negative for all the substances under investigation, the MRO will inform the employer of a pass.

heroin and is not found in poppy seeds and is not a metabolite of any other opiates. When interpreting codeine and morphine only results, or when both are present, the ratio of one to the other and/or free morphine can aid in determining the substance of origin.

Cocaine

There are very few differences between American and UK/EU MRO interpretations of cocaine metabolite positive tests as there are few alternative legitimate medical explanations for a cocaine positive. Frequently the MRO is faced with the donor adamantly denying use.

Metabolism

Cocaine is a naturally occurring alkaloid that is extracted from the coca plant, *Erythroxylon coca*. It is usually in the form of cocaine, HCl, suitable for nasal insufflation (snorting). It can also be smoked and the freebase (crack) form is normally prepared for smoking. The majority of cocaine users snort the drug, less smoke it as crack and a minority inject it.

Cocaine is rapidly and extensively converted by the liver to the major metabolite benzoylecgonine (BZE). This is excreted in urine and is the target compound for drug testing. BZE is not pharmacologically active and its presence only demonstrates prior use. In some users unchanged cocaine and ecgonine methyl ester can also be detected, though these are not measured in workplace testing. Following a usual intranasal dose of cocaine (about 100 mg in a 70-kg subject or 1.5 mg/kg), BZE can be detected for 2–3 days.[27] In chronic users (who sometimes take more than 10 g/day) BZE has been detected 22 days after the last consumption.[28]

Passive exposure

As cocaine can be smoked, the question of passive exposure arises, since smoking of freebase adds crack vapours or ambient crack smoke to the atmosphere. Cone *et al.*[29] studied realistic passive exposure to smoked cocaine and demonstrated that BZE was present in the urine of exposed personnel, although the maximum level was 6 ng/mL, significantly below the GC-MS confirmation level of 150 ng/mL.

Bank notes

Initially viewed as anecdotal, there is a belief that all bank notes are 'covered' in cocaine. Several studies have demonstrated that some bank notes are impregnated with cocaine as a result of drug use. At MRO review individuals may claim that they were handling money before providing a sample. However, they forget that all donors are observed washing their hands before a sample is provided; and furthermore it is not cocaine that is measured in the urine but BZE, which is only produced after ingestion of cocaine.

Herbal teas

There have been several documented cases of cocaine ingestion by drinking coca or herbal teas, and also unknowing ingestion of cocaine spiked into food or drink. One such case concerns 'Health Inca Tea' which is imported into the United States and has 'decocained' coca leaves listed among the ingredients, however on analysis each teabag was found to contain 4.8 mg of cocaine. After a single volunteer consumed one cup of 'Health Inca Tea' urine samples were collected and analysed by GC-MS using the workplace cut-off level of 150 ng/mL. BZE was present in the urine 2 hours after consumption, with the first negative result appearing in the sample collected 29 hours after consumption.[30]

The Jockey Club of Great Britain commissioned research into claims that the cocaine metabolites measured in jockey samples originated from Mate de Coca tea.[31] An infusion was prepared from a single teabag by immersing it in 250 mL of boiling water for 25 min. Analysis of the infusion indicated that the teabag contained 2.5 mg of cocaine. Analysis of urine samples collected after consumption of the tea showed that it remained positive for BZE for at least 24 hours following ingestion.

Since herbal teas are not an alternative medical explanation, and reputable manufacturers of such teas do not use ingredients such as 'decocainised coca leaves', the MRO is faced with little option other than to uphold the positive laboratory test report.

Innocent ingestion of spiked food or drink may be impossible to verify through the normal procedure and increasingly MROs are using alternative samples, namely hair, to verify frequency of exposure. If hair analysis is offered, the MRO is advised to collect the sample at the same interview. Consent from the employer may be necessary for the additional investigation and the MRO may need to communicate the donor's explanation to obtain consent. Technically this is not medical information and therefore not confidential, however it would be best practice to obtain consent from the donor, as advised to British MROs by the General Medical Council (GMC) in 2004.[32]

Medicinal use

Cocaine is a local anaesthetic with legitimate medical use, mainly in certain dental and ear, nose and throat (ENT) procedures. Should a donor be tested within a few days of receiving cocaine for such treatment, they may test positive for BZE. In these situations, the MRO is advised to contact the treating healthcare professional and request details of the quantity and times of administration of the drug.

Box 10.4 Case study

A 21-year-old male, subject to a workplace substance misuse policy, was randomly selected for unannounced testing. At the time of urine collection the donor declared the use of paracetamol (twice, 2 days before the collection) and daily use of a nasal spray only in the last 14 days. He tested positive for benzoylecgonine, a cocaine metabolite, and the concentration determined was approximately 950 ng/mL (the cut-off level is 150 ng/mL). The sample passed all the adulteration tests.

The donor attended a medical review to discuss these findings and at this consultation revealed he had been treated in hospital for a nasal fracture, 2 days before the collection. With the donor's consent, the medical review officer wrote to the hospital for details of the donor's treatment. The following information was released:

Reduction of the fractured nose was by 1 mL of cocaine paste (500 mg cocaine hydrochloride as a 25% paste with adrenaline 0.1%). This was applied topically to the mucosal lining of the nose.

Cone *et al.*[33] reported that an intranasal dose of 32 mg will achieve a maximum mean concentration of 13 681 ng/mL in urine, requiring 3 days for total elimination. Therefore it can be concluded that a dose of 500 mg would most likely result in a urine concentration of greater than 900 ng/mL after 48 hours. The laboratory findings indicate that a large dose of cocaine had been ingested and after considering the information from the hospital and the timescale disclosed, it was concluded that in this case the high benzoylecgonine concentration could be the result of the treatment. However, it should be noted that the laboratory would not be able to distinguish between additional use of cocaine and this medication.

Frequently a donor will claim a topical anaesthetic such as lidocaine and others ending in 'caine' as the reason for testing positive. MROs should be aware that there is no structural similarity between these anaesthetics and cocaine and its metabolite BZE and they do not give a positive result with any of the tests for cocaine (see Box 10.4).

Amphetamines

Historically, amphetamine and methamphetamine have been the only analytes in this drug class that are included in a workplace drug testing programme and this continues to be the position in the United States. Drugs from the ecstasy class of amphetamines have become popular drugs of abuse in the UK/EU and so the test for amphetamines in these countries has been extended to include the popular ecstasy type compounds (e.g. 3,4-methylenedioxyamphetamine (MDA), 3,4-methylenedioxymethamphetamine (MDMA) and *N*-ethyl-3,4-methylenedioxyamphetamine (MDEA)). Amphetamine and methamphetamine are usually ingested orally, although methamphetamine can also be smoked and both can be injected. They are sympathomimetic drugs and powerful CNS stimulants.

The amphetamines immunoassays used by workplace drug testing laboratories have been developed to have low cross-reactivity to all but the compounds of interest. Therefore a standard amphetamines test panel including ecstasy would rarely indicate the presence of other sympathomimetics such as phentermine, ephedrine and phenylpropanolamine which are found in over-the-counter medications; and this greatly decreases the number of samples requiring confirmation (see Table 10.1).

Metabolism

Amphetamine is metabolised by deamination and hydroxylation. Twenty-four per cent of the dose is excreted unchanged in urine although this varies widely with pH. Over 24 hours 80% of a dose is excreted unchanged if the urine is strongly acidic and this proportion can be reduced to 1–4% if the urine

Table 10.1 CEDIA amphetamine/ecstasy assay[34]

Compound	Concentration tested (ng/mL)	% Cross-reactivity
Phentermine	25 000	3.3
d,l-Phenylpropanolamine	500 000	0.3
d-Pseudoephedrine	160 000	0.9
l-Ephedrine	250 000	0.5

CEDIA, cloned enzyme donor immunoassay.

is strongly alkaline. Approximately 50% of a methamphetamine dose is excreted unchanged in the urine with a small portion being demethylated to amphetamine. The effect of urine pH on methamphetamine excretion is similar to amphetamine.

The plasma elimination half-life of MDMA is approximately 8 hours with 65% of a dose being eliminated unchanged and approximately 10–15% converted by demethylation to MDA. The UK/EU has recognised the increased use of 'ecstasy' type compounds and have incorporated MDA and MDMA into the amphetamine panel of drugs as a minimal additional requirement to amphetamine and methamphetamine.

Internet purchase of diet tablets

The Internet has made the purchase of various medicinal products possible without a prescription. Drugs for conditions such as male impotency, hair loss and weight reduction are among the most popular internet purchases. Individuals who buy weight loss pills may not be aware or claim ignorance regarding the contents. Many of these tablets contain amphetamine or related substances that metabolise to amphetamine, which would produce a positive drug test. Without records to support the clinical condition and/or the medication, MROs should fail the donor.

Medicinal use

Amphetamine has a number of medicinal uses, such as bronchodilator, CNS stimulant, appetite suppressant and treatment of hyperactivity in children. Individuals with medical conditions such as narcolepsy or who have been prescribed medication overseas may be prescribed amphetamines and form part of the workforce subject to drug testing. Medicinal use of amphetamines would explain the findings of their drug test, however a responsible MRO needs to look beyond this and ask why these drugs are prescribed and what are the safety implications? Faced with this dilemma, the MRO must decide whether to inform the employer of the potential safety risks.

Amphetamine and methamphetamine exist in two optical isomeric forms; *d*- (dextro or +) and *l*- (levo or −), where the *d* or *l* indicates the direction that the isomer will bend a beam of polarised light. The *d*-isomer has much greater pharmacological activity than the *l*-. Manufactured medicines contain 100% *d*-amphetamine while 'street' amphetamine is an approximate 50 : 50 mixture of the two isomers. Immunoassays have been developed which are sensitive to *d*- and not *l*-, however it should be noted that GC-MS assays do not distinguish between *d*- and *l*- forms. When interpreting amphetamine reports it is essential for the MRO to be aware of the testing procedures and specificity of the methods used.

The *d*- and *l*- isomers can be determined separately by using a chiral assay.[35] The ratio of *l*- to *d*- can assist the MRO investigate whether illicit amphetamine is being ingested in addition to prescribed drug.

One method described to differentiate between *d*- and *l*-amphetamine involves liquid/liquid extraction of the urine samples followed by on-column derivitisation with *N*-trifluoroacetyl-1-prolylchloride (1-TPC) and separating the *d*- and *l*- derivatives on an a chiral column prior to mass spectroscopic detection. The authors analysed urine samples from two patients both of whom were inpatients receiving *d*-amphetamine but they were also permitted to leave the unit on a daily basis and thus access 'street' amphetamine. Subject no. 1 showed $<20\%$ *l*-/*d*- ratio of amphetamine after 3 days of *d*-amphetamine only, but subject no. 2 had an *l*-/*d*- ratio of $<30\%$ recorded on a single occasion; the remaining values were 40% or greater. These findings were similar to those of Palfrey and Labib,[36] where patients compliant with *d*-amphetamine only excreted approximately 4% *l*-amphetamine, while patients taking 'street' amphetamine with or without prescribed *d*-amphetamine excreted approx 50% *l*-amphetamine.

Interpretation rules for the *l*-/*d*- ratio (%) now stated as:

- $\leq 20\%$: donor has taken only (*d*-)amphetamine
- 20–50%: donor is either using (1) prescribed medication in addition to street amphetamine or (2) has access to prescribed amphetamine as well as using street amphetamine
- $\geq 50\%$: donor is most likely to be using street amphetamine only.

In the United States, it is *d*- and *l*-methamphetamine that need to be differentiated from each other and the interpretation of *l*-/*d*- ratio is currently:

- $>80\%$ *l*-methamphetamine: could be associated with Vicks Inhaler or the metabolism of medications such as Selegiline.
- Only *d*-methamphetamine: 'ice' or crystal methamphetamine has been smoked as the synthesis of 'ice' requires the recrystallising properties of pure *d*-methamphetamine.
- $>20\%$ *d*-methamphetamine indicates the use of some source of *d*-methamphetamine other than obtained from an inhaler.

MROs should be aware that products with the same name may vary in formulation from one country to another (e.g. Vicks Inhalers).[37] Though not related to workplace drug testing, the case of Alain Baxter in 2002 who became the first British skier to win an Olympic medal is a salutary lesson. He used the American Vicks nasal decongestant which contains the banned International Olympic Committee substance levametamfetamine, even though the British equivalent does not.[38]

Benzodiazepines

Benzodiazepines are the most commonly prescribed tranquillisers known. They are anxiolytic agents, prescribed for anxiety relief. Many of this large group of drugs are also hypnotics for the promotion of sleep. They were at one time seen as safe, non-addictive drugs, an alternative to barbiturates, but it is now recognised that dependence to benzodiazepines is a real issue. Until recently in the UK, possession of benzodiazepines without a prescription, with the exception of temazepam and Rohypnol®, was legal. They are prescription-only medicines, and an individual in possession of benzodiazepines who cannot prove a legitimate prescription for them can be arrested.

A benzodiazepine can be categorised into one of three groups according to its plasma elimination half-life (i.e. the time it takes the body to decrease the plasma concentration of a drug to half of the starting value). Some benzodiazepines have active metabolites that contribute to the effects of the drug. Furthermore, their elimination can be impaired as a result of liver damage and genetic factors.

The classification of the groups is as follows:

- short-acting: a half-life of 1–8 hours (e.g. midazolam and triazolam)
- intermediate-acting: a half-life of 8–40 hours (e.g. flunitrazepam and temazepam)
- long-acting: a half-life of 40–200 hours (e.g. diazepam and chlordiazepoxide).

While benzodiazepines are widely prescribed in the United States, they are not included in the Federal testing panel. However private companies frequently test for them, thus reflecting the use within society. In UK/EU workplace drug testing benzodiazepines are routinely included in the test panel of drugs.

As stated in the introduction to this chapter, immunoassays for benzodiazepines are developed to detect many members within the group, but ability to do so varies with cross-reactivity of the antibody and large differences in dose between the individual drugs. Confirmation services rarely cover the whole group and are normally limited to a few drugs that are agreed between the laboratory and the customer.

MROs should be aware that while their service provider has the ability to look for a wide variety of benzodiazepines, since there are more than 30 different drugs within this group, expectations have to be realistic. Furthermore, prescribing practices vary between countries and this will be reflected in the services offered in each country.

Metabolism

Benzodiazepines undergo extensive phase 1 metabolism via *N*-dealkylation, hydroxylation and these metabolites then undergo phase 2 conjugation prior to elimination as glucuronides. Those drugs with a hydroxyl group on the 3 position of the benzodiazepine ring undergo direct conjugation with glucuronic acid. Some of the metabolites are pharmacologically active with similar potency to the parent substance; for example diazepam (Valium®) is rapidly absorbed after oral administration after which *N*-demethylation and 3-hydroxylation occur to produce the major active metabolites desmethyldiazepam (nordiazepam), oxazepam and temazepam. The three metabolites subsequently undergo glucuronide conjugation and 70% of the dose of diazepam is excreted in urine, mainly as oxazepam glucuronide, with smaller amounts of temazepam glucuronide and desmethyldiazepam glucuronide.[39]

A number of benzodiazepines are metabolically interrelated (see Figure 10.1).

Herbal products

There have been reports of Asian teas with 'natural' benzodiazepines that assist sleeping[41,42] or in some instances pharmaceutical compounds have been added to herbal products.[43] If the donor still has access to the tea, the laboratory may be able to analyse a sample. However, as many are purchased over the Internet or are loose material when acquired (and so unregulated), the MRO must fail a donor that tests positive for benzodiazepines and claims herbal products as the reason. Again, the company must provide clear guidance to all employees stating that herbal products will not be accepted as a reason for a positive drug test.

Drug-facilitated sexual assault

While involvement with drug-facilitated sexual assault (sometimes called 'date rape') is not a primary role of an MRO, employees may approach the occupational health service following an incident rather than the police. Drug-facilitated sexual assault is the 'secret' administration of a substance

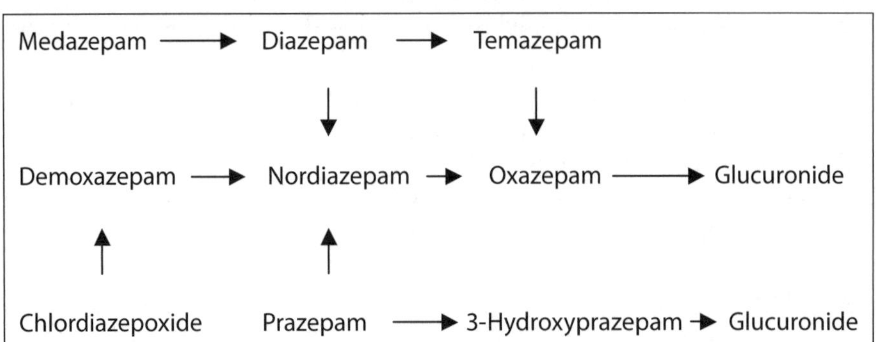

Figure 10.1 Metabolism of selected 1,4-benzodiazepines.[40]

to an individual with the intention of incapacitating them prior to committing a sexual assault. The drugs used are typically very potent (i.e. a small dose is required for effect), tasteless and fast acting but their effects continue for a long time. As a result interval between ingestion and sample collection can be long and specimens must be analysed with sensitive techniques.

Speculation about Rohypnol (flunitrazepam), which is a very potent benzodiazepine that can be easily slipped into a drink, started to appear in the UK popular press as the drug which was frequently used, but the Forensic Science Service undertook a study of 1014 cases of suspected drug-facilitated sexual assault in 2005 and showed that no Rohypnol was detected in these cases. Rather, 46% of victims had consumed alcohol and 34% illicit drugs, with only 2% indicated to be possible drug-facilitated sexual assault.[44] Subsequent information has led to Rohypnol being removed from the UK marketplace but it is still available via the Internet.

Medicinal use

Benzodiazepines are used for the treatment of anxiety, panic attacks, stress-related conditions, insomnia, epilepsy, withdrawal from other drugs and alcohol, also as a pre-operative sedative. Since they are all prescription-only medicines, tracing the origin is relatively easy and a UK/EU MRO would, with the donor's consent, write to the family doctor to verify the source. In the United States the responsibility would rest with the donor to provide proof.

Although prescribed medication may explain a positive test result, the MRO must consider the subject's job role and whether there is a safety risk. In these situations they might issue a pass for the drug test with the caveat that the case has been re-classified as clinical.

Alcohol

Measurement of ethyl alcohol/ethanol within the workplace can be undertaken either in urine and/or breath. Breath provides at point of contact a direct measurement which can be used to determine whether an individual is intoxicated with alcohol, above a prescribed limit. It requires calibrated breathalysers from approved (in UK by the Home Office) manufacturers and breathalyser technicians must be trained in the operation of the device and associated procedures when dealing with the results.

Workplace policies may refer to alcohol in the context of 'under the influence'. Organisations and MROs must remember that urine is not a suitable specimen to test for claims of 'under the influence' unless collected as a second void sample. A urine specimen collected using the second void method is the only sample that can be interpreted properly. Organisations are tending to move away from urine in favour of breath alcohol measurements (see Box 10.5).

Box 10.5 Second void collection

In a second void urine collection the first specimen is discarded as it relates to urine generated over an unknown time period relative to the events. A second sample is collected one hour later and analysed to determine the alcohol concentration. The second specimen is considered current as it was generated over a one-hour period of time when the donor had no access to uncontrolled liquids that may contain alcohol and thus the potential for a hip flask defence.

Metabolism

Following oral ingestion, alcohol is rapidly absorbed and the majority is metabolised mainly in the liver with a small amount in the kidneys and some is excreted unchanged in urine and breath. A healthy liver has the capacity to metabolise a maximum of about 170 g of alcohol per day. If large amounts of alcohol are ingested regularly, the hepatic enzymes involved in alcohol metabolism are stimulated, thus causing their activity to increase. More alcohol is then required to achieve the desired effect, which encourages the individual to increase their alcohol consumption, which can develop into high level abuse and alcoholism.

Ethanol is oxidised to carbon dioxide and water in a process involving three steps: (1) the oxidisation of ethanol to acetaldehyde by alcohol dehydrogenase, which requires NAD as a coenzyme, (2) conversion (mainly in the liver) of acetaldehyde to acetyl coenzyme A by aldehyde dehydrogenase, which also requires NAD and (3) conversion of acetyl coenzyme A to carbon dioxide and water in peripheral tissue (e.g. muscle).[7]

Normal individuals are able to eliminate alcohol from their blood, mainly by metabolism at a rate that decreases the concentration by between 6 mg and 25 mg of ethanol/100 mL/hour at an average of 15 mg/100 mL/hour.

If an organisation adopts 'zero tolerance' with respect to the alcohol cut-off level, it should be noted that low levels of alcohol can be generated by what is sometimes called autobrewing. In this condition microflora in the gastrointestinal tract produce alcohols (methanol and ethanol). Adopting a zero tolerance puts considerable pressure on laboratories to distinguish between endogenous and consumed ethanol.

Logan and Jones[45] reviewed the literature from 1958 to 2000 and concluded that except in well-defined and exceptional cases, normal healthy individuals cannot generate sufficient ethanol to test positive at 50 and 80 mg/dL, the commonly used drink–drive limits. Exceptional circumstances were reported in a study on Japanese subjects who generated vast amounts of ethanol after eating a carbohydrate-rich food such as rice. Many of the individuals had been diagnosed with chronic yeast infections as well as other gastric problems and some had undergone abdominal and gastric surgery. It was concluded that the explanation for the extremely elevated blood alcohol levels observed was a chronic yeast infection in the gut combined with microbial fermentation of the carbohydrate-rich rice and additional factors that diminished the individuals' ability to eliminate alcohol.[46,47]

Al-Awadhi *et al.*[48] reported a study of blood ethanol concentrations in 1557 individuals of 13 nationalities and both genders who provided samples as a prerequisite for a job appointment or residency renewal. The concentrations ranged from 0 to 3.52 mg/dL with little difference between the genders, which demonstrated the issues faced by organisations with a zero tolerance alcohol policy.

Medicinal use

Since 2005 there has been widespread introduction of alcoholic hand rubs placed near patient beds and this has increased the number of enquiries about possible accidental ingestion and misuse. A recent report focused on the accidental ingestion by children and elderly or confused patients,[49] but healthcare professionals also have access to these products and may abuse them. The bottles are 500 mL or larger in size and contain between 30 and 80% ethanol which, if consumed, can result in potentially fatal alcohol poisoning.

Alcohol is also present in some over-the-counter medications, such as Covonia Cold and Flu Formula (160 mL) with 15% ethanol. The advised therapeutic regimen states one dose (20 mL) every 4 hours, with no more than four doses in 24 hours. However if excessive quantities of Covonia are consumed (5 bottles over 18 hours) with a social pint of beer, there is sufficient alcohol in the body to exceed the UK Road Traffic Act level, 80 mg of ethanol/100 mL of blood.[50]

Other commonly used products containing ethanol include mouthwashes; for example, Listerine Antiseptic Mouthwash Original, sold in 100-mL bottles, contains ethanol (95%) IP 26.9% v/v, and the recommended use is to wash the mouth with 20 mL, twice daily. Individuals with an alcohol misuse problem can buy these products easily and without attracting attention. Increasingly, alcohol-free versions of products are being manufactured partly to prevent this misuse.[51,52]

Medications containing ethanol are clearly labelled and contain only small quantities of ethanol so as not to infringe the UK Road Traffic Act, however there may be implications for employees within the air transport industry as their allowed levels are considerably lower (20 mg/dL in blood as stated in the Railways and Transport Safety Bill). Other everyday items also contain various alcohols, both ethanol that people can safely drink and methanol, which is unsafe to drink.

Other drugs

While this chapter has focused on the five drugs and alcohol that generally feature in a workplace drug programme, there are many more drugs that a MRO may need to review and interpret. Furthermore, while screening methodology for the common workplace drug testing panels has been automated for rapid analysis there are a number of drugs that are being increasingly misused for which automated immunoassays are not yet commonly available (e.g. ketamine and pethidine). Initially they were only available to healthcare professionals but now such compounds are becoming more widely abused.

Barbiturates

Manufactured for medical use since 1903, these drugs were widely prescribed for anxiety, depression and insomnia. Concerns with accidental overdose and also their deliberate use for suicide has resulted in a considerable reduction in barbiturate prescribing and the gap being filled since the late 1970s by benzodiazepines and more recently by the 'Z' hypnotics (zolpidem, zopiclone and zaleplon). In 2002, only about 20% of all depressant prescriptions in the United States were for barbiturates.[53]

Most barbiturates are extensively metabolised: less than 5% of a dose of amobarbital or pentobarbital is excreted unchanged, but 25% of a dose of phenobarbital is excreted unchanged, with 17% as total 4-hydroxyphenobarbital, about half of which is the glucuronide conjugate. Urinary excretion of the unchanged phenobarbital increases when the urine is alkaline. In the UK, phenobarbital is the most frequently encountered barbiturate, either as a parent substance or as a metabolite of primidone, since both are still prescribed to treat epilepsy. Phenobarbitone is also encountered intermittently as a cutting agent, most notably for heroin.[54]

Prescription of barbiturates in the UK has dropped from 16 million in 1966 to 5.1 million in 1987 and continues to move downwards.[55] However, in May 2004 the EU borders were opened to countries of the former Soviet Eastern Bloc and with the increased diversity of the workforce came the challenge of different prescribing practises within these countries. Laboratories involved with workplace and clinical testing for drugs have reported an increase in the number and variety of barbiturate-positive samples. The re-emergence of barbiturates may be a new challenge for some laboratory toxicologists and MROs alike.

MROs must be aware that some testing laboratories do not routinely analyse samples for barbiturates and some industries have chosen not to include these drugs in their profiles. The rail industry in the UK does not require the analysis for barbiturates, even though phenobarbital is prescribed for the treatment of epilepsy, a medical condition that prohibits sufferers from track-side duties.

MROs may be faced with individuals whose claimed use of phenobarbital provides a satisfactory explanation for the positive test report, however the underlying medical condition could exclude them from certain duties. A review of the job role, full safety evaluation and review of the pre-employment medical questionnaire should be undertaken, as well as dialogue with the donor's family doctor before the donor is allowed to return to work.

Propoxyphene

In January 2005 co-proxamol, also known as Distalgesic®, was withdrawn from the UK marketplace after it was linked to both suicides and accidental deaths. A study of 4162 drug-related suicides in England and Wales between 1997 and 1999 showed that 18% involved co-proxamol alone and that in the 10–24 age group a higher proportion were due to co-proxamol than in any other age group.[56]

Norpropoxyphene is the main metabolite that is formed by *N*-demethylation of propoxyphene and 35% of a dose is excreted in a 24-hour urine, 13% as norpropoxyphene and 5% as unchanged drug.

Co-proxamol, which contains a combination of 325 mg of paracetamol and 32.5 mg of dextropropoxyphene was a prescription-only medicine. It has a long history of use by individuals suffering from postsurgical pain, arthritis, and musculoskeletal pain. It will take some years for all stocks of this medication to be consumed, however, concerns are already being raised about replacement drugs in the workforce. Increases are expected in prescriptions for not only codeine and dihydrocodeine, but also some of the newer analgesics (e.g. fentanyl and tramadol). While the codeine and dihydrocodeine are easily detected in urine, immunoassays for the new analgesics are not yet available and these drugs are not currently included in the test panels.

Methadone

The UK Guidelines require detection of either the parent drug or its main metabolite, 2-ethylidene-3,3-diphenylpyrrolidine (EDDP), and immunoassays are available which are specific for either parent drug or EDDP (Table 10.2).

Table 10.2 CEDIA product information sheets[57,58]

CEDIA assay	Methadone	EDDP
Methadone	100%	<0.02%
EDDP	<0.016%	100%

CEDIA, cloned enzyme donor immunoassay; EDDP, 2-ethylidene-3,3-diphenylpyrrolidine.

An appropriate immunoassay and confirmation method must be selected and correctly documented on the laboratory report, which should specify whether methadone or EDDP was the target.

Following absorption, methadone undergoes *N*-demethylation resulting in a substance which spontaneously cyclises to form the major metabolites: 2-ethylidene-1,5-dimethyl-3,3-diphenylpyrrolidine (EDDP) and 2-ethyl-5-methyl-3,3-diphenyl-1-pyrrolidine (EMDP), both of which are pharmacologically inactive. Individuals on methadone maintenance programmes excrete up to 60% of a dose in urine in 24 hours, with approximately 33% as unchanged drug, 43% as EDDP and between 5% and 10% as EMDP.

Explanations for methadone-positive drug tests may include the subject being on a methadone maintenance programme, which is easily checked. However methadone is widely available for street purchase and misuse, though it is rarely seen on its own in street users, but usually in combination with benzodiazepines and/or morphine/codeine.

The US Federal drug testing programme does not require testing for opioids such as methadone, though some organisations may include them in their programme.

Lysergic acid diethylamide (LSD)

Although not a frontline drug of misuse, LSD is monitored in certain job areas, such as the military in the United States, and in the UK, London Underground transport workers.

Until the mid-1990s, radioimmunoassay (RIA) was the only method available for screening of LSD. As a consequence, many organisations did not test for this. In 1996 a non-radiolabelled immunoassay was introduced that could be automated which made initial screening easier, however confirmation is difficult because doses of this very potent drug are in the microgram range and thus very sensitive analytical techniques are required. LSD is extensively metabolised and only about 1% of an ingested dose, which typically is only 50–100 micrograms, is excreted unchanged in urine in 24 hours. Confirmation techniques must be extremely sensitive and it is only since the introduction of LC-MS and LC-MS/MS that routine confirmation has become possible.

LSD is difficult to synthesise, but there are a number of clandestine laboratories manufacturing doses which tend to then be regionally available.

There are currently no medicinal uses of LSD, so interpretation of LSD-positive laboratory reports is straightforward.

Phencyclidine (PCP)

Phencyclidine (1-(1-phenylcyclohexyl)piperidine) (PCP) was initially synthesised in the 1950s as an anaesthetic but its human use was discontinued because many patients reported unpleasant effects and disorientation on waking. Its use as a veterinary anaesthetic has continued.

The drug can be ingested orally, by nasal insufflation or smoked. Following absorption PCP undergoes hepatic metabolism to produce two hydroxy metabolites that are excreted in the urine as glucuronide conjugates. Up to 70% of a dose is excreted in the urine in 10 days; 16% as unchanged drug and the rate of unchanged drug excretion is increased in acidic conditions.

PCP is one of the five drugs that form the Federal drug testing panel, however, in reality the drug is not widely abused in the United States. Its use is quite regional, mainly in San Francisco and Los Angeles on the west coast and Washington DC on the east coast. Historically, cannabis has been laced with PCP, resulting in donors testing positive for both within seven days of use. PCP use within the UK/EU is practically unheard of.

Interpretation of PCP-positive results is easy as there are no medical conditions for which it is prescribed in either the United States or the UK/EU. However, since this drug is encountered so rarely in the UK/EU, MROs are advised to verify a positive result with the testing laboratory since they are the last quality check before releasing the result.

Methaqualone

Methaqualone is a potent sedative–hypnotic of the quinazoline class and has a high potential for misuse. The oral use of methaqualone (Quaalude®, Mandrax®) has waned in Western countries since the mid–late 1980s, but the practice of smoking the drug with cannabis is a serious public health problem in South Africa, other parts of Africa and India. The South African police referred 6064 methaqualone-related cases to their laboratory in 2002.[59] The practice of smoking methaqualone with cannabis is known as 'witpyp' (i.e. white pipe) or WP.

Methaqualone is extensively metabolised and up to 50% of the dose is excreted in the urine during the first 72 hours after ingestion, mainly as conjugated metabolites, with only 2% being excreted as unchanged drug.

Methaqualone was withdrawn from the US marketplace in the 1980s and positives are rare. Most companies that request methaqualone in their testing profiles will have a global footprint. An immunoassay is available for methaqualone screening and suspected positives can be confirmed by routine chromatographic/MS procedures.

As with PCP positives, these will be rarely seen by MROs unless based in specific regions and so all reports should be verified with the testing laboratory.

Summary

The need for an MRO in the UK/EU is still not fully acknowledged or understood by many organisations. Some companies operate under the belief that

HR managers are capable of interpreting laboratory results and this denies the donor the opportunity to discuss private medical issues with the MRO. In addition it adds a responsibility to the HR manager for which they are neither trained nor qualified.

UK/EU MRO procedures have drawn much from those used in the United States though with a slightly different emphasis on the role of the donor. The burden of proof in the United States is clearly placed with the donor, who is responsible for providing information regarding medication, whereas in the UK/EU the MRO writes, with the donor's consent, to other healthcare professionals to gather this information. As more UK/EU companies engage the services of MROs it is likely that there will be a shift of responsibility for providing proof to the donor.

As alternative biological samples, such as hair and oral fluid, become increasingly used for workplace drug testing, the MRO will need to ensure that they are familiar with testing these samples and interpretation of results. Information about the analytical techniques involved with testing such samples and in particular the sensitivity and specificity must be available from the laboratory along with technical support. UK laboratory guidelines for point-of-collection devices (urine and oral fluid), alcohol (oral fluid and breathalysers) and drugs (oral fluid) are in draft, as of April 2010.

The main function of an MRO is the interpretation of laboratory results. Unlike forensic toxicology, where a very wide range of analytical investigations may be carried out, workplace drug testing laboratories analyse samples for a pre-agreed test panel and within each drug group, a limited number of compounds at agreed cut-offs. This difference needs to be clearly understood to prevent unreasonable expectations and conflict between organisations, laboratories and MROs. Clear defined terms and conditions between all parties will provide the framework in which to operate.

This chapter has reviewed the major drug groups and the most common interpretive dilemmas. Over time the reason offered by donors for positive drug tests will change. This may be a result of a change in prescribing practices by healthcare professionals, or changes in substance misuse trends or drugs available (e.g. mephedrone). The Internet has provided an easy access forum where ideas can be exchanged about drug and alcohol testing programmes, adulterants, new drugs and mechanisms of use and much more. The MRO must stay abreast of these changes, including those in specimen validity testing.

References

1. Shultz TF. *Medical Review Officer Handbook*, 8th edn. London: Quadrangle Research, 2002.
2. The 49 CFR Part 40 (Code of Federal Regulations title 49, Transportation, part 40 Procedure for Transportation Workplace Drug Testing Programmes) Issued 01 August

2001, updated 31 August 2009. www.dot.gov/ost/dapc/new_docs/part40.html (accessed 1 September 2009).

3. UK Workplace Drug Testing Forum (2001) United Kingdom laboratory guidelines for legally defensible workplace drug testing. Version 1.0. http://ltg.uk.net/pages/monographs/guidelines.asp (accessed November 2010).
4. European Workplace Drug Testing Society (EWDTS) (2002) Draft guidelines for the collection part for urine and oral fluid and the entire procedure for hair for feedback. Version 1.0. www.ewdts.org/guidelines.html (accessed November 2010).
5. US Department of Health and Human Services (DHHS) (2004) Mandatory guidelines (effective 1 Nov 2004). http://workplace.samhsa.gov (accessed 1 September 2009).
6. Faculty of Occupational Medicine. Guidance on alcohol and drug misuse in the workplace. Faculty of Occupational Medicine of the Royal College of Physicians, London, July 2006.
7. Bowman WC, Rand MJ. *Textbook of Pharmacology*, 2nd edn. Oxford: Blackwells, 1984.
8. United Kingdom National External Quality Assessment Service (NEQAS) returns instructions. Created 10 December 2008, version 1.0. www.Heathcontrol.com (accessed February 2009).
9. Cone EJ, Johnson RE, Darwin WD *et al.* Passive inhalation of marijuana smoke: urinalysis and room air levels of Δ9-tetrahydrocannabinol. *J Anal Toxicol* 1987; 11: 89–96.
10. Cone EJ, Johnson RE. Contact highs and urinary cannabinoid excretion after passive exposure to marijuana smoke. *Clin Pharmacol Ther* 1986; 40(3): 247–256.
11. Mule SJ, Lomax P, Gross SJ. Active and realistic passive marijuana exposure tested by three immunoassays and GC/MS in urine. *J Anal Toxicol* 1988; 12: 113–116.
12. *DrugLink* 2006; 21(4): Jul/Aug.
13. Anon. (27 June 2006) Iced marijuana tea to debut in British health food shops. www.breitbart.com (accessed 2007).
14. The Hemp Shop (2009) Swiss hemp iced tea. www.thehempshop.co.uk/product-26.htm (accessed 2 September 2009).
15. Goodness Direct. www.goodnessdirect.co.uk/cgi-local/frameset/script/search.html (accessed 28 December 2007).
16. Callaway JC, Weeks LP, Walls HC, Hearn WL. A positive THC urinalysis from hemp (cannabis) seed oil. *J Anal Toxicol* 1997; 21: 310–320.
17. What is Marinol and how does it work? www.marinol.com/aboutmarinol/index.html (accessed 18 December 2007).
18. Reynolds JEF, ed. *Martindale: The Extra Pharmacopoeia*, 31st edn. London: Royal Pharmaceutical Society, 1996.
19. Sativex® Oromucosal Spray. www.gwpharma.com/sativex.asp (accessed 18 December 2007).
20. Rohrig TP, Moore C. The determination of morphine in urine and oral fluid following ingestion of poppy seeds. *J Anal Toxicol* 2003; 27: 449–452.
21. Thevis M, Opfermann G, Schanzer W. Urinary concentrations of morphine and codeine after consumption of poppy seeds. *J Anal Toxicol* 2003; 27: 53–56.
22. King MA, McDonough MA, Drummer OH, Berkovic SF. Poppy seed tea and the baker's first seizure. *The Lancet* 1997; 350: 716.
23. Braye K, Harwood T, Inder R, Beasley R, Robinson G. Poppy seed tea and opiate abuse in New Zealand. *Drug Alcohol Rev* 2007; 26(2): 215–219.
24. Hayes LW, Krasselt WG, Mueggler PA. Concentrations of morphine and codeine in serum and urine after ingestion of poppy seeds. *Clin Chem* 1987; 336: 806–808.
25. Cone EJ, Welch P, Mitchell JM, Paul BD. Forensic drug testing for opiates: I. Detection of 6-acetylmorphine in urine as an indicator of recent heroin exposure; drug and assay considerations and detection times. *J Anal Toxicol* 1991; 15: 1–7.
26. Cone EJ, Dickerson S, Paul BD, Mitchell JM. Forensic drug testing for opiates: V. Urine testing for heroin, morphine, and codeine with commercial opiate immunoassays. *J Anal Toxicol* 1993; 17: 156–164.
27. Hamilton HE, Wallance JE, Shimek ELJ *et al.* Cocaine and benzoylecgonine excretion in humans. *J Forensic Sci* 1977; 22: 697–707.

28. Weiss RD, Gawin FH. Protracted elimination of cocaine metabolites in long-term high-dose cocaine abusers. *Am J Med* 1988; 85: 879–880.
29. Cone EJ, Yousefnejad D, Hillgrove MJ, Holocky B, Darwin WD. Passive inhalation of cocaine. *J Anal Toxicol* 1995; 19(6): 399–411.
30. ElSohly MA, Stanford DF, ElSohly HN. Coca tea and urinalysis for cocaine metabolites. *J Anal Toxicol* 1986; 10(6): 256.
31. Turner M, McCrory P, Johnston A. Time for tea, anyone? *Br J Sports Med* 2005; 39: 37–38.
32. General Medical Council (GMC) (2004) Confidentiality: Protecting and providing information. April. www.gmc-uk.org.
33. Cone EJ, Tsadik A, Oyler J, Darwin WD. Cocaine metabolism and urinary excretion after different routes of administration. *Ther Drug Monit* 1998; 20: 556–560.
34. Product Package Inserts Revision 5 Part No. 10008452; CEDIA® Amphetamine/Ecstasy Assay pack insert 10006576-0 2003 01.
35. Tetlow VA, Merrill J. Rapid determination of amphetamine steroisomer ratios in urine by gas chromatography-mass spectroscopy. *Ann Clin Biochem* 1996; 33: 50–54.
36. Palfrey S, Labib M. A simple HPLC method for separation of amphetamine isomers in urine and its application in differentiating between 'street' amphetamine and prescribed D-amphetamine. *Ann Clin Biochem* 1996; 33: 344–346.
37. Vicks Vapor Inhaler. www.vicks.com/vapour-inhaler-info.php (accessed 17 December 2007).
38. Anon. (2002) He couldn't believe he had won it. Now ski hero mourns loss of miracle medal. *Guardian*, 22 March. http://sport.guardian.co.uk/print/0,4379406-108645,00.html (accessed 17 December 2007).
39. Swarbrick J. *Clarke's Isolation and Identification of Drugs*, 2nd edn. London: The Pharmaceutical Press, 1986.
40. Kueffer H, ed. (2009) Drugs of Abuse Testing Guidelines, last updated 2009-04-02. www.cscq.ch/agsa (accessed 10 September 2009).
41. Leong K (2009) Can green tea help you relax? http://healthmad.com/nutrition/can-green-tea-help-you-relax/ (accessed 10 September 2009).
42. Lu K, Gray MA, Oliver C, Liley DT, Harrison BJ, Bartholomeusz CF, Phan KL, Nathan PJ. The acute effects of L-theanine in comparison with alprazolam on anticipatory anxiety in humans. *Hum Psychopharmacol* 2004; 19(7): 457–465.
43. Eachus P. Positive drug screen for benzodiazepine due to a Chinese herbal product. *J Athl Train* 1996; 31(2): 165–166.
44. Scott-Ham M, Burton F. Toxicological findings in cases of alleged drug-facilitated sexual assault in the United Kingdom over a 3-year period. *J Clin Forensic Med* 2005; 12: 175–186.
45. Logan BK, Jones AW. Endogenous ethanol auto-brewing syndrome; as a drunk-driving defence challenge. *Med Sci Law* 2000; 40(3): 206–215.
46. Kaji H, Asanumo Y, Saito N, Hisamura M, Murao M, Yoshida T, Takahashi K. The auto-brewery syndrome – the repeat attacks of alcoholic intoxication due to the overgrowth of Candida (albicans) in the gastrointestinal tract. *Mater Med Pol* 1976; 8: 429–435.
47. Kaji H, Asanumo Y, Shibue H, Hisamura M, Saito N, Kawakami Y *et al.* Intragastrointestinal alcohol fermenatation syndromes: report of two cases and review of the literature. *J Forensic Sci Soc* 1984; 24: 461–471.
48. Al-Awadhi A, Wasfi IA, Al Reyami F, Al-Hatali Z. Autobrewing revisited: Endogenous concentrations of blood ethanol in residents of the United Arab Emirates. *Sci Justice* 2004; 44(3): 149–152.
49. Archer JRH, Wood DM, Tizzard Z, Jones AL, Dargan PI. Alcohol hand rubs: hygiene and hazard. *BMJ* 2007; 335: 1154–1155.
50. Covonia Cold and Flu Formula – 160 ml. www.covonia.co.uk (accessed 11 September 2009).
51. Listerine® Antiseptic Mouthwash Original. www.listerine.com/product-original.jsp (accessed 16 September 2009).
52. Colgate Plax Alcohol Free. www.colgate.co.uk/app/PDP/ColgatePlax/UK/AlcoholFree.cvsp (accessed 16 September 2009).

53. Nationwide Medical Review (2002) Drug free workplace – barbiturates. http://www.drugfreeworkplace.com/drug-pages/barbiturates-ref.php (accessed 23 June 2003).
54. Strang J, Gossop M. *Heroin Addiction and the British System: Origins and Evolution.* London: Routledge, 2005.
55. DrugScope (2007) Barbiturates. www.drugscope.org.uk/resources/drugsearch/drugsearchpages/barbiturates.htm (accessed 19 December 2007).
56. Hawton K, Simkin S, Deeks J. Co-proxamol and suicide: a study of national mortality statistics and local non-fatal poisonings. *BMJ* 2003; 326: 1006–1008.
57. Product Package Inserts Revision 5 Part No. 10008452; CEDIA® Methadone Assay pack insert 10006542-0 2002 01.
58. Product Package Inserts Revision 5 Part No. 10008452; CEDIA® Methadone Metabolite (EDDP) Assay pack insert 10006492-0 2002 08.
59. South African Police Service (2002) Drug effects–methaqualone. www.saps.gov.za/drugs/meth.htm (accessed 8 January 2008).

11

Guidelines for workplace drug testing

Leendert J Mostert and Ronald Agius

Key points

- Workplace drug testing has been practised in the United States for over 20 years; a historical outline of the main events is given.
- The key stages of workplace drug testing are specimen collection, laboratory analysis and reporting and interpreting the analytical results.
- The three widely used guidelines regulating workplace drug testing in Australia/New Zealand, the United States and Europe are thoroughly compared, outlining similarities and differences.
- The harmonisation of workplace drug testing guidelines remains a challenge for the stakeholders involved, including toxicologists, medical review officers, human resources personnel, legal personnel and policy makers in order to assure fairer tests and judgements and safer workplaces.

History

The development of guidelines for workplace drug testing has its origins in the United States. In the late 1960s and early 1970s there was a growing public concern about increasing drug use (specifically heroin). Facts that led to a strong political interest were:

- the increase in the 1960s of the absolute number of addicted individuals
- the spread of the problem from urban ghettos to smaller communities and the middle and upper classes
- the rise in narcotic use among adolescent and pre-adolescent youths

- the increase of crime, attributed in large part to the growing addict population
- the reports of widespread narcotic use by American military forces and a growing concern over the impact of thousands of addicted soldiers returning to the United States.

President Nixon was the first to formulate a national drug policy in which supply reduction was balanced with demand reduction. Treatment of addicts became possible from then on. After a loss of interest it was President Reagan who, in 1986, signed Executive Order 12564[1] (Drug-Free Federal Workplace). This established the goal of a drug-free Federal workplace and made it a condition of employment for all Federal employees not to use illegal drugs at any time.

In 1987 Public Law 100-71 passed Congress. This law was designed to establish uniformity among Federal agencies' drug testing programmes, reliable and accurate drug testing methods, employee access to drug testing records, confidentiality of the test results and centralised oversight of the drug testing programme. Federal agencies were provided with the Model Plan for a Comprehensive Drug-Free Workplace which described the components of the Federal agency plans and the Mandatory Guidelines for Federal Workplace Drug Testing Programs. These Mandatory Guidelines describe the scientific and technical aspects to be used by agencies and the laboratories testing Federal employees.

In 1988 the Drug Free Workplace Act[2] was introduced, which require Federal contractors and recipients of Federal works and grants to maintain programmes aimed at keeping the workplace drug free. In 1991 the Omnibus Transportation Employee Testing Act[3] was introduced, under which safety-sensitive transportation employees in aviation, trucking, railroads, mass transit, pipelines and other transportation industries are required to submit to mandated alcohol and drug testing.

Since 1988, more and more private companies have introduced drug-free workplace programmes incorporating drug testing. In 1988, 21% of companies in the United States conducted drug testing; the number rose to 81% in 1996.

General principles of workplace drug testing guidelines

In general, guidelines describe the best practice for laboratories providing workplace drug testing in order to ensure that the entire drug testing process is conducted to give accurate and reliable information about drug use of the employee. Furthermore, the drug testing process from collection to reporting of the results should be legally defensible. Also of importance is that the privacy of the employee is respected and all information considered as confidential.

The drug testing process consists of three key stages:

1. obtaining the specimen from the donor
2. analysis of the sample for the presence of drugs
3. review, interpretation and reporting of the analytical results.

Specimen collection

For decades, urine was the preferred specimen for drug screening and all initial screening methods were mainly immunoassays. Recently, alternative matrices such as oral fluid, hair and sweat are increasingly being used. Consequently, workplace drug testing guidelines are being revised to include these alternative matrices. The latter complement each other, depending on the reason for illicit drug use investigation.[4] Specimens need to be collected under circumstances that respect the dignity of the individual while ensuring that the specimen is authentic. Suitable records must be made when the specimen is collected to prove that the specimen collected is the sample received by the laboratory. This is the first step in the chain-of-custody process that can be used to prove that the final result belongs to the specimen collected.

Specimens have to be collected by trained personnel (collection officers or collectors) who understand the principles of chain of custody. The collection procedure must ensure:

- the privacy and security of the collection site during specimen collection
- the specimen is freshly supplied
- the prevention of sample tampering and adulteration
- the proper identification of the donor and of the specimen
- the formal written consent of the donor for the analysis of the specimen
- the disclosure of recent medication or cosmetic treatment, in the case of hair analysis which may influence the drug testing result.

In addition, the collector must ensure that:

- enough specimen is collected to ensure a possible counter-analysis
- in case of segmental hair analysis, the hair strand should be fastened with a string before cutting and the root tip indicated
- each specimen collected is adequately shipped (or picked up by the laboratory's courier) in a timely fashion.

Laboratory analysis procedure

The laboratory is crucial in the whole drug testing process, as it is not only responsible for the analytical testing, but also of the equally several important pre-anayltical and post-analytical steps. These include:

- the initials checks on the sample's integrity
- validity testing
- screening and eventual conformational analysis
- result certification and reporting
- sample storage/disposal
- completion of the chain of custody.

Reporting and interpreting the analytical results

The laboratory usually reports the analytical result together with observations concerning the sample integrity (specimen validity result) to the medical review officer (MRO).[5] The MRO:

- will review the result
- may interview the donor if the result is non-negative
- will interpret and report the final result to the employer.

Comparing workplace drug testing guidelines

After outlining the essential elements of workplace drug testing guidelines, we now provide a detailed comparison of the three mostly applied workplace drug testing guidelines, namely the Australian/New Zealand Standard Procedures for Specimen Collection and the Detection and Quantitation of Drugs of Abuse in Urine,[6] abbreviated as AS/NZS 4308-2008, the Mandatory Guidelines for Federal Workplace Drug Testing Programs,[7] abbreviated as SAMHSA 2008 and the European Laboratory Guidelines for Legally Defensible Workplace Drug Testing,[8] abbreviated as EWDTS 2002. Even though all above mentioned guidelines include other matrices apart from urine, for clarity's sake, only the guidelines for drug testing in the urine matrix are compared in Table 11.1.

Conclusion

Table 11.1 shows that the three workplace drug testing guidelines are similar in the basic elements, namely:

- pre-analytical aspects ensuring the identity and integrity of the sample
- measures to ensure the highest quality of the analytical results
- competence in the result interpretation
- post-analytical measures to ensure the safe storage of the records and the sample.

There are differences, however, for instance in the drug profiles to be analysed for and the cut-offs used. A serious deficit of all guidelines is the

Table 11.1 Comparison of guidelines for workplace drug testing in urine

Described item	**AS/NZS 4308-2008**	**SAMHSA 2008**	**EWDTS 2002**
On-site screening	Necessitates the implementation of quality controls, proficiency testing, verification of testing devices, competency-based training and accreditation	POCT enabled by the 2004 revision	Not specified
Collection site			
Secured	Yes	Yes	Yes
Authorised access	Yes	Yes	Yes
Use of chain-of-custody form	Yes	Yes	Yes
Minimal content of the custody form:	(a) Verification of donor's identity (b) Two identifiers unique to the donor (c) Date and time of collection (d) Confirmation by the donor that the specimen was their own and was correctly taken (e) Name and signature of collector (f) Declaration by the collector that the specimen has been collected and if applicable tested on-site in compliance with this Standard (g) Requesting authority details (h) Results of specimen integrity checks carried out at the point of collection	The date, purpose and individuals involved in each handling of the specimen must be documented, from the time the specimen is collected to the final storage and disposition of the specimen	a) Information identifying the donor b) Date and time of collection c) Name of testing laboratory d) Names and signatures of all individuals who had custody of the sample during the collection process
Privacy donor	Yes	Yes	Yes
Precautions regarding integrity/identity of sample	Yes	Yes	Yes
Toilet bluing	Yes	Yes	Yes

(continued overleaf)

Table 11.1 *(continued)*

Described item	AS/NZS 4308-2008	SAMHSA 2008	EWDTS 2002
Restricted source of water	Yes	Yes	Yes
Photo identification of donor	Yes	Yes	Yes
Donor shall remove unnecessary outer garments	Yes	Yes	Yes
Donor shall wash and dry hands before collection	Yes	Yes	Yes
Sample collection			
Procedure for difficulties with providing sample	Yes	Yes	Yes
Temperature withins 4 min after collection	33–38°C	32–38°C	32–38°C
Procedure/criteria for direct observation	Allowed when 'there is an unacceptable risk to the integrity of the specimen'	Yes	Not described
Observed transfer of urine to specimen bottle by donor	Yes	Yes	Yes
Use of tamper-proof label	Yes	Yes	Yes
Donor signs label and chain-of-custody form	Yes + labels with collection date and min. two unique identifiers	Yes	Yes + specimen labelled with unique identifier at collection site
Donor signs informed consent	Yes	Yes	Yes

Secured sample storage by collector until shipment	Yes	Yes	Yes
Split specimen procedure	Yes	Since 2008 revision – obligatory (Section 2.3)	Yes
Minimal volume split specimen procedure (bottle A/B)	Enough to perform all testing	Min. 30 mL/15 mL	Min. 30 mL divided into two bottles (bottle A and B)
Procedure when donor unable to provide a specimen	No	Yes since 2008 revision (see Section 8.5)	No
Direct observed collection	No	Yes, since 2008 revision under special conditions listed in Section 8.8.	No
Procedure for shipment to the laboratory	Yes, containers sealed and transported accordance with this Standard	Yes	Not considered necessary as all samples and documents are sealed in packages that would indicate tampering during transport
Procedure for re-confirmation by second lab	Yes	Yes	Yes
Laboratory personnel			
Described professional, educational, organisational qualifications for employees working in the drug testing laboratory	Yes	Yes	Yes
Laboratory analysis			
Documentation of entrance of unauthorised visitors to the laboratory	Yes	Yes	Yes

(continued overleaf)

Table 11.1 *(continued)*

Described item	AS/NZS 4308-2008	SAMHSA 2008	EWDTS 2002
Inspection of custody and control form (CCF) and information on the seal, specimen bottle	Yes	Yes	Yes
Sample inspection for tampering, adulteration, substitution (by lab or MRO) when received in the laboratory	Yes	Yes	Yes
Criteria for observed discrepancies to reject the specimen for further testing	Yes	Yes	Yes
Subcontracting	Not allowed	Not allowed	Allowed with strict adherence to chain-of-custody procedures
Initial drug test			
Immunoassay	Yes	Yes, FDA approved	Yes
Other analytical screening methods possible	Yes mentioned in 4.2	No	Yes mentioned in Appendix D
Multiple initial drug tests allowed (re-screening)	No	Yes	Not described
Customer informed about cross-reactivity of related compounds and expected sensitivity	Not described	Not described	Yes
Screening cut-off in ng/mL			
Alcohol	Not described	Not described	Not described

Marijuana metabolites	50	50	50
Cocaine metabolite/s	300	150	300
Opiates (morphine) 6-acetylmorphine	300	2000 10 (regardless of morphine concentration)	300
Amphetamines MDMA (ecstasy)	300	500 500	500
Phencyclidine	Allowed but not described	25	25
Benzodiazepines	200	Not specified	200
Methadone (or metabolites)	Allowed but not described	Not specified	300
Barbiturates	Allowed but not described	Not specified	200
Buprenorphine (or metabolites)	Allowed but not described	Not specified	5
LSD (or metabolites)	Allowed but not described	Not specified	1
Methaqualone	Allowed but not described	Not specified	300
Propoxyphene (or metabolites)	Allowed but not described	Not specified	300
Confirmatory drug tests			
Only on samples screened positive on the initial test	Yes	Yes	Yes
Required analytical method	GC-MS, however GC-MSn and LC-MSn are allowed if certain criteria are met	GC-MS	GC-MS or LC-MS

(continued overleaf)

Table 11.1 *(continued)*

Described item	AS/NZS 4308-2008	SAMHSA 2008	EWDTS 2002
Confirmation cut-off in ng/mL			
Alcohol	Not described	Not described	Not described
Marijuana metabolite (THC-COOH)	15	15	15
Cocaine metabolite	150 (benzoylecgonine and ecgonine methyl ester)	100 (benzoylecgonine)	150 (benzoylecgonine)
Morphine	300	2000	300
Codeine	300	2000	300
Dihydrocodeine	Not specified	Not specified	300
6-acetylmorphine	10 (optional)	10	10
Buprenorphine (or metabolites)	Not specified	Not specified	5
Amphetamine	150	500	200
Methamphetamine	150	250 (when amphetamine $\geq$ 100)	200
MDMA (ecstasy)	150	250	200
MDA	150	250	200
MDEA	Not specified	250	200
Other members of amphetamine group	500 (phentermine[a], ephedrine[a], pseudoephedrine[a], benzylpiperazine[a])	Not specified	200
Temazepam	200	Not specified	100
Oxazepam	200	Not specified	100

Desmethyldiazepam (nordiazepam)	200	Not specified	100
Other members of the benzodiazepine group	200 (diazepam) 100 (7-amino-clonazepam, 7-amino-nitrazepam, 7-amino-flunitrazepam, α-hydroxy-alprazolam)	Not specified	In agreement with customer
Phencyclidine	Not specified	25	25
Methadone (or metabolites)	Not specified	Not specified	250
Barbiturates group	Not specified	Not specified	150
Propoxyphene (or metabolites)	Not specified	Not specified	300
LSD (or metabolites)	Not specified	Not specified	1
Methaqualone	Not specified	Not specified	300
Validity testing			
Creatinine	>200 mg/L	>1.77 mmol/L (20 mg/dL)	>2.0 mmol/L
Specific gravity	May be used to prove dilution	If creatinine <20 mg/dL	If creatinine ≤2.0 mmol/L Between 1.001 and 1.020
pH	Not described	Between 3 and 11	Between 4 and 9
Oxidants	Not described	Yes, presence	Optional
Nitrite	Not described	≤500 micrograms/mL	≤500 mg/1
Chromium(VI)	Not described	≥50 micrograms/mL	Optional
Halogens (bleach, iodine, fluoride)	Not described	≥200 micrograms/mL nitrite eq.	Optional

(continued overleaf)

Table 11.1 *(continued)*

Described item	AS/NZS 4308-2008	SAMHSA 2008	EWDTS 2002
Glutaraldehyde	Not described	Yes, presence	Optional
Pyridine	Not described	$\geq$ 50 micrograms/mL Cr(VI) eq.	Optional
Surfactant	Not described	$\geq$ 100 micrograms/mL dodecylbenzene sulfonate-equivalent	Not described
Procedure and criteria for additional validity testing	Request for second sample if suspected to be adulterated, diluted or substituted	Yes	Not described
Confirmation of a positive validity test by another analytical method	If creatinine <200 mg/L another method may be used	Yes	Further investigation of a positive validity test
Reporting of results			
Results reported to MRO	Not described	Yes (within 5 working days)	
Report 'adulterated' (SAMHSA) Report 'sample integrity failed' (EWDTS)	Not specified	pH <3 or ≥ 11 nitrite ≥ 500 mg/L Cr(VI) ≥ 50 mg/L Halogens, glutaraldehyde and/or other adulterants present	pH <3 or ≥ 11 nitrite >500 mg/L or when other tests indicate adulteration or sample otherwise unsuitable for analysis or creatinine ≤ 0.5 mmol/L and s.g. outside the range
Report 'substituted'		Creatinine <0.18 mmol/L (2 mg/dL) and s.g. ≤ 1.0010 or ≥ 1.0200	Not reported

Report 'dilute'	Creatinine $<$ 200 mg/1	Creatinine between 0.18 and 1.77 mmol/L (2–20 mg/dL) and s.g. between 1.0010 and 1.0030	Creatinine between 0.5 and 2.0 mmol/L and s.g. within range
Report 'invalid result'		Creatinine $<$0.18 mmol/L and s.g. between 1.0010 and 1.0200 or s.g. $\leq$1.0010 and creatinine $\geq$0.18 mmol/L (2 mg/dL) or pH between 3 and 4.5 or pH between 9 and 11 or nitrite between 200 and 500 mg/L or Cr(VI) $\geq$50 mg/L or presence of: halogens, glutaraldehyde, oxidants, surfactants or interference on two separate aliquots on immunoassay or confirmation or physical appearance suspect to damage instruments or appearance bottle A and B different and reported 'invalid' and/or screening result of bottle A negative	Not reported
Procedure for rejecting samples (fatal flaws)	Yes	Yes	Yes
Reporting all non-negative test results	Yes	Yes	Yes

(continued overleaf)

Table 11.1 *(continued)*

Described item	AS/NZS 4308-2008	SAMHSA 2008	EWDTS 2002
Reporting quantitative (confirmatory) results	Yes	Only on request of MRO	Always
Quantitative results for confirmed positive opiates >15 000 micrograms/L morphine or codeine	Not described	Yes	Not described
Electronic result transmission (secured)	Not described	Possible	Possible
Results provided verbally	Not described	Not allowed	Not allowed
Semi-annual statistical reports to the (Federal) agency	Not described	Yes	Not described
Archiving of testing-related documents and sample storage			
Storage of records of urine specimens	Min. 2 years	Min. 2 years	For positive samples an agreed period and longer if under legal challenge
Criteria for (secure) short-term sample storage	2–8°C, unit monitored	Max. 7 days at 6°C	At 4°C
Long-term sample storage of positive samples	Freezer, min. 3 months	–20°C, min. 1 year	–15°C, min. 1 year (unless otherwise authorised in writing by the customer)
Quality assurance and quality control			
Criteria for calibrators	Not described	Not described	Yes, use of certified reference materials, demonstrated traceability back to primary standards

Calibration of the initial drug test	According to manufacturer's instructions	Not described	Once a week
System suitability test prior to analysis (screening and confirmation)	Not described	No described	Yes
Each analytical run (initial test) should include:			
(Certified) negative samples	Yes (known negative)	Yes (certified)	Not necessary
Minimum of 1 control at 25% above cut-off	Yes	Yes	Yes
Minimum of 1 control at 25% below cut-off	Yes	Yes	Yes
Calibrators	Not necessary	Yes	Not necessary
% QC samples of total samples	10%	10%	5%
Blind samples of total samples	Not necessary	1% with a minimum of 1	Not necessary
Each analytical run (confirmation) should include:			
(Certified) negative samples	Yes (known negative)	Yes (certified)	No
Minimum of 1 control or calibrator 25% above cut-off	Yes	Yes	No
Minimum of 1 control or calibrator 25% below cut-off	Yes	Yes	No
Positive calibrators and controls	Not described	Yes	No
One control at approximately the cut-off concentration	Yes	No	Yes

(continued overleaf)

Table 11.1 *(continued)*

Described item	AS/NZS 4308-2008	SAMHSA 2008	EWDTS 2002
% QC samples of total samples in a batch	10%	Not described	At least 5%
Requirements for calibrators (confirmation)	Yes, 3-point calibration + blank, use of internal standards	Yes	Yes, min. 3-point calibration; must bracket the cut-off concentration + blank, use of internal (deuterated) standards
Other requirements for confirmatory analysis (acceptance criteria):			
S/N ratio	>3	Not described	Not described
Maximum retention time deviation	±2% of calibrator in SIM *m/z* >50		±3 s or 2%
Criteria for SIM or full scan identification	± 20% (SIM)		Yes
Maximum permitted tolerances for relative ion intensities	± 30% (full scan)		20%
Use of deuterated internal standards	Yes		Yes
Blind sample programme	No	Yes	Not necessary
QC levels	± 25% of the cut-off	± 25% of the cut-off	approx. ± 25% of the cut-off
Acceptance criteria for QC	Both controls shall be within ± 20% of the expected value	Not defined	Not defined
Participation in recognised external proficiency testing programme	Yes	Yes	Participation in an external quality assessment scheme

Determination of the uncertainty of measurement	Yes	Not described	Not described
Review of results			
MRO review of non-negative results	Not described	Yes (licensed physician)	Best carried out by an MRO although a toxicologist is allowed to carry out a toxicology review
Donor request for retest a positive sample (reconfirmation)	Yes, reconfirmation is possible	Through MRO within 72 hours	Requires authorisation of donor and customer
Positive result consistent with legal drug use	Not described	Reported as negative	Reported as negative however only by an MRO (not a toxicologist)
Procedure for a failed to reconfirm result	Not described	Yes	Yes, criteria for reporting the result
Protection of the employee	Not described	By privacy act	By data protection legislation
Individual access to test and laboratory certification results	Not described	By written request	Not described
General certification requirements			
Required quality system	Lab should be accredited	Lab should be certified; forensic toxicologist advice is often needed	Lab should be accredited according to ISO 17025
Required accreditation	Not described	Not described	Accreditation by accrediting body working with the EWDTS guidelines

(continued overleaf)

Table 11.1 *(continued)*

Described item	**AS/NZS 4308-2008**	**SAMHSA 2008**	**EWDTS 2002**
Capability to test for 5 drugs using initial immunoassay and confirmatory GC-MS methods and validity tests	Yes, marijuana, amphetamines, opiates, cocaine, benzodiazepines	Yes, marijuana, amphetamines, opiates, cocaine, phencyclidine	Not described, all combinations possible
Initial and confirmatory drug tests performed at same place	Yes	Yes	Not necessary
Evaluation of PT sample results			
Initial certification procedure of applicant laboratories	No, lab should be accredited	Yes	No, lab should be accredited
Evaluation of laboratories	Participation in external quality assessment scheme Periodic visits by the accrediting body	Yes, e.g. requirement of no false positives; identify and confirm 90% of the total drug challenges; correctly quantitate 80% of total drug challenges at ±20% or ±2 SD of the reference group mean; no false result for validity testing; requirement to identify and confirm 80% of the total specimen validity testing; requirement to correctly quantify 80% of the total specimen validity testing	Participation in external quality assessment scheme Periodic visits by the accrediting body
Results of inadequate performance			
Failure to comply with any aspect of the guidelines	Not described	Revocation or suspension of certification	Not described
List of certified laboratories	No	Yes	No

[a] Optional.

GC-MS, gas chromatography-mass spectrometry; LC-MS, liquid chromatography-mass spectrometry; MRO, medical review officer; POCT, point-of-collection testing; PT, QC, quality control; s.g., specific gravity.

absence of testing for alcohol, the cheapest and the only socially accepted drug, almost worldwide. The cut-off is a very important point in guidelines, as above this value a drug test will be reported as positive, meaning that the donor has used or was exposed to a drug or drugs.

The evolution of guidelines depends strongly on the legislation they have to fulfil, which explains why the SAMSHA guidelines are very elaborate and technical compared with the EWDTS guidelines. The latter are based on the UK guidelines, since the UK has the longest history of workplace drug testing in Europe. This by no means indicates that the EWDTS guidelines are followed by all the 27 European countries.[9] Definitely more needs to be done in Europe, but the aim of these guidelines is to provide a common legally defensible basis for those European countries where workplace drug testing is or will be carried out.

From an international point of view more needs to be done, especially with regard to harmonisation of the cut-offs. This was a general outcome of several speakers and participants at the International Forum for Drug and Alcohol Testing (IFDAT) held on 13–15 April 2010 in Barcelona,[10] who were critical regarding the unrealistically low percentage of confirmed positives, especially in the United States. The challenge to lower the cut-offs and to revise the drug profiles to be tested for requires more sensitive analytical methods, competent toxicologists/MROs and continuous teamwork with human resources personnel, legal personnel and policy makers. Workplace drug testing guidelines should be living documents, open to discussion in the interdisciplinary groups mentioned above, continuously revised, based on the latest scientific developments in order to assure fairer tests and judgements and, above all, safer workplaces.

References

1. Executive Order 12564, Drug-free Federal workplace. *Federal Register* 51(180), 32889–32893, 15 September 1986. www.archives.gov/federal-register/codification/executive-order/12564.html (accessed November 2010).
2. US Department of Labor. Drug-Free Workplace Act of 1988. www.dol.gov/elaws/asp/drugfree/screen4.htm (accessed November 2010).
3. Fort Lewis College (1997) Omnibus Transportation Employee Testing Act, 1991. www.fortlewis.edu/administrative_services/flc_policies/04_human_resources/4-12.aspx (accessed November 2010).
4. Bush DM. The U. S. Mandatory Guidelines for Federal Workplace Drug Testing Programs: Current status and future consideration. *Forensic Sci Int* 2008; 174: 111–119.
5. Ropero-Miller JD, Goldberger BA. *Handbook of Workplace Drug Testing*, 2nd edn. Washington DC: AACC Press, 2009.
6. SAI Global. Procedures for specimen collection and the detection and quantitation of drugs of abuse in urine (AS/NZS 4308 : 2008). http://infostore.saiglobal.com/store/Details.aspx?ProductID=996711 (accessed November 2010).
7. US Department of Health and Human Services. Mandatory Guidelines for Federal Workplace Drug Testing Programs, Federal Register 2008. http://workplace.samhsa.gov/DrugTesting/Level_1_Pages/mandatory_guidelines5_1_10.html (accessed November 2010).

8. European Workplace Drug Testing Society (EWDTS) (2002) European Laboratory Guidelines for Legally Defensible Workplace Drug Testing. www.eapinstitute.com/documents/EWDTSGuidelines.pdf (accessed November 2010).
9. Lillsunde P, Haavanlammi K, Partinen R, Mukala K, Lamberg M. Finnish guidelines for workplace drug testing. *Forensic Sci Int* 2008; 174: 99–102.
10. International Forum for Drug and Alcohol Testing (IFDAT), 13–15 April 2010, Barcelona.

12

Case studies

Per Björklöv

Key points

- In the UK, the concept of drug and alcohol testing was a result of a rail crash in which a train crew member tested positive.
- Initially it was only drugs (and not alcohol) that were routinely tested for on all candidates prior to employment for safety-critical posts and on promotion or transfer to another safety-critical job.
- In Germany, randomised drug screening is prohibited by law, therefore, only pre-employment drug screening can be performed.
- Degussa has developed a training programme about 'the worker, risk factor and reliability' which all managers must undergo.
- In Sweden, the safety committee decided together with the unions that drug testing should be implemented.
- A blood test that indicates high consumption of alcohol and a hair test where a lifestyle that includes drugs can be detected are used for pre-employment screening.
- A random programme of oral fluid tests and a breathalyser are used.
- Expertise was included in the beginning of the policy-making process.

Introduction

Workplace drug testing in Europe differs from country to country. There are as many legal systems as countries. In some countries employers can use drug tests with few legal problems. In other countries random testing is not legal but pre-employment testing is or pre-employment testing is not legal but random testing is. Cultural differences between countries also contribute to how workplace drug testing is used in Europe.

In this chapter three companies tell of their own experiences about workplace drug testing. We have asked them to describe why they decided to start it, how they implemented it, problems along the way and about any benefits they have gained.

The companies come from the UK, Germany and Sweden.

UK: South West Trains Drug and Alcohol Programme

Information provided by Barbara Davenport, Head of Occupational Health, South West Trains.

Introduction

The railway industry, formally British Rail (BR), has undertaken drug and alcohol testing since 1993 and has a wealth of experience in this field. The concept of drug and alcohol testing was introduced as a result of the Transport and Works Act 1992, which in part followed the 1991 Cannon Street rail crash in which a train crew member tested positive for drugs.

It is a criminal offence under the Transport and Works Act 1992 for anyone in control of the movement of a train or working in a maintenance capacity to do so when unfit to carry out that work because of impairment through either alcohol or drugs.

The first published British Rail Alcohol and Drugs Policy was produced in July 1993, this was superseded by a Railway Group Standard on Alcohol and Drugs, which was published in August 1996 for implementation from December 1996. This has since been reviewed and republished, the last revising being December 2008. When the drug and alcohol testing regime was first implemented it was in a very different form to how it looks today.

Initially it was only drugs that were routinely tested prior to employment for all candidates for safety-critical posts and on promotion or transfer to another safety-critical job. At the same time it was decided to randomly test annually 5% of the safety-critical employees across the network. This was an administrative nightmare which at the time involved running a national database to select the individuals to be tested, then sending a letter to them via their manager which was handed to the employee no earlier than 48 hours before the test. They then attended for testing and returned to work on their next shift. The results were sent to their local personnel department once received in occupational health (OH). Again it was only drug testing that was performed randomly.

The other type of testing undertaken was 'for cause' screening to find out whether drugs or alcohol were a causal factor in an accident or incident, or for behaviour giving cause to suspect that a person was unfit to continue work.

The only alcohol testing that took place was either for behavioural reasons or for cause following some type of operational incident.

Employee awareness

South West Trains was privatised on 6 February 1996, and continued to implement the BR Drug and Alcohol Policy, along with the testing methods they had adopted.

As part of the South West Trains safety case, the company drug and alcohol policy was comprehensively reviewed and revised in 2001 and rebriefed to all employees.

The policy was briefed as promoting a safe and efficient workplace, and to enable the company to demonstrate due diligence under the relevant legislation, but more than that to fulfil our duty to both employees, customers, the general public and shareholders to run as safe a railway as possible, which includes, where possible, preventing risks caused by the consumption of alcohol or drugs at work. It was easy to demonstrate to employees that a clear link exists between the use of alcohol and drugs and safety.

The policy was put in place with the aim of preventing employees reporting for duty, or attempting to report for duty while unfit due to alcohol or drug use, and also that neither alcohol or illegal drugs are consumed or used while on duty.

The policy applied to all South West Trains employees, all employees of other companies operating on lines within the South West Trains operating areas, and all contractors and others working on South West Trains premises.

Not only were we briefing employees on use of alcohol or illegal drugs, but also on the correct use of prescribed and over-the-counter medications that can affect performance, particularly antidepressants, sleeping pills, some antihistamines, analgesics and some cough and cold medicines. It is the responsibility of the individual employee to inform their manager of any medication they have consumed in order that they can be verified as safe to take while in the workplace.

All staff are aware that they will be tested for drugs at their pre-employment medical. This is undertaken in the OH department under chain-of-custody arrangements. They are informed that on promotion or transfer to a safety-critical post they will be tested, and also the reasons for post-incident, for cause and behavioural testing. All safety-critical employees are aware that at least 10% of that population will be randomly tested annually.

All employees are aware of the consequences of either producing a positive drug and/or alcohol test or refusing to undertake a test when requested to do so.

An individual will probably be dismissed if they have a positive drug or alcohol test.

The briefing given to all employees, and for which they sign to confirm they have been briefed on is as follows:

You WILL be dismissed if you

- *Test positive for drugs, for which there is no legitimate medical need for either the use or quantity of drugs detected*
- *Test positive for alcohol with a breath test of greater than 13 µg/100 ml breath or 39 mg/100 ml urine*
- *Refuse to take an alcohol or drugs test without good cause*
- *Report or try to report for duty when unfit through alcohol or drugs*
- *Consume alcohol or drugs whilst on duty*
- *Decline or discontinue without good cause an approved course of treatment for an alcohol or drugs problem.*

In addition, if you seek help for an alcohol or drugs problem AFTER you have been called for a test, AND you fail that test – you will ALMOST always be dismissed.

Changes to random drug screening process

At the same time the policy was reviewed, changes were made to the random process. It was recognised that the 48-hour notice period given to individuals would allow most illegal substances to be excreted from the body if the individual abstained from use. In order to be able to demonstrate continued due diligence as an employer we decided to introduce unannounced random drug and alcohol screening.

Moral and ethical considerations

Controversy often surrounds the need to achieve the goal of a drug-free workplace. By actively promoting drug and alcohol free values and norms, while carefully controlling conditions under which unannounced random drug and alcohol screening takes place, the organisation hopes to foster both employee and public trust. Justification for unannounced drug and alcohol screening comes from the assertion that impairment is not always physically evident. It is also important to remember that unannounced testing also has a deterrent effect.

Employees have individual rights and civil liberties, including rights to privacy and confidentiality. The balance will shift depending on what work they do, in safety-sensitive areas where there is a significant risk to other workers or the public, a more proactive approach to testing should be taken.

Changes to process

We continue to use pre-employment testing, and all candidates are tested, irrespective of the post they have applied for, on promotion or transfer to a safety-critical post, and for cause, post incident or for behavioural reasons.

We fundamentally changed the way we undertook random testing by undertaking the testing on site. A collection officer goes to test individuals at one of our workplaces, rather than calling the employee up to the OH department for testing.

The contracted agency for our drug and alcohol screening undertakes random selection of site and personnel to be tested at a date and time decided by them. Once these details are selected, the local HR manager is informed and a responsible manager appointed to oversee the testing on the day. A list of all safety-critical employee pay numbers is sent to the lab not less than 24 hours before the testing is due. At least 10% of those eligible for testing are selected and the company are informed who will be tested.

The responsible manager is accountable for allocation of suitable accommodation in which to undertake the testing, and to ensure the selected employees attend the screening. The collection officer attends, takes the samples and the individuals go back to work. One significant difference from the BR policy is that the random testing process includes testing for alcohol and drugs, not just drug testing.

The results are sent to the OH department, from where they are inputted into the HR database and disseminated to HR/local managers.

Eight years on from instigating this process for unannounced random drug and alcohol screening, the procedure has been refined to reduce the amount of administration behind it. The process is essentially unchanged, apart from the fact that the collection officer independently selects the employees for testing once he or she arrives on site. This change is a result of problems encountered when individual employees have been selected for testing, but are in fact out working on a train when the collection is due to be taken.

It is important to note that the trade unions were consulted regarding changes to the policy, which resulted in them supporting the changes and this was then communicated to our employees, their members.

Assistance for employees who declare a problem

As part of our drug and alcohol policy, we do offer assistance for anyone who declares a problem which they want help to deal with. There are several routes that individuals can use to make the initial declaration:

- tell their local manager/HR manager who will arrange a referral to OH
- tell OH directly that they have a problem and wish to be helped
- declare their problem to the company Employee Assistance Programme, who are instructed to refer back to OH.

Once an individual has come forward they will be assessed by the OH adviser and/or OH physician. Informed consent will be obtained to discuss rehabilitation with a nominated line manager. This is essential when looking at returning the individual back to the workplace. A treatment plan will be devised to include:

- detox if necessary
- referral to professional drug and alcohol team
- suitable alternative work placement found (if necessary)
- regular review with OH.

Once a treatment plan has been agreed an employee contract will be drawn up, the core elements of which include:

- details of detox plan (if appropriate)
- minimum attendance with key worker
- minimum attendance with support groups (if appropriate)
- the need to be tested randomly for drug and alcohol
- blood tests (if appropriate)
- reviews with OH
- consent
- boundaries.

Time spans for care are difficult to judge as each case is dealt with on its individual merits, however we would usually look for a 12-month period of abstinence before allowing the individual back into a safety-critical post.

As is often the case, there may be periods of relapse for the individual involved. During the initial rehabilitation period discretion is used, however we do make it clear to these employees that they will only be supported once through the whole rehabilitation process by the company, and if at any time during the process they have a positive drug or alcohol screen they will be dismissed.

Conclusion

Drug and alcohol policies and testing have been part of the UK railway industry since 1992, and on the whole the concept of drug and alcohol-free workplace is well embedded in the whole of the railway industry and culture.

This is a crucial policy as part of our suite of policies and procedures, which make up our safety case, and as such, has a high profile within the company. We will continue to review and revise our policy and testing regime, and are particularly interested in watching how methods of testing are evolving with the use of new technology.

Germany: Degussa policy with respect to drug screening

Information provided by Rolf Breitstadt, Occupational Health Physician, Degussa.

Introduction

Evonik Degussa, formerly known as Degussa, has been involved in the topic of pre-employment drug testing since 1996. The motive to do so was to some extent the spectacular, open drug scene in Frankfurt and other big cities, which inevitably made the drug problem quite visible for everyone to see.

At that time the drug problem was not perceived as a cross-social problem on an intra-enterprise level, but as the exclusive problem of certain marginal groups.

Based on this high prevalence of drug use, it was decided to collaborate with the forensic medicine group in Frankfurt and a renowned wholesale laboratory in order to make drug screening possible as a component of the routine pre-employment medical examinations.

In Germany, randomised drug screenings are prohibited by law, therefore, only pre-employment drug screening can be performed.

Annual reports outline the number of drug tests performed as well as the number of positive result rates.

Identifying patterns in illicit drug use: is this the tip of the iceberg?

It does not come as a surprise that the number of positive drug screening result rates reflects the pattern of drug consumption in the region, nor is it surprising that, after having initially observed an elevated rate of positive findings we are now facing a regional variations, but overall experiencing a 1% average positive rate when it comes to pre-employment testing. This is still a remarkable number of positive test results taking into consideration that the prospective employees knew prior to reporting for their medical examination that drug testing would be conducted during their pre-employment medical examination.

While the initial goal was not to achieve a drug-free company, we succeeded in setting a clear expectation and impression. All things considered, the drug screening has now developed into a routine part of the examination. It is now expected that drug users will be identified and dealt with, meaning that dealing with drug abusers is now taken for granted.

Drug screening during the pre-employment medical examination is no more and no less than a serious statement by the company that it is not willing to accept illicit drug consumption and the resulting adverse effects at our work facilities. It means that a high standard has been established for safety, even if it means not following the general social trend.

Indicative drug testing confined by limits

Considering that forensic toxicologists state there is a 7% incidence rate of compensated drug consumers, we realised that only very few people are sent to our medical services because of peculiar behavioural traits or on suspicion of suffering from chronic or acute drug effects. We have therefore developed a training programme which all managers at all major Degussa sites must enter. A publication dealing with the subject of drug effects, behaviour changes in general and safety aspects, entitled 'The Worker-Risk Factor and Reliability?', was distributed to all participants during the training.

We also instructed and motivated the management to concentrate on tracking peculiar behavioural traits and encouraging the employee to pay a visit to the medical service for further clarification or evaluation. Nevertheless we have to face the fact that, despite our best efforts, the 'response rate' in this context is still low. There are various possible reasons for this, for example, the problem of drug users may not be present in the company or the drug users don't show any behaviour changes while in the working environment.

In Germany we simply lack investigations such as those that exist, for example, in the United States, where compulsory or mandatory drug testing is performed after accidents.

Drug screening upon initial hiring

Preliminary physical examinations upon hiring serve to verify a potential employee's fitness for the tasks he or she is to perform in the context of the position for which the candidate has applied. The tests conducted depend on the job-related demands, specific to the applicant's aspired position. Since June 1996 Degussa AG has been screening for illegal drug use as a part of these preliminary physical examinations. Aspiring employees receive leaflets that inform them of such a drug test in advance and they must declare their consent to the test in writing. As a result of such advance notice we initially observed that a number of individuals avoided the preliminary exam by not showing up. Currently, fewer than 2% of those screened test positive for drug use. By now the company's drug policy is known to young applicants, which means that we have experienced a continual decrease in the number of positive test results among aspiring employees.

By consenting to drug screening an employee actively contributes to the promotion of his or her personal and general safety. In any event they agree to an encroachment upon their personal privacy, a fact which the company acknowledges and appreciates.

The current legal situation permits drug screenings only in the context of pre-hiring physicals. Random drug test are currently not allowed by German law and are therefore not conducted.

Since regular drug users do not manifest visible signs of impairment, respond in socially well-adapted ways and do not behave in typically conspicuous ways, they can only be identified through drug testing. However, even random testing could not determine with any degree of certainty or guarantee that a particular workplace is 'drug free'. Nevertheless we have reason to believe, because our workforce mirrors the general population, that there are between 5 and 7% of drug users within our workforce. We are also aware that in the absence of the ability to conduct random drug screening in Germany, we are able to only partially respond to the problems presented by drug users.

Guidelines for the implementation of drug screening programmes

Every endeavour to screen for drugs represents a particularly sensitive situation, as it always constitutes an encroachment upon an employee's personal rights and since positive results will generally have far-reaching consequences, ultimately having legal ramifications.

In view of the legal difficulties in particular, quality is of utmost importance. To ensure that tests are conducted in a reliable and proper manner, we have outlined mandatory guidelines which will ensure that legal stipulations are adhered to while the personal rights of employees are respected.

These guidelines detail:

1. The assessment criteria
2. The handling of samples with respect to ensuring continuous surveillance
3. The documentation of results, as well as their reporting and filing
4. Selecting a drug-screening lab
5. The quality of the confirmatory tests, so that they will measure up to the standards for forensic evidence
6. Communication between human resources and test persons

Our primary aim with respect to these drug screenings conducted during pre-hiring physicals is not to determine whether a given case is one of 'drug addiction' versus 'occasional' or 'controlled' use. It is not possible to do so given the constraints of the pre-hiring physicals and proactive testing.

Training management is necessary

In response to the sensitive nature of drug testing, we have initiated a mandatory training programme for management personnel to provide them with the knowledge and skills needed to deal with the problem of drugs in the workplace in a competent manner.

Our research into this issue has shown that the primary demand placed upon management (i.e. to inquire into conspicuous behaviour among employees) puts particular demands on their leadership skills. In the context of their leadership role, management sees itself confronted with a whole range of human behaviours, including drug and alcohol consumption. An important task is therefore to observe employee behaviour, interpret it adeptly and to follow up anomalies without compromising personal rights or management's integrity.

Since anomalous behaviour is usually not attributable to drug use, a training programme was necessary to provide management with the skills needed to intervene through dialogue. The aim is not to put management in a position to diagnose whether drug use is an issue or not, but to enable it to deliberately direct the employee in question to occupational health services so that the latter may clarify the circumstances underlying the behaviour. Such a programme also was needed to lay the foundations for a more informed discussion with employees on the issue of drugs and addiction.

We have therefore created a brochure that attempts to break down the complex issue of 'who is a risk' (i.e. when a person becomes a risk to him- or herself or to others with respect to 'safety'). In addition, a mandatory training seminar was instituted for all management personnel at all locations in Germany.

Sweden: Drug testing, case study from a Swedish transportation company, Flygbussarna Airport Coaches

Background

Flygbussarna (Airport Coaches) is a service supplier of bus transportation. They offer bus services to and from all the major airports in Sweden. The company has its headquarters in Stockholm. The company has about 380 employees.

The current alcohol and drug policy is from the year 2006. The aim was a drug-free environment when discussions started about the drug policy and tests in the company. A combination of bus driving and a use of drugs and/or alcohol is a major contribution to road injuries and fatalities.

Other reasons for drug tests are to prevent illness and injury at the workplace, and also to create a good working environment for all employees. The prevalence of drug use in society was another reason – if drugs are available, there is a greater chance they will be found in the workplace as well.

How it was implemented

The decision to implement drug testing was taken in the safety committee together with the unions. The human resources (HR) department was responsible for the implementation. It started with training for the HR department and the unions. The purpose of the training was to create a knowledge platform so that a discussion and planning of the procedures could take place. The training was carried out by an expert on drugs and alcohol, testing procedures and policy making.

After the training the HR department and the unions agreed on what test methods should be used, what drugs should be tested, which staff categories should be included in the test programme, how the random selection should be structured, procedures if a test is positive. It was also emphasised that this was not a programme to get rid of the employees with an alcohol or drug problem.

The programme should help employees with alcohol and drug problems as well as deter them from drinking too much or using illegal drugs. The programme includes the entire staff, not just bus drivers. Two staff members from the HR department were selected to be designated employer representatives. This is a function that should make the alcohol and drug programme effective and ensure the workplace achieves the aim of the policy. The designated employer representatives get an in-depth training in collection procedures, how to take care of positive test results, how to handle refusals, etc. They then qualify as experts within the company in this area of expertise.

An alcohol and drug policy was then written and approved.

An overview of the programme

The programme includes:

A pre-employment testing
B random testing
C testing after incidents
D suspicious cause testing.

A Pre-employment testing

All new employees are drug tested. We test for both overconsumption of alcohol and use of drugs. For alcohol we use a blood test called carbohydrate-deficient transferrin (CDT). The CDT test shows if the donor has had an overconsumption for a week or longer in the last six weeks. For drugs we use a hair test. This hair test shows if the donor has used drugs regularly within the last three months. If either of these tests are positive the donor has the possibility to explain and/or challenge the test result. The company's norm is not to hire people who have tested positive.

B Random testing

We have a test quota at 25% of the employees per year. At start we had a random testing programme where an external provider gave us a list of employees who should be tested each month. This selection method did not fit our administration so well and therefore another selection method was implemented after a while.

The current selection method is that the collection provider makes a random selection of which site should be tested and what date and time. The collector comes to the site and tests the drivers that come in to the site at that time. The number to be randomly selected is decided before the testing takes place.

At the random testing we use a breathalyser for measuring possible alcohol and oral fluid testing for illegal drugs.

C Testing after incidents

If an accident/incident occurs, the employees involved are tested. Tests used are breathalyser for alcohol and oral fluid for illegal drugs.

D Suspicious cause testing

Supervisors are educated and trained to detect drug use and overconsumption of alcohol and/or if the employee behaves in a suspicious manner. In that case the supervisor contacts the designated employer representative, who then contacts the suspected person and evaluates if it is necessary to order a test.

Under these circumstances we usually use a more extensive test panel that also screens for legal drugs. Methods used depend on the situation but can include blood, hair and oral fluid testing. Consideration will, of course, be taken to medication that the employee may be taking.

How we handle test results

Negative test result

If the test result is negative the test result will not be sent out to the donor.

Positive test result

If the test result is positive a medical review officer (MRO) will call the donor and discuss the test result. If it is a confirmed positive test result, a discussion/questioning will take place between the employee, the manager and the rehab coordinator at the company. Rehabilitation is undertaken according to the company policy. Only employees are offered rehabilitation by the company. Job applicants are not offered rehabilitation.

Refusals

The company and the unions are in agreement with the policy and therefore make it difficult for the employees to refuse the undertaking of a drug test.

This has just happened a few times. After discussions with the designated employer representative the employees have accepted the test in all cases. The applicant has always the possibility to refuse, but will not be offered a job if he or she refuses.

Summary

As we developed the policy together with the union we have had very few problems. The policy is well received by the majority of all employees and they understand the importance of having such a policy.

We have had positive test results among applicants and among our employees both for alcohol and drugs, however, we believe that the most important thing is the result of having this rather stiff policy which will act as a means of deterrence for the abuse of drugs, alcohol and/or drinking too much.

We think that applicants with drug-related abuse problems will not consider looking for jobs at our company and that the users we perhaps have had have stopped or use less.

The alcohol and drug programme was not implemented for the purpose of finding as many abusers as possible. It was implemented to deter people from using drugs or drinking too much.

One very positive result is that we do not have as many accidents since the implementation of the policy.

Advice

A good recommendation is to include expertise in the beginning of the policy making process and to get as many facts as possible. It is very important to understand how to do things, what is necessary and then obtain good examples from other working places. This may be a valuable tool in how to avoid poor or ineffective programmes or methods.

13

Australian perspectives

John H Lewis

Key points

- Workplace drug testing is well established in Australia's heavy industries.
- The main aim of drug testing is to manage risk of accident or injury in the workplace.
- There are various Occupational Health and Safety Acts in Australia.
- There is a responsibility for managers to comply with these Acts.
- Urine testing has been the preferred drug testing technique in identifying risk of drug-induced impairment.
- There is continuing controversy from union groups as how to best measure impairment.
- Many employees oppose urine testing, but would agree to oral fluid testing.
- Despite Australian Standards for both urine and oral fluid, there is concern that current on-site devices for cannabis in oral fluid will fail to adequately address risk of impairment in the workplace.

Introduction

Drug testing within sections of the Australian workforce is now a well-established practice, particularly in the primary resources industries, such as coal, minerals and petrochemical. Australia is a major world supplier of raw materials, including wool, beef, uranium, bauxite, gas, iron ore and coal, and as such employs a large workforce, much of it in remote parts of the country. It has been suggested that worker isolation, combined with a high disposable income, may contribute to substance use in these environments; however, there is no evidence to suggest that employees of these industries have a greater disposition to using illegal or recreational drugs than employees in major cities or people in the general Australian community. Unlike the United States, there are no equivalent federal or state government laws on the use of illicit drugs in the workplace. Implementation of random drug testing has, and continues, to be based on principles of occupational health and safety.

Background

Although workplace drug testing commenced in an ad hoc manner around 1994, during the 1980s, a need was recognised to ensure personnel involved in safety critical tasks were free from the influence of drugs and alcohol.[1] Although there are scant data on drug-related fatalities or injuries within the workplace, one case was widely reported. Following a fatality involving a driver of a haul truck at a large mine site in Western Australia, a coronial inquest found the driver had a large concentration of tetrahydrocannabinol (THC) in her blood as well as smoking implements in the vehicle.[2]

The impetus to introduce random drug testing, particularly in the mining industry, arose from interpretations of Mine Safety Acts within each state. For example, the objectives of the Western Australia Mines Safety and Inspection Act 1994 are, inter alia, to promote and secure the safety and health of persons engaged in mining operations; and to protect employers and employees against risks associated with the mines and operations by eliminating those risks.[3] However, although a small number of industries commenced random drug testing in the period 1994–2000, it was the release of legislation in each state and territory from 2000 onwards that empowered employers to seriously consider random and 'for cause' drug testing.

WorkCover NSW and its equivalent in other parts of Australia is a statutory authority with responsibility for ensuring safe work practices. The organisation has been responsible for publication of the Occupational Health and Safety Act 2000.[4] This Act, binding on all employees and employers, has, inter alia, objectives to:

- **a** secure and promote the health, safety and welfare of people at work,
- **b** protect people at a place of work against risks to health or safety arising out of the activities of persons at work,
- **c** promote a safe and healthy work environment for people at work that protects them from injury and illness and that is adapted to their physiological and psychological needs,
- **d** provide for consultation and cooperation between employers and employees in achieving the objects of this Act,
- **e** ensure that risks to health and safety at a place of work are identified, assessed and eliminated or controlled.

Many industries throughout Australia have introduced a duty of care policy by taking measures to reduce the risk of accident or death due to drug and alcohol-affected employees and thereby ensuring compliance with this Act. Although there has been much focus on identifying drug use within the mining, steel and petrochemical industries, there is evidence of potential drug problems in such diverse areas of winemaking[5] and deep sea fishing.[6,7]

In Australia there have been three competing forces affecting the introduction of drug testing programmes. First, as discussed earlier, there is an Act of Parliament requiring employers to minimise risk of accident to employees by eliminating or controlling for hazards (drug-affected behaviour). Second, many union movements have objected to drug testing, claiming that as urine testing cannot identify impairment, it has no place in the workplace. Third, a report by the Privacy Committee of New South Wales[8] concluded that workplace drug testing was privacy invasive, in terms of physical privacy and information privacy. The report expressed concern at the inaccuracy of testing, but conceded that as workplace safety was of such importance, then, in some circumstances, workplace drug testing for safety reasons may be justified.

Objections to urine drug testing based on privacy have largely been overturned in a number of court cases, for example, *Pioneer Construction Materials Pty Ltd* v. *Transport Workers Union of Australia*.[9] More recently, the Victorian Law Reform Commission, in a report on workplace privacy,[10] while deeming drug and alcohol testing to be inherently intrusive, recommended regulation by mandatory codes. Importantly, in the Workplace Privacy Act 2005,[10] the Commission declared that an employer had the right to undertake certain actions, including drug and alcohol testing, if there were reasonable grounds for believing that a worker's non-work-related activity may have a direct and serious impact on the business or reputation of the employer. In other words, employees who take recreational drugs on a regular basis, but outside their hours of employment, may still pose a risk to the organisation.

Contemporaneously with the issues of reliability and privacy in drug testing, Standards Australia produced AS 4308[11] in 1995. Apart from the United States' SAMHSA Guidelines,[12] Australian Standard AS 4308 was the world's first national standard for medico-legal drug testing. The document was revised in 2001 as a joint Australian/New Zealand Standard AS/NZS 4308 and has since been extensively revised in 2008.[13]

Although not mandatory, companies wishing to implement drug testing have had a choice of testing procedures since 1995. In Australia, laboratories must be accredited to the level of testing offered to the public (i.e. either clinical or medico-legal toxicological testing). The National Association of Testing Authorities (NATA)[14] is the sole body in Australia responsible for laboratory accreditation. Assessment is conducted every 2–3 years by a staff field officer and a scientific expert in the field. In order to gain accreditation, a laboratory must demonstrate compliance with requirements under ISO

17025[15] if the laboratory undertakes chemical analysis or ISO 15189[16] if the laboratory is involved in medical/pathology testing. Acceptable criteria for accreditation includes, inter alia, robust methodology, traceable documentation, acceptable performance in quality assurance programmes, quality control and staffing. It is perhaps the latter that is of some concern. Although there are good data indicating satisfactory performance by the majority of Australian laboratories accredited to undertake workplace drug testing,[17] many laboratory personnel have little experience in publications, provision of expert opinion or court appearances, all of which are prerequisites for accreditation to the Standard. Thus, while the workplace can be reassured of the accuracy of laboratory results, there is often a paucity of experts prepared to provide opinion in a court of law.

Drug use in the Australian workplace

Workplace testing programmes opt for the drug groups included in the Australian Standard (i.e. amphetamine-type substances, benzodiazepines, cannabis, cocaine and opiates). Although there are no officially published data, laboratory test results indicate the most commonly found drugs in random testing programmes to be cannabis, methylamphetamine and codeine. Apart from the first two, which are illicit, codeine is the most common therapeutic drug found. Preparations containing codeine up to approximately 15 mg are available in Australia without a prescription. Codeine use presents two problems in workplace drug testing. First, as on-site testing is used throughout Australia, many tests show a positive reaction to opiates. As the majority of workplace drug and alcohol policies stipulate that employees cannot return to work until a presumptive positive test has been confirmed, there is significant pressure on laboratories to confirm the opiate test as soon as possible. Invariably, codeine is identified.

Second, although the Australian cut-off for opiates is set at 300 ng/mL (micrograms/L), raising it to 2000 ng/mL, as was done in the United States, could eliminate up to 30% of codeine positives, which are, in general, merely a nuisance. However, as urinary levels of codeine are often found in the hundreds to thousands of micrograms per litre, simply raising the cut-off to an arbitrary value is of dubious merit. As described earlier, virtually all opiate positives derive from codeine use and therefore one can conclude there is currently very little evidence for heroin use within industries currently undergoing random drug testing. There is also very little evidence for cocaine use within these industries. Laboratory results are supported by data produced from the Illicit Drug Reporting System (IDRS)[18] that indicates there is very little cocaine use by intravenous drug users in Australia other than in Sydney.

Until recently, pseudoephedrine has been the second most common legal drug used within the workforce. In general, like codeine, this is a nuisance drug as it has been part of common cold and flu preparations. Fortunately, both with on-site screening tests and certain laboratory-based immunoassays,[19] there is often a deliberate poor cross-reactivity of methylamphetamine tests to pseudoephedrine. Use of these newer immunoassays has significantly reduced identification of pseudoephedrine and thus costs in confirmatory testing. Furthermore, because of problems of pseudoephedrine diversion for methylamphetamine production, over-the-counter cold and flu medications no longer contain pseudoephedrine, and this will further reduce the number of nuisance positives.

Laboratory interpretation

The interpretation of cannabis, methylamphetamine and benzodiazepine results is, in general, relatively straightforward. However, there are risks of inaccurate interpretation when codeine is detected. Although the metabolism of codeine and morphine has been well documented,[20] interpretation of their presence in urine relies on accurate quantitation of the deconjugated metabolites. Although quality assurance programmes are used to monitor the accuracy of laboratory tests, they tend to submit free drugs that have been spiked into urine, rather than challenge laboratories with realistic metabolites that are found as glucuronide conjugates. Thus, while laboratories can easily identify morphine and codeine, they often have poor hydrolysis techniques and frequently underestimate one or both of these drugs, leading to a misinterpretation of what a person actually took. While morphine is relatively easy to hydrolyse,[21] codeine requires more vigorous conditions.[22] Results from the Austox proficiency programme,[17] have shown that when urine samples pooled from codeine users are submitted to laboratories, a wide range of concentrations are often reported. An example from such a challenge is shown in Figure 13.1.

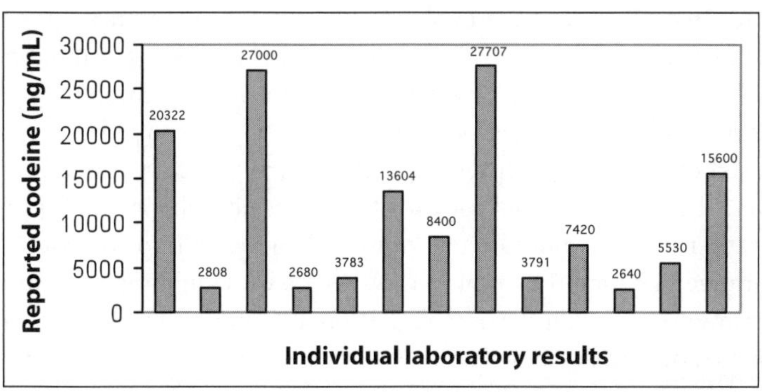

Figure 13.1 Example of variation in reported codeine results when challenged with pooled patient urine containing codeine glucuronide. (Source: Austox proficiency programme 2005.)

On-site drug testing in Australia

The vast majority of industries undergoing random drug testing utilise some form of on-site screening, either a lateral flow colloidal gold device or a cup type. Most, but not all devices use cut-offs similar to those in AS/NZS 4308. There are both advantages and disadvantages of organisations opting for on-site testing. First, as many industries are isolated from major cities, the use of on-site devices allows employees to return to work immediately following a negative result. A disadvantage of these devices is that many of them are more sensitive than their equivalent laboratory-based screening test. This is a contentious issue between some laboratories and on-site testers. One argument is that on-site devices are designed to be more sensitive or 'aggressive' than their nominal cut-off, in order to minimise false negatives. The counter argument is that there are some inconsistencies in a small number of cases when urine samples are further subjected to a laboratory's immunoassay as was required in previous Australian Standard protocols.

Unfortunately, once an on-site device shows a 'positive' reaction to a drug group, it becomes difficult for management to accept a negative laboratory report. Often, they question the accuracy of either the on-site device or the laboratory testing. Under earlier versions of AS 4308 it was mandatory to perform a laboratory screening test following an on–site 'presumptive positive'. Under current guidelines, this is optional; the laboratory is now only required to perform mass spectrometry following an on-site screening test. While this procedure marginally speeds up turn-around, it also removes ambiguity when screening tests are around the cut-off (when on-site screen is positive and laboratory immunoassay is below cut-off). The downside is that there is less consistency in screening. Removal of mandatory laboratory-based screening with multi-point calibration and proper controls effectively creates an unlevel playing field for employees in different industries subjected to different screening devices.

In Australia, arguments have been made over this issue of inconsistency in on-site testing. Cut-offs have evolved over many years of urine testing and there is international agreement for many of these values (e.g. cannabinoids at 50 ng/mL). A cut-off is a value set by the operator of an analyser by way of calibration, and there are defined limits of acceptability for batches of samples, based on calibration curves, quality controls and absorbance changes. However, the term 'cut-offs' for on-site devices is perhaps an inappropriate name; rather devices should have 'nominal' values due to the wide concentration range in which they function. Whereas we would reject a laboratory-based immunoassay run if controls fell outside, for example, 20% of their target value, on-site devices need only show a negative reaction at 25% of the cut-off and a positive reaction at 150% of the cut-off.[23] In other words, on-site devices, by their very design, have much wider latitude for indicating positives or negatives than laboratory-based immunoassays. Does this matter? From a management perspective, perhaps not, but for employees, there remains an inconsistency in testing protocols, which catches some and allows others to escape detection.

In order to provide a more consistent approach to screening, AS/NZS 4308 now requires on-site devices to be verified by an independent and duly accredited laboratory. This process involves testing a minimum of 10 urine specimens spiked with the target analyte in each class at –30% and +25% of the screening cut-offs. Using mass spectrometry, the Standard deems that not more than a total of 10% shall return either a positive at –30% of the cut-off and/or a negative at +25% of the cut-off.

Extent of drug testing in Australia

It is difficult to calculate the extent of workplace drug testing in Australia. Unofficial sources suggest over 500 000 tests per annum are conducted, about half of these utilising on-site devices. With a total Australian population of approximately 22 million, these numbers imply 1 person in 44 is being drug tested. This is not in fact the case; the majority of professions and industries do not undertake drug testing.

Alternative matrix testing in the workplace

Although many industries have accepted the introduction of random urine drug testing, there is still some resistance to its implementation. However, some employees have argued for the introduction of oral fluid testing as a preferred alternative to urine. Their arguments are generally based on an assumption that first, saliva is less invasive than urine and second, as urine cannot measure impairment, saliva testing would be more appropriate. The issue of intrusiveness (of urine) and claims that urine testing cannot identify impairment, continue to cloud the real issues of whether oral fluid is the more appropriate matrix for minimising a risk of accident or injury due to drug use within the Australian workforce.

A minority of industries already use oral fluid testing in their programmes. Many had trialled it and reverted to urine, while others are satisfied that it meets their needs. As oral fluid screening devices are currently too insensitive to cannabis,[24–28] from a risk management perspective, oral fluid testing may fail to identify a large number of cannabis users within the workforce, and this could actually encourage employees to smoke marijuana more frequently and even in the workplace.

In 2006 an Australian Standard for oral fluid testing was released;[29] however, its impact on workplace drug testing practices will not be known for some time. As technology improves, oral fluid testing will have an established place in routine medico-legal drugs of abuse testing. At present, for industries wishing to comply with their duty of care obligations under the various Occupational Health and Safety Acts, urine testing appears to be the most appropriate means of reducing risk of drug-related accidents in the workplace.

The impact of random drug testing in the workplace

Most drug testing is conducted at mine sites and other high-risk environments; and as employees are often paid high salaries in these jobs, there is an incentive to cease recreational drug use or risk losing their livelihood. There is some anecdotal evidence that implementation of random drug testing has had a marked effect on reducing the incidence of drug use in these industries.

The future

With the release of an Australian Standard for both oral fluid testing and a revised Standard for urine testing, there will be some developments in existing drugs of abuse testing procedures. Although oral fluid testing will appeal to those sections of the workforce opposed to urine testing, there will be the unresolved issues of sensitivity, laboratory accreditation, satisfactory performance in quality assurance programmes and interpretation of results. In time, it is hoped that most of these problems will be resolved and alternative matrix testing will be a routine tool in substance abuse testing.

Laboratory-based urine testing has significantly matured, with the release of an updated Standard and some confirmatory test cut-offs lowered to reflect an increase in recreational drug use. There will be greater emphasis on validity testing and there will be better control over the use of on-site screening devices. In Australia, the need to comply with occupational health and safety legislation has been, and continues to be, a major contributing factor in the implementation of random workplace drug testing.

Conclusion

Workplace drug testing is now commonplace in many industries throughout Australia. With a requirement for independent verification of urine on-site devices for those wishing to comply with Australian Standard AS/NZS 4308, there is greater confidence in testing procedures. However, there are on-going arguments, often in the industrial courts, regarding the relative merits of urine versus oral fluid testing. The mandatory requirements to comply with occupational health and safety legislation and the availability of good scientific data on the strengths and weaknesses of both types of devices should enable organisations to select the most appropriate form of testing.

References

1. Dell G. In: *Safety in Australia* 23 No. 2 August 2000. Adelaide: Walsh Media Services.
2. BHP Iron Ore Pty Ltd and Construction, Mining, Energy, Timberyards Sawmills and Woodworkers Union of Australia Western Australian Branch. Western Australian Industrial Relations Commission No. CR 274 of 1997, 19 June 1998.
3. Western Australia Mines Safety and Inspection Act 1994. www.austlii.edu.au/au/legis/wa/consol_act/msaia1994276/s3.html (accessed December 2010).
4. New South Wales Government. WorkCover Authority of NSW (2003) Occupational Health and Safety Act (NSW) 2000. www.workcover.nsw.gov.au (accessed December 2010).
5. New South Wales Government. WorkCover Authority of NSW. Wine Industry code of practice for workplace health and safety. WorkCover Authority of NSW Cat. No. 129 January 1999. www.workcover.nsw.gov.au/formspublications/publications/Pages/WC00129 (accessed December 2010).
6. Carruthers Susan, Boots K, Midford R. Perceived and self-reported licit and illicit drug use among fishing industry workers on the mid-north coast of Western Australia. *Drug Alcohol Rev* 2002; 21: 357–361.
7. Evans A, Tait R, Harvey P, Newbury J. Recreational drug use within the employees of the mariculture and seafood industry in South Australia. *Drug Alcohol Rev* 2005; 24: 67–68.
8. Drug Testing in the Workplace. The Privacy Committee of New South Wales. No. 64 October 1992. Sydney.
9. *Pioneer Construction Materials Pty Ltd v. Transport Workers' Union of Australia, Industrial Union of Workers, Western Australian Branch.* Western Australian Industrial Relations Commission 2003 WAIRC 10049.
10. Workplace Privacy Final Report. Victorian Law Reform Commission Melbourne October 2005.
11. Standards Australia. Procedures for the collection, detection and quantitation of drugs of abuse in urine. AS 4308 : 1995. www.standards.org.au (accessed December 2010).
12. Mandatory Guidelines for Federal Workplace Drug Testing Programs. Federal Register 53 FR 11979 April 1988.
13. Standards Australia. Procedures for specimen collection and the detection and quantitation of drugs of abuse in urine. AS/NZS 4308 : 2008.
14. National Association of Testing Authorities Sydney. www.nata.asn.au (accessed December 2010).
15. ISO/IEC 17025: 2005. www.iso.org (accessed December 2010).
16. ISO/IEC 15189: 2007. www.iso.org (accessed December 2010).
17. Austox Urine Toxicology Drugs of Abuse Proficiency Programme. www.austox.com (accessed December 2010).
18. National Drug and Alcohol Research Centre (NDARC). Findings from the Illicit Drug Reporting System (IDRS) Australian Drug Trends 2004. NDARC Monograph No. 55, National Drug and Alcohol Research Centre, University of New South Wales Sydney, 2005.
19. CEDIA® Amphetamine/Ecstasy Assay. Microgenics Corporation, Fremont, CA, USA.
20. Posey B, Kimble S. High performance liquid chromatographic study of codeine, norcodeine and morphine as indicators of codeine ingestion. *J Anal Toxicol* 1984; 8: 68–74.
21. Combie J, Blake J, Nugent T, Tobin T. Morphine glucuronide hydrolysis: superiority of β-glucuronidase from *Patella vulgata*. *Clin Chem* 1982; 28: 83–86.
22. Lin Z, Lafolie P, Beck O. Evaluation of analytical procedures for urinary codeine and morphine measurements. *J Anal Toxicol* 1994; 18: 129–133.
23. Agilent Technologies. Onsite Cupkit™ Pro 5. Varian, CA, USA. www.varian-onsite.com (accessed December 2010).
24. Rosita. Evaluation of different roadside drug tests. December 2000. www.rosita.org.
25. Kintz P, Bernhard W, Villain M, Gasser M, Aebi B, Cirimele V. Detection of cannabis use in drivers with the Drugwipe device and by GC-MS after Intercept device collection. *J Anal Toxicol* 2005; 29: 724–727.

26. Iten P, Baumgartner M. Experiences with the DRUGWIPE® saliva drug test at the roadside. Poster presentation at The International Association of Forensic Toxicologists Congress, Seoul, Korea September 2005.
27. Verstraete A, Raes E (eds). ROSITA Final Report. Ghent University, Belgium, March 2006.
28. Blencowe T, Pehrsson A, Lillsunde P. DRUID Driving under the influence of drugs, alcohol and medicines. Analytical evaluation of oral fluid screening devices and preceding selection procedures. Project No. TREN-05-FP6TR-S07. 61320-518404-DRUID. Finland, 30 March 2010.
29. AS 4760-2006. Procedures for specimen collection and the detection and quantitation of drugs in oral fluid. Standards Australia. www.standards.org.au (accessed December 2010).

14

Canadian perspectives[1]

Barb Butler

Key points

- Canadian employers began to provide greater direction to employees on alcohol and drug issues in the late 1980s with the transportation and oil and gas sectors leading the way in response to specific United States initiatives. The policies they began to introduce set clear rules around use and possession, and introduced alcohol and drug testing in specific situations.
- In the 20 years since, employers in many industry sectors have recognised their due diligence obligations around safety in the workplace, and the need to proactively eliminate risk associated with alcohol and other drugs. They also recognise their obligations under human rights laws to accommodate employees with an alcohol or drug dependency.
- Those most proactive employers are in higher risk industries including forestry, mining, construction, manufacturing and warehousing, other transportation (not affected by the US cross-border requirements for truck and bus drivers), utilities, construction, municipal transit, and other sectors with distribution operations.
- There has been limited survey research on alcohol and drug use patterns in the Canadian population and in workplace settings. The survey data suggest that a relatively high percentage of Canadian adults remain heavy alcohol drinkers and current marijuana users, and that use of other illicit drugs has risen over the past few years. Drug use and heavy alcohol use are significantly higher for males than for females, presenting additional concerns around safety for employers in 'risk sensitive' industries where there are a significantly higher percentage of male workers.

- There are no laws at the federal or provincial level that would specifically address alcohol and drug issues beyond the Controlled Drugs and Substances Act (CDSA) and the Criminal Code. As such, employers wishing to implement alcohol and drug policies that include testing requirements must interpret a series of legal decisions to determine what they can and can not do. The degree of risk in the workplace, or in the specific position a worker holds, can make a difference in when and how testing may be initiated.
- One constant, though, is that employee testing can only be initiated if it is part of a comprehensive alcohol and drug policy tailored to meet the specific needs of each workplace. In addition, the programme should be seen as a reasonable and responsible response to those stated needs, presenting an appropriate balance between health and safety (due diligence) and respect for individual rights and privacy.
- Alcohol and drug testing of employees in Canada is not required by legislation or regulation, nor is it illegal for an employer to introduce a policy that requires testing in specific situations. However, high standards must be met to ensure technical accuracy, and employees who test positive and have a dependency must be accommodated by the employer.

Introduction

Canadian companies have been in a difficult position when considering whether to implement alcohol and drug testing programmes. Unlike the United States and some European countries, the Canadian government has decided not to issue regulations requiring testing in certain industry sectors, and as a result there is no guidance on appropriate policies/programmes, or Canadian standards or procedures for the testing process. Our federal and provincial governments to this point have remained 'neutral' on the issue. However, the federal and some provincial human rights commissions have issued policies which provide some guidance to employers on when testing would be appropriate, as well as their accommodation obligations for individuals who have a dependency. It is acknowledged, though, that these policies are not the law. A number of legal decisions have resulted from individual complaints to certain human rights commissions, or from labour challenges to testing programmes in certain industries. With no direction from government, Canadian companies must determine what is acceptable for their policies and testing programmes by interpreting these legal decisions.

Canadian organisations in a variety of industry sectors are concerned about alcohol and drug use patterns and the need to take appropriate steps to deal with employees who may be impaired on the job. Many have provided assistance programmes to help those with current or emerging alcohol or drug problems. Some have work rules around alcohol and drug use, while others may have some reference to 'fitness for duty' requirements in a health and safety policy. However, many employers are recognising this may not be enough in order to minimise safety risk and associated liabilities. They are implementing comprehensive alcohol and drug policies, and are supplementing their approach with alcohol and drug testing under certain circumstances.

This report:

- provides some context around current alcohol and drug use patterns in Canada and workplace safety concerns
- outlines some of the trends in the development of workplace alcohol and drug policies and associated testing programmes
- highlights the direction and boundaries being set around testing programmes through key legal cases in the absence of legislative direction and
- outlines the direction Canadian policies have taken in light of these decisions.

Alcohol and drug use patterns in Canada

There is limited information available to examine the nature and extent of the alcohol and drug problem in Canada. An extensive government study of the transportation industry in 1989 and an internal survey of employees at a national oil company the next year provided some data, but their findings are substantially out of date. Health Canada conducted a national survey of Canadian adult use patterns in 2004 and updated the information in 2008. This provides information nationally and by province. Supplementing this is a 2002 workplace survey conducted in one of the provinces by the Alberta Alcohol and Drug Abuse Commission, which provides information by industry sector. Between them they provide some information on drug use trends Canadian employers may be facing.

Canadian Alcohol and Drug Use Monitoring Survey

The recently released Canadian Alcohol and Drug Use Monitoring Survey provides the most recent information on alcohol and drug use patterns for Canadian adults.[2] The following highlights are of interest and the full survey is found through the web base in the endnote:

- Seventy-seven per cent of Canadian adults are current drinkers (past year), with males more likely to be current drinkers than females (81.4% vs. 73.5% F). Males are more likely to be heavy frequent drinkers (7.9%

vs. 2.6% F) and of those who drink, men were more likely to report alcohol harm in the past year (10.6% vs. 6.8% F).

- Patterns differ across the country. The province of Quebec has the highest percentage of current drinkers (80.9%) while Newfoundland and Labrador (NFL) has the highest percentage of heavy frequent drinking (9.4%) followed by New Brunswick (7.3%). In addition, 8.7% of Canadian drinkers reported harm from alcohol use in the past year, with the highest levels found in British Columbia (9.9%), Nova Scotia (9.6%) and NFL (9.6%).[3]
- In the period since the 2004 national survey, the current level of alcohol use by males remained the same, while it decreased slightly for females. There was also an overall reduction in heavy frequent drinking (from 7.1% to 5.1%) with the greatest reduction for males (11.6% down to 7.9%). Reported harm from alcohol use did not change between the two surveys.
- The number of current (past year) marijuana users decreased from 14.1% in 2004 to 11.4% in 2008. This reduction in use levels was found for both men and women. 14.4% of males reported being current users, compared to 8.6% of females. Substantially higher use levels were reported for individuals age 15–24 (32.7%) compared to those age 25 and older (7.3%).
- As with alcohol, marijuana use patterns differ with the region of the country, being highest on the east coast (Nova Scotia 13.4%) and the west coast (13.1% in British Columbia) followed by Alberta (12%) where massive construction and extraction of the oil and gas resources is now taking place.
- With regard to other drugs, 3.9% of Canadians reported using an illicit drug other than cannabis in the past year (cocaine, speed, ecstasy, hallucinogens or heroin), with hallucinogens (2.1%) and cocaine (1.6%) the most frequently reported. Use levels of illicit drugs other than cannabis were substantially higher for those aged 15–24 (15.4%) compared to those aged 25 and older (1.7%). Higher levels were found in Quebec (5.7%) and western Canada (Saskatchewan 4.1%, Alberta 3.9% and British Columbia 3.7%). There was an increase in the use of drugs other than cannabis since the 2004 survey.

Substance use and gambling in the Alberta workplace (2002)

The most recent survey of working adults was conducted in the western province of Alberta by the Alberta Alcohol and Drug Abuse Commission (AADAC). They reported that since their 1992 survey, substance abuse remains an issue throughout the province and found use patterns reflected the general population results.[4] There have been no other studies of employed individuals in the country.

- The percentage of current (past year) alcohol users remained about the same at 81%, with no change in the percentage reporting regular moderate to heavy (9%) or very heavy (5%) drinking. 4% reported using alcohol within 4 hours of coming to work. And 11% of employed individuals reported using alcohol while at work, although the majority said this was less than once a month.
- There was an increase from 6% to 10% of workers who reported using illicit drugs in the past year, marijuana being the most commonly used drug. The percentage reporting use of other drugs did not change from the last survey for cocaine (1%) and hallucinogens (1%), while amphetamine/other stimulant was reported at 1% for the first time in 2002. 1% of workers reported using illicit drugs while at work, and 2% reported drug use within four hours of coming to work.
- Workers in a number of at risk industries, including construction, utilities, forestry/mining, public administration, and finance/insurance/real estate were most likely to report substance use at work, at-risk use, multiple substance use or gambling issues. AADAC reports 'The safety-sensitive nature of many at-risk industries heightens concerns that substance abuse or use while at work may have serious implications for job performance and safety.'

Although there has been limited survey research in Canada, these two surveys, including the trend data, provide Canadian employers with a picture of the likely patterns they may find in their own operations. Anecdotal data finds a significant number of employers in all industry sectors are introducing alcohol and drug policies focused on fitness for work and minimising risk of accidents and injuries. Court and arbitration decisions have confirmed employers do not need 'proof' of a problem before taking proactive steps in this area to ensure workplace and public safety.

Organisations challenging Canadian workplace alcohol and drug policies and testing in the early 1990s tried to argue that drug abuse was a US issue and that Canada should not be 'importing' US solutions for a US problem. That argument is not a factor 20 years later as it is increasingly acknowledged that there are indeed legitimate concerns around illicit drug use and heavy/hazardous drinking levels in Canada and recent research suggests use levels are comparable.

To put the Canadian situation into perspective internationally, the United Nations 2007 World Drug Report stated Canadians lead the industrialised world in marijuana smoking and are four times more likely to have smoked pot in the past year than residents of nearly every other country. And the UN's 2009 World Drug Report pointed out that 'Canada has grown to be the most important producer of MDMA for North America' and stated that there has been a significant increase in the amount of methamphetamine manufactured and exported for the US market as well as many others. It also pointed out that since 2003–2004 Canada has emerged as the primary source of ecstasy-group substances for North American markets, and increasingly for other regions in the world.

Alcohol and drug policies and testing programmes: recent trends

With its close proximity to the United States, Canadian industry has been significantly influenced by their very strong anti-drug stance, and their acceptance of testing as one solution to workplace drug problems. US law requires Canadian commercial motor vehicle drivers who operate into the United States to be subject to testing programmes as a condition of entry. US companies are increasingly demanding Canadian workers on their sites to be subject to testing as a condition of contract. Others are requiring Canadian subsidiaries to implement testing programmes similar to the parent company, but these must still be compliant with Canadian law. One result of the US initiative is that Canadian testing procedures, for the most part, mirror theirs, and Canadian laboratories are accredited for employee testing programmes directly by the US Department of Health and Human Services.

Transportation sector

The issue first came to the forefront in the mid to late 1980s. That was when the US Department of Transportation issued regulations for their own industry that would also impact motor carrier, rail, marine, aviation and pipeline operations entering US territory. The requirements were put on hold while the Canadian government agreed to examine its own direction in this area. Transport Canada undertook extensive research, including a survey on use patterns in the industry across the country, and after consultation with industry and labour representatives, developed draft legislation requiring policies, assistance programmes and testing. The legislation was directed at the federally regulated transportation sector (airports, aviation, extra-provincial truck and bus, rail and marine industries). The intent was to respond to the US government initiative by legislating an appropriate approach for Canadian industry, and to seek a mutual recognition of each country's requirements even if they differed in the end. As a result, many transportation companies, in anticipation of government regulation, began to implement more comprehensive workplace policies. A number introduced the option of testing in reasonable cause and post-incident situations, as well as pre-employment testing for applicants to safety-sensitive positions.

In December 1995 Transport Canada reversed direction and decided not to introduce legislation to require testing in Canada's transportation industry, leaving companies to their own devices to set policies and programmes. In the absence of Canadian legislation, the US government made their regulations covering cross-border operations effective for large motor carriers that transport people or products into the United States in July 1996; smaller carriers had until July 1997 to comply.

Companies were obliged to have comprehensive alcohol and drug testing programmes (including pre-employment and random testing) in place as a condition of operating into the United States. Most felt obliged for health and safety reasons to extend their policies to all employees, and implement appropriate policy standards for 'Canada-only' drivers who have the identical duties as those who cross the border, as well as their other employees. However, the legality of requiring 'Canada-only' drivers to be in the random testing programme was unclear at the time, and many simply left them out of the random pool.

Companies in other sectors who have a distribution arm (e.g. manufacturing, food and beverage, utilities, oil and gas, retail, etc.) are also affected by the US testing regulations if they transport their product into the United States. Rather than focusing their programmes solely on the cross-border drivers, many have also set appropriate standards and procedures for all employees at the same time as they meet their regulatory obligations. The regulations therefore led to policies being introduced in other industry sectors.

Oil and gas sector

Parallel to this, after the Exxon Valdez incident off the coast of Alaska in the late 1980s, many companies in the oil and gas sector began to introduce comprehensive policies with testing triggered in a number of circumstances. The Exxon subsidiary in Canada (Imperial Oil) also introduced random testing, but it was not widely embraced by the rest of the industry. Most companies in this sector had programmes by the mid 1990s and many have reviewed and updated these programmes in recent years as the legal situation around testing has become clearer.

Policy development and testing programmes are playing a major role in this sector in Northern Alberta where extensive expansion of the oil sands resource has resulted in massive construction and extraction projects. With thousands of employees and contract workers moving into the area for short or longer periods of time, there is a target demographic for drug or heavy alcohol use (young males, high income, shift work/remote location/travel status) throughout the region. These have all been designated high-risk sites and the large oil and gas companies and major contractors are setting strong policies to address their safety risk. Although most have operations across

Canada, and ultimately do set policies for their entire organisations, the primary focus of activity for implementation is presently in this geographic area.

Employers are requiring reasonable cause and post-incident testing at all of these sites, and have strong return-to-work conditions if a worker violates site policies; if allowed back on a project, they will normally be subject to unannounced testing as well as the expectation that they get help for any problem they may have. Three of the first major companies in the area also introduced pre-site access testing (the worker must have passed a drug test within a limited period of time before going on site); as new projects are opening up, all employers are setting the same requirement. The theory is that they do not want to employ someone who was unable to pass a test for another site. Whether this approach is effective or not, it is now a universal requirement in Northern Alberta, though rarely used elsewhere in the country.

The contractors are heavily unionised on these projects, and one initiative of the Construction Owners Association was the development of a 'model' in consultation with the unions that would allow their members to be compliant with the various site alcohol and drug policies. Although each site has its own unique policy requirements, there is enough commonality that a construction contractor can adopt the principles of the 'model' and for the most part be in compliance with these requirements. It sets out core standards around fitness for work and alcohol and other drug use and possession. The unions agreed with reasonable cause and post-incident testing under these circumstances, provided there is education, training and an opportunity for members in contravention of the rules to get assistance for a problem and be reassigned to the site. A new version of the 'model' issued in February 2006 includes the option of formalising pre-site access testing, would allow for random testing, and sets out the requirement for mandatory assessments for a problem. Most unions have not signed on to this version. This agreement which includes testing is unique to the Northern Alberta situation, however the British Columbia and Saskatchewan construction organisations have initiated similar programmes in the last year, and it is being examined in other parts of the country as a joint labour/management initiative.

A final initiative in Northern Alberta is rapidly expanding and becoming a model that other organisations are looking at. Called the Rapid Site Access Program (RSAP) it reflects the nature of construction projects and supplements the 'model' in a unique way. All the sites now require site access testing prior to a contract worker being able to begin their job, and this can be a significant problem for the site owners and contractors if there is a delay in receiving test results. The worker cannot get on the site without a negative test, and particularly in 'shut down' situations (when a large number of people are rapidly needed on site), this can be a logistical problem severely affecting operations. RSAP was set up to deal with this. It is a voluntary programme through which a worker can pass a drug test, and be put in a random 'pool' through which he or she can be tested at any time. Owners that have accepted the programme will waive the site access requirement provided the worker's status remains 'active'.

There is an independent Third Party Program Administrator/Case Manager with an extensive database monitoring the active and inactive members. Any RSAP member who refuses to be tested, or fails a required test would be removed from active status, sent for an assessment to determine whether there is a dependency, the worker would be expected to comply with any recommended treatment, and would be subject to a monitoring programme for a specific period of time on returning to active status. All contractor companies who are members of the Construction Owners Association of Alberta are participants in the programme. Most of the owner sites have accepted the programme although with some caveats. And the majority of the trade unions are now participating (fall 2009), in particular because of the change to analysis of oral fluid for drug testing earlier this year. The programme remains voluntary, and the number of volunteers began to increase with the change in testing method, but remains at fairly low given the many thousands of workers on these oil sands projects. Other organisations in the construction industry are in the process of developing similar programmes, but it will be some time before their success can be known.

Other sectors

Employers are recognising that relatively high levels of alcohol use in the population and ready availability and use of high potency illicit drugs, as well as the increasing use of performance-impacting medications all are affecting health and safety in the workplace. In order to minimise safety risk and liabilities, Canadian employers in many other industry sectors are implementing alcohol and drug policies which establish appropriate standards around possession and use, offer education, training and access to assistance, provide methods to investigate policy violations, and set out consequences for violation. One investigative tool many are now turning to for detection and deterrence is alcohol and drug testing. The most active areas are in higher risk industries including forestry, mining, construction, manufacturing and warehousing, other transportation (not affected by the cross-border requirements), utilities, construction, municipal transit, grocery and other industries with distribution operations, etc. Some municipalities and healthcare facilities are beginning to look at the issue as well.

The courts have made it clear that occupational health and safety obligations extend to contractors, and earlier policies also referenced application to contractors, although in many, it was unclear what their testing obligations were. In the mid to late 1990s many companies in a variety of industry sectors who had their own comprehensive policy became more specific in their expectations, and required their contractors to introduce workplace policies as a condition of contract. In many cases, this has included the ability to trigger alcohol and drug testing – primarily in post-incident and reasonable cause situations. These contractor requirements are not limited to the construction trades in Northern Alberta, but are a requirement across the country.

Legislation and guidelines

There are no laws at the federal or provincial level that would specifically address alcohol and drug issues beyond the Controlled Drugs and Substances Act (CDSA) and the Criminal Code. The CDSA prohibits the importation, exportation, production, sale, provision and possession of a wide variety of controlled drugs and substances except where permitted by regulations. The CDSA provides authority for police to arrest, search and seize for controlled substances. The Criminal Code establishes standards and penalties for impaired driving/operating infractions involving the care and control of a motorised vehicle, vessel, railway equipment or airplane. Provincial legislation also provides for administrative licence sanctions for impaired driving. So both of these areas of legislation can assist employers; they can involve the police in investigations where there are grounds to believe there are drug possession or trafficking concerns in their workplace, and they can take action if an employee operating a company vehicle is charged by police with impaired driving under the Criminal Code.

Separate from this, Canadian employers face a variety of potential legal issues that may be related to alcohol and drugs and are best addressed through consistent implementation of a clear and reasonable policy. This can include addressing the liabilities associated with the actions of impaired employees at work, due diligence responsibility around workplace safety, actions in response to possession or trafficking of illicit drugs, and the duty to accommodate those with a chemical dependency in accordance with human rights provisions. In fact, a recent court decision confirmed that

> human rights legislation fits within the entire legal framework within which enterprises must function ... and ... that framework includes other standards that also reflect deep values of the community such as those established by workers' compensation legislation prohibiting an employer from placing an employee in a situation of undue risk, and the standards of the law of negligence.[5]

The Court stated that this fuller legal framework must be considered when a company's occupational requirements are being assessed. The key responsibilities follow:

- Occupational Health and Safety Legislation places the onus on employers to ensure the health, safety and welfare of employees; employers must prove diligence in minimising or eliminating all potential safety risks, including those associated with independent contractors. Organisations can be liable for any negligent or wrongful acts committed by an employee acting within the scope or course of employment, which could include negligence in allowing an alcohol or drug-impaired employee on the worksite or on a public highway once declared unfit to work, and negligence when returning someone to a risk-sensitive job after treatment or after a policy violation where sufficient monitoring mechanisms are not in place and a substance-related incident results. The company policy should have provisions to address these responsibilities. The courts have clarified that occupational health and safety responsibilities can extend to contracted workers and subcontractors. As a result, increasingly companies are not only introducing policies for employees, they are also introducing requirements for contractors (generally by issuing a 'Statement of Expectations for Contractors').
- Reinforcing these safety obligations, Canada's Criminal Code has been amended to set rules for attributing to organisations, including corporations, criminal liability for the acts of their representatives. There is a legal duty for all persons directing work to take reasonable steps to ensure the safety of workers and the public. In essence, criminal negligence is established where the organisation or individual, in doing anything or in omitting to do anything, that is its/his/her legal duty to do, shows wanton or reckless disregard for the lives or safety of others. It is expected that this legislation will impact how organisations deal with substance abuse issues.
- Driver liability makes the owner of a vehicle accountable for any injuries or damages caused by a person driving the vehicle with the owner's consent. This is why companies must be clear that the rules around alcohol and drug use apply when someone is operating a company vehicle and/or operating a vehicle on behalf of the company. It is also why policies address reporting, and the consequences of receiving, an impaired driving charge in these situations.
- Hosting liabilities associated with the provision of alcohol to others or hosting alcohol-related events can include the provider of the alcohol, the occupier of the premises where the problem occurred, and the sponsor of the event. If they are in any way implicated in an event involving alcohol use, the company can be held responsible for injuries the person who drank may receive, and for any third party they may injure. This is why Canadian companies must have clear rules around when alcohol can be used, as well as procedures for social and business hosting where alcohol use may be involved. This includes procedures to minimise the possibility

that someone may leave in an intoxicated state that could result in injury to themselves or a third party.

- Supreme Court of Canada direction on the concept of a bona fide occupational requirement has been established, and this now sets a standard on how companies must act when developing an alcohol and drug policy. The Court's direction has been used in a series of subsequent cases involving alcohol and drug policies and testing programmes by other courts, arbitrators, and Human Rights Boards and Tribunals. Specifically, in two key decisions, the Supreme Court of Canada confirmed that to make what may be considered a discriminatory work standard acceptable (e.g. no alcohol use during the day, or individuals are subject to testing under certain circumstances, etc.), companies must meet the following tests:[6]
  1. The employer must show the standard was adopted for a purpose rationally connected to performance of the job.
  2. The employer must establish that the standard was adopted in an honest and good faith belief that it was necessary to the fulfillment of that legitimate work-related purpose.
  3. The employer must establish that the standard is reasonably necessary to the accomplishment of that legitimate work-related purpose; it must demonstrate it is impossible to accommodate individual employees without imposing undue hardship on the employer.
- Federal and Provincial Human Rights Legislation prohibits discrimination on the basis of a disability. Current or former dependence on drugs or alcohol is considered a disability under the federal Act, and has been interpreted in the same manner at the provincial level. Issues around reasonable accommodation, and establishing a bona fide occupational requirement (bfor) for treating someone differently need to be addressed. Prevention initiatives including access to assessment, assistance, treatment, and follow-up services, as well as modifying hours or duties in certain circumstances would all contribute to accommodation responsibilities.

All of these legal issues come into play in the development and the implementation of a company policy and testing programme in Canada.

Guidance from human rights commissions

Each province and the federal government has a commission which sets policies and adjudicates cases dealing with discrimination issues in light of the legislation in their jurisdiction. Several of these commissions have been active in providing guidance to employers who are considering alcohol and drug testing programmes. This is not law – the tribunals and courts hearing the various cases set the law – but these policies can help employers understand their obligations when it comes to addressing human rights issues. A number of provincial commissions have set policies which would limit testing to very specific situations, for example, only in reasonable cause and post-incident situations as part of a broader programme of medical assessment, monitoring and support.

In 2009, the Alberta Human Rights and Citizenship Commission issued a new policy in which it stated it did not have jurisdiction to tell an employer when or whether they could require alcohol or drug testing. Instead, the Commission focused on alcohol and drug dependencies, and the obligations of employers to accommodate those individuals who have a dependency and therefore a disability. The Commission also confirmed that recreational (casual) use of alcohol or drugs does not constitute a dependency and therefore, the provincial legislation would not protect those individuals.

In the same year, the Federal Human Rights Commission took a different approach to the issue. Their guidance would apply to federally regulated industries (e.g. transportation, postal, nuclear energy, banking, etc.). The Commission conducted extensive consultation on this issue, reviewed key Canadian case law and provided an analysis of the direction workplace programmes are taking, as well as advice for employers considering policies that include testing. In particular, the Commission Policy states testing would be acceptable in the following situations:

- alcohol and drug testing for 'reasonable cause' where an employee reports for work in an unfit state and there is evidence of substance abuse
- alcohol and drug testing after a significant incident or accident has occurred and there is evidence that an employee's acts or omissions may have contributed to the situation
- following treatment for drug or alcohol abuse, or disclosure of a current alcohol dependency or abuse
- on a random basis for alcohol provided the employee holds a safety-sensitive position.

Testing in these situations would not be limited to safety-sensitive positions, however, pre-employment and random would be limited to those positions presenting higher risk if someone was under the influence of alcohol or other drugs on the job. In other words, pre-employment and random alcohol and drug testing is acceptable for truck and bus drivers, and may be acceptable for other safety-sensitive positions provided the company can establish testing is a bona fide occupational requirement, and then provides guidance on making that determination. Finally, the policy provides guidance to employers in a number of areas, noting that employers are encouraged to adopt comprehensive policies beyond just testing, that include access to assistance, education, peer or supervisory monitoring and off-site counselling and referral services.

Canadian alcohol and drug policies

Policy development

There are a number of key areas that policies must address, and several difficult decisions that need to be tackled. The first step is to establish a background to the specific policy decisions that follow. There are some valid reasons for taking a 'two-step' process. The courts/arbitrators/human rights tribunals have found the reasons for establishing the policy – the thought patterns that go behind it – are just as important as the policy components themselves (see test no. 2 in the Supreme Court list above). The process should involve consultation with representatives of key parts of the organisation and ensure that the policy ultimately implemented results from an assessment of the organisation's specific requirements and responds to those requirements. This would include:

- identifying all current practices, policies and services, including provisions in occupational health and safety manuals, the collective agreement, employee benefit programmes, etc.
- ensuring the policy builds from this base
- identifying gaps or missing pieces
- determining what can be improved and ensure the policy addresses this
- assessing the degree of risk in the operations, identifying any past problems or incidents
- looking at external factors including recent legal decisions, trends and practices of others in the industry, general information on use patterns, impacts and effective solutions
- identifying likely stakeholder expectations and how conflicting expectations will be handled
- setting out overall objectives for the programme, which will be a foundation for its implementation.

Policy components

Various adjudicators have indicated that simply putting in place a policy copied from a US parent, or someone else in the industry will not meet the Supreme Court test. There is no 'typical' policy or programme; if the steps above are followed, each programme will reflect the unique corporate culture and values of the company, the fundamental aspects of the business it is in, the regulatory environment within which it must operate, and most important, the specific programme needs. However, there are a number of key areas that policies must address, and several difficult decisions that need to be tackled.

And it should be clear throughout the following sections that assistance for those who may have a problem is an important part of a balanced approach.

Canadian companies cannot simply implement a testing programme or policy. Testing may play a role as an investigation tool or deterrence tool, but must be part of a broader approach that includes the following:

1 awareness and education programmes, both at policy introduction and ongoing
2 access to assistance, through an internal or contracted employee assistance programme, or as appropriate, community resources
3 training for supervisors on their role under the policy, including both performance management for early identification of potential problems, and appropriate steps to take to investigate a possible policy violation
4 a variety of tools to investigate if someone may be in violation of the policy.

Each of these components should be included in any company programme. The policy statement itself should:

- be written down and broadly communicated to all employees
- provide clear direction on the objective and application (who is covered and under what circumstances)
- outline the applicable rules and responsibilities, including any higher standards for risk- or safety-sensitive positions
- clarify avenues to access assistance, reinforce the importance of obtaining assistance for a problem before it impacts the workplace, and outline conditions for return to duty, including aftercare provisions on a case by case basis
- set out the procedures which will be followed to investigate a possible policy violation (e.g. investigation and escort procedures if someone is unfit for work, accident investigation, impaired driving situations, searches, alcohol and drug testing)
- set out consequences for a policy violation and any conditions for continued employment, including provisions for a substance abuse professional assessment to determine whether the individual has a problem in need of accommodation.

Finally, in order to be effective, it must be carefully communicated so everyone knows what is expected of them and where to get assistance if they need it. Supervisors also need specific training on their responsibilities around performance management, investigating possible policy violations, and making referrals for an alcohol and drug test.

Someone must be in charge of the overall programme, usually called the programme administrator, who will ensure consistent communications, education and training all take place, and who will contract for necessary external resources including testing services, Employee Assistance Programme and substance abuse professionals to provide specific assessments in a post-violation situation.

Canadian unions, human rights bodies, privacy commissions and civil liberties organisations have not questioned an employer's obligation to provide a safe workplace and the importance of setting out clear and well-communicated policies to this end. Their major concerns have focused on the investigative tools used to ensure compliance, the introduction of alcohol and drug testing, the consequences for a violation, and ensuring those with a problem receive appropriate accommodation.

Introduction of alcohol and drug testing

Many Canadian employers are questioning whether they should introduce alcohol and drug testing programmes for their employees. Faced with increasing responsibilities for the actions of their employees, aware of current alcohol and drug use patterns, and faced with the possibility of decriminalisation of marijuana, employers are looking at testing as a way to deter use and identify those who may be placing their co-workers and others at risk. As a result, a number of employers, particularly those in higher risk industries, are choosing to include testing in certain circumstances as part of their company policy.

However, they cannot simply implement a testing programme and assume it will be found acceptable by employees or the courts. The most recent arbitration and court decisions have provided better guidance on the allowable circumstances for testing, and some of the minimum programme and policy standards which must be met. Any testing that is introduced should be within the context of the company's overall approach to health and safety, and its specific requirements with respect to alcohol and drug issues.

Therefore, companies need to first make a careful assessment of whether alcohol and drug testing should or should not be included in the overall policy – in other words, be able to explain how it contributes to the company's overall safety objectives. The introduction of testing in any workplace is a controversial decision, and should be made with full understanding of the role it can play, and consideration of whether it is justified for certain employee groups. Decisions are needed on who to test, under what circumstances, for what substances, using what technology, and what will be the consequence for failing a test, or refusing to be tested.

Testing circumstances in Canada have included:

- pre-employment as a final condition of hire
- pre-assignment/certification (e.g. to a risk- or safety-sensitive position)
- prior to assignment to a specific task or job site ('pre-access testing')

- after a significant accident or incident as part of a full investigation
- with reasonable cause (to believe someone is unfit due to alcohol or drug use) as part of an investigation
- on a purely random basis at a specified rate per year
- as a condition of return to duty after treatment or a policy violation
- as a condition of continued employment after a policy violation (e.g. last chance agreement)
- as part of a monitoring agreement after treatment.

Some companies may conclude testing will not play a role in the implementation of their policy. Others may conclude testing should be triggered for all employees under certain circumstances, or for certain groups of employees (e.g. high risk) under other circumstances. Each policy must be absolutely clear on when testing applies, and the procedures which will be used, as well as the justification for its introduction.

Testing technology

Currently, the standard practice is to collect a urine sample for analysis in a Department of Health and Human Services (DHHS)-certified laboratory. The core testing panel is marijuana, opiates, amphetamines, phencyclidine (PCP) and cocaine, although protocols can be set up to test for other drugs as required under the circumstances (e.g. for a post-treatment follow-up testing programme, in locations where there are particular concerns about drug abuse for other drug classes, or in special client circumstances). Technology has also been developed that would allow an oral fluid (saliva) sample to be tested for drug presence, and this technology will increasingly be looked at as an alternative in the coming years. It is already being used in a few Canadian workplaces to provide a closer link to recent use and greater likelihood of impairment than urine testing. This alternative methodology may be a key requirement to meet legal standards that are emerging for random drug testing in particular.

A calibrated breath analyser is normally used for alcohol testing, although a saliva test (to 'screen' out negatives) and a second urine collection for lab analysis has been used in remote locations if a breath machine is not readily available. Careful steps are needed in collection and conversion of results to blood-equivalent levels. Originally on-site urine testing screens were primarily being used in remote locations where turnaround on a test result can take several weeks. Since 2009 these devices have become much more sophisticated when it comes to testing for sample adulteration, and as such, are increasingly being used across Canada, particularly to speed the site access testing process, and in reasonable cause and post-incident situations. Any 'non-negative' result must be confirmed in a certified lab.

Finally, before drug test results are reported to the company, a positive test, or a tampered/adulterated laboratory test result must be reviewed by an independent and qualified medical review officer (MRO), who will discuss the situation with the employee to determine if there is a legitimate medical reason for the finding. If there is no legitimate medical explanation, it will be reported to the company as a positive or tampered test result as appropriate to the finding.

Testing programme implementation

A comprehensive network of trained collection facilities was established to meet the motor carrier needs across the country (for US cross-border regulations), while at the same time providing the means to meet the needs of those in other industries who chose to introduce testing programmes. Three Canadian laboratories were certified by the US DHHS to provide fully accurate testing services for Canadian companies introducing programmes, and a number of Canadian occupational health physicians took the appropriate training to be certified as MROs – an essential part of any workplace testing programme. The labs and other medical facilities set up collection sites, and in many areas breath testing for alcohol is available. As such, an infrastructure has been established, and companies exploring the option of including testing under their policy can be assured of reliable and accurate results – provided they used qualified and experienced service providers. Although not universally available, collection capability has grown in many regions as demand for testing has grown.

Unfortunately, as in any situation where there is demand for a new service, product manufacturers with quick and cheap solutions which do not provide accurate test results, unqualified collectors, doctors claiming to be qualified MROs, and non-certified labs have shown up and started promoting their services. In the absence of any government standards employers have been at the mercy of product promoters; without knowing the right questions to ask, some have ended up with highly ineffective programmes, or programmes that would not be defensible if challenged. It is very much a 'buyer beware' environment, but the increasing desire of employers to begin testing has caused many to not be sufficiently cautious when setting up their programme.

Where testing has been approved by courts and arbitrators, the programmes have met the higher standard as set out in the US testing regulations, using US certified labs and trained collectors and qualified and experienced MROs. Programmes using less qualified providers have not yet been put under scrutiny in the courts, although one arbitration ruling made it very clear that the highest standards for collection and respect for donor privacy must be met.

Testing legality

There are at present no provincial or federal laws that would specifically prohibit drug testing, or provide employers with any kind of direction on when and how it may be utilised in a company programme. There have been no specific Supreme Court decisions in this area, although their direction on human rights obligations has specifically affected how employers implement policies and testing programmes. No matter how solid their policy is, and no matter how high the standards are in their testing programme, Canadian employers can still face a legal challenge, for example:

- a complaint through a human rights commission centred on discrimination and/or accommodation concerns
- a wrongful dismissal action
- a grievance against the policy itself or actions towards an individual employee
- in a government or certain regulated organisations, a challenge of the policy itself under the Charter of Rights and Freedoms.

A number of recent decisions across the country provide some guidance on where the law may stand on this issue. An interesting twist in the last few years has made legal interpretation a bit more complicated. The human rights laws apply to all individuals, and decisions would accept testing in a number of situations, with the key limitation being the requirement for applicant and random testing to be only acceptable for safety-sensitive positions where a bona fide occupational requirement can be established. However, a number of arbitrators have concluded there may be higher standards to meet in a unionised setting, leading the way to limiting reasonable cause and post-incident testing to safety-sensitive positions or safety-sensitive working environments.

Although each case has its own unique aspects, it appears the trend has been to find testing acceptable:

- as part of an investigation in an unfit for duty (reasonable cause) situation where there is evidence alcohol or drug use may be a contributing factor
- as part of a full investigation into an accident/incident situation, without reasonable cause, provided testing is only for those whose acts or omissions contributed to the situation
- as part of a monitoring programme after treatment to support continued recovery, normally on the advice of a substance abuse professional or treatment programme
- as a condition of return to duty after a policy violation and on an on-going follow-up basis
- as a condition of 'certification' or qualification to a higher risk position for new hires and existing employees transferring to the position

- on a random basis for alcohol in higher risk (safety-sensitive) positions with the qualification noted below.

In one significant human rights hearing, the Federal Human Rights Tribunal upheld alcohol and drug testing on a pre-employment and random basis for safety-sensitive positions in the motor coach industry.[7] The Tribunal also ruled that any individual who tests positive and has an alcohol or drug problem must be provided with assistance and accommodation for that problem. This means employers must have a process in place to ensure that professional assessment is done. The Federal Human Rights Commission's new policy resulted from this decision and would allow for random testing for other safety-sensitive positions where justification can be established (testing meets a bona fide occupational requirement for the position).

At the provincial level and in other industries, random testing is still being challenged and a few key decisions have been issued which better clarify an employer's options in this area. There is no question random testing would have to be limited to the highest risk 'safety-sensitive' positions in any operation, and even then random drug testing may not be upheld beyond the motor carrier industry, or if upheld, be limited to using the newer oral fluid testing technology. However, it appears the law is taking a different perspective in a unionised setting. A series of labour arbitration rulings have stated that to introduce random testing in a unionised setting in Canada, employers either have to have prior union agreement or evidence of an out of control drug culture.

Conclusion

Many Canadian employers have concluded that one of the most effective ways to prevent workplace alcohol and drug problems, and to effectively investigate and take corrective action, is to first establish a clear and comprehensive workplace policy. Each company must decide what will work best in their own environment; there is no model policy. Each programme should be tailored to meet the specific needs of each workplace, and should be seen as a reasonable and responsible response to those stated needs. The result should be an appropriate balance between health and safety (due diligence) and respect for individual rights and privacy. This means finding a balance between measures to control or deter use (clear standards, investigation tools and consequences/discipline) and prevention measures (education, training and employee assistance). Alcohol and drug testing has been introduced in a significant number of workplaces in Canada and in particular in higher risk industry sectors, but these programmes are only defensible if they are part of a more comprehensive approach, and the highest standards are used for the testing process. There remain some challenges to introducing random alcohol and drug testing, particularly in a unionised setting.

Endnotes

1. More information on Canadian policy and testing issues can be found at www.butlerconsultants.com
2. Canadian Alcohol and Drug Use Monitoring Survey 2008. www.ccsa.ca/Eng/Statistics/Canada/GHAS/Pages/default.aspx
3. This would be at least one of eight harms to self: physical health; friendships and social life; financial position; home life or marriage; work, studies or employment opportunities; legal problems; difficulty learning; housing problems.
4. Substance Use and Gambling in the Alberta Workplace, 2002, Alberta Alcohol and Drug Abuse Commission. www.aadac.com/87_491.asp
5. Oak Bay Marina Ltd (Painter's Lodge) and B.C. Human Rights Tribunal and Robert Gordy, B.C. Court of Appeal, September 2002. www.lancasterhouse.com/decisions/2002/sept/bcca-gordy.htm
6. SCC file No. 26274, September 9, 1999 (Meiorin). www.lexum.umontreal.ca/csc-scc/en/pub/1999/v013/html/1999scr3_0003.html. These tests were confirmed in *British Columbia Superintendent of Motor Vehicles* v. *British Columbia Council of Human Rights*, SCC file No. 26481, December 16, 1999 (Grismer). www.lexum.umontreal.ca/csc-scc/en/pub/1999/v013/html/1999scr3_0868.html.
7. Salvatore Milazzo and Canadian Human Rights Commission, and Autocar Connaisseur Inc. (Coach Canada), Federal Human Rights Tribunal, November 6, 2003. www.chrt-tcdp.gc.ca/search/view_html.asp?doid=502&lg=_e&isruling=0 and www.chrt-tcdp.gc.ca/search/view_html.asp?doid=586&lg=_e&isruling=0.

15

A New Zealand perspective

Susan Nolan

Key points

New Zealand (NZ) companies have been introducing drug and alcohol-free workplace policies and programmes, including testing, since 1992. This chapter covers the following key topics:

- history of workplace drug testing in New Zealand and related industry trends
- the legislative issues and some relevant case law
- the medico-legal testing requirements (i.e. testing to the latest version, currently 2008, of the Australian/New Zealand Standard AS/NZS 4308: 'Procedures for specimen collection and the detection and quantitation of drugs of abuse in urine')
- legally robust workplace drug and alcohol policies and the associated procedures
- NZ drug abuse trends and statistics relevant to workplace positive tests
- status of oral fluid testing.

Introduction

Most 'safety-critical' industry sectors are now embracing drug and alcohol testing as part of comprehensive programmes which also have a strong focus on education and rehabilitation. Lawful drug testing in New Zealand should be conducted to the strict medico-legal requirements of the most recent Australian/New Zealand Standard, AS/NZS 4308 'Procedures for specimen collection and the detection and quantitation of drugs of abuse in urine'.[1] This chapter gives an overview of the NZ experience, highlighting the mix of testing options employed, the industry sector trends, the categories of drugs misused, the influence of significant Employment Court Judgments, the changes in the 2008 version of AS/NZS 4308 and current position of oral fluid testing.

It is important to emphasise that some of the figures referred to relate to the statistics from tests conducted by the Institute of Environmental Science and Research Limited (ESR). ESR is a Crown Research Institute (CRI), and is considered to be a New Zealand leader in providing analytical services and advice related to drug and alcohol-free workplaces. The laboratory is accredited to provide testing services in compliance with AS/NZS 4308.

History

New Zealand has a population of 4.3 million. The introduction of workplace drug testing as part of a company's drug and alcohol-free workplace programme (DAFWP) commenced in the early 1990s. Initially this was in response to US companies requiring their global subsidiaries to adopt policies and procedures which mirrored the US programmes. In 1992 the NZ Navy also introduced drug testing programmes and the other Armed Forces followed. During the mid to late 1990s, the industries which pioneered DAFWP programmes that included testing were in the forestry, fishing, mining and aluminium manufacturing sectors. Since 2000 most of the other 'risk' industry sectors have introduced organisations with comprehensive programmes in place.

Figure 15.1 shows the increase in workplace drug testing urine specimens tested by ESR from June 1998 to June 2006. In 2006 there were other agencies (both laboratory and 'on-site' screening) providing testing services and the author estimates that the total number of tests for 2005/2006 was at least twice the ESR statistics (i.e. greater than 60 000). Since 2006 there has been a significant increase in workplace drug testing and the total number of tests conducted during 2009 is estimated to be greater than 100 000. While many of these tests are conducted in full compliance with AS/NZS

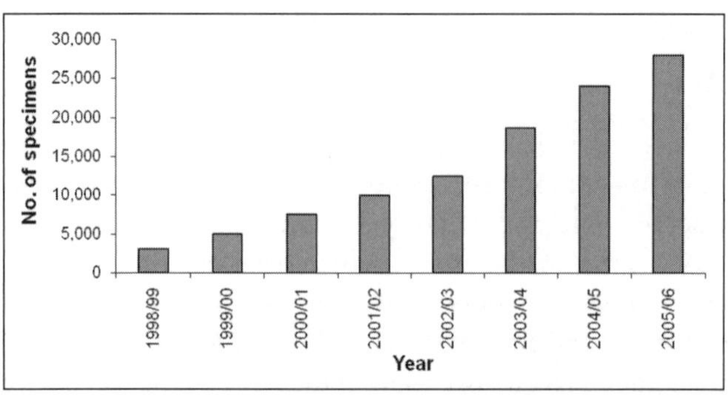

Figure 15.1 Workplace drug testing urine specimens analysed by ESR between June 1998 and June 2006.

Table 15.1 Top 12 industry sectors: drug testing distribution

Industry sector	% of total urine specimens analysed		
	2003/2004	2004/2005	2005/2006
Roading/horizontal construction	16	20	21
Forestry	19	18	15
Transportation	18	16	13
Dairy	13	10	10
Meat/poultry	6	10	11
Fishing/shipping	5	5	6
Aluminium smelter	4	4	4
Mining	4	3	<2
Personnel consulting/ training	4	3	<2
Manufacturing	2	4	2
Vertical construction/ engineering	2	<2	2
Oil/power/energy	<2	<2	3

Source: Institute of Environmental Science and Research Limited statistics.

4308 : 2008, unfortunately a proportion are conducted using 'on-site' screening only and without mass spectrometry confirmation of tests that have screened not negative.

Table 15.1 and Figure 15.2 illustrate the proportion of total specimens tested for drugs by ESR for the top 12 industry sectors. The statistics from June 2003 to June 2004 are compared with those from June 2004 to June 2005 and June 2005 to June 2006.

The 1990 industry leaders (forestry, fishing/shipping, mining, aluminium) have remained well represented. From 2000 to 2003 the dairy, transportation and road/horizontal construction industries embraced testing. During 2004–2005, many meat/poultry industries introduced programmes. Since 2006, the industry sectors which have either introduced or substantially increased drug testing are vertical construction, agriculture/farming, personnel consulting and some local and central government agencies (including NZ Customs Department). Another industry sector that is gaining momentum is the tourism/hospitality sector. Training institutions associated with the 'risk' industry

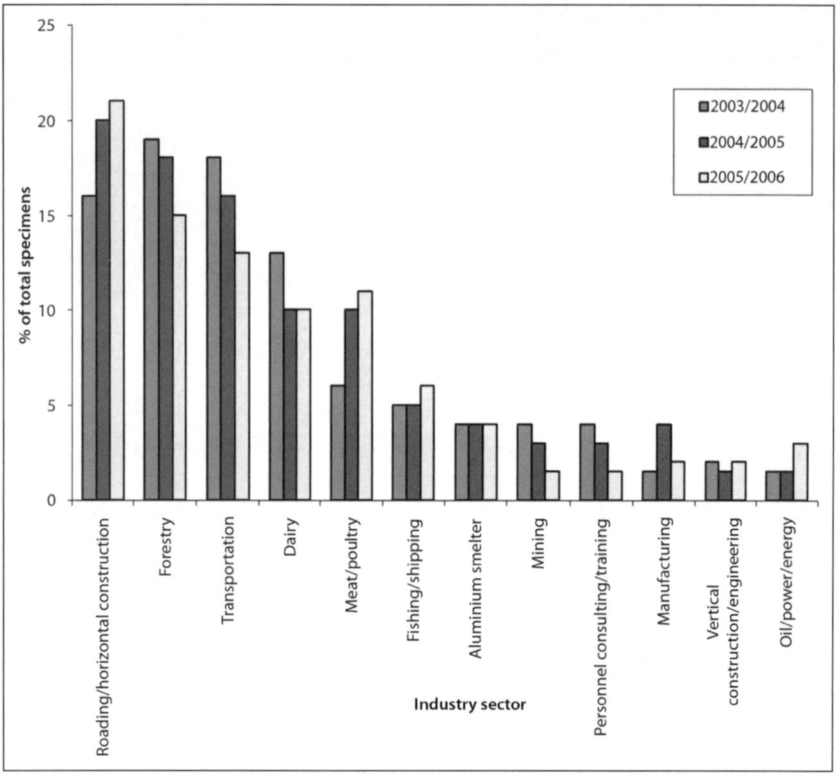

Figure 15.2 Drug testing distribution in top 12 industries (ESR statistics)

sectors are also increasingly being required to provide a pool of 'drug-free' potential employers.

Legislation and standards

The rapid increase in the number of organisations adopting DAFWPs is the result of two overlapping NZ trends and influences: the increase and change in the use and misuse of drugs of abuse and the ongoing use and misuse of alcohol combined with the introduction of the Health and Safety in Employment Act (1992) and its Amendment (2002). This legislation requires employers to take 'all practicable steps' to ensure the safety of employees while at work. The courts have interpreted this obligation as meaning employers must be alert to potential hazards and take measures to prevent injury and accidents. An alcohol or drug-impaired employee is stipulated as a potential hazard in the 2002 amendment and the introduction of DAFWPs with testing, particularly in safety-sensitive industries, is one way of employers meeting their obligations.

Other NZ legislation which should be considered when developing workplace policies and programmes include:

- Human Rights Act (1993)
- Privacy Act (1993)
- Bill of Rights Act (1990)
- Employment Relations Act (2000)
- Common Law
- Maritime Transport Act (1994).

In April 2004, a landmark employment court judgment[2] impacted positively on the development of DAFWPs. Six industry unions challenged the proposed Air New Zealand drug and alcohol policy which included random testing. Three employment High Court Judges heard the case in October 2003. Pre-employment was accepted and not challenged. The judgment was that Air New Zealand can randomly test those employees who are in 'safety-sensitive' areas and jobs, while testing post-accident/incident and/or for reasonable cause is permissible for all staff. An important proviso of the judgment was that the specimen collection, testing and reporting must be conducted in strict compliance with the latest edition of the Australian/New Zealand Standard (AS/NZS 4308) and should be part of a comprehensive DAFWP model. Any lesser testing regime was not acceptable.

The Australian/New Zealand Standard, AS/NZS 4308: 2008 'Procedures for the specimen collection and the detection and quantitation of drugs of abuse in urine'[1] is the latest edition. The initial AS 4308 Standard[3] was developed in 1995 in response to the rapidly developing medico-legal urinalysis market. This was updated and made a joint AS/NZS Standard in 2001[4] and a further extensively revised edition released in 2008.

An Australian Standard for Oral Fluid Testing (AS 4760-2006) titled 'Procedures for specimen collection and the detection and quantitation of drugs in oral fluid' was released late 2006.[5] New Zealand was represented on the committee developing this standard.

Practices, policy and procedures

Drug and alcohol-free workplace model

The comprehensive DAFWP model shown in Figure 15.3 has been promoted by ESR and Instep Limited since 1995 and has now gained acceptance by many other advisors in the field. It has also become the model endorsed by employment courts and most unions.

The model has four critical components which all must interact harmoniously for the programme to be successful in eliminating the abuse while providing assistance to the abuser. The components are:

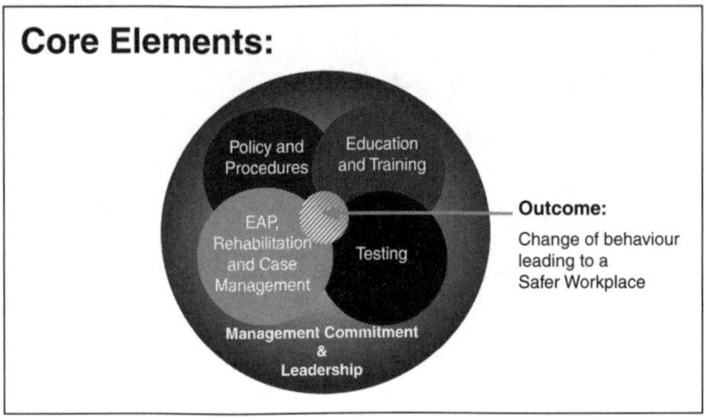

Figure 15.3 Drug and alcohol-free workplace model. (DAFWP Model designed by ESR and Instep Ltd (www.insteplimited.com) for NZ Forestry Industry Association, 2000.)

- development of policies and procedures that 'fit'
- education and training
- testing
- rehabilitation and case management.

Development of policies and procedures that `fit'

Initially policies and procedures must be developed which are legally robust, operationally sound and 'fit' the culture of the company.

Consult and communicate the intent

- Determine the aim (e.g. 'Create a drug and alcohol free workplace and workforce')
- Determine the objectives and ensure they are measurable (e.g. 'Reduce unacceptable risks of drug and alcohol misuse in the workplace')
- Achieve improved safety/operational performance
- Comply with legal obligations under the Health and Safety in Employment Act 1992 and 2002 Amendments
- Support and rehabilitate staff with drug and alcohol problems
- Treat all staff consistently in selection/testing/application of procedures
- Protect staff privacy and confidentiality
- Ensure all drug tests administered are legally defensible
- Consult with union, employee representatives, staff, other stakeholders.

Develop policy and procedures

The policy should contain:

- Its purpose, aims, objectives
- Legal issues including privacy and disciplinary matters

- Testing categories: pre-employment, internal transfer, reasonable cause, post-accident/incident, random, follow-up/post rehabilitation
- Role of education and training
- Rehabilitation: voluntary and after a positive test.

The procedures should contain:

- Definitions of terms used
- List of drugs of abuse
- Detailed processes and diagrams for each category of testing
- Cut-off concentrations for drugs in urine (AS/NZS 4308 : 2008 or any updated version)
- Target concentration for drugs in oral fluid (new 2006 standard)
- Alcohol testing level: either zero alcohol or NZ land transport drink driving level
- Procedures following a positive test or an 'invalid' specimen
- Disciplinary consequences of refusing to consent to a test
- Rehabilitation processes: voluntary or after a positive test
- Disciplinary process for serious misconduct
- Evaluating and auditing.

Education and training

A variety of educational options are considered to be crucial during the policy implementation phase to ensure the success of the programme.

Training for managers and supervisors

These workshops (typically half day duration) train and empower managers, supervisors and team leaders to intervene constructively in situations where they have reasonable cause to believe that a worker may be an unacceptable risk due to substance abuse. The training also focuses on compliance with company policy and an in-depth understanding of the procedures required for managing a drug and/or alcohol test.

General education for all employees

Education programmes for all staff focus on facts about alcohol and drugs, NZ trends, effects on health and safety, issues relating to the drug and alcohol tests, substances tested for and amounts, testing programme options and results management according to the company policy and periods taken to eliminate drugs.

Specialist medical advisor workshops

Periodically, two-day workshops are run for general practitioners and occupational health practitioners who wish to be trained as medical advisors (equivalent to medical review officers) for workplace drug and alcohol programmes that include testing. The focus is to gain expertise in advising and assisting companies in the development, implementation and ongoing operation of DAFWPs and to understand the issues relating to interpreting results.

Testing

Legally defensible workplace drug testing in NZ must be conducted by a mix of service providers who strictly adhere to the principles of the latest AS/NZS 4308 Standard (for urine). Laboratories conducting screening and confirmatory testing must have the relevant accreditation. The NZ laboratory accreditation body is the International Accreditation New Zealand (IANZ).[6] A technical assessment is conducted every three years by a staff field officer and a scientific expert familiar with AS/NZS 4308. In addition, annual surveillance visits are carried out. To gain accreditation, the laboratory must demonstrate full documentation of procedures, acceptable performance in quality assurance programmes, quality control and staffing with experience in publications and providing expert evidence for courts. The primary accreditation criteria are based on ISO/IEC 17025 : 2005. There are currently three accredited laboratories in NZ: LabPLUS (Auckland District Health Board's Laboratories), Canterbury's District Health Board's Laboratories) and ESR.

Appendix A of AS/NZS 4308 : 2008 sets out the procedures for 'on-site screening' for drugs in human urine. The previous editions of this standard did not accommodate on-site screening. The procedures are very stringent. Devices used must be verified to ensure trueness of results with respect to the screening cut-offs (Appendix B of AS/NZS 4308 : 2008).

Temperature and creatinine tests are mandatory at the time of collection and other panels of integrity tests are recommended. Quality controls (both positive and negative) must be conducted each day prior to any testing being conducted at a site. Subsequently at least one quality control is run after each batch of 25 specimens on a given day. Screening results are reported as either 'negative' or 'not negative'. It is mandatory to confirm all not negative screens by mass spectrometry tests at an accredited laboratory. The collecting agencies providing on-site screening services are also required to join a proficiency testing programme.

A urine specimen collector must have successfully completed a course of instruction for specimen collection and on-site screening (if applicable), handling, storage and dispatch of specimens and have received a statement of attainment in accordance with the New Zealand Qualification Authority (NZQA).[7] There are two qualifications (called unit standards) required (US 25458 'Perform urine specimen collection in the workplace for drug testing' and US 25511 'Perform urine drug screening in the workplace'). Since 2009 many collectors have achieved these qualifications but, unfortunately, others are still operating without upskilling.

A collecting agency providing both urine collection and on-site screening is required to obtain accreditation from IANZ. The accreditation process in NZ has only became available during 2010.

The 2006 Oral Fluid Standard has similar high quality collection and analytical protocols and accreditation requirements. The testing categories are discussed below.

Rehabilitation and case management

An Employment Assistance Programme (EAP), which specialises in substance abuse counseling, should be in place before testing for current employees commences. Employees can either voluntarily self-refer or be directed to the EAP through management intervention. The troubled employee is assessed within 24 hours and directed to the appropriate treatment facility:

- Employees assessed as alcohol or drug abusers only are directed to addiction counselling: 4–6 session short-term counselling model.
- Employees assessed as alcohol or drug dependent are directed to addiction facilities that best meet abstinence-based recovery. Detoxification and residential or outpatient treatment may be required.
- Case management permits the treatment provider and the EAP to liaise with the company regarding employment issues that require change once the employee resumes work.
- The final step in the rehabilitation contract requires the employee to undergo periodic, unannounced drug and/or alcohol testing on resuming work to ensure that he or she is no longer an unacceptable risk in the workplace.

Testing options

Company DAFWP policies can include varying mixes of the testing options listed below. The donor should sign an informed consent form prior to a specimen being collected.

- Pre-employment
- Internal transfer
- Post-accident or incident
- Reasonable cause
- Random
- Follow-up or post rehabilitation random.

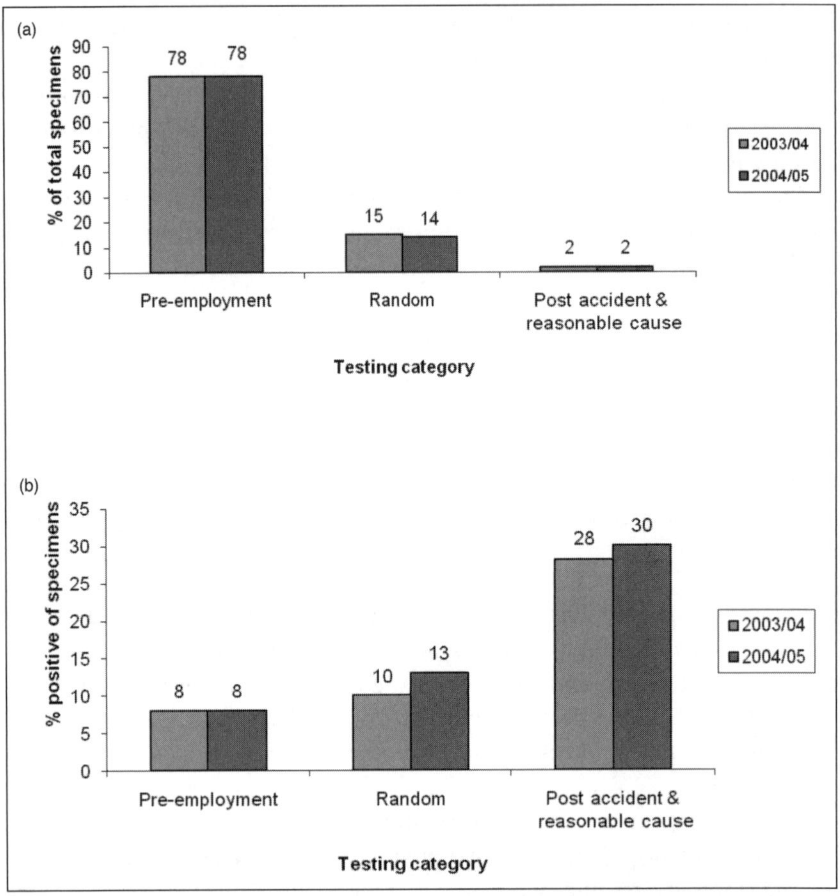

Figure 15.4 (a) Percentage of total specimens in testing categories and (b) percentage of specimens testing positive (ESR statistics).

Figure 15.4 illustrates the proportion of drug tests conducted by ESR nationwide in some of the above categories and compares the percentage of positive results over the two years June 2003/2004 and June 2004/2005.

Pre-employment testing

This is the most popular testing option and applicants must test negative to be considered for appointment. The companies inform applicants in employment advertisements or when initial contact is made that this is a requirement. Many employment placement agencies are now required to drug test their pool of job-seekers and only make available 'clean' temporary or permanent employees. On average 8% of pre-employment tests are positive.

Internal transfer

This option exists in some policies for situations when:

- part-time or temporary employees are offered permanent position
- an employee is applying to move to a new safety-sensitive job within the company.

Post-accident/incident

Employees involved in any significant accidents, incidents or 'near misses' are tested immediately to identify whether drugs or alcohol were a factor. Depending on the severity of the accident/incident and the wording of the company procedures, the testing will either be mandatory or as a result of a 'just cause' judgment by a trained manager. While the immediacy of the specimen collection process may be interrupted by essential medical treatment and other obvious operational impracticalities, the focus should always be on the urgency and priority of the tests.

Reasonable cause

Employees are requested to undertake a test where there are reasonable grounds for suspecting drug or alcohol misuse is impacting on performance or safety.

Random

Approximately 25% of companies with policies currently have random testing in place and many others are planning to introduce such programmes. In these programmes all employees or an identified group (e.g. those in safety-sensitive positions) are tested on a random unannounced basis. Random testing can involve either the random selection of a proportion of employees for testing or all employees within a group being tested at random times within a certain period. Most companies contract out to a third party the selection process and timing of the testing.

On average, from 2003 to 2005, between 10% and 13% of random testing specimens have had positive results (Figure 15.4).

Follow-up/post-rehabilitation

Testing usually occurs during a rehabilitation programme to measure progress. On return to work employees are randomly tested over a 12- to 24-month period to detect relapses (e.g. six tests annually). Depending on the company policy, an employee will face serious misconduct and dismissal after either the second or the third positive result.

Epidemiology: New Zealand drug trends

Drug trends

The drug classes which are available in New Zealand and included in the normal suite tested for in workplace programmes are discussed. Other drugs can be added to the mix but must still be tested to the same criteria dictated by AS/NZS 4308.

Cannabis

After alcohol, cannabis is the most prevalent drug used. For years cannabis has been grown in abundance throughout New Zealand both outdoors and indoors hydroponically. During the 1990s, there was also a significant number of hash oil clandestine laboratories extracting the resin from the surplus (mainly leafy) parts of plant material and producing hash oil.[8] Hash oil production has decreased since 2000 resulting in only 170 hash oil items being presented, by the NZ police, to ESR for analysis in 2003/2004 and a further reduction to 75 items in 2004/2005.

Amphetamine-type substances (ATS)

The drug scene has changed dramatically since 2000. NZ gangs started to manufacture methamphetamine (MA) in its crystalline/ice form from pseudoephedrine and this has caused huge problems for society, workplaces and families. The NZ-manufactured MA is called ‘P’: P for pure and P for point bags (containing 0.1 g of MA), which is the normal mode of distribution. The

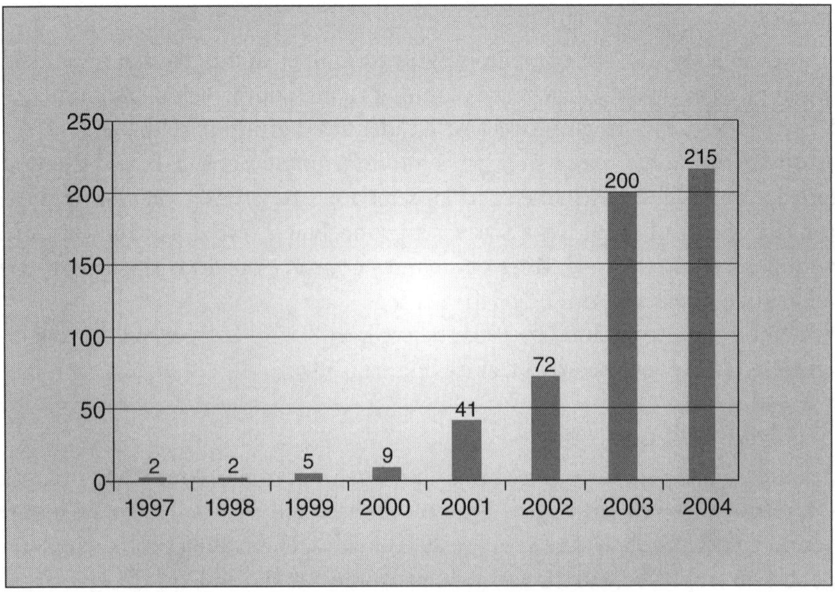

Figure 15.5 Methamphetamine 'P' clandestine laboratories seized (ESR statistics).

steady increase in the clandestine laboratories investigated and dismantled by the NZ police and ESR forensic scientists is shown in Figure 15.5. The 2005 statistics were similar to 2004. MA is also imported along with other amphetamine-type substances such as ecstasy (MDA, MDMA, MDEA) and the 2C analogues.

During 2009, the following analogues of methcathinone have started to emerge on the NZ drug scene:

- 4-methylmethcathinone (4-MMC): also known as 'miaow miaow'
- 2-(methylamino)-1-(4-methylphenyl) propan-1-one (also known as mephedrone)
- methoxymethcathinone (also known as methedrone).

Methcathinone and its analogues are all class C controlled drugs under the Misuse of Drugs Act 1975 and its relevant amendments. However they are not listed in AS/NZS 4308 : 2008 as drugs which are automatically tested for in a workplace drug testing programme (see Table 15.3). Hence the laboratory needs to be asked specifically to analyse for these substances where they are suspected.

According to the 2005 World Drug Report 2005,[9] NZ now has one of the highest usages of amphetamine-type substances per cent of population in the world.

Party drugs

Benzylpiperazine

Preparations containing the synthetic drugs benzylpiperazine (BZP) and trifluoromethylphenylpiperazine (TFMPP) were legal to use and sell in NZ to persons over the age of 18 until 2008. Many different brands were readily available at a variety of accessible outlets. The individual dosages of BZP ranged from 60 to 500 mg and the quality of the products vary considerably. While BZP is an anthelmintic medication, when used as a party drug the effects are said to be similar to ecstasy, though less intense. It is estimated that more than eight million dosages were sold between 2000 and 2008. BZP was classified as a class C controlled drug under the Misuse of Drugs Act in 2008 (Misuse of Drugs Act 1975, Amendment Act 2008 (08/5)).

BZP is included in the suite for workplace drug testing and accounted for 30% of the positive amphetamine-type substances until 2008. It has also been added to the list of amphetamine-type substances that are tested for in table 2 of AS/NZS 4308 : 2008 (see Table 15.3).

Other party pills

Since BZP was classified as an illicit substance, other 'new generation' party pills have been introduced to the market. One which has gained popularity is 1,3-dimethylamylamine (DMAA). This drug has caused concerns and, during 2010, should be scheduled as a restricted substance. This provides stringent controls around so-called 'new generation party pills', including a prohibition on:

- selling or supplying DMAA to anyone under 18 years of age
- advertising DMAA in the media
- offering DMAA as a gift or reward
- the sale and supply of DMAA from or within premises where alcohol is sold or from service stations
- the sale of DMAA from or within any premises where children or minors gather.

Opiates

During the 1970s NZ had a significant heroin importation problem. A NZ syndicate called 'Mr Asia' was importing pure heroin in large quantities from the 'Golden Triangle'. However with the collapse of the Mr Asia syndicate, imported heroin dried up. To compensate, NZ ingenuity came to the fore with the establishment of 'home bake' laboratories. Relatively small quantities of impure mixtures of heroin and morphine are manufactured in kitchens and sheds by extracting codeine from medications and using a pyridine demethylation process to chemically convert the base to morphine and heroin on a small scale.[10] While the 'home bake' epidemic has largely been replaced by 'P' manufacturing, this practice still exists in some regions.

Because of the relatively low incidence of heroin abuse, the majority (>80%) of 'not-negative' opiate screen results are interpreted, from mass spectrometry analyses, as being present due to legitimate intake of medicines containing codeine. Preparations containing codeine up to approximately 10 mg are available in NZ without a prescription. Occasionally poppy seed consumption can be shown from mass spectrometry to be the cause of the 'not-negative' opiate screen.

LSD, cocaine and benzodiazepines

Compared with other countries, NZ used to have a relatively high LSD usage which has decreased with the upsurge in availability of amphetamine-type substances and party drugs. LSD analysis is offered by the accredited laboratories as an optional addition to the routine workplace drug testing suite.

Cocaine abuse is low compared with global trends but importations are evident due to the increase in popularity of the stimulant drug market.

Benzodiazepine abuse has also increased as these prescription or illicit medications become more readily available for purchase via the Internet or on the 'black market'.

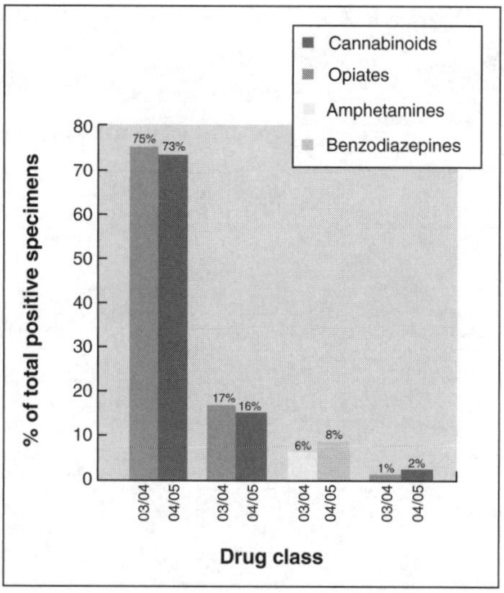

Figure 15.6 Drug class positives as percentage of total positive specimens.

Workplace drug positives

The distribution over two consecutive years, 2003/2004 and 2004/2005 of urine drug positives amongst the classes commonly tested for in workplace programmes is illustrated in Figure 15.6. Cannabis (73–75%) was significantly higher than opiates (16–17%). As discussed previously, the majority of opiate positives can be traced back to legitimate medicinal use. Amphetamine-type substance positives (6–8%) are increasing each year as are the benzodiazepines (1–2%). At this stage NZ has a minimal cocaine problem in the industries conducting testing.

Australian/New Zealand Standard: AS/NZS 4308 : 2008

As discussed previously, the 2008 edition of AS/NZS 4308, 'Procedures for specimen collection and the detection and quantitation of drugs of abuse in

Table 15.2 Immunoassay initial test cut-off concentrations: AS/NZS 4308 : 2008

Class of drug[a]	Cut-off level (micrograms/L)
Opiates	300
Amphetamine type substances	300
Cannabis metabolites	50
Cocaine metabolites	300
Benzodiazepines	200

[a] For drugs that may be optionally tested within each class, the specified cut-off levels may not apply and other methodologies may be more appropriate.

Table 15.3 Confirmatory test cut-off concentrations (as total drug): AS/NZS 4308 : 2008

Compound	Cut-off level (micrograms/L)
Morphine	300
Codeine	300
6-Acetylmorphine	10
Amphetamine	150
Methylamphetamine	150
Methylenedioxymethamphetamine	150
Methylenedioxyamphetamine	150
Benzylpiperazine[a]	500
Phentermine[a]	500
Ephedrine[a]	500
Pseudoephedrine[a]	500
11-nor-Δ9-tetrahydrocannabinol-9-carboxylic acid	15
Benzoylecgonine	150
Ecgonine methyl ester	150
Oxazepam	200
Temazepam	200
Diazepam	200
Nordiazepam	200
α-Hydroxy-alprazolam	100
7-Amino-clonazepam	100
7-Amino-flunitrazepam	100
7-Amino-nitrazepam	100

[a] These drugs may be optionally tested within each class and the specified cut-off levels shall apply.

urine', puts a greater emphasis on specimen integrity testing and some of the confirmatory cut-offs concentration have been lowered. Screening using verified 'on-site' screening devices and laboratories performing 'screen-only' tests have been accommodated. The emphasis is on using quality devices and procedures that mirror the strict requirements for laboratories performing full laboratory-based urine testing.

The AS/NZS 4308 : 2008 immunoassay screen cut-off concentrations are listed in Table 15.2 and the confirmatory test cut-off concentrations are listed in Table 15.3.

Oral fluid testing in the workplace

During 2004/2005 there was pressure on some workplace sectors to introduce oral fluid testing and to follow Australian trends. Hence the requirement for Standards Australia to release a standard by late 2006. The arguments for oral fluid are based on the assumption that collecting a saliva specimen is less invasive than urine and that a positive oral fluid test is a better indicator of impairment. There have been a number of issues still to be resolved before oral fluid testing is robust enough. Some of these include:

- Stability of drugs in the collecting devices (particularly THC). ESR's research on three different collecting devices showed two of the devices quickly lost very substantial amounts of THC (>60%).[11] Since this research was published, there have been collecting devices produced which show stability of THC.
- Most oral fluid 'on-site' screening devices are currently too insensitive to satisfactorily detect cannabis use.[12–15] Hence full laboratory screening and confirmation in an accredited laboratory is currently the only viable option for this drug. In NZ cannabis is still the drug (after alcohol) most widely misused so testing systems must be sensitive enough to detect this drug for acceptable period after use.

A significant Employment Court Judgment (December 2007)[16] has influenced the use of urine versus oral fluid testing in NZ. The Maritime Union (MUNZ) challenged the lawfulness of the Toll Owens Limited's (TLNZ) workplace drug and alcohol testing policy. One of the MUNZ challenges was the use of urine drug testing. They argued that oral fluid testing was the only appropriate methodology. On 21 December 2007, Chief Judge GL Golgan recognised the lack of sensitivity of current oral fluid tests (particularly on-site screens) for detecting THC and recommended that urine testing was the most appropriate form of testing for cannabis in workplace programmes.

There is still minimal oral fluid testing being conducted in NZ workplace programmes. Urine drug testing dominates the market.

Conclusion

During the 1990s many NZ companies were hesitant about introducing DAFWPs which included testing. However the past 10 years have seen a steady increase in companies in the high-risk industries embracing the comprehensive approach, with a focus on education and rehabilitation harmoniously supporting the testing regime. Most high-risk industry sectors are now well represented. Industry case studies are emerging highlighting the positive outcomes from DAFWPs.

Urinalysis predominates supported by the strict quality requirements dictated by AS/NZS 4308 : 2008 for collection, detection, quantitation and reporting. This edition allows for 'on-site' screen testing and has dictated the criteria for verification of screening devices, procedures to be employed and qualifications of the service providers. In spite of this, the use of inferior testing processes and, in particular the inappropriate use of 'on-site' screening testing, has continued to permeate the market.

Oral fluid testing has only gained minimal appeal in sections of the workforce but there remains naivety and misinformation about the stability of drugs in the collection devices, sensitivity of 'on-site' tests for some drugs (particularly cannabinoids), quality assurance programmes and interpretation of results. The Australian Standard, AS 4760-2006, has addressed these issues but very few service providers comply with the standard.

While alcohol and cannabis are still the substances most commonly misused, the use of amphetamine-type stimulants, particularly methamphetamine (commonly referred to as 'P'), has rapidly increased since 2000. The new generation of 'non-BZP' party pills are widely used and abused because the legal status in NZ allows some of them to be readily available.

Acknowledgements

The author wishes to acknowledge the figures in this chapter which were from ESR's statistics and publications.

References

1. Standards Australia and Standards New Zealand, Procedures for specimen collection and the detection and quantitation of drugs of abuse in urine. AS/NZS 4308 : 2008.
2. Goddard TG, Travis BS, Colgan GL. NZ Amalgamated Engineering Printing and Manufacturing Union Inc et al v Air New Zealand Limited, AC 22/04, ARC 42/03, April 2004.
3. Standards Australia International Ltd. Recommended practice for the collection, detection and quantitation of drugs of abuse in urine, AS 4308 : 1995, 1995.
4. Standards Australia International Ltd and Standards New Zealand. Procedures for the collection, detection and quantitation of drugs of abuse in urine, AS/NZS 4308 : 2001.
5. Standards Australia. Procedures for specimen collection and the detection and quantitation of drugs in oral fluid, AS 4760-2006.
6. International Accreditation New Zealand. www.ianz.govt.nz (accessed December 2010).
7. New Zealand Qualifications Authority. www.nzqa.govt.nz (accessed December 2010).
8. Nolan SL, Bedford KR, Valentine M. Making a hash of it. In: *Proceedings of the 13th Meeting of the International Association of Forensic Sciences*, 22–28 August 1993, Düsseldorf, Germany. Published in *Advances in Forensic Sciences* 1995; 5: 246–249.
9. United Nations Office on Drugs and Crime (UNODC) (2005) *World Drug Report 2005*. New York: United Nations. www.unodc.org/unodc/en/world_drug_report.html (accessed July 2005).

10. Bedford KR, Nolan SL, Onrust R, Siegers JD. The illicit preparation of morphine and heroin from pharmaceutical products containing codeine: 'Homebake' laboratories in New Zealand. *Forensic Sci. Int* 1987; 34: 197–204.
11. Dickson S, Park A, Nolan SL, Kenworthy S, Nicholson C, Midglay J *et al.* The recovery of illicit drugs from oral fluid. *Forensic Sci Int* 2007; 165: 78–84.
12. Verstraete AG, Raes E. *Rosita-2 Project: Final Report.* Ghent, Belgium: Academia Press, 2006.
13. Verstraete A, Labat L. Use of onsite tests for the detection of drugs in oral fluid at the roadside and at the workplace. *Ann Toxicol Anal* 2009; 21(1): 3–8.
14. Kintz P, Bernhard W, Villain M, Gasser M, Aebi B, Cirimele V. Detection of cannabis use in drivers with the Drugwipe device and by GC-MS after Intercept device collection. *J Anal Toxicol* 2005; 29: 724–727.
15. Iten P, Baumgartner M. Experiences with the DRUGWIPE® saliva drug test at the roadside. Poster presentation at the International Association of Forensic Toxicologists Congress, Seoul, Korea, September 2005.
16. Colgan GL. *Maritime Union of New Zealand (MUNZ) Inc* versus *TLNZ Ltd*, Employment Court Judgement.(AC51A/07; File No: ARC 34/07).

Index